Knocking on Heaven's Door

Knocking on Heaven's Door

Six Minor Leaguers in Search of the Baseball Dream

Marty Dobrow

University of Massachusetts Press

Amherst and Boston

Copyright © 2010 by Marty Dobrow
Printed in the United States of America

LC 2010027868
ISBN 978-1-55849-843-3 (paper); 842-6 (library cloth)

Designed by Richard Hendel
Set in Scala and ITC Franklin Gothic by Weschester Book
Printed and bound by Thomson Shore, Inc.

Library of Congress Cataloging-in-Publication Data

Dobrow, Marty, 1960–
Knocking on Heaven's door : six minor leaguers in search of
the baseball dream / Marty Dobrow.
    p. cm.
Includes bibliographical references and index.
ISBN 978-1-55849-843-3 (pbk. : alk. paper)—
ISBN 978-1-55849-842-6 (library cloth : alk. paper)
 1. Minor league baseball—United States.
 2. Baseball players—United States.   I. Title.
GV875.A1D62 2010
796.357'64—dc22
                    2010027868

British Library Cataloguing in Publication data are available.

For the remarkable team around me:

Sarah at first, Josh at second,

Jeremiah at the hot corner, Peter at shortstop;

Mom and Dad in center, Julie leaning left,

Joe doing the right thing;

I look in for the sign and see Missy-Marie—home,

where my heart most definitely is.

Contents

Knocking on Heaven's Door

Prologue
"If They Make It, We Make It"
West Brookfield, Massachusetts

When the cell phone rings, Jim and Lisa Masteralexis shake their heads. It is late on a summer night, and their three young children have finally fallen asleep. Toys and puzzle pieces and picture books are strewn around the living room. Dinner dishes still sit on the kitchen table, macaroni and cheese on the floor.

Looking at the caller ID, Jim sees it is one of their newer clients, Randy Ruiz: high maintenance, big bat. A first baseman/DH for the Reading Phillies, he is tearing up the competition. He is leading the Eastern League in batting and is second in home runs—despite having missed the first fifteen games of this 2005 season after testing positive for steroids at the end of the previous year. Jim snaps open the phone and says, "What's up, Randy?"

Ruiz is hysterical. He is calling from the team bus in the midst of a 430-mile journey from Akron, Ohio, to Trenton, New Jersey. His manager, Steve Swisher, has just informed him that he is going to be suspended without pay for thirty days for failing another steroids test. Fighting back tears, he insists he is innocent. "I swear to God, Jim. Give me a Bible, put me in front of a church, and let lightning strike: I didn't do it." Here he is, having absolutely the season of his life, seven years into the grueling minor league journey, finally on the cusp of his dream, a kid who grew up in the South Bronx with nothing, and now the whole sweet story is unraveling.

"Are you sure, Randy? Are you absolutely sure?"

"Straight up, Jim. I swear. I haven't touched it the whole year."

"All right, big fella. Pull yourself together. I'll see what I can do."

Jim talks it over with Lisa deep into the night. They find the contact information for Quest Diagnostics, the lab authorized by Major League Baseball to conduct drug tests. In the morning they put in a rush order and arrange to have Randy tested right away. After rifling through some papers, they begin to file an appeal. Part of the application requires them to fill out a complete list of drugs Randy has taken in the last few months, the so-called "therapeutic use exemptions." One of the drugs on the list catches Jim's attention: Viagra.

"Randy, man, you're twenty-seven years old. What do you need that for?"

"Jim," he says, pausing. "This shit works."

Jim can only laugh. This merely confirms what he often says to Lisa about life in the minor leagues. It is a "testosterone soap opera."

● Their first date, on June 15, 1988, took place at Fenway Park, a Red Sox–Yankees game.

Jim had grown up just seven miles away in Watertown, listening to the Sox pretty much every night, Ned Martin's voice echoing through the kitchen while Jim's mother, Esther, rolled out Greek pastries. Several times a year Jim would trade three or four bucks for a ticket in the bleachers, where he'd bop the occasional beach ball, cheering hard for Yaz or Rico or Dewey. He doesn't really remember the Impossible Dream team of 1967 (he was only five), but in '75 he reveled in Carlton Fisk's boyish dance to keep it fair. It was the sport's iconic image: waving, waving, waving, jumping for joy. The next night, Game 7, Jim was there with tickets from a family friend, his hopes riding with every pitch. All these years later he can still see it, two outs in the top of the ninth, the score tied, the bloop off the bat of Joe Morgan falling too fast, plunking onto the outfield grass, the 4–3 Reds win, the acid taste of falling short.

On Opening Day 1976, however, he was back, ducking out of Watertown Junior High at noon, hopping aboard an MBTA bus for Kenmore Square, and bounding through the turnstiles, a move that would land him his first and only suspension from school. Jim couldn't get enough of the scene. There was something mesmerizing about Fenway, Updike's lyric little bandbox of a ballpark, so much caring inside it, a sense, however preposterous, of its mattering in the grand scheme. He vowed that one day he would be an important person here.

It hadn't happened as a player. A catcher ("because I was the fat kid"), Jim had been small-town good. He was an East Watertown Little League All-Star, and a regular at the Ted Williams Baseball Camp fifty miles away in Lakeville. He had soft hands behind the plate, a strong arm, and a competitive streak that usually trumped his insecurity. He was good enough to become the captain at Watertown High, good enough to make a Division I team at the University of New Hampshire, good enough—in the words of Roger Kahn—to dream.

But not good enough to bring that dream to life. In college there were curveballs that buckled his knees, a coach he disliked, and the realization of just how exceptional you had to be to succeed. Already there had been so much winnowing, so many players who had not made it as far as he had. Still, he realized, he wasn't anywhere near getting drafted, joining that ultra-elite crew who were selected by big league teams in the first week of June.

He began his senior year by going hitless in his first twenty-three at bats. The Wildcats made it to the first round of the NCAA tournament that year, played at McCoy Stadium in Pawtucket, Rhode Island, the Triple-A home of the Red Sox, and the site three years earlier of a thirty-three-inning game, longest in professional history. Batting ninth against the University of Connecticut, Jim went hitless in his first three at bats, striking out twice. But in his final plate appearance in the eighth inning, Jim smacked a line drive that banged off advertisements on the left-field fence, and he puffed into second with a double. He stood in the middle of a diamond where far better players toiled, guys who were just one phone call away from the big leagues. He was twenty-one years old. A few minutes later his baseball career was over.

He left the game behind him and took his political science major to Washington, D.C., working as a staff assistant for David Obey, a Democratic congressman from Wisconsin. Despite being relegated to the menial tasks of answering phones and opening mail, Jim enjoyed the pulse of politics and the self-important Washington scene. By night he prowled Georgetown, sometimes working as a bartender, admiring the bevy of attractive, ambitious young women. He liked to flirt with waitresses: "Do you take Visa? Do you take American Express? Do you take an IOU?"

In 1986 he returned to Boston to begin law school at Suffolk University. The first year was brutal, with huge chunks of dense reading, case studies to memorize, papers to write. Living at his parents' house, he worked into the wee hours, asking his mother to type his homework. There was, however, one distraction: the siren call of the Red Sox. They were a powerhouse team in that fall of 1986, with Wade Boggs, Jim Rice, and young Roger the Rocket Clemens (born twelve days before Masteralexis) leading the team and the city to the very brink of joy. In the bottom of the tenth inning of Game 6 with two outs, Jim turned to his father on the living room couch and said, "Dad, I can't believe it: The Red Sox are going to win the fucking World Series." He was already planning his trip to Kenmore Square for the wild celebration, when suddenly there were three singles, a wild pitch, a little ground ball down the first base line.

The next year he hit his stride in law school. In the fall he ran for Town Council in Watertown and won, becoming by far the youngest member of the nine-person board. He set up an office in the basement of his parents' house, taking calls about snow removal and cable television contracts. In the spring he met a vivacious first-year law student named Lisa Pike. She hailed from the other side of the state, the small rural town of Huntington. She had gone to UMass, as a dance major initially, before turning to sport management. She was smart. She was tough. Also thin and blonde with a taste for bright red nail polish. And one more thing—she was a gargantuan baseball fan. For Jim, this seemed too good to be true.

In a way it was: Lisa was a devout Yankees fan. The radio had always been on in her house, too, but rather than Ned Martin, she tuned in to Phil Rizzuto, whose "Holy Cow!" rang forth with every blast by Reggie Jackson, or every diving stab at the hot corner by Lisa's favorite player, Graig Nettles. Her family got only one station on television, so she and her younger brother would wait for their father, Butch, to come home from banging nails, curl up with him, and listen to the game on the radio. "My father just loved the Yankees so much," she says. "He was a pretty big construction guy. But the one thing that would make him cry would be the Yankees."

It was a steamy night at the ballpark, that first date, Jim sweating so profusely that he was embarrassed. But he found the scene, as always, intoxicating. It was baseball, and the Red Sox, and Fenway, and a young woman who made his heart race. What's more, the Sox won, 7–3.

● Their life had become a juggling act on a tightrope: his day job as a lawyer specializing in labor and contracts, hers as the head of the sport management program at UMass; their three active kids, five-year-old Nathan, already with a sweet swing from the left side of the plate, and the curly-haired twins, Taylor and Justin, in the midst of their terrible twos; and of course DiaMMond Management, the mom-and-pop baseball agency they had opened together in November 1992. To succeed, they felt they had to keep things small and personal. They had to be the agents who knew the dog's name, and what kind of perfume the girlfriend liked to wear. Over the years they had built up a client base of two dozen players, all but one of them minor leaguers, most hailing from New England.

They were a rare husband-and-wife team. Jim was the front man, the primary talent scout, the hard-edged negotiator. Lisa, one of just four women among the 402 agents certified by the Major League Baseball Players Association, provided legal fine-tooth-combing, a soft touch with players' families, and a disarming presence at the negotiating table. By this point Jim's head of still-thick brown hair had become flecked with gray. Lisa was still blonde and trim and filled with energy, though the right side of her face sometimes sagged from Bell's palsy, a localized paralysis that set in just before she gave birth to the twins.

Their family life was suffused with the game. Eight days after Nathan was born in 1999, Jim was driving up to Montreal to see the major league debut of one of their first clients, Peter Bergeron. Lisa watched on television, the tears streaming down, a mixture of maternity blues and pride in a young man whose family she had come to know quite well.

Three years later, gingerly settling into the passenger seat between contractions with the twins, she heard the familiar sound of Jim's cell phone. He picked it up as he started driving to the hospital. Red Sox minor league director Ben Cherington was furious. Manny Delcarmen, Jim and Lisa's client, had just gone AWOL from his team in Georgia and was driving north to Massachusetts, repeatedly hanging up on Cherington. "Ben," Jim said, flying down the road, "I'll see what I can do."

They had run the business in the red almost the whole time. The money would leak out in lots of ways. Each year, for instance, the agency provided thousands of dollars' worth of new equipment for its entire stable of players. This was primarily the territory of Jim and Lisa's other partner, Steve McKelvey, who joined the agency in 1998. Like Jim a former catcher and captain of his high school team, Steve was forever working the phones with Nike and Wilson and Adidas, trying to persuade an account clerk to throw in another glove or another pair of turf shoes, or to send out the Under Armour shirts by overnight mail. "Although Bob Feller was able to do it," Steve says with a straight face, "no pitcher today can pitch without these shirts." (As much as anyone, Steve had seen the infuriating yet somehow delicious unpredictability of the sport. Back in 1986 he was working in corporate marketing for Major League Baseball, and in this role he was helping to set up the championship trophy for the Red Sox at Shea Stadium during Game 6 behind a plastic champagne shield, only to have to whisk it away after the Bill Buckner blunder.)

More costly to the agency than the direct flow of funds was the hemorrhage of time. Jim was forever shaving hours from his law job, infuriating the partners at Brackett and Lucas by yielding to his baseball habit. Day after day he would travel to high school and college diamonds, trading intelligence with the scouts, wooing the prospects and their families. Often he'd find himself in unfamiliar territory: a city slicker tracking deer in the snow with a high school pitcher who could throw heat, steeling himself at the family dinner table for the venison stew. Summer days meant on-the-fly exchanges with babysitters, quick pecks on the cheek for the kids, and trips to minor league outposts, nine innings of uneven baseball, a steak dinner with one of his guys. "If they make it," he often told Lisa and Steve, "we make it."

● Somehow the Baseball Dream lives on. Long after the national pastime lost its status as the center of the American sporting world, and even in an age when the game's fundamental integrity has been called into question, yearning to be a big league ballplayer remains an iconic quest.

It is, of course, a difficult journey. The long weeding-out process begins in Little League. Even the star players there, those stamped for greatness, almost always fall short. They come to realize they are not good enough at the thing they love. By high school, baseball's game of "Survivor" has voted almost everyone off. Of the whittled-down crew who make their varsity teams, only a small percentage will go on to play college ball; fewer still will ever know the thrill of getting drafted. That is the dream come true.

Except that it isn't. No one grows up dreaming of being a minor league player.

The hard slog through the minors rarely has a happy ending. Ninety percent of minor leaguers—young men who can hit the ball four hundred feet or throw it ninety-plus miles per hour—will never play a single inning in the big leagues. Sure, their life has a charm to it: summer nights in small towns, the fuzzy mascots, the tee-ballers leaning over the dugout for autographs, the halter-top hopefuls arriving from the local community college. But beneath the charm lurks tremendous pressure on the players and on their families who have latched on to the dream. Minor leaguers are commodities that can be uprooted overnight by a trade, or released without remorse. They make up a culture of ferociously competitive individuals looking for any possible edge. It is an icy fact: one player benefits from the failures—even the injuries—of others, especially teammates.

Those few young men who climb into the ranks of the high minors, to Double-A and Triple-A, live in a world of *almostness*, so close to something they want so much, something they have always wanted—and still they are not likely to get it.

Minor leaguers lead a life of economic privation. Most make under $15,000 a year. Meanwhile, the minimum major league salary ($400,000 in 2009) and the average ($3.2 million) dangle incredible possibility just beyond the horizon.

● There are almost seven thousand minor leaguers under contract with a Major League Baseball team. Each of them has a unique story.

The two dozen players represented by DiaMMond Management agents Jim and Lisa Masteralexis and Steve McKelvey offer a small sample of the mosaic. In the 2005 season that the first three-quarters of this book focuses on, there were seven thousand worthy tales. The stories of the five minor leaguers and one soon-to-be drafted college player whose lives are recounted in the following pages necessarily simplify a complex world.

There is Randy Ruiz, with his hardscrabble upbringing in the South Bronx and controversy over steroids. There is Brad Baker, a former first-round draft pick, carrying the hopes of his tiny rural town on his slender shoulders. There is Doug Clark, the understudy to Barry Bonds, who spends his off-seasons as a substitute teacher at the inner-city high school he once attended. There is Manny Delcarmen, a kid from Boston who grew up idolizing the Red Sox and wound up getting drafted by the team. The college kid is Matt Torra, whose world is about to change forever. And unlikeliest of all, there is Charlie Zink, the son of prison guards who went to art school and then developed a knuckleball that gave him a chance.

We find them on the cusp of a difficult dream that still shines in a cynical age.

Spring Training 2005

Crash Davis Territory

Scottsdale, Arizona

A few weeks in the Southwest have awakened Doug Clark's freckles from hibernation. They have blossomed on his powerful forearms. They have started to create sheet music on his slightly lined forehead. And they have cropped up on the temples flanking his hazel eyes— alert, penetrating eyes that are now focused on a television screen in his room at the Days Inn.

As the cameras settle in on Sammy Sosa and Mark McGwire, Doug cannot help flashing back to 1998. That was the year when these two larger-than-life stars carried the sport on their broad shoulders. Together the ebullient Sosa, hop-stepping after each moon shot over the ivy, and the Bunyanesque McGwire, blasting baseballs deep into the St. Louis night, had taken aim at one of the gold standards of sport: Roger Maris's single-season home run record of sixty-one. Maris, of course, had eclipsed Babe Ruth's thirty-four-year-old record of sixty back in 1961. Thirty-seven baseball seasons had come and gone, with grand sluggers named Mays and Aaron, Killebrew and Banks, Robinson and Jackson, Schmidt and Griffey all falling well short of the mark. But in 1998 Sosa somehow hit sixty-six—a truly remarkable feat, and still four shy of the seventy smashed by Big Mac. That season was a national love fest, with *SportsCenter* paeans on a daily basis, charts in every newspaper, fans flocking to the ballpark, ready to invest their money and their faith. Many credited Sosa and McGwire with nothing less than saving the sport from the taint of 1994, when owners and players, unwilling to divide vast riches, had canceled the World Series.

That summer of the great long-ball duel coincided with Doug Clark's first year of pro ball. He hit three home runs that year playing for the Single-A Salem-Keizer Volcanoes in Oregon. He lived in the basement of his host family's house and took long bus trips to play teams like the Yakima Bears and the Tri-City Dust Devils. There were times when he almost couldn't believe his good fortune. He was a professional athlete, getting paid to play the game. Yes, it was only $850 a month (not even in the same galaxy as Sosa's 1998 salary of $8,325,000 or McGwire's $8,928,354), but still, it felt like some childhood fantasy come to life. In a family of seven kids, he had grown up sharing a basement room with two older brothers, three thousand miles away in Springfield, Massachusetts. Now here he was, on a big green field between the Cascades and the vast sweep of the Pacific. Sometimes when he left the ballpark at night, he would just look up at the sky. He couldn't believe how many stars there were.

Breathing in the stale air-conditioned air, Doug watches the usually effervescent Sosa speak haltingly, suddenly unable to answer in English after years of charming fluency in postgame interviews. Slammin' Sammy's prepared words are meek, their meaning carefully parsed: "To be clear, I have never taken illegal performance-enhancing drugs. I have never injected myself, or had anyone inject me with anything. I've not broken the laws of the United States or the laws of the Dominican Republic. I've been tested as recently as 2004 and I am clean."

Doug stares at the mighty McGwire, looking like a man sitting on a tack, stammering and sputtering his way through one non-answer after another, repeating the limp mantra "I'm not here to talk about the past."

He takes in the sight of the dapper Rafael Palmeiro, wagging his finger defiantly at the cameras and stating, "Let me start by telling you this: I have never taken steroids—period. I don't know how to say it any more clearly than that. Never."

There they are, three of only twenty men in the grand history of Major League Baseball to hit five hundred career home runs.[1]

And of course there is Jose Canseco, author of "only" 462 homers, and author also of *Juiced*, a 304-page book released a month earlier that swaggered its way through confession and accusation. Canseco alternately extolled the virtues of steroids, for extending the human potential and expanding the range of the possible, and cautioned about their risks—making the soul (and certain organs) contract. Canseco is resplendent in his navy blue suit, all but wearing the scarlet "S" as an accessory while accusing others of doing the same.

For Doug, though, the most riveting testimony does not come from the stars. It comes from the parents of Rob Garibaldi and Taylor Hooton, two young ballplayers who had taken steroids in the quest for baseball greatness.

Garibaldi had grown up in Petaluma, California, just north of the Bay Area. At age seven he had told his mother, Denise, a clinical psychologist, that he wanted to be a baseball player. For years he was single-minded in pursuit of that goal. He used to videotape McGwire's at bats. At Casa Grande High School he was a scrawny star who began ingesting an array of supplements, which gave way to "Andro" (androstenedione, the steroid precursor that was legal in Major League Baseball when McGwire admitted using it in 1998). After graduating, Garibaldi drove to Tijuana with a friend and purchased steroids. He got bigger and better and bigger still, starring for a community college, and then earning a full scholarship to the University of Southern California, a perennial baseball power. After one great season, though, he began to tumble out of control: chasms of depression, stretches of unpredictable behavior, fits of rage. One day, sitting in a car around the corner from his home, he pointed a stolen .357 Magnum at his temple and fired.

"There is no doubt in our minds," Denise Garibaldi told Congress, "that steroids killed our son."

Taylor Hooton grew up in Plano, Texas. The cousin of former big league pitcher Burt Hooton, Taylor aspired to stardom on the mound. Told by a coach during his junior year of high school that he would need to be bigger to become a dominant pitcher, he embarked on an aggressive course of steroid use. Taylor built himself up, broke himself down. He was seventeen years old when his mother found him hanging from the door of his childhood bedroom. He left a vial of steroids in his room, wrapped in an American flag.

"It's a real challenge for parents to overpower the strong message that's being sent to our children by your behavior," Taylor's father, Donald Hooton, said to the assembled stars. "Players that are guilty of taking steroids are not only cheaters—you are cowards."

Just a few weeks before, Doug Clark had been surrounded by kids who were not all that different from Taylor Hooton. The students he taught as a substitute at Springfield Central High School were a restless lot. There were two thousand of them, roughly a third black, a third white, a third Hispanic. Beneath all of their posturing Doug sensed the familiar hunger, the yearning to stand out. He understood. He had come out of the same inner-city high school some years before. In each of the last seven off-seasons he had come back to teach.

With a biology degree from the University of Massachusetts, he was comfortable manning a science class and overseeing most levels of math. He could fake his way through history and pinch-hit easily in PE. During downtime he liked to regale the trim and elegant Mena DeCarvalho (his former Spanish teacher and onetime coach of the cheerleaders) with tales from his winter league experiences in Mexico and the Dominican Republic. Mostly he was drawn by the kids, by the battles of innocence and angst, by the lights that had not yet gone out. Corny or not, he believed in being a role model.

After school he would sometimes talk about the students with his mother, Peggy, a former teacher herself. Often he'd persuade his cousin and close friend R. J. Joyal, a local high school principal, to go out for a beer; or he'd catch a college basketball game with his younger brother Connell, a middle school math teacher. Teaching was the family path.

At night he would crash at the family homestead, going down to the basement room he once shared with older brothers Will and Andrew, now both married and fathers of young children. On the wall, still, was a reminder of Doug's other line of work: a poster made of baseball cards from the 1998 Salem-Keizer Volcanoes, thirty-three fresh-faced kids starting out their pro careers, all determined to make it to the big leagues. Almost all of them had long since abandoned ship or, more commonly, been pushed off the plank.

Doug has been good enough to stay on board. Through seven seasons he has managed a career batting average of .291. He spent the last five in the so-called "high minors" of Double-A (primarily) and Triple-A, close to the Promised Land. A year ago, in 2004, he hit .292 with ten home runs, seventy-one RBI, and thirty-three stolen bases for the Norwich Navigators, Double-A affiliate of the San Francisco Giants. He has played all three outfield positions and played them well. Talk to his minor league managers and you will hear a familiar refrain: Doug is a hard worker, a good guy, a true professional.

But he has never spent a single day in the major leagues.

One thing Doug has not demonstrated is a lot of pop. He has never hit more than eleven home runs in a season. At six foot two and a stony 207 pounds, Doug does have what some call gap power (twenty-three doubles and a league-leading thirteen triples a year ago), but he is playing in an era when there is a lust for the long ball.

It has been seven long years. Seven years of doing things on the cheap. Never before has Doug made more than $2,400 a month, paid only from the first day of the season in early April until the final game on Labor Day, meaning $12,000 for the year. True, 2005 will be different. Having completed seven full seasons, Doug had been eligible for the first time for minor league free agency. He and his agent, Jim Masteralexis, had gotten some interest from several teams but decided ultimately to re-sign with the Giants for a sizable raise. The $6,500 a month will give him a living wage from baseball for the first time, more than $30,000 for the year.

Still, that is a far cry from major league money. Playing just three weeks in the bigs at the prorated minimum salary of almost $2,000 per game would easily eclipse his yearly salary at the minor league level. In the minors, of course, he would continue to get a per diem on the road, meal money of $20. But in the majors that figure would be $80.50. Pizza versus prime rib.

Doug knows that the threshold of talent separating top-level minor leaguers from entry-level major leaguers is razor thin. The disparity in income, though, is enormous. Baseball is unlike most career fields that way; after all, near-great doctors are still quite affluent.

He has lived a big chunk of his life in the contradictory culture of the minors, at once charming and ruthless. For all the family-friendly entertainment the players provide, they live in a world that militates against forming any sort of friendship, one in which the temptation to cut corners—to cheat—is enormous. Many of them have little else to fall back on after baseball. Their identity and all their eggs are tucked into this one basket. There is a yearning to become just a little bit better. A little more bat speed, an extra two miles per hour on the fastball, and maybe, just maybe, you will get the call.

Doug's perspective on baseball's darkening cloud of steroids and performance-enhancing drugs doesn't just come from his status as a minor leaguer trying to make it big, or a teacher trying to keep it real. It goes beyond his academic background in biology. There is also the little matter of his professional affiliation. He has spent his whole career as an outfielder—primarily a left fielder—with the San Francisco Giants' organization, where he has worked in the most formidable shadow in the world of sports.

Doug is fascinated by Barry Bonds. How could he not be? In this intensely competitive arena, here is a guy who seems to stand above the game. Sometimes at the Giants' spring training facility, around the edges of his own workouts, Doug can't help staring at the batting cage when Bonds takes his hacks. It is always an event: the short and beautiful swing, the enormous blasts into the desert sky. This is the hardest thing to do in sports, it is often said—hit a round ball with a round bat, and hit it square. Nobody does it better. "He has so much power up there," says Doug, "that you can't even fathom it."

Back in 2000 Doug had gone to major league spring training for the first time as a non-roster invitee. He got to stay at the major league hotel, the Marriott, and basked in the luxury of it all. In the clubhouse, his locker was just two away from Bonds's. He went about his business, tried to act as if he belonged, put on his sanitary hose without yielding to peripheral vision. One day, though, he was introduced to the slugger by Bonds's father,

Bobby Bonds, himself a former Giants outfielder who now worked with minor leaguers. "This guy," Bobby told his son, "can hit."

A few days later, when Doug was, not surprisingly, sent down to minor league camp, Bonds gave him a bat. Doug thanked him, perhaps too profusely, and carefully placed the lumber in his bag. Later that day the bat was stolen, almost certainly by one of Doug's minor league teammates.

In 2001 Doug was back at big league camp for a few weeks. He made a home video for his eldest brother, Will, who was getting married back in Springfield on Saint Patrick's Day. Approaching veterans such as Eric Davis, Shawon Dunston, J. T. Snow, and Marvin Bernard, Doug asked for their thoughts about marriage and got replies from "Have tons of kids" to "Don't do it!" Part of the video shows Bonds asleep in the training room. Of course he awakened to hit a record seventy-three home runs that season, while Doug, toiling in Shreveport, Louisiana, managed six.

He continued the grind, the bus trips to Wichita, to Mobile, to Trenton, living out of a suitcase for months at a time. He ate hundreds of meals at Denny's. In stints with the Fresno Grizzlies at Triple-A in 2002 and 2003, he touched the highest rung of the minor league ladder. One of the supposed perks there was flying to road games. Often what that meant in practice was coming home to the two-bedroom condo he shared with three other players after a Thursday night game, sleeping for an hour or two, then waking for a 3:30 a.m. shuttle bus to the airport. There he would catch a flight to Tucson or New Orleans for a Friday night game. By not flying right after the game, the team saved on hotel bills.

In the off-season Doug took to spending two months as an "import" for winter league teams in the Dominican Republic and Mexico. The money was decent and the opportunity was clear: a chance to get better. Still, he struggled, far from home, dealing with Montezuma's revenge, sputtering his way through the Spanish he remembered from Mena DeCarvalho, breathing in the smoke wafting to the back of the bus during twisting rides through the mountains. Sometimes when his Navojoa team played in Mexicali, he would wait in a long line to cross the border into Calexico, California, where he'd stock up on Pop-Tarts at Wal-Mart and revel in the cell phone reception, calling home to his dad. It was a hard life, a lonely one, but the quest demanded it. He yearned to find that edge, "to be that person they want."

After his third year of winter ball, he came back to Springfield in January 2005, spent time with his family, and worked as a sub at Central High. In February he flew out once again to Arizona for his eighth year as a pro.

He was amazed at the world he encountered. The usual tranquillity of spring training had been replaced by a wild buzzing of activity. Reporters swarmed everywhere. The congressional hearings were looming. Barry Bonds would not be appearing because of an ongoing grand jury investigation regarding his testimony in the BALCO case from the fall of 2003, but he had become ever more the elephant in baseball's living room.

Bonds arrived at spring training with 703 home runs, within range of the most hallowed record in sports—twelve more to pass the Babe, fifty-three to eclipse Hammerin' Hank. He also arrived in the immediate aftermath of the leaking of his grand jury testimony, published by the *San Francisco Chronicle* in December 2004. The weeks ahead would be filled with discussion about "the cream" and "the clear" and Bonds's mysterious knee injury.

When Doug showed up at the ballpark in Scottsdale, he was greeted by television trucks and a bevy of reporters with notepads and tape recorders. There was a gag order on the team in terms of talking about Bonds, but still the cameras were following his every move. "It was almost," Doug said, "like he was above life."

On March 4 Bonds broke his silence, speaking to two reporters. The greatest hitter of his generation was not the usual defiant Giant that day, but instead spoke in terms that were almost philosophical and as close to confessional as he would ever summon. "So we all make mistakes," he said. "We all do things. We need to turn the page. We need to forget about the past and let us play the game. We're entertainers. Let us entertain." He turned around a question about whether people taking performance-enhancing drugs were cheating. "What is cheating?" he asked. "You can't see, things look fuzzy, so what do you do? You go get glasses. Is that cheating? You get glasses so you can see, so you can do your job. What's the difference?"

The next day the *San Francisco Chronicle*'s Henry Schulman began his story with these words: "Barry Bonds' testicles have not shrunk and his hat size has not grown. So said the man himself as he ratcheted up his attack on critics."

This was the state of baseball, our national pastime, on March 5, 2005, Doug Clark's twenty-ninth birthday.

Twenty-nine is still young for a man in most parts of early-twenty-first-century America, but for a minor leaguer it is getting to be baseball old. Deep in his heart Doug knew he was approaching Crash Davis territory. Time was running out.

Three days later, having gone 3-for-9 (.333) in major league spring train-ing games, Doug was sent down again to the Triple-A Fresno Grizzlies. He packed up his gear, slung a duffel bag over his shoulder, and moved out of the Marriott.

Twelve days after that, he sat glued to the television set in his room at the Days Inn. That was where the minor leaguers stayed.

Can't Miss

Peoria, Arizona

This is the part he hates.

The pressure on the mound? That comes with the job description. Going after the three toughest outs in the game as a closer? Brad Baker can deal with that. Hadn't he proved it? He was recently named the 2004 Southern League (Double-A) Pitcher of the Year, going 2–1 with thirty saves and a 1.57 ERA; then he absolutely blew away hitters in the last month during his first ever call-up to Triple-A. That is why he is here in spring training in Peoria, Arizona, on a major league forty-man roster for the first time in his seven years as a pro.[1] He can stand the heat.

But having to perform at "Padre Idol" before a hooting crew of veterans? That is something else altogether. For a shy young man who loves to wait in a tree stand with his bow and arrow during the first snowfall, or sit for hours in an ice shack on the Harriman Reservoir in Vermont with his fishing line plunging through an augered hole, this is something to dread. Every night he calls his young wife, Ashley, back home in Massachusetts and pleads for advice about what to sing. Ultimately they settle on Big & Rich's "Save a Horse, Ride a Cowboy." Feeling like an idiot, he goes over to Wal-Mart and buys some boots, a cowboy hat, a flannel shirt, and a couple of plastic pistols. The next morning he heads to the ballpark, heart pounding. All things considered, he would much rather face Barry Bonds with the bases loaded.

● Bradley Donald Baker has an appealingly wholesome face. His thick brown eyebrows and long, almost delicate lashes guard hazel eyes that look earnest. His shy smile reveals prominent cheekbones and big, very white teeth. He is reserved, faintly uncomfortable in his skin, unfailingly polite. For the first few years of his professional career, he referred to reporters as "sir." His first minor league pitching coach, Herm Starrette, once told him, "If I had a son, I'd like him to be like you. If I had a daughter, I'd want you to be the guy ringing the doorbell."

At first glance Brad's story appears to have been torn from Norman Rockwell's sketchbook. He grew up in the rural town of Leyden, Massachusetts, just below the Vermont border. Leyden has no stores or streetlights.

There is a cemetery with lichen-covered stones dating back to the early 1800s, a single covered bridge above the Green River, and, according to the 2000 census, 772 residents, 758 of them "White alone."

Three modest homes sit at the top of what the locals call Baker Hill, a plateau with views of more than thirty mountaintops in three states. At one end stands the home that Jim Baker built out of hardwoods from the adjacent forest. Jim and his wife, Vicki, raised three children here, Brad, Colby, and Jill. Fishing poles fill a bucket on the porch. The living room walls are lined with deer racks and a bear pelt, a black one with huge teeth. Brad felled the bear with a single shot at age thirteen.

Across the large front lawn sits the home of Brad's grandparents, Donald and Irene. Donald is a lifelong smoker, and he can be gruff when he drinks too much, but Brad has always sensed his softer side. Retired from his days working railroad construction, Donald now walks to his part-time job as a janitor at the Pearl Rhodes Elementary School, going down the hill by the pasture where he keeps Holsteins as pets. Irene is a devout woman, the mother hen, committed to her family, the Bible, and baseball. When she is not serving up her legendary pancake breakfasts, she is often following Brad's career, clipping articles and tuning in to the webcast of games. Last August, when Brad got promoted to Triple-A in Portland, Oregon, the games wouldn't start until 10 p.m. in the East, and since Brad is a closer, he typically wouldn't come in until after midnight. Irene would root for a Portland lead in a close game, waiting for the magic words from Rich Burk on Sunny KKAD, 1550 on your AM dial: "Now warming up for the Beavers, Brad Baker." That's when she would take out her tape recorder.

Between these two houses and set back a bit farther toward the woods is the home of Brad's uncle Jeff (Jim's younger brother, Donald, and Irene's son). He and his wife, Cheryl, have two kids in elementary school, Kyle and Brooke. Jeff is the white-collar guy in the family, a financial planner for Money Concepts down the hill in Greenfield. His office is a shrine to his nephew. A baseball signed by Brad sits next to one signed by Carl Yastrzemski. Part of one wall is covered with Brad's minor league cards, the shy smile tucked beneath caps of teams like the Augusta GreenJackets and the Mobile Black Bears. Tacked up by Jeff's computer is a San Diego Padres schedule. He admits particular interest in some games in July, when the Padres come east to play the Mets and Phillies. That's when he plans to drive his specially equipped van down to watch his nephew pitch in the big leagues.

Long ago Jeff had been a star athlete in this small town. He was the starting catcher on the Pioneer Valley Regional High School baseball team. An admitted daredevil, he had also earned a spot on the U.S. Developmental (pre-Olympic) ski jumping squad. In his office, right next to a photo of Brad throwing heat in a high school game, sits a framed shot of Jeff flying through the air, his focus apparent beneath his goggles, leaning over his Kneissl skis, the very vision of youthful invincibility.

Of course that was before the accident. It was a sparkling day in the first week of August 1979. Scheduled to take the test for his driver's license later in the week, Jeff got a ride that day from his buddy Jeff Davis. They drove four miles down the hill to the pumping station, past tall cornfields and wispy Queen Anne's lace, to a dirt road that led to the covered bridge.

It is a place with an eerie history, a site of the "Deerfield Massacre," in which fifty-six Puritan colonists, most of them women and children, were killed by French and Indian troops. A nearby sign proclaims: "The cruel and bloodthirsty savage who took her, slew her with his hatchet at one stroke. The Reverend John Williams of Deerfield, 'the Redeemed Captive,' so wrote of his wife, Mrs. Eunice Williams, who was killed at this place, March 1, 1704."

Still, it is a wonderfully serene spot, the postcard-perfect wooden bridge spanning the river, leading to a meandering dirt road that heads up into the woods. The dam that sits just upstream produces a breathtaking waterfall. The water then collects and widens, creating deep pools that are popular with teenagers and other wildlife. Jeff had made the dive off the bridge successfully dozens of times before. He hit his first one that day perfectly, thriving on the adrenaline rush and sense of power, not noticing that the water level was low. Clambering back up, he took easy, hungry strides to reach the wide boards of the bridge. There he stood, glistening, surveying the scene, before plunging yet again, straighter this time, splashing triumphantly into the water. He never felt his head slamming into the sandy bottom. There was no pain, just a sense of warmth and sleepiness, some vague awareness of the ambulance siren.

He had severed his fifth vertebra, a "C5 complete." He would never take another step.

Brad was born the next year, the first child of the new generation. From the beginning he had a deep connection with his uncle. Jeff would often take him for a spin in his wheelchair, down to see the cows, out to watch the full moon rising over the mountains. As Brad got started in Little League, Jeff was a fixture behind the backstop, listening to the pitches pop into the catcher's glove. In 1990, at age nine, Brad climbed into his uncle's van, the one Jeff operates with the back of his head (pushing buttons for blinkers and horn) and pins attached to his wrist (connected to two levers for gas and brake). They drove east a hundred miles to Fenway Park to see the Red Sox play the Yankees. Sitting behind home plate in the handicapped section, they cheered wildly when Mike Greenwell hit an inside-the-park grand slam home run, one of the rarest feats in the game. It was the first time Brad had ever set foot in a major league stadium.

His odds on getting back there in the way he most wanted to were prohibitively low. Sure, he was a local hotshot, long and lean with a live arm and a smooth delivery. He dominated the best athletes in Leyden, and in regional All-Star games he generally blew away the finest hitters from Orange, Erving, and Turners Falls. Oftentimes a whispering chorus behind the backstop would ask, "Who is this guy?"

Occasionally Jeff would look up from his Quickie wheelchair and explain that the fireballer on the mound was his nephew Bradley, who hoped one day to pitch for the Red Sox. Some people nodded their encouragement. Others scoffed. "Sure, the kid is good, but he's a big fish in a puddle. He'd be competing with people from all over the world. You gotta be realistic."

There was no doubting Brad's love for the game. He could tell you all the Red Sox statistics, give you scouting reports on the top prospects in Pawtucket. From Opening Day until the inevitably disappointing finish, the Sox were constantly on the radio or on television up on Baker Hill, usually in all three houses. Up in the loft which Brad shared with Colby, his bed was made up with baseball card sheets. Even in the winter, people traveling by could often hear the plink of aluminum bat on ball from the cage that Jim had built for his boys, or the thwack of Brad's pitches landing in Colby's glove as they stood in their Sorels atop the snow pack.

Brad's mechanics were startlingly good. His motion was free and easy, his head still, his balance point consistent, the whiplike action of his arm repeated pitch after pitch. The ball just seemed to flow out of his hand. Amherst College baseball coach Bill Thurston, the local pitching guru, was stunned by his coiled grace. Thurston had coached a pair of future big league hurlers (John Cerutti and Rich Thompson), and he had been running off-season pitching clinics for area youths for almost three decades. Even among polished professionals it was rare to find such a smooth and efficient delivery. Thurston wound up featuring Brad prominently in his instructional video.

Another thing that set Brad apart was his command of the changeup. It is a pitch that strong-armed high school pitchers don't usually develop, both because it's difficult and because it's not really needed to get the vast majority of teenage hitters out. But fooling around with Colby one day in ninth grade, Brad hatched a unique delivery that would in time become his signature pitch. It wasn't the typical circle change, held like an "okay" sign, or a palmball, choked deep into the hand. Improbably, he would hold his thumb and pinkie on the seams at the narrowest point of the horseshoe and place his three middle fingers on top, gripping the ball like a claw. The resulting action left Colby wide-eyed. The pitch seemed to slow precipitously in front of the plate, then dart sharply down—not unlike Wiley E. Coyote going over a cliff in the old cartoons. (In years to come, even Brad's professional coaches would be dumbfounded by the pitch. Gary Lance, who would be his pitching coach for three years in the Padres organization, said, "It's something he's got that's his alone. I wouldn't teach it to anybody else, and I wouldn't tinker with what he's doing. I'm kind of afraid of it. When I see it in his hand, I don't even want to look at it. . . . I don't want to interfere with the magical aspects of it. It's almost mystical.")

● Life began to change for Brad in his junior year in high school. In November, when he generally had whitetail deer on the brain, Brad found himself thinking a lot about a ninth grade girl with blond hair and milk chocolate eyes. Her name was Ashley Kachelmeyer. She had a lively spirit and a love for sports. Her family hailed from the neighboring town of Bernardston, where they were known for their basketball prowess; her dad was a coach, her brother a thousand-point scorer. She was a good player herself, and focused most of her attention there, though she was flattered by the attention in the school cafeteria from the soft-spoken star of the baseball team.

During spring break, Ashley, her mother, and her aunt Jill went away for a brief vacation. One night the phone rang and Jill answered it. Hearing a polite and nervous voice at the other end, she announced, smiling, "It's a boy for Ashley."

When Ashley returned from vacation, she started showing up at all the baseball games. She wasn't alone. Northeast regional scouts from many major league teams had started making the journey up to little Pioneer Valley Regional High School, where Brad's class of seventy-three was unusually large. They rode past stone walls and dairy farms and the Northfield drive-in theater. When they arrived at Pioneer, they parked their cars on the grass and snapped open their chairs, oblivious to the red-tailed hawks gliding above and the rumble of freight trains in distant left center field. They pointed their radar guns out at the mound and jotted notes on legal pads: *90-plus. Unusual command of changeup. Lots of bite. Throws on a downward plane. Free and easy delivery. Wiry body: can put on pounds of muscle.*

Out of the woodwork, too, came some slick and overdressed men, oddly free at 3:30 on weekday afternoons. Representatives of Scott Boras and Bob Woolf Associates, they would often sidle up to Vicki Baker in her red and white lawn chair with the homemade needlepoint designs of ball and bat.

By the end of the American Legion season in the summer of 1998, Jim Masteralexis had become a fixture. He'd look Brad's parents in the eye and say: "We're not a big agency like Scott Boras. We really focus on local kids and their families, and give them a lot of individual attention. It's a family model. I started the agency with my wife six years ago. Lisa teaches over at UMass, and she loves baseball as much as I do. Our first date was a Red Sox–Yankees game at Fenway Park. I couldn't understand how she could grow up in a small Massachusetts town and be a Yankee fan. For years I've been trying to get her some professional help."

Jim had a huge advantage with Brad in that he was representing Peter Bergeron, the best-known baseball player in western Massachusetts. Hailing from the comparative metropolis of Greenfield (population eighteen thousand), Bergeron had grown up just twenty minutes down the road from Leyden. He was rapidly moving up through the ranks in the Montreal Expos' farm system (and would ultimately make his big league debut in September 1999). Seeking their own scouting report, the Bakers called up the Bergerons, and also contacted the family of Doug Clark, who had signed with Jim after being drafted in the seventh round by the San Francisco Giants in June. All reports came back positive.

Jim's wooing continued in the off-season. One February afternoon he found himself halfway up Bald Mountain in Leyden, a southern-facing patch where the snow had started to melt, exposing some brush, food for the winter-thin deer on the Vermont side of the border. He crouched with Colby, while Brad, knowing every inch of these woods intimately, went to rustle up the natives. Sure enough, moments later several deer came racing by right in front of the wide-eyed agent, who had grown up just outside Harvard Square.

Later that day Jim had dinner with the family, and tasted venison stew for the first time in his life. Eventually the talk turned to baseball. For now, Jim said, everything had to be done on a basis of trust. At this point his role would be that of "family adviser" rather than agent. The family couldn't sign any kind of agreement with him because Brad would lose the option of playing college baseball, should he decide he wanted to go that route. In fact the college scholarship offers had started to pile up, and Jim encouraged the Bakers to pursue them actively, even though Brad had his heart set on turning pro. Jim told them that there were too many unknowns about how the senior season would play out and where Brad might get selected in the draft. If things went well and he was projected to be picked in the first three or four rounds, the college scholarship would serve as a bargaining chip to drive up the signing bonus. Although Brad, like all first-year minor leaguers, would have to sign the standard minor league contract of $850 a month (not even covering his housing), top picks could get a sizable one-time bonus. Until the fifth or sixth round, Jim said, that meant six figures. In the first, it meant seven. Jim Baker, who was often out of the house before dawn to pound nails or pour concrete, could only shake his head.

High school seniors were actually in a better position to get big money than college players, Jim explained, because of the scholarship option; in essence teams were willing to bribe top players *not* to go to college. Of course, early-round bonuses typically included a "college fund" of $50,000 to $100,000 held in escrow (though Jim knew deep down most players never used that fund). Also, Jim added, if Brad projected as a very early pick, his arm would be considered an "insurable risk"; he promised to research some policies.

On April 12 at 1:45, Brad looked out the window of his math class and saw the parade of cars starting to arrive for Pioneer's season opener against the Greenfield Green Wave. He had expected some scouts to be there. The Orioles, Yankees, and Cubs had expressed special interest. The Red Sox told him that they would be on hand to see every pitch he threw all season long. Still, the turnout was startling. All thirty major league teams were represented. Like beauty pageant judges, the scouts watched every move of his warm-up. He then pitched four innings, a firing squad of Stalker radar guns aiming at him every time he cocked his arm. When he was given the rest of the game off by coach Dexter Ross, the caravan of scouts disappeared.

All spring the insanity continued. Ross wound up changing the message on his home answering machine to include the date of Brad's next start. Scouts would show up at the Pioneer guidance office to glean what they could about Brad's character. One appeared at Mim's Market, a general store in Northfield, and asked about the Bakers' financial status, trying to gauge Brad's "signability."[2] They made it to game after game, sitting among the starstruck Little Leaguers and local geezers like Charlie Lopinsky, who always wore a blue and white Barbara Mandrell hat atop his polyester ensemble. Brad rolled right through it, throwing shutout inning after shutout inning, talking politely to the scouts afterward, then driving Ashley home in his 1991 Dodge Spirit. It was one shining day after another.

He had accepted an offer of a full scholarship from the University of Florida. His right arm was insured for a million dollars by American Specialty Underwriters. On the mound he was just about untouchable: 7–0 with a 0.67 ERA, 114 strikeouts in fifty-two innings.

The thirty-fifth year of the Major League Baseball draft was set to begin on Tuesday afternoon, June 2, 1999. Unlike the NFL and NBA drafts, which had already become national media bonanzas, the baseball draft was still an underground event with a cult following. The culmination of millions of miles of scouting trips, psychological questionnaires, and intelligence-gathering missions into guidance offices and general stores, the draft played out by conference call.[3] It was a form of baseball speed dating, as each team's general manager, scouting director, national cross-checkers, and scouting staff huddled in "war rooms," where they were required to make each selection within two minutes. It went on for fifty rounds over two days, culling the top 1,500 high school seniors, junior college stars, and juniors and seniors at four-year colleges from the United States, Canada, and Puerto Rico.

Tuesday morning was sparkling, plenty warm by ten o'clock, when Brad took Jim Masteralexis and Steve McKelvey fishing on the Green River, not far from the covered bridge. He baited Jim's hook and watched him get his first cast tangled around a rock. Brad quickly felt the tug of a sixteen-inch rainbow trout and handed the rod to Jim, letting his agent reel in the big one.

By lunchtime Baker Hill was abuzz. Relatives, neighbors, and high school teammates were hovering in and around Brad's house. Local reporters, some toting their own cameras, scrawled notes on steno pads. Vicki Baker stepped outside to snap photos of the TV trucks that had driven up from Springfield, pointing their satellite dishes to the heavens.

Just before one o'clock Brad climbed up to the loft, white socks peering from between his black trousers and dress shoes. Game balls in cases lined a bookshelf. The walls were covered with posters: Lou Gehrig, Pamela Anderson, a Porsche Speedster. He booted up his computer and watched as two other high school seniors were selected with the top two picks: Josh Hamilton from North Carolina was taken first by the Tampa Bay Devil Rays, followed by Josh Beckett of Texas by the Florida Marlins.

The first round came and went, thirty players, none of them Brad. He came downstairs, got a glass of water, mingled with the crowd. Then he plopped down in a rocking chair just beneath the black bear mounted on the wall and beside a prom photo of him and Ashley all aglow. He waited. Everyone waited.

When the phone rang, Brad lifted himself out of the chair, walked purposefully toward the kitchen, and picked up the receiver. He was polite on the phone, soft-spoken, betraying no emotion. His end of the call was filled with uh-huhs, an okay or two, a thank you very much. Then he hung up as the crowd's eyes bore in on him. He offered up exactly two words: "Red Sox." The place almost exploded with joy.

When the hugs and high fives settled down, the Baker clan breathed in the new reality. Brad talked to a giddy crew of local reporters. Jeff Baker sat in his wheelchair beaming beneath his Red Sox cap. Jim Baker called it "the greatest day of my life."

● Ray Fagnant, the burly Northeast regional scout for the Red Sox, pulled into the Bakers' rutted dirt driveway on the evening of June 17. Sitting in the living room with Brad and his parents, he pulled one photograph after another out of his briefcase, showing the family the rungs up the Red Sox' minor league ladder. The journey would start in Fort Myers, Florida, in the Gulf Coast League, then head up the eastern seaboard, landing ultimately at Fenway Park. As Brad would later say, "He sold the dream."

Fagnant talked at length about what a great story it would be for a small-town Massachusetts kid who grew up rooting for the Sox to play for them one day at Fenway. He said it was now time to take the next step. Then he paused for a moment before announcing, "Bradley, I have been authorized to offer you a signing bonus of $600,000."

It was hard not to gasp. For a family that still canned its own tomato sauce, this was an almost unfathomable sum of money. Still, Jim and Lisa Masteralexis had given the Bakers a six-page memo about recent signing bonuses and negotiating strategies. They had role-played an initial negotiation, and Brad knew what to do. He told Fagnant that he wanted to step outside for a few moments. The near-solstice light was finally giving way to nightfall as he walked right over to his uncle Jeff's, where Jim and Lisa, seven months pregnant with their first child, had set up camp. To preserve the option of the college scholarship at the University of Florida (and the bargaining leverage it afforded), the agents were not supposed to be directly involved in the negotiations, but they weren't about to stay away completely. After all, this was a big moment for their tiny agency, the highest draft pick they had ever had. When Brad opened the door, Jim almost leaped with anticipation. He was shocked by the $600,000 figure. Brad had been the fortieth pick in the nation, and based on bonuses from recent years, Jim knew this was way below market value. "Are you fucking kidding me?" he said, sending Brad back home with a counter of $1.1 million.

Fagnant nodded his head and snapped his briefcase shut. He said he would report the counteroffer to scouting director Wayne Britton, but he wanted to make one thing perfectly clear. Leveling his gaze at the young man, he said, "You do want to play, Brad, don't you?"

● To the Bakers, of course, this was a once-in-a-lifetime opportunity; to the Red Sox, it was just part of their yearly business. The battle was under way.

Five days later Brad took the mound at Fenway in the Massachusetts-Connecticut High School All-Star Game. He pitched two crisp innings, then sat in the Red Sox dugout the rest of the night, looking out across the emerald field to the Green Monster, lost in reverie: "I was kind of just imagining . . . Opening Day, hearing my name announced, and running out on the field in front of all those people for my major league debut."

After Brad's stint on the mound, Jim Masteralexis was invited up to Wayne Britton's office. "How long you been in this business?" drawled Britton.

"Seven years," Jim said.

"I've been in this business for thirty years," said Britton. He went on to tell Jim how agents were ruining the sport, driving prices out of control. "Where is it going to stop, Jim? Where is it going to stop?"

The days spilled into weeks with the Red Sox holding tight on their offer. Jim pointed out that the forty-first pick—pitcher Casey Burns—had just signed with the Padres for a bonus of $750,000, 25 percent more than the Sox had offered Brad at number forty. Britton continued to "pound us with speeches," Jim later recalled. He argued that the Red Sox were working within a budget for all of their draft picks, and those at the top end set the pay scale for everyone else.[4] What's more, they had to make huge expenditures at the major league level to stay competitive. Jim seethed at the lectures. He warned that Brad was fully prepared to accept the scholarship to the University of Florida if the Red Sox didn't substantially increase their offer. He felt that the Sox were exploiting the situation, putting the squeeze on him personally, knowing it would be a huge blow to his fledgling business if he didn't sign his first blue-chip client. And he thought the Sox were trying to take advantage of the Bakers, viewing them as an unsophisticated rural family smitten with the dream.

Brad passed the time fishing, shooting hoops with Ashley, renting video after video. He kept his arm fresh by pitching for Manny's Appliances in the Tri-County League, the highest available amateur baseball in western Massachusetts. His teammates consisted of a smattering of college players, former high school hotshots, a guard from the local jail. In the middle of each game, two players would walk among the crowd with a batting helmet, asking for donations for equipment and umpire fees.

In and around Leyden, whispers grew louder that Brad Baker was holding out. Jim Baker bristled. At one point he raised his voice to Jim Masteralexis: "Look, do they want my kid or not?"

Finally, on the evening of July 9, Britton and Fagnant drove across the state to Leyden for another negotiating session. This time Jim and Lisa dropped the pretense and stayed with the family. For almost two hours the conversation danced around the topic of money. Britton, wearing a yellow shirt with the logo for the following week's Major League All-Star Game (which the Red Sox were hosting for the first time since 1961) was full of southern charm. He asked Lisa Masteralexis if she would name the baby after him. He complimented Vicki Baker on her cooking, listened to Jim Baker's stories about hunting trips with his boys. Then Britton shifted gears and asked Brad to lift up his shirt. Flabbergasted, he did so. "Bradley, you got a nice arm," Britton said. "I like your arm. I like your shoulders. I like pitchers with sloping shoulders and infielders with high hips."

Brad had been quiet for most of the evening, but he then turned to Britton and said, "Look, we're at one-point-one. You're at $600,000. You haven't moved. What's your offer?"

There was silence for several seconds, Brad staring at Britton, Jim Masteralexis's heart pounding away. Finally Britton said, "I'm going to offer you $775,000."

In the days to come, Jim Masteralexis felt giddy, knowing that a deal was in range. He took Brad down to the first-ever Futures Game, a showcase of top minor league prospects, including Peter Bergeron, which took place at Fenway Park two days before the All-Star Game. Before going in, they walked around the Fan Fest at the Hynes Convention Center and saw three-story murals of Sox All-Stars Pedro Martinez and Nomar Garciaparra. "Maybe one day," Jim said, "there will be a mural of you."

There were a few more conversations with the Sox in the coming days. Jim kept the Bakers in the loop and made Brad laugh with his outrageous imitations of Britton: "Bradley, you got a nice butt. Bradley, you got a nice set of legs there, boy."

Finally, on July 26, fifty-four days after the draft, Brad stood in the front yard at a makeshift press conference as a warm wind whistled through the mountains. He thanked his family, his agents, and God "for my fastball." After emotional farewells with his grandparents and uncle Jeff, he left with Ashley in the backseat of Jim and Lisa's car. His parents, brother, and sister followed, then a Channel 40 TV van. They dropped a teary Ashley off in Bernardston. Then they were off to Worcester for Brad's team physical, and then to Fenway Park to sign the contract, Brad and his father both beaming in Red Sox caps. Jim Masteralexis almost puffed with pride at the bottom line: $832,500, plus a college fund; after all, the thirty-ninth pick, Jerome Williams of the Giants, had just signed for $832,000.

They all sat down to dinner that night at the Sheraton Boston: the Bakers, Jim and Lisa, Wayne Britton, and Ray Fagnant. Britton congratulated Jim and Vicki Baker on raising such a solid young man. He asked Lisa once again to consider naming the baby Wayne. He shook Jim's hand. Then he gave Brad his plane ticket for the next day and wished him well.

Early the next morning a black Lincoln Town Car arrived. Brad's family got the call: "Limo for Mr. Baker."

● The roster of the Gulf Coast Red Sox provided some culture shock for Brad. There were nine guys from the Dominican Republic, four from Venezuela, two apiece from Japan and Korea, one from Guam, one from Mexico. The American kids hailed from buoyant-sounding places like New Market, Tennessee; Spring, Texas; and Independence, Louisiana. The players were all in their late teens or early twenties. Many had received little or no signing bonus. The cost of their lodging at the yellow stucco Wellesley Inn and Suites was taken out of their bimonthly checks, meaning they cleared $212. No one complained. The sense of possibility hung forever in the citrus-spiced air. Ramon Martinez, brother of Pedro and onetime twenty-game winner with the Dodgers, was down in Fort Myers on rehab. He drove to the ballpark every day in a black Mercedes.

Life at City of Palms Park was pretty much devoid of glamour. The players arrived early in the morning by van, driving past places like Larry's Pawn Shop and Another Chance Finance Inc. After running and workouts, games began. There were no tickets and no concessions. People came if they wanted to watch baseball games played at noon in midsummer in Florida. On August 9, Brad Baker's professional debut, there were exactly seventeen. The crowd included Tom Gardner, the seventy-eight-year-old bus driver for the Bradenton Pirates, who fought at Iwo Jima; eighty-five-year-old Eddie Popowski, who had served more than sixty years in the Red Sox organization; blonde teenagers Kristin and Tracy Tatum from West Palm Beach, draping long, tanned legs over blue seats on the first base side and attracting plenty of interest from the dugout; and Kim Hall, mother of Brad's teammate Andrew Cheek, focusing the zoom lens of her Canon on the action, saying, "He's dreamed of this since he was two years old."

With a "B" on his cap, and "Red Sox" across the chest of his No. 67 jersey, Brad threw a fastball for strike one to begin his career. On a strict pitch count of forty, he lasted an inning and two-thirds, allowing no runs on one hit and striking out three. Back in the hotel that afternoon he made his first call to Uncle Jeff, then to Ashley, then to his parents. At dinner that night, at the Olive Garden, he talked about how he missed his Sony PlayStation, and how some of his teammates lived in mortal fear of the $25 fines for offenses like wearing cleats in the clubhouse or eating more than one pack of sunflower seeds in a game. He was intrigued by the way his Dominican and Venezuelan teammates liked to sing in the clubhouse, while some of the Americans liked to splurge at Rita's Italian Ices and flirt with the help. He tried to envision the road ahead. "I never wanted to work like my dad, pounding nails all the time," he said. "Watching him, I knew that was something I didn't want to do. He was working seven days a week. If everything works out perfect, I will never have to work like he did. And so far everything's worked out great. There's always that chance that something could happen, injuries or whatever. It's all what God put you on this earth to be. Hopefully, it's to be a major league baseball player. I'll just find that out in the next couple of years."

Late that night a phone call awakened Brad and his roommate Garett Vail, a pitcher who had just graduated from Harvard with a degree in mechanical engineering. It was Jim Masteralexis on the phone: "Brad, it's been a dream all your life to pitch in a Red Sox uniform. How was it?"

"Jim," said Brad through a yawn, "it was awesome."

Early the next morning Brad was down in the hotel lobby spooning some Raisin Bran into a Styrofoam cup and reading the sports section of *USA Today*. The top story was about Braves rookie Pascual Matos winning a game with his first major league hit. A skinny catcher from the Dominican Republic, Matos had played eight years in the minors before getting his chance. "If I die tomorrow," Matos said, "that's okay."

● By spring training 2005, five and a half years later, countless baseball dramas had played out. Pascual Matos was still alive, still playing, but that *USA Today* story in August 1999 still chronicled his only major league hit. Most of Brad Baker's teammates on the Gulf Coast Red Sox had long since hung up their spikes. Lots of them were gone after just a season or two, people like Garett Vail, the Harvard grad; and Andrew Cheek, whose mother had photos to prove that once upon a time her son had been a pro ballplayer.

For those players taken high in the draft like Brad, the chances of making it, of course, were better. From the inception of the draft in 1965 until

1995, 858 players were selected in the first round, according to *Baseball America*.[5] Among those 858 were some of the grandest and richest stars of the game, people like Barry Bonds, Alex Rodriguez, and Manny Ramirez.

Such success was far from guaranteed, though. In that group of first-rounders, only 407 (47.4 percent) had gone on to play more than three years in the big leagues. And 307 of them—guys who had heard the label "can't miss" again and again—would never play a single inning in the bigs. Thus, more than 35 percent of that ultra-elite crew never saw a big payday after the signing bonus and had to make their peace with the death of a dream.

Brad's own draft class of 1999 demonstrated the uncertainty of professional baseball even more clearly. There were some grand success stories. The number two pick, Josh Beckett, had already pitched a complete game shutout in the deciding game of the World Series at Yankee Stadium. The ninth pick, Barry Zito, was establishing himself as an elite left-handed starter, an All-Star and Cy Young Award winner who would ultimately sign a seven-year, $126 million contract, the biggest at that point ever given to a pitcher.

Still, four of the first six picks had yet to play a major league game.

Brad's journey through the minors included the archetypal long bus rides, soft mattresses at the Red Roof Inn, dinners at Subway, kids yearning for his autograph, drunken fans questioning his manhood. He ran sprints, "threw bullpens" (working off the mound and showing his full arsenal of pitches), ate enough sunflower seeds to plant every pasture in Leyden. Teammates came. Teammates left. With the Single-A Augusta GreenJackets, Brad became close with a fellow pitcher, Dennis Tankersley, who was married and had a one-year-old daughter. They played cards, talked pitching, traded fishing stories. Then, with shocking suddenness, Tank was traded. Brad helped the family cram what belongings they could into a small car, and Tank asked him to throw everything else out. Hearing the clunk of children's toys landing in the Dumpster hit Brad hard. He talked about it at length with his mother that night.

In 2002 Brad was pitching well (7–1, 2.79 ERA) for Sarasota in the Florida State League, the advanced Class-A Red Sox affiliate, but this was his fourth pro season, and he had yet to taste the "high minors" of Double- or Triple-A. One night in late June, manager Billy Gardner Jr. pulled him from a start because, he said, there might be a trade brewing and it was important not to risk injury. Brad sat alone in the dugout that night, his thoughts far away. The next day it was official. Gardner called Brad into his office and told him that he and Dan Giese had been traded to the Padres for veteran left-handed reliever Alan Embree.

Back in Leyden, Uncle Jeff called Ashley and asked her to come to the house as soon as possible. She found him in his wheelchair in the living room, crying behind his sunglasses.

Brad was okay with it. The trade involved a promotion to the Double-A Mobile Black Bears. Jim Masteralexis flew down to Tennessee to see his first game. They then took a leisurely drive through the Smoky Mountains, taking stock of Brad's career. Jim told him that he was in good shape, not even twenty-two years old, headed in the right direction. A few days later Jim was thrilled to learn that the Padres had picked Brad to play in the Futures Game, the All-Star weekend showcase he and Brad had attended together in Boston in 1999.

Still, Double-A proved to be a huge adjustment for Brad. The players were older. The hitters were better. The culture in the clubhouse was more acidic; some players watched the rising and falling stocks of teammates with the hawklike vigilance of Wall Street brokers. Beneath the minor league sweetness was a clear undercurrent, the message that some people wanted you to fail.

Brad pitched adequately in the remainder of the 2002 season (4–4, 4.48), then hit a wall in 2003. His once perfect mechanics unraveled. He developed a hitch in his arm swing. He lost velocity on his fastball, and hitters began to sit on his showcase changeup.

When Ashley drove down that summer to join Brad for a few weeks, she found his confidence shaken. He had been taken out of the rotation and sent to the bullpen for the first time in his career. He was 1–6, his ERA an alarming 5.68. After one game she was waiting with wives and girlfriends outside the clubhouse when the skies opened up. When Brad emerged in the pouring rain, he was angrier than Ashley had ever seen him before. He had just been told that the Padres were sending him down to their Class-A team in Lake Elsinore, California.

"He wanted to quit," Ashley said. "I was sobbing. It was so frustrating. You try to rearrange your life for baseball, and it doesn't give, ever, in the minor leagues."

At what felt like rock bottom, Brad was greeted by a new pitching coach, fifty-five-year-old Charlie Hough, who had recently taken the position on a temporary basis after a shakeup within the organization. Hough's own big league career had spanned a remarkable twenty-five seasons. He had known success and failure equally: 216 wins, 216 losses. He had been a starter, a middle reliever, a closer. From the beginning Brad felt Hough's kindness, his willingness to listen. Hough told Brad that he just wanted to watch him throw for a while, that he wasn't overly inclined to tinker. In time Hough hatched a radical idea. He noted that Brad had command of two pitches, a fastball of eighty-eight to ninety miles per hour and a wicked changeup. That was really all you needed as a closer, when you were going to face hitters only once. In fact Baker's stuff was very similar to two stand-out big league closers, Keith Foulke of the A's and Trevor Hoffman of the Padres: same two pitches, similar velocity. Hough said that he didn't want to impose this decision on Brad but thought that it might prove a faster path to the Promised Land.

As fate would have it, Hoffman was recovering that summer from shoulder surgery and began his rehab assignment in Lake Elsinore. Quietly Brad studied a man making $9.6 million that year, someone destined to become the game's all-time leader in saves. He watched Hoffman's workouts, the way he got ready in the bullpen. By season's end, Hoffman was back in San Diego, and Brad was closing games for Lake Elsinore and feasting on the challenge.

In 2004 it all came together for him. The Padres sent him back to Mobile, where the ghosts gave way to glory. Whenever Brad entered the game, the BayBears would pipe in Semisonic's "Closing Time," and pretty much every night there would be a handshake on the mound, a clap on the back, another win for the home team. In the last month of the season he was promoted for the first time to Triple-A in Portland, Oregon, where he dominated: 1–0, 0.93, four saves, and seventeen strikeouts in just nine and two-thirds innings.

Back home in October, Brad and Ashley got married in a stone church in Northfield on a gorgeous New England Saturday afternoon. During the recessional, the organist broke into "Take Me Out to the Ballgame." At the reception the DJ kept providing inning-by-inning reports of Game 1 of the 2004 World Series, in which the Red Sox were hosting the Cardinals. Jim Masteralexis sat at the bar, staring at the TV, watching Alan Embree, the guy who was traded for Brad, throw from the mound at Fenway Park.

● In February, Brad says farewell to his family and flies to Phoenix. Ashley remains behind, working as a teacher's aide and in Mim's Market in Northfield, saving money and getting set to join him in the summer—they hope in San Diego. Brad moves into a condo at Laguna at Arrowhead in Peoria, a perk of being placed on the forty-man roster. In the mornings he drives past the sprawling Community of Joy church down to the field to work on the time-honored spring training routines of bunting, covering first base, shagging fly balls, running on the warning track. Red in the face, he endures the indignity of "Padre Idol," then goes back to Wal-Mart that night to return his cowboy gear. On the mound he acquits himself well, giving up two runs in his first outing, but then throwing scoreless innings in his next three games.

On Monday morning, March 14, he is called into the clubhouse by Padres general manager Kevin Towers, manager Bruce Bochy, and pitching coach Darren Balsley. They tell him that he is throwing the ball well, but they don't have many bullpen spots. They want him to dig in at Triple-A for the start of the season, to get in some quality innings. Anything could happen, though: injuries, trades, a poor performance at the big league level. "Be ready," they say. "Be ready."

Before the exhibition game against the Mariners that afternoon, Towers stands outside his office, getting ready to fly to Washington to testify in the congressional hearings about steroids later in the week. He seems grateful for the distraction of being asked about Brad Baker. He says that to his mind Brad has gone from "a prospect, to kind of a suspect, back to a big-time prospect." There is no way of knowing what will happen from here, he admits, but there is reason for optimism. "With the success that he's had, not only in Double-A but in Triple-A, and what he's had in spring training, he realizes that it's now not that far away. It's not just a dream."

As is customary on "cut day," Brad gets the afternoon off. He goes back to his condo and plays "Big Game Hunter," a video game that allows him to go after bighorn elk and moose with a bow and arrow from his living room. Later he steps outside and begins idly fishing in the fountain-sprayed pool in the center of the condo unit—casting, catching, throwing back, again and again. The saguaro-pocked mountains turn purple as the sun begins to set. The western sky seems to stretch out forever. The temperature is starting to drop. It is time to call it a day.

3 | Fluttering Away

Fort Myers, Florida

For three long, unforgiving days, Charlie Zink points his blue Yukon Denali down Highway 10, leaving his native northern California, heading south, then east, mile after mile of cruise control, lots of time to reflect. He thinks long and hard about the rocket ship season of 2003, the crash to earth of 2004. By the time he pulls in at the Ramada Inn, the Red Sox minor league hotel in Fort Myers, he has absolutely no idea what to expect.

He doesn't *look* troubled, but then again, he never does. There is a certain serenity about Zink, a California cool, a Japanese calm, a self-protective shield that keeps people at bay. His face has a placid symmetry to it: big brown eyes, perfect teeth, a diamond stud in each earlobe, a mole right at the center of the chin, all framing an expression that is typically contemplative. There are times when the Red Sox brass wonders if Zink is competitive enough. Does he have the fire?

A year ago there had been no such questions. In spring training 2004 Zink arrived amid considerable fanfare. Rob Neyer, senior writer for ESPN, had just published a story stating that Charlie was "easily the best young knuckleball pitcher in the world," that he was "*likely* to have a career something like Tim Wakefield's. And he might be Phil Niekro." *Baseball Prospectus*, the widely respected crystal ball of the game ("the standard by which all scouting guides should be measured," according to Oakland general manager Billy Beane), had tabbed Charlie as the top minor league prospect in the Red Sox organization, and one of the top fifty prospects anywhere. Within just a few weeks Charlie would get some prominent play in an article in the *New Yorker*, of all places, a piece called "Project Knuckleball."

His ticket seemed to be stamped for the fast track to the major leagues.

All of which was rather preposterous for someone who had gone 9–17 as a pitcher in college—in Division III, no less. Absurd, really, for someone who had not been selected in the entire fifty rounds of the draft when he completed his collegiate eligibility in 2001. His odds of becoming a big league pitcher were prohibitively small; after all, a *Baseball America* survey of the drafts from 1965 to 1995 indicated that more than four out of five players selected in the first twenty rounds—the best of the bunch—never played even one inning in the big leagues.

Without any conscious irony, the Red Sox had signed him on April Fool's Day 2002 to fill out a roster spot in the low minors. He was a so-called conventional pitcher then—fastball, curve, a hint of a change, nothing exceptional. The decision to sign him was based largely on a recommendation from his college coach, who happened to be Luis Tiant, the popular swivel-and-fire pitcher who hurled for Boston in the 1975 World Series. Mostly on guile, Charlie pitched well for the Class-A Augusta GreenJackets, but Boston's front office didn't feel he had "projectable" stuff. His pitches just weren't thrown hard enough, and didn't break sharply enough, they felt, to get professional hitters out at a higher level. He was almost certainly destined for obscurity, a guy who would pitch a couple of years at Class-A, then go off to sell used cars.

That is, until one day in July, when he was playing catch in the outfield before a game and decided to uncork a knuckleball to Darren Wheeler, the team's strength and conditioning coach.

● Even before that fateful knuckler, it had been a long, strange journey for Charlie Zink.

It began at the legendary Folsom State Prison. This is where inmates used to be kept in the dark in four-by-eight-foot stone cells, where a warden was once stabbed to death, where ninety-three convicted murderers were executed between 1895 and 1937: "hanged by the neck until dead." Immortalized by the Johnny Cash hit "Folsom Prison Blues," it is a place of mythic stature, one that conforms to the most stereotypical visions of prison life. Yes, this is where California's license plates have been made for over seventy years. And yes, there is a quarry; some of the granite, in fact, provides the foundation of the State Capitol in nearby Sacramento, where Ronald Reagan and Arnold Schwarzenegger have held sway. The prison is cut off from the world by a natural boundary, the American River.

Home at one time to serial killers Charles Manson and Charles Ng, Folsom is also where Charles Tadao Zink served the first eighteen months of his life, in a little house on the periphery of the prison. It is a place his mother, Joyce, refers to kiddingly as "a gated community."

Joyce worked as a prison guard at Folsom back then. You would never peg her for the role. She is a petite and polite five-foot-one Japanese American woman who likes to tend her garden, a legacy from her parents, who once owned a small vegetable farm. That was before they were sent to an internment camp following the attack on Pearl Harbor. They had two children at the time. Two more were born at the camp. Joyce came later. Her father died when she was eleven, her mother when Joyce was fifteen. A few years later, in a sociology class, she took a trip to a prison and discovered her calling. In 1970 she began working at a women's correctional facility. By 1973 she was at Folsom, mentioned in a *Time* magazine piece on "women's lib" as one of the first three women in the state to work as a guard in a men's prison.

One of the many reasons you didn't mess with Joyce was because she was married to Ted Zink. Ted was an imposing six foot three, 260 pounds of menace, topped off by a commanding voice and the nickname "Cobra." Like his father and two brothers, Ted made a life in corrections. He was the toughest of them all, rising from sergeant to lieutenant to captain to the associate warden at Folsom.

In 1979 the Zinks had their only child. Charlie was born a few miles away in Carmichael, but he learned to walk in the little house just beyond the Big Yard. Even after the Zinks moved to upscale El Dorado Hills, Folsom was never far away. Their house, where Joyce Zink still lives, is surrounded by towering pine and oak trees, with a creek running through the backyard. Visitors include deer, wild turkeys, hawks, and vultures, but still, when the wind is blowing just right, the haunting noon whistle from the prison comes through clear as day. Growing up, Charlie would sometimes sit at the dinner table and look at the knives fashioned from license plates and toothbrushes that his parents had confiscated that day. "It made me keep a straight line," he says.

Ted Zink had seen so many boys gone bad, and he was absolutely determined that his son would take the right path. Sports would be the ticket. Above all, Ted loved the controlled fury of football. He often spent his Sundays yelling at the 49ers on television. Out back, he liked to whip a football around with his son, and he delighted in Charlie's strong arm, his ability to throw tight spirals. Ted hoped that one day his boy would be the next Joe Montana.

Charlie wasn't really suited for that dream, though. Unlike his dad, Charlie wasn't a boisterous leader. He was more cerebral, more mellow, with a touch of offbeat irreverence. He favored tae-kwon-do and skateboarding, once breaking his wrist on a jump.

Ted got Charlie out on the golf course by the time he was four, and he broke par for the first time at twelve. Ted wasn't quite like the former soldier Earl Woods, screaming during his son's backswing to hone Tiger's concentration, but he wasn't far off. He was tough, and his expectations were high. Charlie describes him as "a man I really, really wanted to please."

Baseball brought them together in a big way. Charlie pitched. Ted coached. Charlie starred. Ted towered. Charlie was good. Ted was proud—enormously proud.

At Oak Ridge High School, Charlie started messing around with a knuckleball on the side, though he never threw it in a game. For one thing, he didn't need it. His fastball was good enough to blow past most high school hitters. Also it was not the kind of pitch his father would approve of: too gimmicky, almost feminine. Ted had retired from Folsom in 1993 and devoted himself largely to following his son's baseball career, never in a subtle fashion. "Ted was 'that Dad,'" said Ryan Fickle, a longtime American Legion teammate who wound up rooming with Charlie in college. "You always knew where Ted was at a ballgame. He would stand behind the dugout, and yell and scream, and cuss and fit about every little thing. If you asked about Charlie, Charlie could do no wrong."

In Charlie's junior year the Zinks got into a dispute with Oak Ridge baseball coach Mike Isherwood, a former minor league catcher in the Yankees' organization. During a preseason scrimmage Charlie was late covering home plate on a passed ball, and Isherwood laid into him. Isherwood knew that Ted Zink, the loudest fan at any game, had coached most of these kids, and now Ted's son had screwed up. Isherwood sat Charlie down for several games, and Ted Zink's lava began to boil. After a week the Zinks started looking at the possibility of transferring; they considered the mighty program of Serra High School, the alma mater of Barry Bonds, who had recently returned to the Bay Area with the Giants. Ultimately, feeling he had made his statement, Isherwood brought Charlie back to the mound, where he became one of the team's aces, alongside good friend Dave Russell.

Charlie's senior year began with the biggest jolt of his young life when Russell was killed in a car accident. Ever after Charlie would begin each inning by drawing Russell's number, 16, in the dirt behind the rubber and saying a prayer. It was a somber, surreal spring, but Charlie became a force on the mound for the Oak Ridge Trojans. At one point he threw a perfect game against Oak Ridge's main rival, the Folsom Bulldogs. Ted basked in all the articles in the *Mountain Democrat*. Charlie was not someone the scouts were after, not someone fielding Division I scholarship offers, but he was small-town great, and there was, Ted felt certain, a big future laid out before him.

When it came time to choose a college, Charlie was divided. On the one hand, he wanted to break free, to yield to his growing wanderlust. He felt some tension with his dad around a few of his life choices; Ted, for instance, hated the idea of his son wearing an earring. On the other hand, Charlie was deeply attached to his family and his friends. Ultimately he decided to stay close to home and enter Sacramento City College in the fall of 1997. Ted was delighted. Sac City is a junior college baseball powerhouse. Even though Charlie was not by any means the team's best pitcher, with a couple of years of good coaching, anything seemed possible.[1]

The intensity of the place wore on Charlie from the start. Early morning workouts were followed by a few hours of classes, then long hours of practice under a blazing afternoon sun. "It was not what I wanted," Charlie said. "They made it too much baseball. It just got to the point where I wasn't having fun playing anymore." Though his team went 44–2 and won the national junior college championship in 1998, Charlie was miserable.

● Fate intervened in the form of an art school in Georgia and a Fu Manchu'd Cuban known in baseball circles as "El Tiante."

Luis Tiant, veteran of nineteen big league seasons, was one of the game's most vibrant personalities. He pitched with a panache rarely seen before or since. His corkscrew delivery saw him turn his back to the plate, then return to release any of a huge array of pitches from every conceivable angle: slow curves from behind his ear, sidearm sliders, palmballs from over the top. In Boston he was beloved as "Loo-ie." He was famed for his stellar performances on the mound (ninety-six wins over a five-year span), for emerging from the shower with a cigar in his mouth, and for weeping openly at Logan Airport late in the 1975 season when he was reunited with his father, who had been held for fourteen years against his will by Fidel Castro. After retiring in 1982, Luis Tiant toiled for years as a scout and minor league coach. In the fall of 1997 he surprised many in the baseball world by accepting the head coaching position at the Savannah College of Art and Design.

The school was well known to students of architecture and jewelry making, but it was not, to be charitable, an athletic power. SCAD president Richard Rowan hired former NBA great Cazzie Russell to coach basketball and Tiant to coach baseball, believing that they could bring the sort of publicity to the school that it would never get from its majors in furniture design or art history. While there are no athletic scholarships allowed in Division III,[2] Russell and Tiant were given considerable discretion to distribute "presidential grants," which just happened to bring to Savannah some basketball and baseball players who wouldn't have to pay for their college education. Through a contact in northern California, Tiant connected with Charlie Zink. Though Charlie had taken exactly one art course in high school ("I had to work so hard just to get a C"), he sensed in Tiant a kindred spirit.

Ted, of course, liked Tiant's pedigree. Sure, it would be hard to see Charlie leave the nest, but playing for a guy who'd won 229 major league games seemed too good to be true.

Charlie loved the life in Savannah. It was elegant and hip at the same time, and he felt richly alive in its midst. For the first time he was on his own. There was a laid-backness to the place that suited his sensibility. He played golf at majestic courses, and spent nights drinking beer, playing poker, and flirting with long-legged belles whose accents made him melt.

Though smart enough to consider law school seriously, he was lukewarm about the academic experience. The best part was studying historic preservation with a sports-loving professor named Marlboro Packard, who took his students out to old cemeteries with maps and chisels for freshening the worn-down headstones of former slaves and Confederate soldiers. In class, Charlie and his teammates dealt with some resentment from serious-minded art students with big portfolios and bigger debt. According to Ryan Fickle, who joined Charlie at SCAD a year later, this attitude stemmed from a re-creation of the high school social divide, something the art students had expected to avoid: "This is *our* school. Why are *they* here? And why are they getting treated better than us? Why are they picking on us, and why are they getting the girls? Why is this happening again?"

Still, Savannah was a sanctuary for Charlie, a place where he felt at peace. This was where he made the best friends he had ever made in his life. Savannah quickly became a second home.

Baseball was fun again. For three years he pitched for the SCAD Bees, becoming their all-time strikeout leader, despite winning only nine of twenty-six decisions on a bad Division III team that played such foes as Brewton-Parker, Maryville, and Ferrum. Tiant was, in truth, not a great teacher of the game, baseball having come too easily to him, but his child-like spirit was infectious. He would hold court, spinning stories about life in the bigs. He cussed and laughed more than any of the college kids, the laugh coming from someplace so deep in his chest that everyone around him felt more alive. The road trips were unforgettable. Tiant's budget seemed to have no limits. In Atlanta, the team stayed at the Marriott Marquis when the Phillies were in town and had breakfast with manager Terry Francona. In Boston, it was first class all the way, including box seats at a Red Sox game. Charlie was amazed by the electricity at Fenway as Pedro Martinez struck out seventeen Tampa Bay Devil Rays. At one point El

Tiante's traveling show took the Bees out to Texas, where Charlie was surprised by his father, who presented him with two diamond studs. Life had never been so good.

After his college eligibility ran out in 2001, he figured he was done with baseball. There were 1,500 high school and college players selected in June's draft, Charlie not among them. He did, though, get an offer to play that summer for an independent team called the Yuma Bullfrogs. The experience quickly sucked the joy right out of the game: dictatorial coaching, harsh conditions, no camaraderie on the team. Charlie hated dealing with heat that often topped 110 degrees. He lived with a host family who kept ten ferrets and four cats in a two-bedroom house with sporadic air conditioning. On the field, he pitched exactly five innings over four games, compiling a 0–0 record and a 5.40 ERA. The season couldn't end soon enough. "It wasn't anything I wanted to do, ever again," he said.

He had also become worried about his father. His parents had come to one of Yuma's games in Petaluma, California, and Charlie was alarmed to hear Ted's hacking cough. He was still a vibrant man of sixty-one, and he had given up smoking years ago, but this cough just wouldn't quit. Several days later Joyce dragged Ted down to the doctor's office. At first, X-rays didn't show anything, but further tests revealed the telltale signs of lung cancer. He began chemotherapy. The doctors were optimistic that they had caught the cancer pretty early.

Still several credits short of graduating, Charlie returned to SCAD in the fall of 2001. He called home almost every day, and got good reports from his mom. He sank back into the life of leisure, long hours of golf, beer, and Wiffle Ball with his buddies, cracking open an LSAT study guide once in a while. He hadn't picked up a baseball in months when he got a call from Tiant, who had left that year to take a minor league coaching job with the Red Sox. Tiant told Charlie there might be a roster spot or two for a pitcher in the low minors, and he thought it could be worth a shot. As bemused as he was excited, Charlie flew to Fort Myers to try out at a mini-camp with thirty to forty other guys. Donning a Red Sox uniform felt odd and wonderful. Pitching at the minor league complex adjacent to the field where Pedro Martinez took the mound made him feel like an imposter. But he did his best, and nodded his head when the organization's minor league director, Ben Cherington, thanked him for coming down and said they might give him a call.

Returning to Savannah, he figured he at least had a good story to tell. After a couple of days of classes, he was shocked to get a phone message:

the Red Sox wanted to see him in game conditions. If he did well, they would offer him a contract. When the Sox broke camp a few weeks later, Charlie signed on the dotted line to pitch for the Augusta GreenJackets in Class-A ball. He would make $850 a month. His signing bonus was exactly nothing.

Ted Zink was absolutely overcome with pride. He told Charlie that he would fly to Georgia as soon as he could, but for now he wanted to hear everything. What number was he wearing? What were the coaches saying? How hard did the other pitchers throw? What were the buses like? The hotels? How long did it take the top players to make it from Augusta to the major leagues?

Charlie filled him in as best he could. He told him that Augusta was beautiful, a golfer's paradise, that his condo was not far from the famed course where the Masters was played. The team's name, after all, was the GreenJackets. He told Ted that he was making some good friends. He was living with the team's strength and conditioning coach, a 280-pound former college football player from Kansas named Darren Wheeler. And he was spending a lot of time with one of the top prospects in the Red Sox organization, a pitcher from inner-city Boston named Manny Delcarmen. Manny was a good kid from a good family, Charlie said. He had been a second-round pick, and got a signing bonus of three-quarters of a million dollars. Ted hung on every word, though Charlie noticed that the hacking cough seemed to be returning. "It's nothing," Ted insisted.

Joyce discovered the wonders of webcasts that spring, listening to the GreenJackets' games over the Internet and setting up her trusty microcassette recorder in case she heard the magic words "Now warming up for Augusta, Charlie Zink."

Working in long relief, often when his team was well behind, Charlie pitched effectively, ultimately posting a 1.68 ERA in twenty-six games. After each outing he heard his dad's voice on his cell phone, softer than he could ever recall, but "very, very proud—it was a little embarrassing how proud he was."

Ted and Joyce had tickets to come see Charlie in June, but as the day approached, Ted's health began to fail. His cough was constant, his weight dropping more and more. On the day of the flight, the former Folsom warden known as Cobra turned to his tiny wife and said, "I don't think I can make it." He was hospitalized and diagnosed with pneumonia. When Charlie called on Father's Day, Ted could barely speak. After the game that afternoon, he took off for the airport and caught the next plane for San

Francisco. His mother met him at the airport that night, and they drove directly to Folsom Mercy Hospital, where Charlie could not believe his eyes. There was his larger-than-life father, the most commanding presence he had ever known, hooked up to a maze of tubes, gaunt and gasping.

The next morning Ryan Fickle got a phone call he would never forget: his buddy's usually jaunty voice, sobbing, saying simply, "It's over."

Back in Augusta, Charlie felt adrift. He hung out with Manny Delcarmen, sipping beers, spitting tobacco juice into empty bottles, playing video games. In the bullpen he would sometimes make up his own little golf course, tapping a baseball with the barrel of his bat to pass the time. One scorching afternoon he waited in the outfield for his turn to "throw a bullpen," demonstrating all of his pitches before the watchful eyes of minor league pitching coordinator Goose Gregson, who was in town to check on the progress of Augusta's staff. Charlie realized by this point that Gregson was really there to evaluate the guys labeled "prospects," people like Manny or first-round draft pick Phil Dumatrait. Sure, their statistics weren't as good as his, but they were the guys the Red Sox had invested in, the guys who were pegged as potential big leaguers.

Hot and bored, waiting his turn, he tossed a ball back and forth with Darren Wheeler, who goaded Charlie to throw some knuckleballs, something he still messed around with on the side for fun. The first few pitches sank. Then, according to Wheeler, the next one soared at the last moment. It glanced off the top of his glove, knocking his hat off, and sending the lenses flying out of his Oakley sunglasses and the frame smashing into his head just above the left eye. "Dude," Charlie said, "you're bleeding."

Wheeler needed three stitches to close the wound. Years later, still working as a trainer in the low minors, Wheeler said that whenever he looked at the scar, he thought of Charlie.

● Almost everyone who has ever played baseball has experimented with the knuckleball. It is the sport's most charming and exasperating pitch, subject only to the laws of physics and the whims of God. When it's going well, it can make Barry Bonds look like Barry Manilow. When it's not, it can make Fat Albert look like Albert Pujols.

Only a tiny fraction of baseball players will ever be able to throw ninety miles per hour, far fewer with control. But any decent high school hurler can throw the ball in the high sixties: knuckleball speed. Hence it holds out the most tantalizing of hopes. Being able to throw this one slow pitch well was basically enough to pave the path of Hoyt Wilhelm and Phil Niekro to the Hall of Fame. In the modern era it has been the almost singular ingredient in turning a below-average minor league infielder, Tim Wakefield, into a millionaire many times over.

But the truth is that the knuckleball almost never delivers on the promise that it dangles before you. Almost no one has been able to master its idiosyncrasies. Knuckleballers were never a thriving lot; by the time the 2002 season ended, they had become a truly endangered species. Of the more than 330 pitchers on major league rosters, exactly two were knuckleballers: the thirty-seven-year-old Steve Sparks, the embodiment of the charming baseball term "journeyman" (a 56–63 record, an ERA of almost 5.00 in seven humdrum years with three teams), and the thirty-six-year-old Wakefield, the leading practitioner of the game's most peripatetic pitch.

Drafted by the Pirates as an infielder in 1988, Wakefield proved that summer that he couldn't hit professional pitching, batting just .189 in Class-A ball. The next year at spring training, the clock already ticking on his career, he was fooling around with a knuckleball on the side when he was "discovered" by one of the team's coaches. He was sent to the mound, and . . . shazam! By 1992 he was in the big leagues, not just as a rookie but as a dominant pitcher, going 8–1 with a 2.15 ERA and then winning two games in the playoffs, which were watched on television in northern California by thirteen-year-old Charlie Zink. In 1993 Wakefield was the Pirates' Opening Day starter. Greatness beckoned.

And just like that, the Midas touch turned to rust. There were walks by the bushel, flat pitches sent banging off outfield walls. Before long he was back in the minors for the rest of the '93 season and all of '94, trying in vain to reclaim the magic. The Pirates concluded that his brief mastery of the knuckleball was an aberration. Manager Jim Leyland later said, "It's just a freak pitch. It's the darnedest thing I've ever seen. We couldn't help him." The following spring Wakefield was released.

The Red Sox salvaged him from the scrapheap in a move that would prove to be one of the great steals of the modern game. The magic came fluttering back as he started the 1995 season with a 14–1 record and a 1.65 ERA. Then just like that, it vanished, as he sputtered to the finish with a 2-and-7 mark and an ERA over 7.00. Such was the rollercoaster of the knuckleball.

In the years to come, though, Wakefield would emerge as Boston's most versatile and durable pitcher. He started, he pitched long relief, he closed. The Red Sox were willing to live with the capriciousness of the pitch because over the long haul, Wakefield provided undeniable value: someone who could chew up innings, a guy who could accomplish the fundamental pitcher's job of getting outs.

• When the Sox convened for spring training in Fort Myers in 2003, the coaching and development staff were suddenly very interested in Charlie Zink. They saw the action on his knuckleball and began to believe that Wakefield's clone had arrived, the one guy in a million, the pitcher with the winning Powerball ticket. After a couple of weeks, Goose Gregson and farm director Ben Cherington confronted Charlie with an edict: from now on you will be a knuckleball pitcher. You will throw the pitch 95 percent of the time.

Charlie was shocked. Hadn't he pitched well with his conventional arsenal a year ago? Yes, he was told, his results had been good; but they didn't believe he had the proverbial right stuff. He wasn't going to make it as a big leaguer on his fastball, curve, and change. This was his chance. Take it, or kiss the dream good-bye.

The Sox provided what instruction they could in the form of a tutorial from Wakefield. He told Charlie that he essentially had to unlearn the pitching mechanics he had been developing for a dozen years. The long arm swing and powerful leg drive to generate velocity had to be replaced with a short arm motion and a four-foot stride. He had to work with a stiff wrist rather than whiplike action, leading with his palm. Wakefield told him to strive for a repeatable delivery, over and over, aiming at the catcher's mask. The one piece of individuality Charlie was permitted was his unique hybrid grip: thumb underneath, knuckle of his index finger against the hide, middle fingernail digging in.

He began the 2003 season in Fort Myers in extended spring training, the dreaded instructional program, while most of the players in the organization were dispatched to minor league teams. After a long week he was sent to Sarasota, the Sox Class-A team in the Florida State League, where he was told he was going to be a starting pitcher. His new identity, the knuckleballer, placed him in a role even stranger than that played by place-kickers in the culture of a football team (since every team has one). He felt peripheral, like the resident freak, his athleticism questioned in a world of young jocks.

The isolation was, in some ways, familiar. After all, Charlie was an only child, the son of prison guards, a guy who had played baseball at an art school. He had to find his own way. Catchers weren't used to the knuckleball. No one else on the staff threw one. Coaches were not really trained to deal with the pitch. Charlie's instructional guides consisted of little more than Tim Wakefield's cell phone number and a couple of DVDs of Wakefield's starts. A few weeks into the season he was 0–3 with an ERA of 5.19. In one start he walked eight batters in five and one-third innings. He longed for the days of being able to throw his fastball, to "challenge" hitters in a way that would have made his father proud. His sense of separation was magnified when his roommate and best friend on the team, Manny Delcarmen, blew out his elbow in late April and left the team for surgery to reconstruct his ulnar collateral ligament—the famed "Tommy John" procedure.

In time, though, the grand experiment began to show promise. Charlie gained comfort with the delivery. More and more he was able to throw the ball without spin and began to get some great diving action on the pitch. Some of the swings against him looked absurd, sending teammates into fits of laughter on the bench. In May he allowed just a run and five hits while striking out seven and walking no one in eight innings against the Daytona Cubs. On June 1 he pitched a complete game three-hitter in beating the Lakeland Tigers. As the season developed, he was becoming a force.

In late July he was summoned into manager Billy Gardner's office and told that the Red Sox had promoted him to Double-A in Maine with the Portland Sea Dogs. That promotion, from Class A to Double-A, is often thought of as the hardest one in baseball. Most organizations have three or four Single-A teams, and just one apiece at Double-A and Triple-A—the so-called "high minors." Suddenly you encounter players with major league experience, and others who will get called directly to the big leagues. It is, for many, a monumental adjustment.

In his first start, on August 1, he allowed just two hits over five and one-third innings and struck out seven, but took the loss against the Binghamton Mets. Two weeks later he took a no-hitter into the eighth inning in beating the New Britain Rock Cats. All the way across the country, Joyce Zink sat alone in her home in El Dorado Hills, webcast playing, tape recorder rolling, feeling happier than she had in years.

On August 30, four days after his twenty-fourth birthday and two days shy of the traditional minor league finale on Labor Day, Charlie made his last start of the year at home against the New Haven Ravens, Double-A affiliate of the Toronto Blue Jays.

His knuckleball that night lived up to Hall of Famer Willie Stargell's description of the pitch: a "butterfly with hiccups." It danced all over the place, as New Haven batters chopped and hacked and whiffed. Charlie was throwing the pitch with complete confidence. As the zeroes piled up on the scoreboard, the crowd of 6,891—the largest Charlie had ever played before—began to pulse with every pitch. Entering the bottom of the ninth leading 2–0, the former SCAD Bee was throwing a no-hitter.

He got Danny Solano to pop up. Then came the league's leading hitter, Alex Rios, who chopped the ball to the left side; shortstop Raul Nieves charged in, gloved it, and fired to first, just in time. There was only one more out to go.

"I was as nervous as I've ever been out there," Charlie would say after the game. "I was shaking."

On a 1–1 knuckler, Matt Logan blooped the ball to short left. Nieves sprinted out, while left fielder Kevin Haverbusch raced in. Both players dove, and the ball landed just between them and squirted away for a double. Charlie then surrendered an RBI single to Shawn Fagan before leaving to a standing ovation.

The Sea Dogs held on to win, 2–1. Charlie Zink had become a cult hero.

On September 13 he went to Boston to join other minor leaguers in the organization who had been named the top pitchers or players of their teams. They converged on Fenway Park for a game between the Red Sox and the White Sox, all sitting together in the left field stands. All except Charlie, that is. He was placed in the second row right behind the plate to watch Tim Wakefield in action. Right next to him was Theo Epstein, the first-year general manager, at twenty-nine the youngest in baseball history. After a brief introduction, Theo didn't speak to Charlie all night. "I was just sitting there looking at girls," Charlie later recalled. "It was fun. Everyone thought I was someone important."

He pitched, and pitched well, in the Arizona Fall League, a showcase for top prospects in all organizations. While there, he watched on TV the epic 2003 American League Championship Series between the Red Sox and the Yankees. He was fascinated by studying Wakefield. Sure, there was the bitter end, the eleventh inning home run he surrendered to Aaron Boone in Game 7, adding another chapter to Boston's seemingly endless October anguish. But the enduring image for Charlie was Wakefield dominating the Yanks in winning both of his starts, sending their mighty lineup into fits of frustration. Some of the best hitters in the world were taking one feeble hack after another. The good knuckleball was the game's Kryptonite.

In spring training the next year, Wakefield invited Charlie out one evening, saying they should meet at Saks Fifth Avenue. When he arrived, Wakefield had already purchased two suits. The young pitcher was flabbergasted when Wakefield told him that he would wait while Charlie was measured for alterations. Then they went out for a fancy meal, which ended with Wakefield yelling at Charlie when he reached for his wallet.

When the 2004 *Baseball Prospectus* came out, Charlie saw the list of Top 50 prospects, which contained many soon-to-be stars at the major league level: David Wright, Joe Mauer, Grady Sizemore, Jason Bay, Scott Kazmir, Alex Rios, Bobby Crosby, Ervin Santana, Bobby Jenks . . . and there he was, right there with them, so close he could taste it.

But that year Charlie Zink would get an intimate introduction to the other side of knuckleball life. Starting the season with Portland, he had trouble right away. He had never pitched in a cold climate before, and New England in April was too blustery for him. Long ago he had been diagnosed with Raynaud's disease—a blood vessel disorder that causes the extremities to turn numb in response to cold or stress—and he struggled to get a good grip on the knuckler. Even as the weather warmed, he fought to regain command. Already 0–2, he gave up seven runs in four and two-thirds innings in a loss on May 1, then followed that up with a start in which he was knocked out after getting just four outs, while surrendering four runs on five hits with four walks.

"I was just lost," he would later say. "There really was no one to talk to." In baseball "you've got to wait five more days to pitch. Those five days take forever. You had a bad outing. Now you can't do anything about it. You just have to keep looking at your garbage numbers."

His teammates provided little help. His best friend in the organization, Manny Delcarmen, was down in Sarasota, trying to come back from his elbow surgery. Other members of the pitching staff were not enjoying his struggles, but they were not exactly gushing with sympathy either. If anything, Charlie's wild spree of success in 2003 in his month at Portland had ruffled some feathers. The knuckleball was viewed not much differently from steroids—something unnatural that was used to cut corners.

Charlie began spending a lot of time at the Fore Play Sports Pub in downtown Portland. On the road he found distractions galore. Most alluring were the trips to play against the Norwich Navigators in Connecticut, where Charlie would go to the Mohegan Sun casino for hours on end, sometimes losing hundreds of dollars at blackjack. On the mound, he just couldn't seem to find himself. He began to feel tightness and twinges in his shoulder. Other pitchers were leapfrogging over him in the organization. On July 8 he lasted just three innings in a loss to Trenton, plunging his record to 1–8 and ballooning his ERA to 5.79. The headline he saw in a Trenton paper would sting him to the core: "Zink Stinks." He couldn't argue the point.

After that start, the top prospect in the Red Sox organization was told that he was headed back down to Class-A ball.

In Sarasota he did anything but right the ship. In three starts he went 0–2 with a 5.65 ERA. He was then shut down for the year after an MRI revealed a swollen shoulder capsule. Thus concluded an almost unimaginably bad season.

He stayed with the Sarasota team for the last month of the year, running and rehabbing and watching game after game in Florida in August. The days seemed to last for weeks. When the minor league season came to a merciful close on Labor Day, Charlie was told to report to extended spring training in Fort Myers. There it was more of the same: running and bunt defenses and covering first base on ground balls hit to the right side, again and again. September crawled into October and he was there still, reporting to work in shorts and a Hooters or Bob Marley T-shirt, changing slowly into his baseball gear. After a long day of workouts, the team would order pizza and wheel a television set into the clubhouse and watch the Red Sox play in the 2004 postseason. It seemed so far away. Even as the Sox fell behind three straight games to the Yankees, and then Dave Roberts stole second and the whole baseball world became some sort of Red Sox Fantasy Island, Charlie wanted nothing more than to get the hell out of there.

When it was all over, when the "long-suffering" Red Sox had finally done it, Charlie drove home to California, more relieved with every mile. He enveloped his mother in a huge hug. He downed one Sierra Nevada Pale Ale after another while watching the 49ers. He drove out to Lake Tahoe to gamble with his old buddy Ryan Fickle, once a Division III All-American baseball player, now an assistant manager at Enterprise Rent-A-Car. He slept late. When he got up, he sometimes just walked out into the backyard by the creek beneath all those old oak and pine trees where he used to catch the bullet passes from his dad. He breathed deeply, looked out into the foothills of the Sierras, and heard that haunting noontime whistle.

4 Manny Being Manny

Fort Myers, Florida

In the grand scheme, eighty-six years is a heartbeat, but in New England the period of time from September 1918 until October 2004 had been a historical epoch along the lines of the Pleistocene Era or, more accurately, the Dark Ages. Had ever a people suffered so much? Always the sweetest of fruit had been dangled, always it had been snatched away. It wasn't just losing. It wasn't just not winning. It was the anguish of almost.

Now the Curse of the Bambino had lifted. After their back-from-the-crypt comeback against the Yankees, the Red Sox had made quick work of the St. Louis Cardinals. Beneath a full lunar eclipse, they had won it all. Throughout New England it was said over and over again: Now I can die in peace.

In truth, most of the fans didn't perish quite yet. They enjoyed a winter of the most extreme content. They pinched themselves silly and turned basking and savoring into art forms.

In mid-February they revel in the annual *Boston Globe* photo of the equipment truck leaving Fenway Park, heading south. Many follow, more pilgrimage than vacation, flocking to Fort Myers, Florida, to greet the conquering heroes as they try to do it again. They are people like Frankie Jurkowski, a mailman in Northampton, Massachusetts, who always wears a Sox cap when making his appointed rounds. Late in October, Frankie had walked with his son to a nearby cemetery, poured some champagne over his father's gravestone, and said simply, "Dad, they did it."

On March 4, for the first time since the World Series win, men in Red Sox uniforms take the field to play. They split their squad in two and take on Northeastern University and Boston College in a pair of seven-inning games. For years the Sox have scheduled games against college teams in their first few days of Florida action. For the college kids, playing against the Sox is a photo for the scrapbook. For the pros, it is a gentle adjustment to competition, a way to dip their toes in the water. Invariably, the Sox win big.

Game 1 proves even more of a romp than expected, as five major and minor leaguers combine for a no-hitter, with Boston winning, 17–0. Game 2 is a more reasonable rout: 11–5. For all Red Sox players it is a glowing day.

All except one, that is. In his first-ever game in big league camp, Manny Delcarmen gives up all five runs on three hits, two walks, and a wild pitch in just one-third of an inning.

● No player in the Red Sox organization enjoyed the World Series victory more than Delcarmen. Though he wasn't on the big league roster during the win—he had never even played Double-A ball for that matter—the team and its history were deep in his bones. Who else could navigate every stop of the MBTA bus line, much less call one of its drivers, Javy Colon, a lifelong friend? Who else knew what it was like to live in a triple-decker? Who else preferred candlepin bowling? Even as rambunctious teenagers, Manny and his friends used to flock to Ron Covitz's ten-lane operation, the one with the Keno games and the homemade ice cream, a place where, as one reviewer deftly noted, patrons could get both a banana split and a 7–10 split.

The hub of his youth, though, was the place his old Irish high school baseball coach John Conley called "Fenway Pahk." Manny had sat in virtually every section of the famed ball yard, often showing up early, stretching his dark, sinewy arms over the railing, imploring Wade Boggs, or Dewey Evans, or Roger the Rocket Clemens for an autograph. Sometimes he sat in the bleachers and watched the pitchers warm up from just a few feet away: crack, crack, crack, sliders on the black. He played his own ball on the skin infields of Jamaica Plain and Roxbury, holding hard to that common and unlikely dream, to grow up and play ball for the Sox.

The absurdity of the dream was even more pronounced in inner-city Boston. For all the region's devout worship of the Red Sox, the city's public high schools had not produced a single major league draft pick since 1966.

Manny came by his love for the game honestly. His father, Manuel de Jesus Del Carmen (known to all as "Kuki"), had grown up in the pueblo of San José de los Llanos in the Dominican Republic. By the early seventies, when Kuki came of age, the Dominican had become established as a baseball proving ground, yielding several prominent players. Those included the Alou brothers, Matty, Felipe, and Jesus (the one with the continual crick in his neck), and the euphoniously named center fielder for the great teams of the Big Red Machine, Cesar Geronimo.

A scrappy shortstop, Kuki signed with the Phillies in the summer of 1973 at the age of seventeen. Like the vast majority of minor leaguers, he was damn good but not good enough. He languished in the low minors for years, playing for teams like the Pulaski Phillies in the Appalachian League and the Peninsula Pilots in the Carolina League, never making anywhere near a thousand dollars a month. Still, he loved it. When the dream thudded to a halt in 1977, he sobbed.

In search of a new life, he and his wife, Belen, moved to the Dorchester neighborhood of Boston, then to Jamaica Plain, which had become a thriving bastion of Dominican culture, the streets pulsing with salsa and merengue and the smell of chicharrón (pork rinds). Soon after, he opened Kuki's Auto Repair in Hyde Park, at the southernmost tip of Boston. He had part of a brick warehouse next to Feeney's Welding. Six days a week he'd come home with grease on his hands. Years later the family moved into the first floor of a triple-decker on Sunnyside Street, not even a half-mile from the shop.

Their first child was Sabrina, all girl. Then came Manuel Jr.—Manelito—and Eddy. All grew up speaking Spanish at home. Almost every Christmas they would go down to Los Llanos, where the world revolved around family and baseball. Manny remembers being awakened each morning by roosters and jumping up to grab his glove.

Even as a child, Manny had a presence. Beneath dark, curly hair tipped gold by the summer sun was a big smile tinged with a hint of mischief. He was an effervescent and headstrong kid. When the games he loved to play didn't work out, the volcanic tantrums followed. "Very stubborn," recalls Sabrina. "If it wasn't his way, he would throw a fit."

The thing that calmed him down the most was the simple joy of throwing a ball. Even as a young kid, he had natural whiplike mechanics. He was a fixture on the sidelines at his dad's softball games for a team called the Red Hats, and Kuki's teammates marveled at young Manny's velocity. Each crack in the pocket of the catcher's glove filled him with a sense of pride and power. So, too, with the candlepin bowling; he'd fire the three-pound balls down the lane with savage speed, sending the thin pins clattering.

In 1998, when Manny was a sophomore at West Roxbury High School, the Red Sox unveiled their new ace, Pedro Martinez. Never before had Dominican culture been embraced by such a wide swath of mainstream America. Pedro's starts at Fenway were events: the Dominican flags, the songs, the theatrical flair on the mound, ninety-seven miles an hour up and in. "That," Kuki would say with pride, "is how you play the game."

During the school day Manny was a fun-loving kid, not always the most mature. High school classmate Anaclarice Silva recalls that he used to delight in coming up from behind in the hallways, tapping you on one shoulder, and passing on the other side. One day when she was walking down the stairs in her tight ROTC uniform, Manny snapped a photo of her butt and held on to it like a trophy.

On the field he was more serious, taught from a young age to respect the game. As his body filled out, his starts became events in their own right. Area scouts with MapQuest directions littering their backseats pulled in behind the backstops at city schools to observe a young man who could run his two-seam fastball up to ninety-three miles per hour and snap off 12–6 curveballs. They pointed their radar guns out toward the mound every time Manny cocked his wrist. In his first start as a senior Manny struck out twenty batters. In the neighborhood there was a palpable buzz, a sense of *orgullo*: the local kid was about to make good.

Early on draft day in June 2000 he took off, sitting by himself for hours among the mostly elderly patrons at the Old Country Buffet in suburban East Walpole, hiding from the attention of friends and family and media. The selections, dutifully followed by his family on the Internet, began at one o'clock. Shortly after three, Manny returned. Before he even got to the front yard, he was intercepted by a hug from his teary mother. It was then he learned that he had been picked in the second round, sixty-second overall—by the Red Sox.

In late August, after a protracted negotiation, Manny sat next to his dad in the team's executive offices at Fenway Park, resplendent in a new tan suit and new Sox cap. Reading from a crumpled piece of paper, he told reporters: "What can I say? It's a dream come true. Before anything, I'd like to thank the Red Sox for selecting me. My family and I feel blessed that Boston has such faith in me. I know how much this means to the Spanish community in Boston. I'd like to thank my mother and father for being with me every step of the way."

● Up until 2005, Manny's minor league career had not been all that distinguished. The Sox liked his stuff, and his competitive mien, but not always his attitude. That issue came to a head during the 2002 season, his second full year as a pro. Manny spent the entire year pitching for the Augusta GreenJackets, Boston's low-A team in the South Atlantic League. From the beginning he butted heads with Arnie Beyeler, an old school, by-the-book manager, who, like Manny's dad, had spent a big chunk of his youth in the minors, never breaking through. Beyeler wanted discipline and respect. Manny was a free spirit with a bullheaded streak. He was a twenty-year-old kid from the city, a second-round draft pick who had spent a decent chunk of his $750,000 signing bonus on a low-riding silver Lexus IS 300 with nineteen-inch rims, interior neon lights, and a supercharger. He came to the park in his wraparound Oakleys with his cell phone on his hip. Beyeler thought he needed to be chopped down to size.

Manny lost his first four decisions that year, failing for the first time in his life on the baseball diamond. It was a long, hot summer, filled with Comfort Inns and Waffle Houses and southern-accented abuse cutting through the humid air from small-town fans of teams like the Greensboro Grasshoppers and the Savannah Sand Gnats. He missed his friends and the frappes back at the bowling alley in Hyde Park. He missed his dad. He had a hankering to go out with Ana Silva. The girl whose backside he had photographed in high school was now studying economics at Regis College, a Catholic women's school in Weston, Massachusetts. She had gotten his screen name from a friend and began instant messaging him anonymously. Little by little over a period of weeks she revealed more of her identity, at one point hinting that they had gone to school together. Charmed, Manny paged through his high school yearbook and started taking guesses. Ultimately, shaking, hands sweating, she text messaged her name. Ah, yes, Ana.

In August, Manny hit his stride. In his last three starts he didn't allow a single earned run in fifteen innings, surrendering only eight hits, striking out fourteen. The season was set to end on Labor Day, and Manny had one start left, his numbers up to a more respectable 7–8 with a 4.10 ERA. He was feeling strong, regaining his confidence. No minor leaguer in the Red Sox organization had more strikeouts. He wanted to end the year with a bang.

Then he got called into Beyeler's office, where he was told the team was shutting him down for the rest of the summer. Manny was incensed. "Why?" Told he had thrown enough innings and that the Sox wanted to protect his young arm, Manny shook his head in disbelief. "Fine," he said. "I'm outta here."

Doors slammed. Lockers slammed. Soon he was thundering north, airing out that supercharger. The cell phone kept ringing: Beyeler telling him he'd be sorry if he went AWOL. Manny snapped the phone closed. A few minutes later it was Ben Cherington, the director of player development for the Red Sox, way up on the organizational totem pole. Click. Then Cherington again. Click!

Up in Massachusetts, Jim Masteralexis's cell phone rang. At that moment he was helping a very pregnant Lisa into the car. Rivers of sweat were pouring down their foreheads. His heart was hammering. It was not a good time. Still, he saw on the caller ID that it was Cherington, who was both a former student of Lisa's and, more important, his lifeline to the Red Sox organization. Against his better judgment, and with Lisa glaring at him, he snapped open the phone.

"What's up, Ben?"

"Jim, Manny's gone AWOL. He just exploded in the locker room and took off. He keeps hanging up on me. Will you tell him to get his ass back to work?"

"Look, Ben, I'll see what I can do. But I gotta tell you, it's not going to be easy. I'm in the car with Lisa. We're going to the hospital. She's about to have twins."

Manny just kept going, mile after mile, the steam barely dissipating. A little after one in the morning, he stormed over the George Washington Bridge into a city of lights. Barely on the other side, he blasted through a gigantic pot hole, immediately flattening two tires and bending one of those shiny nineteen-inch rims beyond repair. He thudded over to a closed gas station. Grabbing out of the trunk a bat that had been signed by his Augusta teammates, Manny pounded away at the rim. Boom-boom-boom-boom, sparks flying. Boom-boom-boom. It felt good. Boom-boom. He didn't have to take this. Boom!

And then he stopped, thoroughly ashamed. What the hell was he doing? He just wanted to pitch, to compete. But this, he knew, went against the code. This was not what it meant to be a professional ballplayer. This was not respecting the game.

Sheepishly, he called his dad, waking him from a deep sleep in Boston. He waited for hours, night giving way to a languid late-summer dawn. His teammates were back in Georgia finishing up their season like pros. He had made a fool of himself. By the time Kuki arrived, Manny was not merely chastened; he was broke. Some tough-talking teen had seen the fancy car and Massachusetts plates as fair game. He demanded money. Resigned, Manny merely emptied his wallet and handed his bills out the window.

● The 2002–3 off-season was pure salve for Manny. He loved the pulse of the streets in Hyde Park and Jamaica Plain. People would stop him, pat him on the back, ask him when he might make it up to the Sox. Sometimes he hung out at Kuki's Auto Repair, talking cars and pitching with his dad. At Ron Covitz's bowling alley he'd plunk down three dollars for a string of candlepin, pose for pictures with neighborhood kids, and talk smack with his old buddies. Javy Colon always kept him laughing. Javy also reminded him that he needed to be patient and count his blessings. Throwing a ball for a living beat the crap out of driving a bus on Route 23 through Dorchester and Roxbury up to Ashmont Station.

Sometimes Manny drove out to the pristine campus of Regis College. He sat in the bleachers at the volleyball games, hooting and hollering, making Ana Silva recoil with embarrassment. She punched him in the arm afterward. He threw his arm around her shoulder. By November they were going out.

Manny was assigned to the Sox' Single-A team in Sarasota, Florida, for 2003, a season that began with his serving a suspension for his vanishing act at the end of 2002. The reason was never reported in the Boston media. Because he was still in the low minors, Manny's act of defiance was the proverbial tree falling in the forest, but within the organization, it was duly noted. Manny was a fiery competitor, but he was also one stubborn dude.

On April 11 he threw the best game of his young pro career, seven innings of one-hit, eleven-strikeout ball against the Vero Beach Dodgers. Six days later he was sailing along again, working on a four-hit shutout in the ninth, when he uncorked a changeup that left his elbow and fingers vibrating with numbness. The pitch flew out of the park for a game-tying home run. It was the least of his worries.

Manny had been throwing a ball his whole life and had never felt a hint of pain in his arm. He didn't say a word to anyone other than his roommate, Charlie Zink.

"Dude," Zink said, "shut it down. It's too early in the season. You're too young. Don't get hurt."

"Dude," Manny replied, "I'll get people out."

His next outing, in Dunedin against the Blue Jays' affiliate, was going along well enough, Manny's pitches darting around in the low nineties. Then came a two-seam fastball that brought back the explosion of numbness. Still, he tried to throw. There was a fastball at eighty, a curve that bounced way in front of the plate, then a trip to the dugout with his elbow swelling up like a grapefruit.

The Red Sox flew him home to Boston and set up an MRI with Dr. Bill Morgan, not yet famous as the doctor who would practice on a cadaver before suturing Curt Schilling's ankle, creating the famous bloody sock of the 2004 ALCS. Morgan looked at the film and told Manny, "I've got some good news and some bad news. The good news is you did not tear your ligament the whole way. The bad news is you need surgery."

That afternoon Manny watched his brother Eddy hit a home run in a high school game. Afterward he approached his kid brother with tears in his eyes. Later in the day he broke down in front of his father. He was twenty-one years old and scared out of his mind.

Back when Kuki had started in the low minors, a pitcher who tore his ulnar collateral ligament was instantly finished with his career, no matter how promising he might have been to that point. Fortunately for Manny, he was growing up in a different era, one when the term "Tommy John surgery" had become almost an athletic cliché. Back in 1974, John, a left-handed pitcher in his prime with the Dodgers, was sailing along in the middle of a 13–3 season when one pitch felt suddenly, horribly different from all of the thousands in his past. He had torn his UCL, a little connective band in his elbow that had invisibly made his craft possible since he first took the mound in Little League. Desperate, he turned to Dr. Frank Jobe and agreed to be the guinea pig for a maverick surgical procedure that replaced the torn ligament with a tendon imported from his right forearm. Ultimately, Jobe thought, the tendon (which connects muscle to bone) could be trained to serve as a ligament (bone to bone), though he gave John a slim chance of ever pitching again in the big leagues. But after a year and a half of rehab, to the wonderment of many, John returned better than ever. He won ninety games over the next five seasons, and then another ninety-two over nine more in a career astonishing for its longevity.

Since then, the procedure had become a career saver for a great many pitchers. Manny's agent, Jim Masteralexis, told him that several guys had actually demonstrated *increases* in velocity after surgery. So when the Red Sox agreed to Masteralexis's request to set up the surgery with the famed Dr. James Andrews, the Leonardo da Vinci of elbow reconstruction, Manny had reason for optimism. That said, it was hard to crowd the doubt out entirely. Fifteen percent of the operations were not successful, an unsettling number for a young man whose arm was both his meal ticket and his source of self-esteem. On Cinco de Mayo, while his home neighborhood pulsed with life, Manny lay on an operating table in Alabama as a tendon removed from his left forearm was threaded through tunnels that had been drilled through the ulna and humerus bones in his right elbow.

The summer of rehab moved at a glacial pace. Day after day Manny submitted to the pain and drudgery at the Red Sox spring training facility in Fort Myers. After April, Fort Myers becomes the organizational base for rehabbing players and for extended spring training. Then in mid-June it becomes the home of the Red Sox' rookie team in the Gulf Coast League. There they were every day for Manny to see, the latest batch of prospects, young and strong and healthy, full of hope, while he wasn't even allowed to pick up a ball. He got calls all the time from his buddy Charlie Zink, who had found his groove as a knuckleball pitcher. Zink was moving his way up the ladder, getting a call to Double-A, where Manny had never been. He missed the competition, the quest. He had been pitching in baseball games every summer that he could remember. It was like some terrible itch that wouldn't go away. In time he started throwing a ball left-handed just to taste a little bit of the old ambrosia. Perhaps he overdid it; in December he had to go in for minor surgery to tighten ligaments in his left shoulder.

By mid-March 2004, just ten months after the elbow surgery, he was pitching live batting practice. In a *Boston Herald* article by Michael Silverman, director of player development Ben Cherington was quoted as saying: "Manny has busted his ass—he's worked hard and he's ahead of schedule. . . . He has approached his rehab from Tommy John about as well as you can, and now we're seeing the results."

Walking out of the bathroom one day in spring training, Manny was stunned to see Pedro Martinez. "Manny, right?" Martinez said, extending his legendary right hand. "I've heard good things."

Almost immediately, Manny called his dad. The whole Red Sox dream hadn't felt this real for the longest time.

In mid-May he was finally cleared to pitch in games. He returned to Sarasota in the Florida State League, back on the horse again. He couldn't believe how good it felt: looking in for the sign, swinging into the familiar motion, letting it go, hearing that satisfying thwack in the catcher's glove. He threw three innings and didn't allow a hit, striking out four.

From a statistical standpoint, he didn't have a very good year, going 3–6 with a 4.68 ERA. But as the season went on, the organizational reports got better and better. Many of the runs scored against him were coming on cheap hits. He was averaging more than a strikeout an inning; his walks were way down. He was throwing ninety-five, free and easy. The curveball had bite. His changeup was becoming a legitimate weapon.

At year's end he was invited to play in the Arizona Fall League, an instructional league for top prospects. Each team selected six players for the league, the vast majority of whom had some Double-A or Triple-A experience. Manny gladly joined the Peoria Saguaros, and for the first time in his life he threw in relief—and threw well. On October evenings, while many of the players prowled the Phoenix nightclub scene, Manny typically went home to his condo to watch the Red Sox. He couldn't believe the drama playing out before his eyes: the kings of heartbreak were turning history upside down. He knew what this meant. This was not in any biblical sense a miracle, but it was a singularly grand moment, a fervent confirmation of the fundamental *mattering* of the Red Sox.

He was one of them, sort of. In November the Red Sox placed him on the team's forty-man roster for the first time, and gave him his first-ever invitation to major league spring training. Manny practically glowed with the news. Not that he expected to break with the team in April, mind you. Constitutionally impatient as he was, he knew that would be too much to ask—for now. But he was getting all the right signs. He felt as if he were part of the Red Sox' plans. Surely they would grant him his first promotion to the high minors of Double-A or Triple-A. He would be closer to the Promised Land, closer to home. Like his father, Manny had played his whole career at the A-ball level in the South. But the Sox' Double-A team played in Portland, Maine, and Triple-A was in Pawtucket, Rhode Island. In 2005, he felt sure, he would be back playing ball in New England for the first time since finishing high school in 2000. His buddies from the bowling alley could see him play. So could his dad. And Ana.

They moved in together that November. They lived in the small town of Randolph, south of Boston, across the street from a Shaw's supermarket and around the corner from a Dunkin' Donuts, where guys in hardhats gulped coffee while reading the sports section of the *Herald*. Home was a small apartment on the third floor of an institutional-looking red-brick building with dimly lit corridors. They had some old furniture and two cats, a tabby named Little One and a big white fluff-ball named Precious. It was a sweet life. Ana left early in the morning for her job as a secretary at the DA's office in Dorchester, where one of the lawyers, Mike Roberts, loved to talk to her about the Red Sox. Manny slept late, ran and lifted and long-tossed, watched SportsCenter, played hours of MVP 2004 on his Xbox, electronically pitting himself against A-Rod and Jeter. At night he and Ana often went out, walking arm and arm through Faneuil Hall, watching the magicians out front, the Red Sox apparel and conversation everywhere, the city still dizzy with joy.

● The shortest distance between two points, we learn in high school geometry, is the straight line that connects them. This theorem is contradicted by a two-mile stretch of Edison Avenue in Fort Myers, Florida.

Point A is City of Palms Park, the Red Sox' spring training home. It is a veritable shrine. The sidewalk out front features a statue of a towering ballplayer placing his hat atop the head of a child. The accompanying plaque reads, "The greatest hitter who ever lived, an American patriot, a pioneer in the development of the Jimmy Fund, Ted Williams will forever be one of the great heroes in the history of baseball, Boston, and America." Inside, in the concourse right behind home plate, the first thing fans come to is a bank of ATM machines, the better to support the thriving business that unflinchingly charges four dollars for a twenty-four-ounce bottle of water.

The pilgrims in their Curse Reversed T-shirts and crisp twenty-five-dollar New Era caps zoom their digital cameras at young men who are stretching their hamstrings while chatting with one another about home runs or Hooters. These are big leaguers—World Series champions, no less. All will clear six figures this year, many seven, some eight. They work in a rarefied atmosphere. It is sunny and seventy-seven degrees, the palm trees behind the outfield wall swaying slightly. The field is incredibly green.

The line segment to Point B is a straight shot down Edison Avenue. Almost instantly the landscape changes. Within a quarter-mile, you come to a corner store where a yellow and black cartoon character has been crudely painted on the white cinderblock wall. He is smiling broadly, dropping bills from a wad in his fist, surrounded by dollar signs and the words "Larry's Pawn Shop, Inc." Out front in neon flash the words "Pawn," "Guns," "Jewelry Repair," "Gold," and "Tools." Nearby is the Eden Church, where a couple of black kids sit on the porch on game days, trying to lure cars into a dusty lot for five dollars a pop. Across the street are one-story shacks of light blue and yellow, with clothesline-edged yards, abandoned cars, a dog on a chain sitting in the dust, a prominent "No Trespassing" sign. A canal for irrigation is all but dried up, strewn with trash and bottles. There are several auto salvage yards ringed with barbed wire, a boarded-up firehouse, soulless warehouses filled with pallets and big machinery, and businesses with names like Latin American Tire Repair and Gas N Shack—its Citgo sign in no way reminiscent of the famous one towering over Fenway's Green Monster.

It is a stretch of road marked by more than poverty. A dusty sense of boredom and surrender hangs over it, almost palpably. The American Dream feels dead.

But at the end of the road, the bleak stretch yields to a place of possible hope, Point B: the Player Development Complex, the Red Sox' minor league facility. Here, almost two hundred ballplayers, a festival of anonymity, descend on March mornings to try to claw their way to higher ground. They come from American cities and the heartland, from Venezuela and South Korea, from Mexico and Japan, from the Dominican Republic and Australia. They try to throw a little harder than the next talented guy, or prove that they can hit the outside pitch with authority to right field, or make the double play pivot without flinching as a runner barrels in. Some of the players will be cut before April. Some will play the full year and earn four figures. The fortunate ones will make in the low fives. A precious few will get the call.

The complex features eight batting tunnels and sixteen mounds, but the core is five baseball fields, which are laid out by mid-March in a pecking order. Field 1 is for the Pawtucket work group, those players earmarked as of that moment to begin the year in Triple-A. Field 2 is for Double-A; Field 3 for high-A; Field 4 for low-A; Field 5 for rookie ball. Manny Delcarmen is stewing on Field 3.

He had come down to spring training so pumped up. It was hard to bury the awe. He was sharing the same clubhouse with David Ortiz and Johnny Damon (though, alas, not with Pedro Martinez, who had signed with the Mets in the off-season). Just a few months before, Manny had been screaming his head off for these guys in an Arizona condo. He got calls all the time from his dad and Javy and Ana, all wanting to know what it was like. Same way each night at dinner. He was living that spring in nearby Cape Coral with Felix and Ginette Serrano, friends of Kuki's from the old neighborhood who had recently moved south. Their three sons, all addled with baseball, peppered him with questions. They hung on his every word. Manny Ramirez really sprayed guys with cologne in the locker room? Cool!

Every morning he arrived early and plunged into the time-honored spring training rituals, covering first base on balls hit to the right side, shagging flies during batting practice, running on the warning track. He couldn't wait for the games to begin. He would be pitching for the Boston Red Sox. His team was now *his* team. But when that day arrived, it proved to be a disaster. He pitched against a bunch of college kids who would never play an inning of professional ball. He got one of them out. He allowed five runs.

● The ten days that follow are surreal. He is there and not there. Manager Terry Francona never puts his name on the list of possible pitchers to throw in games. Manny sees a parade of pitchers take the mound, stars and prospects and non-roster retreads, hoping for one more piece of paradise. Surely, he figures, he will get another chance. It never comes. He shows up, does his work, watches and watches, stays quiet. It is like the first day of high school; he tries to be cool, to fit in, to show that he belongs. When some of the veteran players routinely leave the field after five innings or so to go fishing or play golf, Manny follows suit. He has put in his time. He isn't on the list. This must be the way things work.

On March 14 the Red Sox announce their first set of cuts, nine players who are optioned back to the minor leagues. Manny is disappointed but not surprised to be on the list. Rookies aren't going to crack the Opening Day roster of a world championship team. That he isn't assigned to the Pawtucket work group stings a little bit more. But when he sees that he isn't with the Portland work group for Double-A either, he absolutely bristles. Instead, he is assigned to the work group for the Wilmington Blue Rocks at Field 3. Field 3!

Peter Woodfork, the team's assistant director of player development, tells Manny the Sox are disappointed in him. A young player shouldn't be leaving the spring games early. What's more, Woodfork says, Manny needs to drop a few pounds.

Manny is stunned. He had worked himself into what he thought was the best shape of his life. Yes, he is a little heavier than a year ago, but it is all muscle in his trunk, helping him to push off, drive the ball to the plate. This is outrageous. He calls up Jim Masteralexis to protest. Jim hears him out and says he'll see what he can do.

Jim likes Woodfork. He is one of the inner circle of bright young executives who work under Boy Wonder general manager Theo Epstein. Woodfork played baseball at Harvard, where he studied psychology. He is a no-nonsense guy who is clearly headed for big things.[1] Jim tells him that Manny's early departures weren't about laziness; he was just trying to fit in. There is nothing he loves more than being part of the Red Sox. As for the weight, are they really sure this is a problem? Manny thinks that he is in tremendous shape.

"Jim," Woodfork says, "have you seen his butt?"

● Each morning thereafter Manny drives the gauntlet of Edison Avenue, passing by the sparkling City of Palms Park, where everyone is smitten with the Red Sox, and descending through the wasteland to the Player Development Complex. He puts his head down and trudges past Fields 1 and 2 out to the Wilmington work group at Field 3, his baseball Siberia. He runs and runs, letting the sweat pour down his body. He throws bullpens. During batting practice, he finds a spot of open green to shag fly balls, baking under the Floridian sun and trying to make sense of it all. How is this possible? A-ball again? Hasn't he paid his dues? Hasn't he busted his tail through rehab and come out the other side? Why did they place him on the forty-man, send him out to the Arizona Fall League, give him the invite to big league spring training? Is it all a big tease? There are so many pitchers at Field 1 and Field 2 he thinks he is ahead of. Even his buddy Charlie Zink is up with Portland a year after going 1–10 with an ERA of 5.77. Are the Sox really going to keep him here?

The more Manny thinks about it, the more he chafes. Yeah, he has just turned twenty-three. To his mind, though, he has been at this for almost five years, and there isn't much to show for his efforts. His dad had spent his whole career in the low minors in the South: Is this going to be his fate, too? That apartment in Randolph, and Ana's loving arms, are a shade over two hours from Portland, Maine; forty minutes from Pawtucket; about the same, God willing, from Fenway Park. But they are a world away from Wilmington, North Carolina. This just doesn't seem fair to him. Every time the Sox give him some hope, they seem to snatch it away. They draft the hometown kid, then let him twist for months with a signing bonus offer well below market value. They praise him for his strong finish in Augusta in 2002, then shut him down before his last start. And now they have given him a taste of what he most wants, the only thing he had ever really wanted, only to yank it away. He doesn't have to take this.

At home with the Serranos, he watches movies with the boys, shoots baskets out front, sometimes goes to the dog track with Felix. In the car he talks about his frustration, his anger, the blossoming idea of just going home if they decide to send him to Single-A when the season begins. People appreciate him in Boston. They don't try to mess with his mind. Felix listens and tries to talk Manny out of it, but he senses the old stubbornness rearing its head. He gets on the phone with his former softball teammate, the guy who used to fix his car in Hyde Park, and tells Kuki Delcarmen he is worried about his son.

Days pass slowly. The Sox shuffle players within their organization like baseball cards, optioning more players back to minor league camp, discarding a few forever, tweaking the piles in the work groups. With Manny there is no change.

Jim Masteralexis is concerned. He senses Manny's anger. He also hears from Kuki Delcarmen, all in a lather, a bullheaded dad in a china shop. Jim knows it isn't going to be easy to calm anyone down. He knows Manny isn't making an idle threat; he's gone AWOL once before. This, though, would be a disaster.

In the past two weeks Jim has spoken to Peter Woodfork on the phone a couple of times, advocating for his client in a lighthearted way. He gives Woodfork what he calls his "Jenny Craig updates" and says that Manny is working his butt off, literally. This time he turns serious.

"Look, Peter, it's obviously your call. You guys have to do what's best for the organization. I'm not trying to blackmail you or anything, but I got to tell you, Manny's pissed. He's a good kid, Peter. You know that's true. But I'm worried that if you send him to Single-A, you just might lose him."

Woodfork is noncommittal. Baseball is a business. There are lots of talented guys in the organization. They all have their own stories. "We'll give it some thought, Jim. Thanks for the call."

It is time to turn the calendar to April. In a few days the Red Sox will be opening their season against the Yankees in the Bronx. Under a blazing sun in Fort Myers, Manny drives down Edison Avenue, past the stadium and the pawnshop and the junkyards. The clock is ticking.

5 A Dream Deferred

Clearwater, Florida; Reading,
Pennsylvania

There was always one question; it was always the
same. When Luz Ruiz would confront her grandson in the Section 8 apartment they shared on East 136th Street in the South Bronx, she would
fold her arms, look him in the eye, and say, "Are you going to go this way,
or that way?"

Life as Luz saw it was a series of decisions. Nothing was more important than making the right ones. God knows there were plenty of wrong
ones being made out there on the streets. The sidewalks were strewn with
bloodstains and vials of crack and the occasional condom—evidence at
least that some people actually used condoms. To an impressionable kid
like Randy Ruiz, the coolest guys were the dealers. They had the badass
cars pulsing with rap, and the hot girls in the tight jeans. They had wads of
money from selling drugs that could transport you, at least for a while,
away from the urine stench and the cockroaches, away from the meanness
and the gnawing sense of no way out. Of course, there was plenty of evidence
about the crash, too, the way gravity smashed that high on the streets.
That's where the crackheads staggered about, sleeping on the grates, pleading for change. Lots of these guys once had promise, the glittering curse of
potential. Now it was, for most of them, too late. Which way are you going
to go, Randy? This way, or that way?

His dad, Randy Sr., had made a choice. At age sixteen he was a big kid,
a good athlete, drawn to the edge. That meant Julia Franco, a pretty young
thing at fifteen, just beginning to yearn for her own way out. But this was
not Shakespeare: when Julia got pregnant, she was overwhelmed; Randy,
barely shaving, was stunned. The woman who would wind up raising this
child was Luz Ruiz. Randy Jr. would grow up calling her "Mamá."

Randy Radames Ruiz was born on October 19, 1977, one day after the
neighborhood team, the Yankees, polished off the Dodgers at the Stadium
for their first World Series title in fifteen years. From a young age, baseball
was his thing. Through his step-grandfather Juan Roman, a chef at the
New York City Athletic Club, Randy could once in awhile score some free
tickets. For a family on food stamps, this was the one and only luxury—
occasional evenings of big league baseball.

Sometimes Randy would go with his dad when Randy Sr. could get some time off from his job at the General Motors plant in Tarrytown. Randy's dad had an abiding love for a team he still calls "my Yankees." He loved to bring his son to the House That Ruth Built, even though those mid- to late-eighties vintage Yankee teams were mediocre at best. Yankee Stadium was still the great cathedral of the Bronx, the beleaguered borough's singular claim to glory. On the way to the stadium, Randy Sr. would tell his son that he had once been a stickball legend who could smack the Spaldeen farther than anyone amid the boarded-up and burned-down tenements by the First Avenue Bridge. Going up the ramp and seeing the first riot of green, he would point toward the outfield monuments and wonder out loud about what the place must have been like back in the days of Ruth and Gehrig, DiMaggio and Mantle. If he hadn't had to work as a teenager, he said, perhaps he would be digging his cleats into the dirt by home plate and hearing the famous baritone voice of Bob Sheppard: "Now batting for the Yankees, Randy Ruiz." That had been his dream.

But when Randy Jr. was coming of age, the best team in town, the one he rooted for with his whole heart, was the Mets. More often than not, his date for the trips to Shea Stadium was Luz Ruiz. He cherished those nights with his grandmother. She would pack sandwiches, and he would grab her hand, almost pulling her down to the subway stop. After taking the No. 6 train, rumbling out of the Bronx, they transferred to the No. 7 to Shea. As they walked across the boardwalk, Randy's pulse would quicken at the scene: the smell of soft pretzels and chestnuts roasting outside the ballpark, the long escalators to the upper deck, the jets from LaGuardia roaring overhead. He loved to watch Darryl Strawberry hit, the way the whole stadium filled with anticipation. Randy knew that Strawberry, too, had come out of an impoverished urban environment with tons of obstacles. Strawberry's body was still young and lithe then, not yet ravaged by addiction. The big road seemed to stretch out before him. He was the prince of New York, making piles of money for hitting a baseball. That beautiful extension sometimes sent the ball soaring into the night. Young Randy was mesmerized by the moment, the majestic arc of the home run, the roar of the crowd, the slow trot around the bases with one fist raised. Being able to hit a ball like that meant deliverance.

Luz Ruiz, who had already raised five kids of her own, understood the hunger she saw in her grandson's eyes. She sensed his love for the sport, chuckling at the way he insisted on sleeping in his Little League uniform the night before a game, his bat right beside him. At his games she often hid behind a tree because Randy said her presence made him nervous.

Baseball, she hoped, could be the path for Randy. "God," she would pray, "please don't let me die until Randy is where he wants to be."

She clung to the power of such prayer. "I have so much faith in God. I believe in God very much. No matter who you are, where you come from, what color you are, any race, whatever, if you have faith in God and you are good people, God helps you."

At the same time, she knew that blind faith was not enough in the South Bronx—especially in the South Bronx. Prayer had to be wedded to discipline. There were too many minefields out there, a lesson she had learned from excruciating firsthand experience. The eldest of her five children, Ricardo, was killed one night in what Luz describes as "a fight over a girl." Randy was just a toddler at the time. Absolutely awash in grief, Luz began watching over her grandson with a fierce protectiveness. He became her great cause in life.

To the degree that she could, she tried to shield him from the perils of the Brook Avenue–Cypress neighborhood, where, Randy says, there were "always drugs, always dealing, always shootouts, always people getting stabbed." Luz created an oasis, a warm home where something was always simmering on the stove, where the gold-leafed living room table was covered with figurines, the couch with protective plastic. The front door had four separate locks, but above it hung a horseshoe. The tile floor in Randy's room was cracked, but from the window he could hear the music of recess across the street at P.S. 43, the elementary school named after the Swedish sailor Jonas Bronck.

Always a big kid, Randy was teased savagely by the neighborhood toughs. He was the fat boy, *el gordito*. He was the mama's boy without the mama. He did whatever Luz said, incurring all manner of abuse from his peers. Randy was terrified of disappointing her, and she was determined that wouldn't happen. He had to do his homework. He couldn't stay out late. He had to stay away from this kid, and that one, and that one, too. For sure, he was not going to get any girl pregnant. If he messed up in any way, Luz told him she would crack open his head. Worse yet, there would be no baseball.

That got Randy where it hurt. More than anything else, he loved the simple joy of hitting a ball. Like his dad, the stickball legend, Randy had great eye-hand coordination, quick wrists, and a powerful, if paunchy, core. When that ball flew off his bat, everything vanished with it, all the taunts, the labels, the sense of powerlessness. He didn't have to accept the limits imposed by anyone.

As a sophomore he made the varsity team at James Monroe High School. Mike Turo had coached some of the best players in the city over the past sixteen years, including a number of guys who had become pros, but few had Randy's explosive bat speed from starting point to point of contact. Sometimes Turo, who commuted an hour each way from his home on Long Island, would drive Randy home from practice, shuddering at the neighborhood scene. He told Randy that if he really worked hard, baseball could take him places.

James Monroe is a school with a rich baseball tradition. Back in the 1920s, a painfully shy son of Romanian Jews, a kid named Hank Greenberg, destined for the Detroit Tigers and ultimately the Baseball Hall of Fame, hit a record thirteen home runs in a single season. That record stood through the Great Depression, Pearl Harbor, and Elvis, until Ed Kranepool smacked fourteen in 1961. Kranepool became a New York celebrity, an original Met as a teenager on the infamous team that lost 120 games in 1962, and a veteran on the Miracle Mets who won it all in '69. His home run record at James Monroe survived Woodstock, disco, and Desert Storm.

Then in the mid-nineties along came Randy Ruiz. He hit some of the longest shots that Mike Turo had ever seen. Years afterward Turo would still rave about the day at Lehman High School when Randy hit one blast far over the left center field wall into a lumberyard, and another over a tree beyond the center field fence onto a distant parking garage. In sixteen league games in the spring of 1996, Randy clouted seventeen home runs. Sure, it was only a school record, but given the previous record holders and the stature of the James Monroe program, the achievement earned mention in several New York papers.

In June of that year Randy was drafted by his beloved Mets. Turo was right: the game was going to take him places.

● Almost nine years later, the Philadelphia Phillies get set to break from their 2005 spring training camp in Clearwater, Florida. By this time Randy Ruiz, a twenty-seven-year-old with a significant facial resemblance to Muhammad Ali in his prime, had floated and stung his way through a true baseball odyssey.

It began with a standoff. After getting drafted in 1996, Randy couldn't wait to join the Mets. Sure, he was disappointed he hadn't been picked until the thirty-sixth round. He couldn't believe that major league teams thought there were 1,067 high school and college players better than he was. Still, the Mets were the team he loved. They were offering him a bonus of $2,500. He had never seen that kind of money before. He was raring to go.

Not so fast, Luz said. She had spoken to Mike Turo, who understood the temptation to sign. This was professional baseball. It was a big deal for Randy and his family. Still, he had expected Randy to be selected by the twentieth round, where the signing bonus would have been substantially more. Turo knew it was tough to make it to the big leagues from the late rounds. Teams tended to give more chances to the early picks. Turo told Luz that if Randy accepted a baseball scholarship at a junior college, he could try the draft again in a year or two. It was a gamble. There were no guarantees.

Luz also spoke to Randy Sr., who was working as a crane operator for GM. He would have loved to play baseball for a living, he said. What an unbelievable opportunity this was. At the same time, he knew from his own experience—dropping out of DeWitt Clinton High School and working long hours of manual labor for years—that a college education could open doors.

Randy sat at the kitchen table, pleading with Luz. He talked about their trips to Shea Stadium, about how incredible it would be for her to see him playing for the Mets. She talked about college, about the importance of making good choices. He talked about his dream; she talked about hers. Then she looked him in the eye. *This way, or that way?* He went to school.

Actually, he went to lots of schools. In the fall of 1996 Randy started at Tallahassee Community College in Florida, where he was stunned by the freedom, the wild parties, the girls with legs that went on forever. He flunked out after one semester.

Luz shipped him off to an intensive intersession biology class at Erie Community College in Buffalo. No pass, she told him simply, no play. For two weeks he was up by six, tromping through the snow to get to class by seven, walking out with his head spinning at four. "It was," he would later say, "the longest two weeks of my life."

Randy then spent a semester at Essex Community College in Maryland, followed by a semester at Garden City Community College in Kansas. The Broncbusters had a strong baseball team but were better known for their program in rodeo.

His next stop was the powerhouse program at Maple Woods Community College in Kansas City. There he played for an intense coach named Chris Mihlfeld, a conditioning maven who required a fierce commitment in the weight room and a practice regimen that included "twenty poles," sprints from the left field line to the right field line that caused more than a few players to spill their guts on the warning track. Randy lifted and ran—and recruited. As the only Hispanic player on the team, he was given the assignment of talking to a local high school player who had been born in the Dominican Republic before settling in Harry Truman's hometown of Independence, Missouri. When Randy left with his associate's degree in sport management in the spring of 1998, he turned over his No. 33 uniform to the incoming Dominican slugger, Albert Pujols.

Undrafted out of Maple Woods, Randy continued the quest, enrolling in the fall of 1998 at Bellevue University in Nebraska. It was his sixth school in six states in just over two years. Home was where his bat was. Somehow, the street-tough kid fit right in on the prairie. Randy marveled at the way coach Mike Evans would always leave his car unlocked and his keys in the ignition. And the baseball was good. Bellevue rolled over teams like Peru State College and College of the Ozarks en route to an appearance in the NAIA World Series. Randy was a menace at the plate, batting .479 with twenty home runs and eighty-four RBI. Still, at season's end he was by-passed again in the draft. He was devastated. Other small-college kids had been drafted, and presented with life-changing signing bonuses. Why not him? Was this just not meant to be?

A couple of weeks later Randy drove his rusty 1988 Toyota Tercel up to Worcester, Massachusetts, to attend an open tryout with the Major League Baseball Scouting Bureau. He knew it was a long shot, but he decided to take it anyway. Once in a great while somebody still got signed from an open camp, even if it seemed like some Norman Rockwell image from a bygone era—all the more so when the guy heading it up was an eighty-two-year-old man named Lennie Merullo. Unbeknownst to Randy, Merullo had played for the Chicago Cubs back in the 1940s, and had become in subsequent years a legendary scout around New England baseball dia-monds. He had a kind word for everyone, but a discerning eye. He looked for late movement on the fastball, quick hands at the plate, a catcher's abil-ity to block pitches in the dirt. Merullo was a baseball Willy Wonka, hand-ing out the rare golden ticket to a place of wonder. He had contacted a se-ries of "area scouts" from big league teams to help him run the tryout at the College of the Holy Cross. One hundred players showed up, high school hotshots and college stars, and young men who had once known a patch of glory at this hard and humbling game.

Alone among this crew, Randy caught the attention of Cincinnati Reds scout John Brickley. The ball seemed to explode off his bat. "He was spe-cial," Brickley recalled years later. "You could see it right away."

A few days later, on Sunday, July 11, 1999, as the game's greatest players arrived in Boston for Tuesday night's Major League All-Star Game at Fen-way Park, Randy sat in Brickley's living room in nearby Melrose, signing his first professional contract. Brickley told him the Reds could offer only a $1,000 bonus to an undrafted player, but Randy didn't hesitate. After eating Julia Brickley's famous homemade ravioli, Randy called his grandmother to tell her the good news. She gave the choice her blessing. Randy stayed over at Brickley's house that night and hitched a ride with him the next morning to Logan Airport. Two days later he made his professional debut for the Gulf Coast Reds, going 0-for-2 with a strikeout against the Gulf Coast Twins.

● For four years Randy played in the Reds organization. At first it was a big adventure. He didn't mind the noon games under the blazing sun in the Gulf Coast League or even the $850 a month slave wages. It was the way they tested rookies, making sure they were hungry to play. He was.

There were fifty-eight young players who suited up at one point or another for the 1999 Gulf Coast Reds. Some had been picked in the top ten rounds of the draft and commanded signing bonuses upwards of $200,000. Several came from the Dominican Republic or Venezuela and were getting their first taste of the American Dream. Others, like Randy, were overlooked talents who had forced their way onto a scout's radar. All fifty-eight players had defied staggering odds to get there. All, presumably, now felt that they were on the path to the big leagues. Only five would ever get that call.[1]

The next year, 2000, the Reds sent Randy to Billings, Montana, a city of ninety thousand people that was the largest metropolis within five hundred miles in any direction. He loved it. A starstruck teenage program seller named Rebecca Hoffman talked her parents into becoming Randy's host family, and soon he was out with the Hoffmans tubing down the Yellowstone River. The sky was enormous. The air was clean. For the first time in his career, Randy played night games on a regular basis, taking the field before 3,500 rabid fans, for whom the Billings Mustangs were a huge deal. Sure, the thirteen-hour bus rides to Orem, Utah, left him stiff and groggy, but Randy was having the time of his life. He won the Pioneer League batting title that year, hitting .381. With it came a plaque from Kentucky given out to all minor league batting champs, a mounted Louisville Slugger bat with the word "Powerized" blazed into the barrel. It would look awfully sweet on the wall in Luz's apartment.

On one level, life seemed to be opening up for Randy. He was contacted by an agent, Tommy Tanzer, who began plying him with free equipment: gloves and bats and spikes. Tanzer told Randy he wanted to help, and that he believed the young player had what it took to make it.

Still, Randy was a long way from the Promised Land. He spent his off-seasons back in Bellevue, Nebraska, living with college friends while working the third shift at the No Frills Supermarket. After hours of ripping open banana boxes, stocking Snickers, and taking inventory of the root beer, Randy would step out into the gray and frigid morning and trudge through the snow. There was no way out of his predicament. He had to make money. Financially, baseball in the low minors was a losing proposition.

Despite solid numbers again in 2001 and 2002, he found himself barely creeping up the ladder with the Reds, maxing out at high-A ball with the Stockton (California) Ports. He never touched Double-A or Triple-A, the on-deck circle to the dream come true. He didn't understand it. Other guys—the high draft picks, the "bonus babies," the guys the Reds were invested in—seemed to move through the system much more rapidly, even with lesser numbers. It didn't seem fair to Randy. There were times when he let his frustration get the better of him. He sulked. He stewed. He spoke his mind, the South Bronx reflexes roaring to the surface.

Late in spring training 2003 the Reds gave Randy his unconditional release—baseball parlance for getting fired. "When you leave an organization, nobody talks to you," he later reflected. "The people you work with, the people who used to help you, who said they wanted to help you, as soon as you leave, forget about it. . . . I learned a few things in life. One, nothing's secure. Two, nobody cares. If you're not on top, nobody cares."

● Randy spent the 2003 season in the Orioles system. He spent most of the year at low-A with the Delmarva Shorebirds, hitting .310 despite an injury to his right wrist that would require off-season surgery. Granted minor league free agency, he signed a deal with the St. Louis Cardinals in January and reported to spring training a few weeks later.

Of the approximately two hundred players in Cardinals uniforms in March 2004, one was afforded true hero's treatment, a guy who had once played at Maple Woods Community College. Albert Pujols had been in the big leagues for three seasons now, clouting more than thirty home runs, amassing more than one hundred RBI, and hitting over .300 every time. His 2004 contract called for Pujols to make $11 million. He was the face of the franchise, the bright young star in the game. Often he traveled around with his personal trainer, Chris Mihlfeld, the former coach at Maple Woods who had once urged Randy to use his influence to lure the young star. Randy was now an afterthought in minor league camp.

Of course, it wasn't just Pujols. Randy had seen several former team-mates rise through the system to the big leagues, where the 2004 minimum salary would be $300,000. Randy couldn't fathom it. Despite playing for five years with a career average of .300, he had never made 5 percent of that amount. He was still spending his off-seasons stocking shelves at the No Frills Supermarket at three in the morning.

Randy was favoring his wrist and struggling to generate his usual bat speed. On March 26 he was given his unconditional release by the Cardinals without having played a single game in their minor league system. He was stunned. Pleading with his agent Tommy Tanzer to get him a job, he was hurt to find out that other teams weren't interested. Some thought he was too one-dimensional, a DH type whose skills were not "projectable" at higher levels. Some questioned his attitude. Some thought he was overweight, a suggestion that made him bristle. He had always been big. He had always been able to hit.

Randy headed home to the Bronx, defeated. There he was, the great hope of the 'hood, back in the Section 8 apartment with his grandma. He slept in his old room, adorned with trophies and plaques that Luz had put on the walls. One read: "MVP. Congratulations, Randy Ruiz, on your excellent, record-breaking season at James Monroe High School. Drafted by the New York Mets, June, 1996. Home runs: 17. Runs batted in: 66. Doubles: 23. Hits: 62. Runs: 66. Average: .594." Another commemorated his All Region XI status when he was at Maple Woods Community College. A third saluted his making the Pioneer League All-Star team in 2000, playing for a team Luz pronounced the "Buy-lings" Mustangs.

It was almost too much for Randy to take; he felt, as he would later put it, "ashamed." All around him the 2004 baseball season was playing out. For the first time since he was a young child, he was not in uniform. He could hear the blue trains clacking along the Grand Concourse, full of fans thronging to Yankee Stadium, some of them throwing down more than a hundred dollars for a ticket. He knew that there were almost seven thousand minor leaguers still in the game, fighting for a chance. His days seemed to drag on forever.

He took a part-time job in White Plains at the Frozen Ropes batting range, giving hitting lessons. Many of his students were rich kids from Long Island or Westchester, driving up with their dads in Saabs and BMWs. Here he was, the single-season home run record holder at mighty James Monroe High School, a former minor league batting champion, twenty-six years old, going nowhere. He told the kids to stay back, to shorten their strides, to keep their elbows up as the mechanical arms delivered pitch after pitch: ffppt, ffppt, ffppt. Sometimes he would stay late at the cages in the chilly April air, cranking up the machines to ninety-plus, feeling the bat in his hands, so familiar, and whipping it through the zone with one satisfying thwack after another until the sweat was pouring down his face. This was what he loved to do. He just couldn't believe it was over.

Finally, in late April, his cell phone rang. Steve Noworyta, the minor league director for the Philadelphia Phillies, said that his organization had always been impressed with Randy. They had an opening for a first baseman for their team in the South Atlantic League, the Lakewood (New Jersey) BlueClaws. It wasn't going to be much money, and it was low-A ball, but if he hit like they knew he could, there would be an opportunity to advance. Was he interested?

Low-A again? As a sixth-year minor leaguer, wasn't he beyond that? Hadn't he proven himself? It would be a difficult summer. Lakewood's status as the northernmost team in the South Atlantic League meant numbingly long bus trips to places like Augusta, Georgia, and Greensboro, North Carolina, cheap hotels, twenty dollars a day in meal money. Randy was tempted to turn it down. He sought advice from John Brickley, the Reds scout who had signed him back in 1999. Brickley told Randy that he could hit, he always could hit. He didn't want to look back on his career with regrets about what might have been. Randy also realized that on some level he was running out of time. Lakewood was right there by Asbury Park in Bruce Springsteen country. This was one more chance to make it real.

Randy's numbers in 2004 were consistent with his track record. When the season ended on Labor Day in Hickory, North Carolina, against the Crawdads, his .288 average was a bit down, his power (seventeen homers and ninety-one RBI) a bit up. There were a couple of numbers that were significantly different, however. One was his weight, down some twenty pounds to 215. The other was his strikeout total of 140, well above previous years. Partly he attributed that to the lingering pain in his wrist, which troubled him until mid-season. But also, he knew, he was swinging for the fences, convinced that in the modern era this was his only ticket.

At season's end, Randy traveled down to Clearwater, Florida, to work with the Phillies' roving minor league hitting instructor Donnie Long. The two men connected well. Long was a baseball lifer in his mid-forties who had spent his entire career in the minors. To Randy, he didn't seem bitter about not making it; he seemed serene. Long was solid on the technical side of hitting, and helped Randy with his coverage of the outside pitch, challenging him to focus on hitting the ball hard to all fields and just letting the home runs come naturally. Long's mental approach was even more effective. He had an ability to get players to evict the negative: the late swing on the previous pitch, the poor history against this pitcher, the anger about somebody else getting promoted. Let it all go. Focus only on the next pitch. That's all you can control. Too often, he suggested, Randy had been his own worst enemy. He had tried to become somebody else. Rest assured, Long told him, the Phillies liked him the way he was. "Just be who you are," he said. "Stay positive."

Away from the field, Randy spent time with his younger sister Jasmine, a dental hygienist in nearby Tampa. Randy had not been raised with any of his eight younger siblings, and he liked to connect the puzzle pieces.[2] They ate meals together, talked about the world they had left behind. Jasmine provided just a little sense of home. That sense, though, was blasted apart when Randy's cell phone rang.

He did not recognize the caller ID. Dickie Noles? Who was that? Noles left a message saying that he was a representative of the Phillies' Employee Assistance Program (EAP), and he needed to see Randy right away. It was urgent. They could meet at the hotel that evening.

Noles had once been a big league pitcher, starting and ending an undistinguished eleven-year career with the Phillies. He was best known, though, for an incident when he was with the Cubs, when he assaulted a police officer in a drunken rage. This earned him the dubious distinction of being one of the only big leaguers in history to serve a sentence (sixteen days) during a season. While he did return to the mound, he never really took hold as a big league pitcher. He finished his career with a record of 36–53, and considered himself something of a poster child for squandered potential. Noles thought about entering the ministry but ultimately turned to anti-drug education. He often spoke to students in Philadelphia schools, and in baseball circles he was the only former major leaguer to be working as an EAP specialist. It was in this capacity that he met with Randy Ruiz in October 2004. He shook Randy's hand, looked him in the eye, and told Randy that he had tested positive in August for the steroid stanozolol.

● In that fall of 2004, the steroid clouds massing over the national pastime had not yet opened up, though there was no question that a storm was gathering.

In June 1995, the year after the World Series was canceled, future Hall of Famer Tony Gwynn told the *Los Angeles Times* that steroids were "the big secret we're not supposed to talk about," while his general manager, Randy

Smith, estimated that 10 to 20 percent of players were on steroids. Fans and media, equally enthralled by the great home run derby of 1998 between Sammy Sosa and Mark McGwire, were ever so briefly troubled in August when a reporter noted a bottle of the over-the-counter steroid precursor androstenedione in McGwire's locker. McGwire, en route to his record-setting seventy home runs, assured a receptive public that it was no big deal, while baseball commissioner Bud Selig brushed it off, telling the *Washington Post*, "I think what Mark McGwire has accomplished is so remarkable, and he has handled it all so beautifully, we want to do everything we can to enjoy a great moment in baseball history."

Three years later, when Barry Bonds smashed seventy-three home runs, the growing sense of wonder and cynicism was muted by the fact that the record was set amid the national shock following the attacks of September 11. In 2002 Ken Caminiti, the 1996 National League Most Valuable Player, came clean in a cover story in *Sports Illustrated*, admitting that his success had been fueled by steroids and claiming that such usage was pervasive: "The game is so whacked out that guys will take anything to get an edge." More recently, in December 2003, Bonds had been one of ten players subpoenaed to testify before a grand jury investigating BALCO, the Bay Area Laboratory Co-operative.

There was increasingly tough talk about a "zero tolerance policy," but to that point in the fall of 2004, Major League Baseball had yet to suspend a single player for a single game.

The use of performance-enhancing drugs in the minor leagues was rampant. In the lobbies of cheap hotels, or over eleven o'clock dinners at McDonald's or Pizza Hut, the only restaurants open after the game in small towns, there was lots of shadowy talk about what worked, what didn't, who was juicing, how much teams really cared.

Selig had implemented a minor league testing program in 2001 for players not on major league forty-man rosters (and thus not protected by the collective bargaining agreement). That first year, the commissioner's office would later report, 9.1 percent of all minor league tests came back positive for steroids.[3] The consequences of a test violation were, according to Senate testimony later provided by assistant commissioner Rob Manfred, "education and counseling." The reported reduction in positive tests (4.8 percent in 2002, 4.0 percent in 2003, and 1.7 percent in 2004) might indicate some effective education and counseling. Or it might indicate greater sophistication in gaming the system, such as the use of masking agents or poorly supervised tests (allowing the substitution of clean urine for the tainted stuff). The reduction likely also was produced in part by the threat of more serious consequences for failing a second test (what Manfred obliquely referred to in his Senate testimony as "serious disciplinary action for subsequent violations").[4] Some minor leaguers were suspended during this era, but they were not identified. Teams were known to invent fake injuries, or to place players on the restricted list for violating some unspecified team rule.

Truly, there was no public outcry about performance-enhancing drug use in the minor leagues between 2001 and 2004—despite 927 positive tests.[5] Remarkably, the results of the testing program were not offered up by the commissioner's office until early 2005—nor were they aggressively sought by elected officials, members of the media, or fans. The collective neglect, far from benign in retrospect, is startling. To the extent that the baseball public was focused on the issue at all, the attention was directed at the big guys making the big bucks in the big leagues.

● As the 2005 season approached, the storm clouds burst, and baseball officials frantically began to roll out the tarp to protect the image of the game. In November, Barry Bonds's BALCO testimony was leaked to the *San Francisco Chronicle*. Shortly after, excerpts from Jose Canseco's bombshell book *Juiced* were released. Defying the locker room code of silence, Canseco accused some of the game's biggest stars of steroid use. Ridiculed for being soft on steroids, Bud Selig succeeded in getting owners and the Major League Baseball Players Association to open up the collective bargaining agreement—no small feat. They reported a strengthening of the drug program, calling for violators to be publicly identified for the first time, and suspended for ten days for a first offense, thirty for a second, sixty for a third.[6] But a draft of the new policy subpoenaed by Congress revealed a sizable loophole: at the commissioner's discretion, players who tested positive might be able to avoid public exposure and suspension by paying a fine. All of that set the stage for the dramatic hearing before Congress, televised live on March 17.

"Over the past century, baseball has been part of our social fabric," Representative Henry Waxman said in his introductory comments. "It helped restore normalcy after war, provided the playing field where black athletes like Jackie Robinson broke the color barrier, and inspired civic pride in communities across the country."

But now, he said, "America is asking baseball for integrity. An unequivocal statement against cheating. An unimpeachable policy. And a reason for all of us to have faith in the sport again."

● At the Phillies' minor league complex in Clearwater, Florida, Randy Ruiz is smacking the ball all over the lot. Even against top prospects, he is hitting line drive after line drive. His swing feels balanced, relaxed, fierce.

Donnie Long comes by every so often to take a look, and says almost nothing, just nodding his approval. Another guy taking note is one of the Phillies' minor league managers, Steve Swisher. He is a guy with a definite presence. A former National League All-Star catcher and later a minor league manager, Swisher is returning now after eight years away from pro ball; as he explains it, he had wanted to be at home in West Virginia to help raise his two sons. One of them is Nick Swisher, a rookie outfielder with the Oakland A's. Steve Swisher knows what a good hitter looks like. He tells Randy simply, "I want you on my team."

That team would be the Reading Phillies in the Eastern League. Double-A, at long last. Randy knows that Reading's big slugger the previous year was a guy named Ryan Howard, who, by season's end, had made it to the big leagues.[7] He can't wait for the season to begin.

But wait he must. Dickie Noles, the EAP, tells Randy that he will have to begin the year by serving a fifteen-game suspension from last August's positive drug test. Nobody will find out, though. If anybody asks, the team will explain Randy's absence by saying he is rehabbing a groin injury. Just stay clean, Noles tells him. Keep working hard. You don't need the stuff. You're good the way you are.

Randy is relieved. The last thing he wants is for his family to find out that he had used steroids. His grandmother would be devastated. Sure, there is worse stuff in the South Bronx every day, lots of it, but for all the hardening of his upbringing and the crucible of the minors, Randy remains a surprisingly sensitive young man who wants, as much as anything, to be the golden boy in Luz's eyes.

What's more, he feels, Noles is right. He doesn't need the stuff. He hadn't felt right the year before, too lean, too muscle-bound. Now his weight is back up. The Phillies tell him they want him to be himself. If that means being *el gordito*, so be it.

He pays only slight attention to the congressional hearings playing out in mid-March.

I'm not here to talk about the past.

I have never taken steroids. Period.

Baseball's image is under attack as the 2005 season begins. On April 3, just before Opening Day, Alex Sanchez, a spindly twenty-eight-year-old outfielder with the Tampa Bay Devil Rays and author of precisely four major league home runs, becomes the first big leaguer ever to be suspended for steroids, getting a ten-game sentence.

The next day there is another announcement from Major League Baseball. As a result of drug tests conducted among the twelve teams that held spring training in Arizona, the first minor league suspensions are being handed out. There are thirty-eight players on the list, identified by name in papers across America.

One major leaguer. Thirty-eight minor leaguers. And there are more suspensions to come, the commissioner's office promises. There are still results pending from the eighteen teams that train in Florida.

The Phillies tell Randy not to worry. His drug test was taken last August. Those names are not going to be revealed. It is a groin injury, Randy. Right?

● On April 22 Randy suits up for his first game at Double-A for a punchless Reading team that has been shut out in three straight games, a rare feat at any level. That first night he bats cleanup and goes 1-for-4 with a double as the Phillies bust out of their slump (though they lose, 9–7.) He is 1-for-4 again the next night, then 2-for-3. After an off day, Reading concludes its homestand with two games against the New Britain Rock Cats. In the first one, on the night of April 26, Randy goes 3-for-4, blasting two home runs and a double and knocking in five runs in a 10–4 win. The next afternoon Randy again cracks two home runs and a double, knocking in six this time to lead his team to victory.

It has been a dizzying twenty-four hours. For fans and media in the gritty town of Reading, it is as if Roy Hobbs had gotten off the train in *The Natural*. Who is this guy? Where is he from?

Randy Ruiz is batting .526 on the season. He is just getting started.

Opening Day
to the All-Star
Break

6

"It's the Life—the One Everyone Wants to Live"

Portland, Oregon

The 2005 Portland Beavers, the Triple-A affiliate of the San Diego Padres, provide a few strands of the rich tapestry of minor league baseball.

Veteran catcher Michel Hernandez is still chasing the American pot of gold he had decided to seek long ago. Back in 1996 at age eighteen, he bolted out of a stadium in Mexico with four Havana Industriales teammates, leaving behind his island nation, family and friends, and the only life he had ever known. His long haul in the minors has been punctuated by a single September call-up, in 2003, and precisely one, deeply treasured major league hit.[1]

Hard-throwing right-hander Clay Hensley, a twenty-five-year-old native of Tomball, Texas, is set to make his first-ever appearance at the Triple-A level—but not right away. On April 4 Hensley is one of thirty-eight minor leaguers suspended for failing a test for performance-enhancing drugs, the first players ever to be publicly identified. He begins the season with a fifteen-game suspension.[2]

The colorfully named Tagg Bozied is coming back to Portland from one of the most bizarre injuries in baseball history. Bozied was considered a top prospect for the Padres the previous summer, batting .315 at Portland with sixteen homers and fifty-eight RBI. The sixteenth homer and the fifty-eighth RBI, though, led to his being carted out of Portland's PGE Stadium via ambulance. After hitting a walk-off grand slam, Bozied rounded third and got set to launch himself into the arms of jubilant teammates at the plate. The leap turned into a disaster when he ruptured the patellar tendon in his left knee. Bozied hasn't played since.[3]

Steve Sparks, who was the only knuckleballer besides Tim Wakefield in the major leagues in 2004, is trying to get back to the bigs once again at age thirty-nine. Sparks is the journeyman supreme, having pitched professionally since 1987. He has hurled for five big league teams over nine seasons and has been mediocre at best: 59–76 with a 4.88 ERA. Still, that has been good enough to earn him more than $10 million in major league salary. He is not quite ready to give it up.[4]

Then there is twenty-seven-year-old Mike Bumstead, whose fame, such as it is, has little to do with baseball. A devoutly religious player the Beavers will ultimately enlist to speak on "Faith Night," Bumstead vowed to hold on to his virginity until he got married. One night in the summer of 2003, playing Double-A ball for the Mobile BayBears, he couldn't take his eyes off the singer of the national anthem, the former Miss Mobile, Christin Kelly. Ultimately he proposed to her on the same spot, right there at Hank Aaron Stadium. Their wedding, in December 2004, was chronicled a month later by Oprah Winfrey's Oxygen network in a reality series about couples tying the knot. A few days before the episode aired, Jason Vondersmith of the *Portland Tribune* wrote: "The Portland Beavers' Mike Bumstead has never pitched a complete game. Before Dec. 11, he hadn't gone all the way, either."[5]

All these Beavers have a single goal: they are eager to get up, or get back, to the major leagues. Thirteen of the twenty-four players on the Opening Day roster have played at least a little at the big league level.

● Brad Baker is on the verge. At least it looks that way. In 2004 he seemingly put it all together as a closer, with combined Double-A and Triple-A numbers of 3–1 with thirty-four saves and a 1.48 ERA. He was named the Padres' co–minor league pitcher of the year, and flew out on the company's dime to San Diego for a banquet, where he was brought up on stage to shake hands with Padres manager Bruce Bochy and general manager Kevin Towers. Brad and his wife, Ashley, married just a few weeks, stayed in a room where one window looked out onto shiny new PETCO Park and the other onto navy ships in the harbor on sparkling San Diego Bay.

The *Baseball Prospectus* for 2005 has given Baker a rosy report, saying that his "devastating change-up . . . baffles opposing hitters," that he has "drawn comparisons to Keith Foulke and the Padres' own Trevor Hoffman," and that he has "gone from serviceable to nearly unhittable."

Towers himself stated in spring training that Brad "realizes that it's now not that far away. It's not just a dream."

Brad is still just twenty-four years old, though it seems to him that he has been at this baseball life for a long, long time. He is about to enter his seventh season. He had fulfilled his childhood fantasy of getting drafted by the Boston Red Sox—and he had known the acid taste of getting traded away by the team he loved. He had been promoted and demoted. He had been a starter and a closer. He had seen his velocity dip, his once flawless mechanics falter. He didn't know quite why. Was it because he had lost the limberness as his body had filled out, from under 170 pounds in his senior year of high school to almost 200 now? Had there just been too many cooks in the kitchen? *Lead with the hip; don't fly open with the front leg. Generate more rotational energy. Don't land on the front heel and lock your leg. Change the tilt and angle. Keep your release point. Develop the curveball. Stick with the fastball and change. Blow the hitter away. Pitch to contact.* Or had the speed diminished because of some invisible injury? Had there been perhaps some undiagnosed fraying of a ligament or tendon?

Whatever it was, he felt as if he had adapted. He found that closing gave him an adrenaline rush, not unlike hunting with his bow and arrow: the long wait, the brief window, the need to deliver under pressure. Granted, he knew that, barring an injury, he was not likely to get promoted to the big leagues as a closer; the Padres, after all, had the best in the business in Trevor Hoffman. But having a chance to close at Triple-A would provide him a stage, a launching pad. Deep down, he wasn't really concerned about the role. "I don't care what it is," he said. "I don't care if it's throwing one pitch a year—as long as I'm up there."

That would confirm everything. The call-up would validate his status as a former first-round draft pick by the Red Sox. It would make good on the Padres' own predictions back when they acquired him in 2002, instantly giving him one of the organization's two slots in the Futures Game in Milwaukee during the All-Star break. Those rosters were filled with players on the fast track: Jose Reyes, Carl Crawford, Miguel Cabrera, Victor Martinez, Justin Morneau. In that game Brad had more than held his own, pitching a hitless inning of relief.

A big league call-up would also have some large financial implications. True, Brad had gotten a first-round signing bonus of over $800,000,[6] but in seven years he had never made even close to $15,000 in a minor league season. The 2005 minimum big league salary of $316,000 and the average of $2.63 million would change the landscape completely.

Most of all, getting the call would make people happy back home. Not that he was doing it for anyone else, mind you. Brad's baseball dreams were his own. Even so, he understood that his making it to the major leagues would be a huge deal in and around the tiny town of Leyden.

Nowhere would that be more apparent than on Baker Hill. His grandparents, at the southern tip of the plateau, would love it. Donald, his seventy-one-year-old grandfather, was a grizzled former naval officer who had served during the Korean War, a retired brakeman on the Boston & Maine Railroad who drank and smoked too much. Donald's soft spot was his grandson with the golden arm. For years they had been bear hunting buddies, spending hours and hours together alone in the woods every September. They didn't talk much, didn't have to. In the spring Donald would be the guy watering and raking the field before Brad's starts, smoothing out the dirt beside the pitching rubber. By game time he was long gone, too nervous to watch. Brad's grandmother Irene, though, never missed a pitch. She was at all the games when Brad was growing up and emerging as the dominant pitcher in western Massachusetts. Over Brad's minor league career she has become addicted to webcasts. Even after Brad got converted to a closer and shipped out west, where the games didn't even begin until 10:05 eastern time, she was faithfully logging on and readying the tape recorder. On Opening Day 2005, she marches across the little plateau to the home of her elder son, Jim, and his wife, Vicki, and announces simply, "It's sleep deprivation time."

Vicki Baker is the one least addled by the dream. She is sensible, practical, efficient. A claims examiner for an insurance company in Greenfield, she runs the show at home, cold-pack boiling the string beans, making bread for the fair at the Leyden Methodist Church. Baseball, though, is in her blood. Her dad had played in town leagues across the border in Guilford, Vermont. She can tell you little nuances about Carl Yastrzemski's stance or Dennis Eckersley's slider. Seated in her red and white lawn chair with needlepoint designs of bat and ball, she spent years watching Brad from behind the backstop. She has watched her son's professional stock soar and plummet and rise again. "He's on top of his game and he's ready," she said in late March. "Now it's just waiting for the opportunity." Her husband, Jim, tries these days to avoid getting too attached to the outcome. He had called Brad's draft day in 1999 "the greatest day of my life," but he still feels some bitterness toward Boston for trading his boy away. ("I still watch the Red Sox all the time, but unconsciously there's a little resentment there. Sometimes I look for them to do bad. I always looked at Bradley as being the one to get them through the curse.") Jim is usually out of the house these days by five in the morning, heading to his construction job with Fontaine Brothers, building dorms and jails and hotels, but still sometimes he can't resist the lure of the late-night webcast. "Even on the Internet," he says, thumping his chest, "it's boom-boom-boom-boom."

In the middle house, closest to the woods, Uncle Jeff has been riding the rollercoaster of Brad's career as closely as anyone. At times Jeff still sees himself as the catcher he once was back at Pioneer Valley Regional High School. When he hears that a batter has pulled Brad's fastball, he knows for sure the killer changeup is on its way. Jeff treasures the memory of driving nine-year-old Brad to Fenway for his first big league game back in 1990, sitting in the handicapped section, watching the 15–1 rout over the Yankees. Jeff has no sensation of heat or pain from the chest down, but he is the emotional center of the family, his cheeks flushing with pride or sorrow. Although he hasn't thrown a ball in over twenty-five years, baseball is still a passion. His allegiances are split. His office at Money Concepts in Greenfield still has a portrait of Ted Williams on the wall, a baseball signed by Yaz, and a painting of Nomar Garciaparra. But in the morning he always logs on to padres.com, and on the nearby corkboard, beneath the "Franklin Templeton Distributions Update," sits the Padres schedule. He knows it almost by heart. Right after the All-Star break, when San Diego visits Shea Stadium, he plans to be in the house. "I can't wait for that call," he said in late March. "I just feel like he's ready."

And of course there is Ashley. She is just turning twenty-two, but she has been riding the minor league rollercoaster for a long time. She remembers the draft day back when she was a sophomore in high school in June 1999, all the jubilation, all the relatives in Red Sox caps, Brad walking away with her and saying, "Oh my God, I can't believe it." She recalls the day in June 2002 when Uncle Jeff—her favorite Baker relative—called to ask her to drive up to Baker Hill; she found him crying behind his sunglasses over the news that the Red Sox had traded Brad to the Padres. There was the galling night in Mobile the next summer when Brad emerged from the clubhouse in the pouring rain to tell Ashley he had just been demoted to Single-A, two thousand miles away. Now, however, Brad has righted the ship after rocketing back onto the Padres' radar in 2004. He and Ashley were married in October, and a few weeks later she flew out to San Diego to be with him at the organization's awards banquet. She loved the sun and the sparkle of the city, the sense of a bigger life that beckoned just beyond the horizon.

For now, though, she stays home saving money, planning to join Brad in the summer in San Diego. She works two jobs. In the morning she serves as a teacher's aide at Bernardston Elementary School. The place is unchanged since the day she arrived as an energetic five-year-old; there are 182 students now, in kindergarten through sixth grade. Lots of them ride their bikes to school, leaving them propped up, unlocked, against the rack. Ashley spends her days giving spelling tests, jumping rope at recess, handing out milk on lunch duty. When she gets a free moment, she logs on to padres.com on the computer in the kindergarten classroom and places her vote for which Padres prospect she would most like to see in the major leagues.

Afternoons and evenings she works at the general store in Northfield, Mim's Market, where signs on the porch advertise everything from "Big Dave's Bait and Tackle" to a "bagpiper for all occasions." She refills coffee, wraps muffins, and, when things are quiet, bounds across the still snowy parking lot to tune into a Padres spring training game on the satellite radio in her car.

"You just try not to get your hopes up because you don't want to be let down," Ashley reasons. Still, she does find herself thinking from time to time what it would be like to get the call. "Next to our wedding, that will be the most special day," she says. "With all the sacrifices from everybody, that's the ultimate payoff."

● It is already after midnight, Saturday April 16 having given way in Leyden to the wee hours of Sunday, when Irene Baker hits the play and record buttons on her tape recorder. Rich Burk, the voice of the Portland Beavers on Sunny KKAD, brings her the action from PGE Stadium all the way across the continent. The Beavers lead the Sacramento River Cats, 6–5, in the ninth inning, with a certain grandson coming in to pitch.

Just up the road, Vicki and Jim Baker are also tuned in. So, too, is Jeff Baker, having just returned from, of all things, a dance, a fundraiser for a local hospice group at the Polish American Club in South Deerfield.

Saturday marks the beginning of April vacation at Bernardston Elementary, so Ashley has some time on her hands. After working from seven in the morning until early afternoon at Mim's, she speeds the seventy miles south to Bradley International Airport in Windsor Locks, Connecticut. Her Southwest Airlines flight through Chicago gets into Portland at 8:40 local time. She takes a thirty-dollar cab ride to the ballpark, tips the driver another ten bucks, then wheels her big purple suitcase up a ramp on the first base side just in time to hear PA announcer Mike Stone say, "Now pitching for the Beavers, No. 31, Brad Baker." She catches her breath as Brad walks the leadoff hitter, Jack Cust. A strikeout and a force play follow, bringing up shortstop Mike Rouse. Like Brad, Rouse is twenty-four years old, a star player all his life, someone who has never quite made it to the top.

The count goes to 1-and-2. Brad comes set, grips the ball with his thumb and pinky beneath a three-finger claw, and uncorks his signature changeup. Rouse swings over the top and misses. The crowd of 3,167 rise to applaud. Ashley Baker is screaming her lungs out.

Everything is falling into place. "It's the story—the one everyone wants to live," Brad's agent Jim Masteralexis says. "He's living what so many people want to live."

● Except that he isn't, not really. Beneath the shimmer there is a kind of trouble in paradise, though it is hard for anyone—even Brad—to see.

Agents Steve McKelvey and Jim Masteralexis help Brad Baker reel in the big one on the morning of the 1999 baseball draft. *Courtesy of Steve McKelvey*

Even at a young age, Brad displays smooth pitching mechanics. *Courtesy of the Baker family*

The journey begins: Brad gets the call from Red Sox scout Ray Fagnant on draft day. *Paul Franz,* Greenfield Recorder

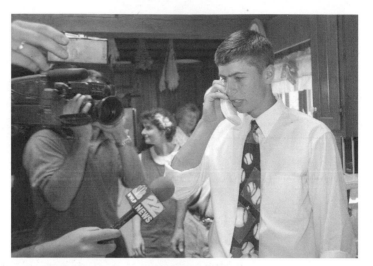

Jeff Baker and his nephew/next door neighbor at Brad's high school graduation. *Courtesy of Jeff Baker*

Brad's parents, Jim and Vicki Baker, in their living room in Leyden. The bear on the wall was shot by Brad at age 13. *Carol Lollis,* Daily Hampshire Gazette

In the summer of 1999, Brad is all smiles
as he begins his professional career with the
Gulf Coast Red Sox. *US PRESSWIRE*

Brad lets one fly for the Portland Beavers in the fateful summer of 2005.
Craig Mitchelldyer

On the one hand, the saves pile up at a prolific rate. On June 6 Brad notches his nineteenth, more than anyone in Triple-A ball, more than anyone in the major leagues for that matter. With three months left in a five-month season, he is on pace to shatter the Pacific Coast League record of thirty-two, provided his path isn't blocked by an injury—or a call-up from the Padres.

But on the other hand, his numbers are a statistical house of cards. Brad has also known his share of "blown saves"—a statistic that personalizes failure more than any other in the world of sports. On June 10 he trots in from the bullpen with a 5–2 lead against the Tucson Sidewinders. With two outs and two on, the home crowd on their feet yearning for one more out, Brad surrenders a game-tying three-run home run to Juan Brito. The Beavers wind up losing in ten innings. Five days later he coughs up a game-tying grand slam against the Tacoma Rainiers for his sixth blown save of the year. His ERA stands at a whopping 5.93.

Off the field, too, there are problems. When Brad left for spring training in February, his grandfather seemed fine. Donald was still walking down to his part-time janitor's job at the Pearl Rhodes Elementary School. He was still tending the pet cows he keeps in a small pasture behind the house. As the maple sap began to plink into buckets throughout Leyden, though, Donald's health took a sharp turn for the worse. The pain came in waves, accompanied by a hacking cough and a vanishing appetite as a once strong body began to wither.

Deep down, all is not well in Brad's relationship with Ashley, either. Ashley is vivacious and revels in social contact. When they are at home in the winter, she loves to go out dancing at the Bella Notte restaurant at the top of Huckle Hill Road in Bernardston; Brad is happier watching a movie or arranging his bait and tackle for ice fishing in the morning. With summer approaching, Ashley wants to go on the road trips to the Pacific Coast League's hot spots, Las Vegas and New Orleans.[7] The bright lights hold little appeal for Brad. When Ashley came to visit in April, Brad was happy to go out and see *Fever Pitch*—a love story about the Red Sox winning it all—but he also showed particular interest in the photos Ashley brought him that were snapped automatically from his tree stand in Leyden, triggered by the movements of deer.

The tension is largely unspoken. Brad and Ashley met so young. The shifting sands of minor league baseball have kept them apart for most of the year, every year. On some level they don't really know each other all that well.

With his teammates Brad isn't particularly social, either. The Triple-A world is a little older than Double-A, a little less innocent, more guys with bigger chips on their shoulders. Brad isn't into the bar scene or the base-ball groupies. Sometimes he plays Halo with teammates, killing one an-other off via the video games that manager Craig Colbert hates. Brad does enjoy one off day spent with teammate Ben Risinger on a ranch outside of Mitchell (a town of 170 people), fishing for rainbow trout and shooting prairie dogs. Mostly, though, he keeps to himself. Even in the bullpen he likes his space, expressing a preference not to have someone else warming up beside him on the second pitching rubber. In the macho culture of the minors, such a quirk isolates Brad, making him vulnerable to barbs from the tobacco-chewing, seed-spitting prospects eying the same golden op-portunity that might never come.

● When Brad signed as an eighteen-year-old, Wayne Britton, who was the Red Sox scouting director, told him that it would be best to avoid making close friends in the minor leagues. He had to be ready for a survival-of-the-fittest mentality. The culture of the minors was too transient. Stay close to your family, Britton advised, and keep your eyes on the prize.

For the most part, Brad has followed the advice. Players come and go all the time. For instance, just a few weeks after they hunted prairie dogs to-gether, Ben Risinger is released by the Padres.

Over the years, the closest friendship Brad has developed in the game is with a a a pitcher named Dan Giese. They were both drafted by the Red Sox back in 1999, but a full 999 picks apart (Baker at number forty overall in the supplemental first round, Giese at 1,039 in the thirty-fourth). For three years their paths crossed only at spring training, as the Sox had them slot-ted for different teams. But in June 2002, when the Sox acquired Alan Embree from the Padres, the package of prospects consisted of Baker and Giese. Suddenly they were cast together as the new guys with the Padres' Double-A team, the Mobile BayBears in Alabama. Giese, who had been drafted out of the University of San Diego, was three and a half years older than Brad, and similarly earnest. He had just gotten married the previous winter, and his wife, Shannon, became close with Brad's girlfriend, Ashley Kachelmeyer. "They're just the greatest people," Ashley says.

In 2003 Brad and Dan Giese became roommates in Mobile. On Easter Sunday, though, Giese was promoted to Triple-A. One week later he was traded to the Phillies for "cash considerations"—baseball chattel, denied the opportunity to make it up to his hometown Padres. "You can't even make friends in baseball," Ashley laments. "You blink your eye, and then they're gone."

Largely because of Ashley's connection with Shannon, however, this baseball friendship stuck. In fact, Dan and Shannon Giese flew to Massachusetts in October 2004 to be in Brad and Ashley's wedding. They sat right in the front of the stone church, tearing up to Shania Twain's "From This Moment On." Later, at the reception, they followed the first game of the World Series as the Red Sox defeated the Cardinals, 11–9, Alan Embree pitching in the eighth inning for the Sox.

In April 2005, after Ashley has spent a few days with Brad in Portland, she carts her purple suitcase up to San Diego to stay with Shannon Giese for a few days. Shannon is pregnant with her first baby. One night they listen to the webcast of Dan's game on the East Coast and then Brad's game on the West. When Brad gets the call-up to San Diego, Shannon says, they can definitely stay with her. Maybe one day they will all be up in the big leagues together.

Things aren't going that well for Dan Giese, though, in 2005. He is twenty-eight, in his third straight year at Triple-A, and he realizes that he doesn't have the "prospect" label which greases the wheels for easier promotion. He is getting tired of the grind, all the travel, losing money to play ball. On June 11, down in Durham, North Carolina, at the ballpark where Kevin Costner once said, "Well, fuck this fucking game," Giese gives up four runs in one and one-third innings, blowing a save and getting the loss, dropping his numbers to 3–4 with a 5.68 ERA.

When he gets word that Shannon has been in a car accident in California, Giese decides he has had enough. Although there are no injuries to either Shannon or the baby, he heads west nevertheless, sure of his path.

It is time to grow up and face reality. Giese decides to finish his degree at the University of San Diego and begins selling cars at Hoehn Honda in Carlsbad.

● On the night of June 22, following a victory over the Fresno Grizzlies, Brad learns that he and Clay Hensley—the pitcher who was suspended at the beginning of the season for failing a drug test—have been named the Portland Beavers' representatives to the Pacific Coast League All-Star team. His league-leading twenty saves was too glittering to pass up, even with a 5.40 ERA.

"The way I look at it, this year I've pitched terribly," Brad admits over a late dinner that night.

He says that the reports on his grandfather are not good, that he is deteriorating rapidly. He nods his head when asked whether Ashley will come join him out west after the All-Star break, and then describes the parade of roommates through his two-bedroom apartment: Tim Stauffer (with Brad, the Padres' co–pitcher of the year in the minors in 2004), who has been called up to the big leagues; Mike Bumstead (the longtime virgin), who has been traded; Jack Cassel (a right-handed reliever from Los Angeles), just promoted from Double-A.

Brad says he is truly surprised by Dan Giese's decision to quit the game, though on some level he understands. No, he hasn't called Dan yet; he doesn't know exactly what to say. He eats his salmon slowly and keeps the conversation safe. The year so far isn't working out quite the way he had hoped.

"The hardest part," he says, "is that you have to perform every day. Most jobs you fail—no problem. But here, you fail, and that could be your career. There's always someone coming up from behind you, so you've got to keep it going. There's no letting up."

7 Opposites Attract

Portland, Maine

In the fog, in the April chill, on the spongy green grass of Hadlock Field, young men play catch. It is a meditative rite of spring. Back and forth. The ball snapping between them. Pop–pop–pop.

They throw in pairs, strong-armed young men who have all sipped the sweet bubbly of success on other fields in other towns. All have been stamped for greatness, been told they could truly believe. And now they are all the way up to Double-A, within range of the goal, though even among this select crew the majority will never play even one game in the bigs. Who will ultimately get the call? Talley Haines? Conor Brooks? Jonathan Papelbon? Marc Deschenes, still plugging along at age thirty-two?

Out in right center field, beneath the fence with an inflatable L. L. Bean boot and the lighthouse that rises after every Portland Sea Dogs home run, two model-handsome characters throw the ball back and forth with some animation. Charlie Zink puts the knuckle of his index finger on the ball, digs into the hide with the long nail of his middle finger, and lets fly. The ball sails without spin through the moist air. At the last second it darts down and smacks Manny Delcarmen in the shin. Hopping mad, he picks it up, and fires back at ninety-five, aiming for the grass right in front of Zink. "Don't get your panties ruffled, you Mexican!" Zink shouts, and the two howl with laughter.

They share a loft in a green condo at the Junipers of Yarmouth apartment complex ten miles north of the ballpark, right off Interstate 295. Downstairs in separate bedrooms live their two other roommates, a couple of laid-back lefties, Kason Gabbard and Jon Lester. The apartment with four pitchers is ballplayer spare: nothing on the walls, dirty laundry piled in the corner, an Xbox with DVDs scattered around the floor, open cans of Bud Light, a few tins of Copenhagen snuff, plastic bottles of Aquafina water filled with brown pools of tobacco juice. They play poker and spend hours with *MLB 2005*, the one with Manny—Ramirez—on the cover.

After games, Manny and Charlie like to go to the bustling Old Port, hitting the bar circuit at places like Gritty McDuff's and Liquid Blue. They usually wind up on Fore Street, snickering at the store called Condom Sense (with its displays of penis pasta and candy bras) and making their way to their favorite joint, the Fore Play Sports Pub. There they play fierce games of pool, with pretty young ladies surrounding the table, the beer flowing, paying sporadic attention to the last inning or two of the Red Sox game playing on twenty-four screens. When they dismount from Charlie's Yukon Denali at the condo in Yarmouth, the Maine night above them is cold and quiet.

● True friendship in the minor leagues is rare. For one thing, the lifestyle is too transient. Players are constantly coming and going, getting promoted, getting demoted, traded, or released. You don't have to spend long in pro ball before you see a teammate getting tapped on the shoulder by the clubhouse attendant, called into the manager's office, and sent packing, sometimes dragging a wife and young kids across the country. Pretty much everyone has known the telltale moment when the clubbie rips the athletic tape with a teammate's name off the top of his locker, wads it up, and tosses it into the trash. As former Red Sox scouting director Wayne Britton advised just-signed draft picks Brad Baker in 1999 and Manny Delcarmen in 2000, avoid getting too close to teammates. Save yourself the trouble.

The larger, more unspoken reason why friendship is uncommon is that beneath the feel-good hokeyness of the minors lies a culture of ruthless competition, particularly among people playing the same position. Simply put, a fellow pitcher or fellow shortstop's success is bad for you. His failure—or injury—is good. Everyone is vying for a few golden spots. Here in 2005, when major leaguers earn a minimum salary of $316,000 and an average of $2.63 million while Charlie Zink pulls in $9,500 ($1,900 a month for five months), you don't see a lot of looking out for number two.

But Charlie and Manny are tight. They first played together in the South Atlantic League in 2002, just days after Charlie's April Fool's Day signing with the Sox. They were two of the forty-one young men, all aged eighteen to twenty-four, who suited up at some point that year for the Augusta GreenJackets. They all lived in an apartment complex just ten minutes from the famous golf course where the Masters is played. A few weeks into the season, Manny moved in with Charlie. From the beginning they shared a laidback irreverence and an appetite for competition of all kinds— everything from playing Ping-Pong to seeing who could flick sunflower seeds closest to a can in the bullpen. There were hours of cards, gallons of beer, lots of ESPN, lots of laughter.

They talked easily about sports and cars and girls. Charlie told Manny amusing stories about his girlfriend Naomi, a photography major who had studied for a while in Italy and France. Manny sought out Charlie's advice when the anonymous instant messages started coming from Massachusetts, from the girl who seemed to know him so well.

They shared the boredom of the minor league grind but also the drama. That was the summer when Charlie uncorked his fateful knuckleball, shattering the trainer's glasses. That was the season that ended with Manny thundering north, calling Charlie from the road, before thudding to a halt in the Bronx.

Their friendship was forged in heavy moments, too. Sometimes Manny would overhear Charlie on his cell phone talking to his dying dad, choking up while telling him about the ballgame that night. "You all right, man?" Manny would ask afterward, picking through pieces of a jigsaw puzzle spread out next to a Domino's box on the kitchen table. Then he'd haul Charlie out to his Lexus and air it out along the back roads lined with fields of red clay, moving faster than any ball they could throw.

The following April, Charlie was the only person Manny confided in about the numbness in his elbow. Charlie urged him not to pitch. "Dude, it's not worth it," he implored. Afterward, while Manny was dealing with the tedium of rehab from the Tommy John surgery, Charlie called him all the time, regaling him with stories from the road. He made Manny laugh, made him work even harder, helped him find his way back.

They were in many respects an odd couple. One was a knuckleballing maverick from California, the son of prison guards of German and Japanese ancestry. One was the fireballing son of a Dominican minor leaguer who grew up in inner-city Boston. One played his last amateur ball at the Savannah College of Art and Design, the other at West Roxbury High School. One was never drafted and didn't get a penny for a signing bonus. The other was a hotshot second rounder who got three-quarters of a million dollars. One occasionally irked the Red Sox brass with his ambivalence; the other did so with his combustibility.

But the bond is clear. Manny says that Charlie reminds him of his buddies from back home. Charlie says of Manny, "It's really hard not to be happy around him."

So close are they that their friendship is the source of some good-natured ribbing from teammates. Manny and Charlie "were just attached at the hip," recalls pitcher Ryan Cameron, another client of DiaMMond Management, who played for a couple of years in the Red Sox organization. "They were real close. A lot of guys made fun of them at some points, because they were just *too* close."

● By the time they move into the condo in Maine in 2005, short-lived baseball fates have changed dramatically. Of the forty-one hopefuls who played for Augusta in 2002, more than half (twenty-two) have already hung up their spikes, none of them voluntarily. Only two, Kevin Youkilis and Wil Ledezma, have made it up to the big leagues. Manny and Charlie are at least still in the game.

For Charlie Zink, 2005 will be his third tour of duty with the Sea Dogs. He is by now well acquainted with the wacky world of the knuckleball. This means a number of things that set him apart from his fellow pitchers.

One is a Valley Girl–esque attention to fingernail grooming. The nail on the middle finger of his right hand is his meal ticket. That is the one that digs into the cowhide just below where the seam of the ball makes a horseshoe. He keeps the nail long, files it meticulously, and avoids prolonged contact with water, his oft-stated excuse for not doing dishes. Before his starts, he paints the nail with three or four coats of extra-strength nail hardener, which he purchased rather awkwardly in a California salon. (His solitary claw makes him unique even among knuckleball pitchers. For generations the small cadre of knuckleballers had also plunged their index nails into the ball, making "knuckleball" a misnomer. But Charlie's unorthodox grip, his index finger bent to put his knuckle right on the hide, pays homage to the early days of the game. Hence, he releases the pitch with just his middle finger extended, sending an unintended but apt message to the hitter.)

He is also the only pitcher on the staff who carries his own catcher's glove with him at all times. The late action on the pitch makes catching it a difficult art, and Charlie tries to minimize the exasperation of his battery mate by providing an oversized glove. It is a light glove with minimal padding, a TPX model actually designed for softball. He is embarrassed to lug such a thing around, but his catchers always use it.[1]

Charlie has also grown accustomed to the isolation of the knuckleballer. Within the macho culture of a team of young athletes, he is the guy who went to art school, the guy with the softball glove and the nail hardener, the guy whose signature pitch doesn't even travel seventy miles an hour. In truth, he senses some resentment at times, as if his pitch were a gimmick, as if he were somehow cheating. The feeling is not without some merit. Ryan Cameron, a teammate with the 2003 Sea Dogs, admitted that Charlie's success that August made some people bristle. "It is unique to see someone come and just settle in and go through it the way he did," Cameron recalled. "Things were just going his way. He was their boy. He was the Red Sox' guy at that point in time. There was some animosity. There were some guys that were a little ticked off about it, a knuckleballer coming through. A couple [of] guys had their starts bumped."

When Charlie struggled mightily in 2004, he sensed a lot of quiet satisfaction around him, if not a festival of snickering.

That is the thing, of course, that is hardest to take about knuckleball life: its maddening unpredictability. Everyone has streaks in the game, slumps and moments of being "locked in," but knuckleball life is pure baseball schizophrenia. Charlie had rocketed his way onto the Red Sox' radar in 2003 with his two near no-hitters, landing himself a seat right next to Theo Epstein at Fenway one night, and a spot on *Baseball Prospectus*'s list of the top fifty prospects in the game. The lavish praise from ESPN senior writer Rob Neyer had been sweet music: "easily the best young knuckleball pitcher in the world."

Then came the plummet of 2004, one terrible outing after another. Charlie would have command for an inning or two, and then it would vanish, some knucklers bouncing to the backstop, some staying up forever in the hitting zone and getting crushed all over the Eastern League. The charmed pitch had become an albatross. Deep down, he had no idea why he was failing so miserably now, or why he had succeeded so grandly the year before. To his mind, he was doing the exact same thing, just trying to throw a spinless pitch at the catcher's mask. He pleaded with his coaching staff to let him go back to being a conventional pitcher. Hadn't he done well that first year in the minors in Augusta? Wasn't his 1.68 ERA better than anyone else's on a staff that included top draft picks? Didn't that show he could pitch effectively against professionals? Couldn't he just try again?

No way, he was told. His stuff wouldn't translate at the higher levels. This was his only path.

At year's end he was back in Class-A, his overall record 1–10, his ERA a humiliating 5.77.

In truth, his shoulder had been sore at the end of the year, and the Red Sox had shut him down with swelling in the capsule of his joint. Charlie wanted to believe that this had played a major role in his decline. During the winter in California, he had worked out extensively for the first time, building arm strength. Maybe the magic would return in 2005.

"The Portland Sea Dogs will feature some of the Boston Red Sox's top pitching prospects. Charlie Zink is not one of them," read the lead of one preseason story in the *Portland Press Herald*. Director of player development Ben Cherington explained to the reporter: "It's such a fine-tuned pitch, you have to be able to repeat the delivery. And his delivery fell apart. He was fighting himself all year."

The article closed with the frank assessment that "Zink looked terrible in 2004 but showed enough in 2003 to allow the Red Sox to keep hoping. 'I want to show I can still be successful doing this,' Zink said."

● His first start comes on a blustery Monday, April 11, 2005. The temperature is just forty-five degrees with strong winds blowing in from right field as Charlie toes the rubber against the New Britain Rock Cats, Double A affiliate of the Twins. Between innings he huddles by a heater in the dugout. It proves to be a glorious day, Charlie's first win in almost a year, as the Sea Dogs shut out the Rock Cats, 1–0. He pitches six innings, allowing just four hits, walking nobody, and striking out two. Perhaps the magic is on its way back.

But in subsequent outings he struggles, his command vanishing for long stretches. On May 1 he has a galling start, lasting just one inning at Norwich, surrendering five runs on two hits and four walks. He is better in his next start, but far from sharp, surrendering five earned runs over six innings while taking a loss at home.

And then, with his ERA at an embarrassing 6.65, he receives some startling news: he is getting called up for the first time to Triple-A. The Red Sox have sustained some injuries to the pitching staff, with veterans Curt Schilling and David Wells on the disabled list, requiring a few reinforcements from Pawtucket. There, too, the staff has been depleted by injuries, so gaps have to be filled. Charlie is now just one level away from the big leagues.

His first call comes in relief on May 10 at Scranton, and it is anything but an impressive debut. In an inning and a third, he surrenders four earned runs on six hits, including a home run. Seven of the eleven batters he faces reach base.

Still, he is thrust into the starting rotation and told he will pitch three days later at home against the Toledo Mud Hens on Friday the thirteenth.

● Manny Delcarmen also pitches on that Friday, back in Double-A in Maryland against the Bowie Baysox. He is dominant, striking out all three batters he faces.

The anger of spring training has faded. With his weight in check, Manny was transferred to the Portland work group and slated to begin the season with the Sea Dogs. He was told that he would work out of the bullpen exclusively, that this was his fastest path to Fenway. For the first time since his high school days, he would be playing ball within range of home. The stands behind the plate at Hadlock Field would fill with Manny's people: Ana, with her flowing mane of black hair; Javy Colon, the MBTA bus driver, wearing a gray cargo cap with earflaps and a Red Sox "B" above the brim; Kuki, his handsome and opinionated father, bursting with pride. At twenty-three years of age, Manny has now taken the dream further than his dad, up to the high minors.

Although he has some rough outings in April, Manny is getting great organizational reports from manager Todd Claus. His fastball is touching the mid-nineties. He has command of the 12–6 curveball. The changeup is becoming a viable third pitch, with deceptive fastball arm motion and late sinking action. He has a locked-in competitive focus on the mound, but he doesn't wear his emotions on his sleeve. Maybe he is easy to over-look on a staff that features a fireballing starter known then as Jon Papel-bon, and a lefty with nasty stuff, Jon Lester, who is on his way to becoming the Eastern League Pitcher of the Year. Still, Manny senses that he is on a good track.

On May 23 he joins a small group of Red Sox minor leaguers sum-moned to Cooperstown to play in the annual Hall of Fame exhibition game at Doubleday Field against the Detroit Tigers. For Manny it is a tantalizing taste of the possible. Being at big league spring training was one thing, when there were dozens of minor leaguers interspersed with the stars. This is far more intimate. He stands there on the grounds of Elihu Phinney's old cow pasture listening to the pregame banter of Kevin Millar and Johnny Damon, and watches with awe as the effervescent David Ortiz wins the home run contest, blasting eight of ten pitches into the just-greening trees beyond the right field bleachers. Ortiz, to him, seems larger than life. All around him the stands are packed with the rock star Red Sox' ever-present entourage. Many have come directly from the Hall two blocks over, where they paid homage to a new exhibit featuring Curt Schilling's bloody sock. (Schilling, on the disabled list, is not on hand that day because of a prior engagement with the Senate subcommittee on steroids).

Manny pitches one inning, a scoreless eighth. Soon after, the Red Sox take off for Toronto, while Manny, buoyed, rejoins the Portland Sea Dogs in Binghamton.

● McCoy Stadium is set amid the gray and decaying factories of working-class Pawtucket, Rhode Island. The stadium, which dates to 1942, has one singular claim to fame: it hosted the longest baseball game in history. On a frigid, windy night in April 1981, the Pawtucket Red Sox and the Rochester Red Wings played to a 2–2 standoff over thirty-two innings before the game was suspended at 4:07 in the morning. It was resumed in late June amid national fanfare (in part because of the ongoing Major League Baseball strike), and ended when Pawtucket scored in the home thirty-third. The game featured a number of players who would go on to the big leagues, including two future Hall of Famers, Wade Boggs and Cal Ripken Jr. It also featured quite a few for whom Triple-A would be the top of the mountain. That group included Dave Koza, whose single finally won the game. Afterwards, prophetically, he said, "Nothing I ever do in life will probably compare to this."

McCoy has turned that night of endless baseball into a shrine. All around the ballpark are posted replicas of articles written to commemorate the contest. Along one huge cinderblock swath of the concourse runs the line score: all those zeroes, speckled with five 1's: one for Rochester in the seventh, a fateful one for Pawtucket in the bottom of the ninth, the maddening matching pair in the twenty-first (Boggs knocked in the tying run in the home half in the wee hours, and later said his wife "didn't know whether to hug me or slap me"), and finally the merciful one knocked in two months later by Koza. The mural stands as a memento of a historic night and also as an unintended commentary on minor league life: it can be an excruciatingly long slog with no guarantee of the big payoff.

On Friday night, May 13, Jim Masteralexis arrives with his five-year-old son Nathan and sits behind the big net in back of the plate. Jim points to the left field wall and tells Nathan that once, long ago, he hit a ball off that fence.

They are there to see Charlie Zink make his first Triple-A start. Jim connected with Charlie through Manny Delcarmen a couple of years back. He finds Charlie to be an intriguing character, more grown up and worldly than most of his other clients, yet unabashedly, perhaps dangerously, fond of beer and gambling and the female form. He is fascinated by Charlie's background and drawn to the mystique of his signature pitch. He refers to Charlie as "a cult figure in the secret knuckleball society."

From his frequent phone contact with the Red Sox, he knows that the front office is growing impatient with Charlie, and that this trial at Triple-A is regarded as something of a litmus test of his viability.

He stands alone on the mound holding his hat over his heart during the national anthem. He scratches the number 16 on the dirt behind the rubber in tribute to his old high school friend Dave Russell. Then he gets ready to face the Toledo Mud Hens. Back in El Dorado Hills, California, his mother, Joyce, tunes in to the webcast, tape recorder whirring.

It soon becomes a disastrous night. The knuckleball stays up in the hitting zone, and the Mud Hens tee off. Charlie is sent to the showers after just two innings, having surrendered eight earned runs on seven hits with four walks and a wild pitch. Later he would admit, "I just remember going out there and feeling like I was overmatched, like I didn't belong there."

Jim sits through another inning or two and sees Nathan yawning and rubbing his eyes. He packs up, and on the way out goes down to the hallway outside the clubhouse. He asks an intern who is guarding access to the area if he would be willing to go in and tell Charlie Zink that his agent wants to talk with him. A few minutes later Charlie appears in the hallway, still in full uniform, looking, as Jim would later recall, "shell-shocked." They talk for a few minutes in the corridor, which is lined with hundreds of small framed photos of men who had once played at Pawtucket and later in the major leagues. The display is not confined to former PawSox; there are lots of opponents as well, some of whom (Mookie Wilson, Aaron Boone) would go on to hold infamous places in Red Sox lore. Nowhere on display, of course, are the countless players who had come only this far.

Jim tries to assure Charlie that he pitched better than his results. He sees Charlie fighting back tears and tells him to keep his head up, that things will surely get better. It sounds pretty empty to them both. Nathan tugs at Jim's arm, and soon they are off, trudging back to the car and heading home.

The next day Charlie is sent back to Double-A and told to join the Sea Dogs in Erie, Pennsylvania. While he is at the airport gate getting ready to board, he gets a call from Red Sox director of player development Ben Cherington, who doesn't sugarcoat his words. Charlie is well into a second straight season of dreadful performance, and it is time to shape up or ship the hell out. "You need to start doing well," Cherington says, "or we're not going to be able to keep you around."

Back with the Sea Dogs, Charlie finds himself immediately placed on the disabled list with a pulled groin—an injury he hadn't suffered. Unofficially, he is on the "phantom disabled list," an illegal but common tactic used by teams to juggle rosters. For Charlie, this baseball limbo is excruciating as the long days stretch out into weeks. He sits in the stands, charting other guys' pitches. At one point there are four straight rainouts against the Binghamton Mets. He plays hours and hours of online poker. The already slow-moving life of the minors grinds to a halt.

● On a drizzly June 1 in Manchester, New Hampshire, Charlie sits in the lobby of the Comfort Inn wearing a red polo shirt, jeans, and sneakers, and trying to make sense of his saga as a professional baseball player. His experience in 2004 was incredibly lonely, he says. "I was just lost. There really was no one to talk to. It's not like a regular pitcher where I can have a coach help me with a mechanical flaw, I was pretty much on my own."

This year, of course, is even worse. He is chafing under the knuckleball edict, and has concluded that success with the pitch is mostly a matter of luck. "My object is to throw the ball without spin. When I throw it without spin and it doesn't move, I don't know what to do. Shit. Those are the days when I don't have a clue, like I don't even want to be a knuckleballer any more. . . . I throw it the way I've always thrown it—it moves when it wants to move. I don't know. I don't have a grasp on it. I just don't feel that confident with it. I never really did. Even when I was having all that success, I wondered how people were missing the ball . . . I don't know. It's a pitch that has just driven me crazy for the last three years."

His candor is startling. A sadness seems to hang over him, almost palpably. He seems worried that his wild youth might be running out. "I don't know how much longer I will be with the Red Sox," he says, his voice flat.

He brightens, though, when Manny Delcarmen comes down to the lobby, his dark, curly hair billowing from beneath his fatigue-style Red Sox cap. During a drive into town to find some lunch, they keep up a steady banter. They bust each other's chops about the latest game of *MVP 2005* in the hotel room. Debating restaurants, Manny says, "You're always looking for some burritos," to which Charlie responds, "I'm trying to take you back to your people." Passing Panera Bread, which advertises free wireless access, Charlie says, "I should bring my computer in there and gamble," which Manny promptly seizes upon as evidence of a problem. Charlie admits that on a recent trip to Mohegan Sun when the team was playing the Connecticut Defenders, he dropped $400 playing blackjack and craps.

Over lunch at Pizzeria Uno, Manny talks about the cutthroat culture of the minors, saying it extends even to agents, who often try to swoop in and steal clients. "We're fighting for a job; they're fighting for clients. We've got to do whatever it takes to get there. They've got to do whatever it takes to get there. They're just like us." Among his fellow pitchers, he says, the competition is fierce. Then he looks over at Charlie and says, "We're both trying to get out of here. But . . . I hope that I move up, and he moves up with me. There's some guys that want you to do bad."

As Manny speaks, Charlie chews absently on a piece of crust. He senses that his buddy is on a different escalator, the one going up. It is hard to tell if he is even listening just then. With a red crayon he is absentmindedly doing the "Uno Word Search" and the "What's on Chef Uno's Pizza" word scramble. His chin rests on his left hand. His right hand is curled around the crayon, the long middle nail digging into the paraffin wax.

8 Baseballtown

Reading, Pennsylvania

In the first summer of the first year of major league baseball, George Bradley was a superstar. Just eleven days after the nation's centennial celebration, on July 15, 1876, Bradley turned in an American classic, pitching the sport's first no-hitter. Hurling for the St. Louis Brown Stockings, one of the charter members of the National League, Bradley dominated the Hartford Dark Blues, 2–0, one of sixteen shutouts he would toss that season, en route to a 45–19 record. An affable fellow with the nickname "Grin," Bradley hailed from the southeastern Pennsylvania city of Reading.

At the time of Bradley's no-hitter, Reading was booming. There was gold in them thar hills, in the form of anthracite coal that was fueling the industrial revolution. The Pennsylvania and Reading railroads were hauling it away, becoming for a time the largest corporation in the world. Tucked under Mount Penn, fifty-eight miles northwest of Philadelphia, Reading was a railroad town through and through. When the game of Monopoly was trademarked in 1935, there was Reading Railroad, right on the board. At the time, the population of the largely German and Dutch city had swelled to 120,000.

But the coal economy went bust, and with it the railroad. The famed line endured multiple bankruptcies before going under completely in the early 1970s. With the demise of the once great railroad, the city's prosperity vanished. In the early twenty-first century, despite an attempt to reinvent itself as a factory outlet showcase, Reading remained a city on the wrong side of the tracks. In 2005 more than 26 percent of the population (now 80,000) lived below the poverty line, twice the national rate. The median household income of $24,026 was just over half the state average. Only 8.6 percent of adults twenty-five or older had a bachelor's degree. More alarming still was the city's murder rate, seventeenth highest in the country, worse even than Philadelphia's.

On weekday afternoons, groups of young men would sit on stoops before brick buildings covered with graffiti, a scene of almost Dickensian grayness. The lack of vitality, the down-and-out feeling, extended to many aspects of life in Reading.

But not to its pride and joy. The love of the national pastime in Reading and in Berks County, which encompasses the city, is so great that in 2002 the region trademarked the name Baseballtown.

Few places in America can claim as colorful a baseball history. Minor league ball has been a staple of the city going back to the late nineteenth century. As early as 1883, widely considered the first year of minor league baseball, Reading had a team in the Interstate League. Fifteen years later, in July 1898, the Reading Coal Heavers earned the distinction of employing the first woman in professional baseball history when Lizzie Arlington pitched a scoreless inning against Allentown. Arlington arrived in style in a carriage drawn by white horses. In pregame warm-ups, according to the account in the *Reading Eagle*, Arlington behaved like a consummate professional "even down to expectorating on her hands and wiping her hands on her uniform."

A decade later the local minor league squad was known as the Reading Pretzels. The third baseman of that 1908 team was a strapping young butcher from Trappe, Maryland, named George Baker. At season's end, Baker's contract was purchased by the legendary Connie Mack of the Philadelphia Athletics. In the majors, "Home Run" Baker would become America's long ball king before a certain George Herman Ruth came on the scene. (Babe, as it turned out, has a place in Reading baseball annals, too. On October 20, 1928, not even two weeks removed from slamming three home runs in the decisive fourth game of the World Series, Ruth and his regal companion Lou Gehrig came to Reading as part of a barnstorming tour. The "Bustin' Babes" defeated the "Larrupin' Lous," 9–8.)[1]

Old-timers in Reading still puff up with pride over homegrown players like "Broadway" Charlie Wagner, who pitched for the Red Sox from 1938 to 1946; George "Whitey" Kurowski, a five-time All-Star third baseman for the Cardinals in the 1940s; and of course the rocket-armed right fielder of the beloved Brooklyn Dodger teams in the late forties and fifties, Carl Furillo—known as "the Reading Rifle."

But the grip of baseball in Reading can be only partially understood by combing the history books and recounting the tales of the nicknamed stars of yesterday. It comes alive in a more visceral way with a night at the ballpark. What is now called FirstEnergy Stadium was originally christened Municipal Memorial Stadium in 1951. It is by thirty-six years the oldest facility in the Eastern League, and it is without question a minor league mecca. For many years running, the Reading Phillies have placed first or second in attendance among the twelve teams in the league. Fans arrive early, pour through the turnstiles, grab their cheesesteaks and mustard-covered pretzels, and immerse themselves in a vivid slice of Americana.

They are welcomed by public address announcer Dave "Frenchy" Bauman, who has not missed a home game since 1978. Bauman touts the area's "rich baseball tradition" and "wonderfully nostalgic stadium," and closes his spiel by declaring that Reading and Berks County "will forever be known throughout the country as the one and only Baseballtown. This is Baseballtown, the home of your Reading Phillies." That sets up a rocking version of "Baseballtown" by gray-haired local songwriter Johnny Jackson: "And beyond this park, those trains keep rolling, just like every day; but in here it might be baseball heaven in the USA."

Dressed in pinstriped uniforms with a black locomotive logo on their caps, the Reading Phillies run out to their positions. They place their hats over their hearts as a teenage girl sings the national anthem. At home plate, the catcher and umpires are joined by no fewer than five mascots: Change-up the Turtle, Bucky the Beaver, Blooper the Hound Dog, Quack the Rubber Ducky, and of course Screwball the Seamhead—his shirt untucked, his tongue hanging out, his eyes bulging. The mascots circulate throughout the crowd all night, each spending an inning at the "Phun House" on the first base concourse, signing autographs and posing for photos.

Other members of the cast emerge as the night of baseball drama unfolds. Before the home half of the second inning, the crowd goes nuts when the hyperkinetic Crazy Hot Dog Vendor unleashes his act. Riding a stuffed ostrich costume and wearing a huge red wig, oversized glasses, and a red bowtie, he yells and frolics, reaching into a satchel and winging wieners into the stands. In the top of the fifth, a long-legged Tooth Fairy comes out with a huge brush to scrub the bases pearly white.

Between-inning promotions include games like the "higher-lower" competition. A male fan is asked to estimate the percentage of, say, Reading Phillies players who wear boxers instead of briefs. A female fan then indicates whether she believes the actual percentage is higher or lower than the first fan's guess. When the electronic scoreboard shows a Reading Phillies player announcing the actual percentage, we learn which of the two fans has earned free tickets to an upcoming demolition derby.

The kitsch, however, does not obscure the appeal of the game itself. This is a savvy fan base; lots of folks still keep a scorebook, and plenty of adults even bring a well-oiled Rawlings in hope of harvesting a foul ball.

"This area is in love with baseball," says Mike Drago, the team's beat writer for the *Reading Eagle* since 1994. "There's no doubt about it."

Nowhere is that more apparent than beneath the stands on the first base side. Here the home clubhouse opens onto the concourse, a rare and intimate configuration that means players must walk through a gauntlet of fans to get to the field. Before games, fans mass outside the door and wait. Many survey the nearby red and white cinderblock wall, which contains the team photos of every squad since Reading first affiliated with the Phillies organization in 1967 (the third-longest ongoing connection between a minor league city and a major league team). They reminisce about the stars of summers past. There are almost a thousand players on the wall here, the vast majority of whom never made it to the big leagues. But there in the 1971 photo is Mike Schmidt; and there in 1980 is Rync Sandberg. Both are enshrined now in the Hall of Fame.

When the clubhouse door swings open and a player or two emerges, spikes clattering on the cement floor, a flurry of activity ensues. Wide-eyed Little Leaguers hold up baseballs and markers. There are pats on the back, "Go get 'em's," "Hey, how you doin's?" cameras flashing and flirtatious winks. In these little moments, reflected in the faces of fans and often the players themselves, it is easy to see why minor league baseball matters so deeply in a place like Reading. It goes beyond the promise of escape, of something to do on a summer night in a struggling city. It speaks to one of the minors' most delicious contradictions.

On the one hand, the presence of these young men provides a sense of validation. The players belong to Reading too; they are, in a sense, one of us. They wear the city's name on their chests, its pride on their sleeves.

And yet, on the other hand, there is also the clear recognition that the success of these young men will ultimately be measured by their transcendence, their ability to get out of town. If all goes well for them, they will before long be leaving Reading, Pennsylvania, in the rearview mirror.

● Randy Ruiz arrives in Reading a couple of weeks into the season. He had stayed behind in Florida for extended spring training, supposedly to rehab a groin injury.

For Randy, Double-A is, if not a dream come true, at least a form of deliverance. After six long years at Single-A, he has at last made it up to the so-called high minors, the promotion many baseball insiders consider to be the most difficult in the sport. It is still a long way from the Promised Land, but this is no small achievement for a guy who had been a thirty-sixth-round pick out of high school—when he didn't sign—and then, three years and six colleges later, been given a meager $1,000 bonus at a tryout camp by the Cincinnati Reds. Those initial nights at FirstEnergy

Stadium awaken in him an old sense of possibility. The crowds are bigger than any he has ever played before, the lights brighter. He can almost hear the trains he used to take as a kid with his grandmother, rumbling off to the great stadium up on 161st Street, or to Flushing to watch Darryl Strawberry swing for the fences.

Here at Reading, a replica train sits atop the right center field wall. When the home team puts runners in scoring position, the steam billows, the whistle blows. And when a Reading Phillie crosses the plate, the tracks light up and fireworks blast. In his first few games, Randy Ruiz practically sets the thing ablaze. After hitting four homers and knocking in eleven runs in the last two games of the home stand, his average sits at .526. The headline in the *Reading Eagle* reads simply, "Power Surge Electrifies R-Phils."

Randy then takes his act on the road. On Sunday, May 1, he cracks a homer and a double and knocks in three runs in Maryland against the Bowie Baysox. The next day he learns that he has been named the Eastern League Player of the Week—in his very first week at Double-A.

That is not the only thing he learns that day, however. In a minor league baseball blog on the website of the *Reading Eagle*, Mike Drago writes:

> A few weeks ago, when Philadelphia Phillies assistant general manager Mike Arbuckle showed up in Reading to catch a game, we talked at length about steroid use in professional baseball, and the effect it was having on the game—and the players.
>
> I ended the [conversation] by telling Arbuckle that, sometime in the near future, I would be calling him for a comment should a Phillies minor leaguer be caught using a banned substance.
>
> Monday that day came.

Drago reveals that Ruiz actually started the year on the restricted list because of a positive drug test at the end of the 2004 season. It had not been a groin injury, after all.

While the drug in question is not identified, Arbuckle describes it in the blog, and in the next day's print edition of the paper, as "not something that was particularly concerning to me individually, or to us as an organization. It was not an issue that was overly alarming; it's not anything of huge consequence."

Arbuckle also tells Drago that Ruiz was the only minor leaguer among the more than 150 in the Phillies organization in 2004 to test positive.

Now, in May 2005, this drama plays out in a context in which players and team officials suddenly have to answer to the burgeoning public relations crisis that followed the nationally televised congressional hearings in mid-March. Ever since home run heroes Mark McGwire, Sammy Sosa, and company were forced to squirm on the national stage, the sport has been reeling. Baseball has to demonstrate that it is taking the issue of performance-enhancing drugs seriously. One of the safest ways for the commissioner's office to do that is to focus on the minor leagues, where the vast majority of players are not covered by collective bargaining.[2] Accordingly, thirty-eight minor leaguers, tested in March at the sites of the twelve teams that hold spring training in Arizona, were suspended for drug violations. Their names were plastered in papers all over America.

Context aside, Drago's investigative work seems to catch both Randy and the Phillies off guard, even though they both knew about the positive test months before. Randy feels that he is being presented as both a cheater and a liar. He can't tell Drago, or anyone else, that he was told by the Phillies to concoct the groin injury. The Phillies are his new employer. They have given him his first chance at Double-A.

In fairness, the Phillies' brass had every reason to believe that the truth about Randy's suspension would never see the light of day. Since none of the minor leaguers who tested positive between 2001 and 2004 had ever been publicly identified, it seemed reasonable that the dirty laundry could be kept in-house. No team was prepared for the avalanche of public scrutiny that followed the congressional hearings.

From Altoona, Pennsylvania, Randy speaks by phone to Drago on Tuesday, May 3. "I've never taken steroids," he claims in the article published the next day. "I know everybody [who gets caught] says that, but I've never taken [steroids]. I'm not into that stuff."

He tells Drago that the positive test was probably caused by an over-the-counter supplement. "I'm not taking anything now. Right now I don't want to mess my career up. I'm staying away from everything. I'm afraid if I take something else I'm gonna get in trouble."[3]

At least initially, Drago gives Randy the benefit of the doubt. In a sidebar to the main story on May 4, headlined "Ruiz Stigmatized by Positive Test," Drago faults Major League Baseball for making no distinction between steroids and over-the-counter products "such as protein shakes." He says that minor leaguers like Ruiz "get thrown under the bus along with admitted steroid-users such as Jose Canseco and Ken Caminiti." He indicates that Randy is now being tested with greater frequency than most other players, including "two or three times" during spring training. He points out that the fifteen-game suspension cost Randy about $750—"roughly one-tenth of his season's salary." Six days later Drago writes that Randy's new-found success at the plate stems largely from an improved mental approach:

"First baseman Randy Ruiz is a big, strong dude. But the strength that's made him so successful this season is located from the neck up."

Still, Randy feels embarrassed, even a little wounded, by being publicly identified as a guy who has failed a drug test. For all his imposing physical stature, for all his South Bronx street toughness, even for all his playful exuberance—the way his Muhammad Ali–like face lights up in a smile— there remains about Randy a surprisingly sensitive, almost thin-skinned side, a capacity for brooding. When he hears even one fan chanting "Steroids" (like the old taunting "Dar-ryl" directed at Randy's childhood hero by Red Sox fans in the 1986 World Series), he bristles. How many of these people judging him had grown up needing food stamps to put dinner on the table? How many had lingered for six years at Class-A, gorging on peanut butter and jelly sandwiches in the clubhouse to keep from losing money as a baseball player? How many had spent their winters working third shift at the No Frills Market in Bellevue, Nebraska, stocking shelves? And how many had cut corners in seeking their own path to success?

Randy later recalled that the sense of isolation was compounded by the fact that he was not getting sufficient support from his agent, Tommy Tanzer. Tanzer had recruited Randy back in spring training of 2001, when he was coming off his batting title and .381 average with the Billings Mustangs. He had liked Tanzer; the agent reminded him of his high school baseball coach in the Bronx, Mike Turo, slight of stature, full of energy, someone who seemed sincerely interested in his well-being. Tanzer's enthusiasm was infectious. But as Randy failed to advance, he felt that enthusiasm waning.

Now, amid the current tension, Randy feels adrift without professional guidance. One day in the clubhouse he talks about his concerns with pitcher Ryan Cameron. A former college teammate of Doug Clark's at UMass, Cameron suggests that Randy talk with his agents. Later that day Cameron calls Jim Masteralexis and tells him about the slugger from the Bronx. He hits everything hard, Cameron says. What's more, Randy is a good teammate, well liked in the clubhouse. There is, however, this little steroid controversy.

When Reading visits the New Hampshire Fisher Cats in late May, Jim drives up for the game. In the stands, he runs into John Brickley, someone he has known since they were baseball-addled teenagers growing up outside Boston. Brickley, as it turns out, is also at the game to see Randy Ruiz, the player he had signed out of a tryout camp six years earlier, someone with whom he has maintained a close relationship ever since. "He's a good-hearted guy, Jim," Brickley says.

Over a late dinner with Brickley and Ryan Cameron, Randy spells out his story to Jim: his upbringing in the Bronx, his years in A-ball, his positive drug test from a year ago. He is clean now, he insists. He has passed all subsequent drug tests. He just wants to put the incident behind him and focus on this new chance at Double-A to chase his lifelong dream. What he is looking for in an agent, he says, is somebody who will really be there for him, even when things are hard. He says he is just not getting that from his current agent.

Jim is struck by Randy's story and his engaging personality, and drawn, of course, by his torrid hitting. He knows the "stealing" of clients is an unseemly part of the agent world. Players can terminate contracts with agents at a moment's notice without penalty, leading to more flirtation and paranoia than you find in a lot of high school hallways. This case is different, though, Jim reasons. Randy is coming to him, rather than the other way around. He really needs help, and Jim thinks that he and Lisa and Steve can provide it, that their "family-based model" is perfect for someone like Randy. Besides, he figures, Tommy Tanzer has already made a small fortune as an agent, representing big leaguers with big contracts such as Dante Bichette, Steve Finley, and Charlie Hayes.

Randy signs up with Jim that very night. Jim leaves his work, cell, and home numbers on Tanzer's machine, and braces for the fusillade. It never comes. Tanzer does not return the call. In his mind, apparently, Randy Ruiz is not worth the trouble.

● Randy has another important source of support in that 2005 season in the person of Reading Phillies manager Steve Swisher. A onetime Major League All-Star who had managed for ten years in the minors, Swisher is returning to the game in 2005 after eight seasons away. "My thing is to just try to get young people to understand that this is the 'American Dream,'" Swisher explained to Mike Drago in a *Reading Eagle* article announcing his appointment in December 2004, "just try [to get them] to be the best that they can be every day."

When Randy arrived in Reading after his season-opening suspension, he was greeted by the silver-haired fifty-three-year-old manager, whose first words to Randy would stay with him all year: "Now let's see what kind of man you are."

In truth, the fiery Swisher is going to have a very bumpy ride in that 2005 season. In late May he is placed on an eight-game leave of absence by the Phillies for what the team deems a "personal issue" following a couple of nights of heated locker room exchanges with players. Another time he is suspended by the league for one game after an on-field altercation with the manager of the Trenton Thunder that has to be broken up by umpires and coaches from both teams.

For Randy, though, Swisher is the ideal manager. Swisher tells him that getting to the big leagues requires constant discipline, making good choices, working hard every single day. Even long after their one season together, Randy will refer to Swisher as "a father figure" and "the best manager I ever had in my life."

Swisher puts Randy in the cleanup spot in the lineup, and the player whom the manager refers to simply as "the big guy" delivers the goods night after night. Randy feels absolutely locked in at the plate. In mid-May he has one torrid stretch in which he gets at least two hits in six straight games, including four home runs and four doubles.

Baseballtown is used to its power displays, from Home Run Baker to Babe Ruth, from Roger Maris (a Reading Indian back in 1955) to Mike Schmidt. Just the year before, Reading fans had seen future National League Most Valuable Player Ryan Howard clout thirty-seven homers in just 102 games and make it up to the Phillies by year's end.

But few in Reading can remember the kind of display being put on by Randy Ruiz. Chewing gum, he begins his routine with his all-black bat (which he still sometimes sleeps with at night). In the on-deck circle he takes five full swings, then steps into the batter's box, digging in with his back cleat and assuming an open stance with his back leg significantly bent. Before every pitch he taps the barrel to the left-front corner of the plate, then makes one or two wide circles of the bat with his left (front) hand. As the pitcher gets ready to deliver, Randy pulls his hands back, lifts his back elbow way up, and moves the barrel in tight little orbits. Then the pitch comes in, and he focuses as always on three things: see the ball, read the spin, explode.

Sometimes he pulls the ball with fearsome power toward the retired numbers of Hall of Famers Schmidt and Sandberg far over the left center field wall. Other times his opposite-field blasts head out toward the swimming pool beyond the right center field wall, or soar out to deep right over the sign that advertises the current Powerball jackpot, often in excess of $100 million.

"It's a show," teammate Chris Roberson says of watching Randy bat, after he bangs out four extra base hits in a win over Binghamton. "You don't know what he's gonna do. He might hit one off the pitcher's head, or he might hit one a mile out of the stadium. It's a show—a big show."

Randy Ruiz during the 2004 season with the Lakeville BlueClaws, his sixth consecutive year in Single-A ball. *Courtesy of Lena Covel*

In 2005, Randy enjoys an unforgettable season in Baseballtown with the Reading Phillies. *Ralph Trout*

Another season, another team: Randy celebrates a home run in 2006
for the Trenton Thunder, Double-A affiliate of the New York Yankees.
Courtesy of Lena Covel

In August 2008, Randy finally breaks through with the
Minnesota Twins. *Courtesy of Lena Covel*

Randy, Lena Covel, and their son, Randy Ruiz III. *Courtesy of Lena Covel*

Randy and his grandmother, Luz Ruiz, in 2009 before a game between the Blue Jays and the Yankees. They are standing in Randy's childhood room in Luz's apartment on 136th Street in the Bronx. *Photo by author*

Randy is interviewed at Yankee Stadium before
a game in September 2009. *Photo by author*

Into June, Randy gives few signs of slowing down. After three hits against New Britain on June 15, he leads the league in both hitting, at .363, and slugging, at .657. The next night he goes 2-for-3, with his fourteenth home run, a double, and two RBI; then the next—on "Renew Your Wedding Vows Night" at FirstEnergy Stadium—he smacks a double and another home run. He is having the time of his life. After all the waiting, he has finally gotten an opportunity, and he is taking advantage of it in a monumental way. He tries not to get ahead of himself, to stay disciplined every day as Swisher had advised. But he can't help wondering just a little bit. Could a call-up to Triple-A be far off, or even a direct promotion to the big leagues?

His grandmother, now sixty-nine, keeps telling everyone in the neighborhood in the South Bronx that Randy is on his way to greatness. "Mamá," he says on the phone, "I'm just getting lucky." He knows it is hard for her to get out these days, that her health is not great, but he wants her to come see him when Reading plays the Yankees' Double-A team in Trenton later in the month.

In the meantime Randy has another set of games circled on his calendar. All season he has looked forward to a four-game series in Akron against the Aeros, an Indians farm team. This will give him an opportunity to see his father, Randy Sr., a crane operator for Delphi, which has just split from General Motors, where he had worked for more than twenty years. Though he was raised by Luz Ruiz, Randy has always maintained close ties with his dad. Baseball has been their bond. Randy Sr. likes to bust his son's chops whenever he is in a slump, or taunt him about the superiority of the Yankees over Randy's beloved Mets. Randy Sr. often tells his son, with a big smile on his face, that he would already have been in the big leagues himself if he hadn't had to go to work to support a family when he was just a teenager. Still, his pride is clear, and Randy always feels it. The call-up, at long last, to Double-A has been a big deal, and Randy knows that his outstanding performance has been deeply satisfying to his dad. Randy Sr. seldom gets the chance to see his son play; after all, he has to leave his house in the Cleveland suburb of Middleburg Heights for the Delphi plant every day by 5:45. The trip to Akron will provide a chance to reconnect.

The whole Ohio family—Randy Sr., his wife of twenty-four years, Denise, and their five children—are in the crowd on Monday night, June 20, when the Reading Phillies arrive. Randy presents a bat and some batting gloves to his stepbrother Jeffrey, then goes 2-for-3 with his sixteenth home run and three RBI to lead Reading to victory. Though he is hitless the next night, he comes back on June 22 to go 2-for-3 with a walk. Then on Thursday night in the series finale, Randy puts on another big display, going 3-for-5 with two doubles in a 9–1 win. Afterward he says good-bye to his family, standing just beside the dugout, offering fists and high fives and little hugs. His dad is beaming.

The team is told to shower quickly and get on the bus for the trip to Trenton, New Jersey. Toweling off and getting dressed, Randy can't help feeling good. He put on a show for his family. His average is up to .370. The team is playing its best ball of the year, having won five in a row. While tying his shoes, Randy feels a tap on his shoulder and hears a teammate say, "Skip wants to see you."

Getting called into the manager's office is a moment filled with anxiety for minor leaguers. Sometimes that call means the end of the road—a trade, a demotion, or worst of all, a release. But Randy knows that can't be the case. Players are also summoned into the office when the news is good. It seems that his time has come. Perhaps it is Triple-A. Maybe, just maybe, it is even better. Randy knows the Phillies have been looking for some extra right-handed power.

His heart hammering, he walks into Steve Swisher's office and is told to close the door. "Randy," Swisher says, looking him in the eye, "I don't know how to tell you this."

"What's up, Skip?" Randy says, smiling at Swisher.

"That last drug test, Randy," he says, his voice trailing off. "It came back positive."

● The long bus ride is an iconic piece of minor league life, part of the romance, part of the grind. Players toss their duffel bags with their personals down into the undercarriage next to buckets of baseballs and bags of bats, trade some of their precious twenty dollars a day of meal money for burgers or burritos at the local mall, then settle in for a journey from point A (typically one struggling industrial city) to some distant point B (typically another). The manager sits up front. The players sprawl behind. Some play solitaire. Some play poker. Most settle into their headphones before long, close their eyes, and doze.

During the 430-mile trip from Akron, Ohio, to Trenton, New Jersey, Randy Ruiz sits in the back, all alone, glaring at the highway. He is shocked at the turn of events. There he is, having the absolute season of his life, seemingly knocking at heaven's door, and now it has slammed shut— perhaps permanently. He is facing a thirty-game suspension and, worse, damage to his reputation that might prevent him from ever getting a chance at the big leagues. In the culture of baseball in 2005, two suspensions for steroid use are the equivalent of wearing a scarlet "S."

When Swisher walks to the back of the bus to try to calm Randy down, he finds him almost inconsolable. "Skip," Randy says, fighting back tears, "I didn't do anything wrong. I'm not an idiot. I was suspended once before. Why would I do that?"

Swisher tells Randy that he believes him, that he believes *in* him, that he will do what he can to help.

A few minutes later Randy takes out his cell phone and calls up his new agents, Jim and Lisa Masteralexis, pleading for help. The test can't be right, he says. It must be picking up something else: an over-the-counter drug, or perhaps some residue of steroids from the previous year that had lingered in his system. He insists—absolutely insists—that he has never gone back to "the stuff."

This is different from 2004, he says. Then he had been desperate, released by the Cardinals in spring training, stewing at home in the South Bronx, spinning his wheels in the batting cages at Frozen Ropes. He had finally hooked on with the Phillies' affiliate in the South Atlantic League, the BlueClaws, but he was despairing about a sixth straight year at Single-A. He knew he was running out of time. His wrist was still hurting from surgery the year before. So he had made a choice, the same choice many hundreds of others had made, lots of them with impunity. At season's end he had been busted, forced to endure that embarrassing meeting with Dickie Noles.

To his mind, he had paid a stiff price: fifteen games with no pay, the humiliation of being outed by the *Reading Eagle* for dressing up the suspension as a groin injury. He had been tested in spring training, and the tests had come back clean. He tells Jim and Lisa that he has absolutely no idea how this could be happening.

"Are you sure, Randy?" Jim asks him. "Are you absolutely sure?"

"I swear to God, Jim. Give me a Bible, put me in front of a church, and let lightning strike: I didn't do it."

● There is not much time to act. Researching the minor league drug policy, Lisa finds that they have just forty-eight hours to file an appeal after Randy was notified on Thursday, June 23. She and Jim spend all of Friday working on the issue. To have any basis for the appeal, they have to call the results of the positive test into question.

The first order of business is to show that Randy is now clean, and that the previous positive result might have stemmed from traces of the 2004 use lingering in his system.[4] They find that Quest Diagnostics, the company that supervises drug testing for Major League Baseball, has three affiliated labs within ten miles of Trenton, where the Reading Phillies are playing that weekend. Randy tells Lisa he will gladly go in the next morning to "pee—I mean urinate—in the cup."

Lisa chuckles. She tells Randy that part of the appeal consists of filling out what is called the "Therapeutic Use Exemption." This calls for Randy to provide a list of all drugs he had taken during the testing period that could have, at least conceivably, influenced previous test results.

Well, Randy says, there was some aspirin for headaches, and occasional over-the-counter cold medication. When he had needed an anti-inflammatory drug after the wrist surgery, he had been prescribed dexamethasone.

"Anything else?"

"Well, yeah."

"What is it?"

"Viagra."

Say what? Lisa dutifully writes it down.

A few minutes later she calls the number for the Health Policy Advisory Committee (HPAC), which is run out of the commissioner's office in New York, to say they will be appealing the decision. The response she gets is pure ice: "Don't bother—he's guilty."

The presumption stuns Lisa. She says that Randy is within his rights to file the appeal within forty-eight hours. Furthermore, he has every right to expect that his name will not be conveyed to the media in the press release announcing the latest round of minor leaguers who are being suspended for failing a drug test.

That press release, she is told, is being faxed out in twenty minutes.

Blood boiling, Lisa sends over the appeal.

On Saturday morning, June 25, Randy goes into a Quest Diagnostics lab and urinates in a cup. The results come back negative for any performance-enhancing drug.

That morning a new round of minor league players are publicly identified as failing tests and facing suspensions. The headline in the *Reading Eagle* reads, "Sources: R-Phils' Ruiz Gets 30 Games." Phillies assistant general manager Mike Arbuckle is quoted as saying, "You want a completely clean organization and we've gone to great lengths to educate guys. One positive [test] to me is more than I want. I get very upset. I have a very low level of patience for that kind of stuff."

Randy speed-dials Jim Masteralexis's cell phone, bristling. Isn't this under appeal? Why is he identified? Why is he presumed guilty? Why? Why? Why?

Jim assures Randy that the appeal has been filed and that he is free to play while it is being heard. He shares Randy's anger that this has been made public and agrees that it is completely unfair. When he senses Randy's anger finally beginning to ebb, he softens his own tone. "So, Randy," he says. "You're twenty-seven years old, man. What's the deal with the Viagra?"

"Jim," Randy says, managing a slight laugh, "this shit works."

That night in a 9–3 victory against the Yankees farm team, the Trenton Thunder, Randy Ruiz hits a pair of home runs.

● The next few weeks pass in a surreal haze, the best and worst summer of Randy's life, played out in Eastern League outposts (where he is often taunted by fans) and at home in Baseballtown.

On June 29 Mike Drago has the lead story in the sports section of the *Reading Eagle*. Beneath the headline "Ruiz: 'I Don't Need to Cheat to Be Successful,'" Drago begins, "His reputation and future in professional baseball might be hanging in the balance, but Reading Phillies first baseman Randy Ruiz doesn't seem fazed by the controversy swirling around him these days."

That night he goes 4-for-5.

On July 4, before a huge fireworks show at FirstEnergy Stadium, Randy smacks his twentieth home run of the year.

Two nights later the stadium is packed. It is one of those magical minor league nights when innocence feels restored. Charlie "Broadway" Wagner, a beloved ninety-two-year-old lifelong Reading resident, is honored before the game and given a World Series ring for his remarkable seventy years of service with the Boston Red Sox, including six seasons as a big league pitcher back in the thirties and forties.[5] Then Cole Hamels takes the mound for the first time at Double-A. Hamels is one of the anointed prospects, complete with all the accoutrements: a seven-figure signing bonus as a first-rounder back in 2002, the legacy of breaking his pitching hand in a bar fight, a girlfriend named Heidi Strobel who is nationally famous from the reality TV show *Survivor* (and will become more so after a subsequent *Playboy* magazine photo shoot). This is an evening of taut baseball on a summer night. During the seventh inning stretch, the crowd of 7,140 fans rises as one to sing "God Bless America." They rise again the next inning when Randy Ruiz blasts a game-tying three-run home run, lighting up the neon locomotive atop the right center field wall.

Though the Phils lose in ten innings, 5–3, Mike Drago waxes rhapsodic. "When Shoeless Joe Jackson walked out of that cornfield in the movie

'Field of Dreams,' he thought he had stepped into heaven," Drago writes to lead off his story for the next day's *Eagle*. "Some people might have had the same feeling walking into storied FirstEnergy Stadium Wednesday on a night as electric as has ever been felt in the old ballpark."

After the home game on Sunday afternoon, July 10—a 10–0 win over Trenton in which Randy smacks his twenty-second home run to tie for the Eastern League lead—most players pause for three days for the All-Star break. In the minor leagues, especially, this time is golden. It provides an oasis from the travel, the monotony, the constant looking over your shoulder.

For Randy, though, there is no chance for a quick trip to Ohio to see his dad, or a jaunt to the Bronx for one of Luz's home-cooked feasts. He is off instead to Portland, Maine, to represent the Reading Phillies in the Eastern League All-Star Game. Batting cleanup for the South team, he comes up in the top of the first inning against Brian Bannister, a touted prospect who will be starting big league games in New York within a year. After ripping an RBI single for the game's first run, Randy stands on first base and takes in the scene. He knows that there are players here on the fast track to big league stardom, guys like Jon Lester and Joel Zumaya and Hanley Ramirez.

None of them—not a single one—is having as good a year as he is.

9 "They Got Him!"

Pittsfield, Massachusetts

Outside Fenway Park at 5:30 on Sunday afternoon, June 5, business is booming. The highest ticket prices in the major leagues do little to dissuade the fans, who have filled the old ball yard for the 171st straight time, and now stream out wearing their souvenir T-shirts paying homage to Big Papi or Manny or Johnny Damon. They pour into the Cask'N Flagon, or hang out at Remdawg's, belting out "Sweet Caroline." Munching overpriced Cuban sandwiches from El Tiante, or sitting under green umbrellas and throwing back the beers, they toast the good times (another late win, 6–3, over the Angels) under a perfect blue sky, temperatures in the eighties, a breeze off the Charles, sparkling June light. Yeah, it is a business. It has always been a business. That's why the Sox sold Babe Ruth to the Yankees all those years ago. But it is a business predicated on passion, on what Sox owner John Henry calls "an affair of the heart."

Jim Masteralexis basks in the bustle. He sits with his buddy and fellow agent Steve McKelvey, sipping $6.50 cups of Bud Light and "marveling at the fabulous breasts of the young women of Boston." Marveling at least until Lisa arrives. It was seventeen Junes earlier when they had met at Fenway on a steamy night for their first date, his Sox defeating her Yankees, 7–3. Now they are converging on the old ballpark once again. This time they've come for the New England College All-Star Game, a contest between top college prospects in the six-state area, slated for this evening after the Red Sox–Angels game.

Jim and Lisa are now the parents of three kids, including two-year-old twins. They have been married for almost eleven years, but their agency, DiaMMond Management Group, dates back even further. In November 1992 they opened what was first called Sport Ventures International, attracting a couple of low-level minor leaguers, a few Canadian Football League players, and the top-ranked player on the International Racquetball Tour. By the time they added McKelvey, Lisa's UMass sport management colleague, in 1998, they represented only baseball players, none of whom had yet made it to the bigs.

Now, in June 2005, the business is still an uphill fight which DiaM-Mond Management tries to wage around the edges of Jim's full-time job as a lawyer and Lisa and Steve's as professors at UMass. Oftentimes they will be with a player for years and never see a penny. Their typical 4 percent commission doesn't apply to minor league contracts, and minor leaguers are basically who they represent. They beat the bushes for top high school prospects, bend over backwards to bond with families, send out lots of top-of-the-line baseball equipment, and set up image-boosting off-season baseball clinics in players' hometowns. They visit players at spring training and occasionally on the road, paying for steak dinners and dispensing all kinds of behind-the-scenes counseling and legal advice.

Once Jim tried—unsuccessfully—to persuade a woman who had slept with one of their clients in a Las Vegas hotel to return over $4,000 worth of clothing she had charged on the player's credit card. Another time, Jim and Lisa took turns on the phone attempting to talk one of their clients into leaving his Independent League team and signing a Double-A contract they had arranged with the Montreal Expos. With the signing deadline just hours away, the client, Jaime Malave, told Lisa, "I'll be honest with you—I haven't gotten a sign yet from God that I should do this." An exasperated Lisa scribbled a note to Jim: "We've lost this one. We're competing with God."

But on this sparkling night at Fenway, the deity may be back on their side. The Major League Baseball draft is just two days away, and DiaM-Mond Management is sitting on a possible goldmine. They have one of the starting pitchers in tonight's game, the top prospect in New England. In the most recent "Draft Tracker" published by *Baseball America*, Matt Torra of the University of Massachusetts was projected as the twentieth pick in the country, someone with "as much helium as any player in the draft."

● Torra, a strapping six-foot-three right-hander, hails from the regrettably named western Massachusetts city of Pittsfield. The small industrial burg is surrounded by the leisure and lavishness of the Berkshires. Within twenty minutes you can pour some chardonnay on the lawn at Tanglewood and listen to the Boston Pops, take in a performance at the famed Jacob's Pillow Dance Festival, or bask in Americana at the Norman Rockwell Museum in Stockbridge. In nearby Lenox the high school teams are unapologetically known as the Millionaires. Pittsfield is the grit beneath the glitz. The downtown features empty storefronts, tattoo parlors, a Family Dollar, and an abandoned convent.

Once Pittsfield had been a thriving General Electric hub. The bustling capacitor and transformer operations opened there in 1903 and quickly became the lifeblood of the city. By 1942 GE employed some 13,500 people in Pittsfield. In the 1960 census, 57,879 people called Pittsfield home, and just about everyone had close family connections to the 250-acre GE facility on the banks of the Housatonic River. With such prosperity, it was hard to argue with GE's rosy jingle, known throughout the land by the 1980s: "We bring good things to life."

But by the 2000 census the city's population had plummeted by more than 20 percent to 45,793. General Electric had stopped making large transformers and all but pulled out of the city, employing only seven hundred people in a separate plastics unit.

The company did not leave without offering some parting gifts, however. Those good things came in the form of polychlorinated biphenyls (or PCBs), a suspected carcinogen that had been used in the production of transformers for almost fifty years. The PCBs, which were used by a number of companies before the EPA banned them in 1977, began showing up in alarming concentrations in the Housatonic and in fill donated by GE to many sites, including the playground at Allendale Elementary School.

With the tax base crippled, Pittsfield plunged into an economic malaise. Recently the city's financial woes have extended even to baseball. Wahconah Park, which had given generations of fans an intimate connection to minor league baseball, was abandoned by one team after another. After the 2000 season the Pittsfield Mets ended a twelve-year run at the ballpark and moved to a brand new stadium in Coney Island. The Pittsfield Astros came in for one year in 2001, but then left for a new facility in Troy, New York. Wahconah's meager amenities—no luxury boxes, no indoor hitting facilities, a dirt parking lot—were no longer up to snuff. Even an institution as down-home wholesome as the minors was showing signs of gentrification. A widely publicized effort to upgrade Wahconah by former Yankee pitcher and *Ball Four* rebel Jim Bouton didn't do the trick. When an independent minor league team, the Berkshire Black Bears, left after the 2003 season, it seemed likely that one of America's quirkiest old-time parks had seen its last professional baseball.

That was a shame, because Wahconah was at the heart of the city's long historic connection with the national pastime. Records of pro ball at the site date back to 1892. The Pittsfield Electrics—a tribute to the city's burgeoning industry—played in the Eastern Association in 1913 and 1914. The ballpark itself dates to 1919, just seven years after Fenway Park was christened. In that era before night games, the ballpark designers thought nothing of orienting the park to the west, giving rise in years to come to "sun delays." Those charming pauses, along with the old-fashioned wooden grandstand (complete with dangling ceramic owls to prevent pigeons from nesting and pelting baseball patrons), provided fans at Wahconah with what *Money* magazine described as "the definitive old-time minor league experience."

The city's baseball heritage predated even the Wahconah swings of players such as Lou Gehrig and Jim Thorpe. The first recorded college baseball game took place in Pittsfield in 1859, a twenty-five-inning affair that saw Amherst College defeat Williams, 73–32. Even that game, seventeen years before the first major league contest, apparently was nothing terribly new for Pittsfield. Baseball historian John Thorn, author of many well-regarded books on the sport's early days, discovered in 2004 a document dating to 1791 that banned "base ball" from being played within eighty yards of the city's new meetinghouse. Thorn's find preceded by many years the first known written reference to the sport in America (the myth of Abner Doubleday inventing the game in Cooperstown, New York, in 1839 having been long ago debunked). Pittsfield mayor James Ruberto seized on the discovery. "Pittsfield," he proclaimed, "is baseball's Garden of Eden."

Matt Torra may not be the city's baseball Adam,[1] but as the 2005 draft looms, he stands on the brink of some significant earthly riches. First-round picks in the draft are now routinely scoring seven-figure signing bonuses. On several occasions leading up to the draft, Torra speaks of his desire to "make Pittsfield proud."

In the city Torra is well known as the kid who began banging nails and laying shingles for his dad's small construction company, Jim's Building and Remodeling, when he was just eleven. Jim Torra had wanted to instill a work ethic in his youngest son, and also to corral his considerable energy. Pretty much out of the womb Matt had been like a bull in the chute at the rodeo. Family friend Mickie Turner, Matt's first babysitter, remembers him as "absolutely wild."

The physical and mental battles with hitters would ultimately harness that energy better even than putting up a roof on a blazing July afternoon, though that effect was not immediately apparent. While Torra was a solid player from his first days on the Burger King–sponsored team in South Little League, he wasn't considered a prodigy. Coming out of Pittsfield High, he was not draft material, and he wasn't widely recruited, staying local at UMass on just a partial scholarship. But as a college player he blossomed, learning to command his low-nineties fastball on a downward plane, tightening a viciously dropping curveball, and developing a serviceable changeup. After his sophomore year in 2004, he earned an invitation to the prestigious Cape Cod League. There he held his own against some of the best college hitters in the country. As winter approached, he began getting all kinds of unsolicited mail.

"Happy Holidays from the Seattle Mariners."

"When filling out the enclosed questionnaire, be as honest as you can when you circle an answer. If you're not sure you're ready for pro ball, please say so. Don't write what you think a scout would like to read, but write how you feel" (from Buddy Paine, Pittsburgh Pirates).

"Happy Holidays to you and your family. . . . On behalf of the world champion Boston Red Sox organization, I would like to wish you the very best this coming season" (signed Ray Fagnant, Northeast Regional Scouting Director).

Entering his junior year, after which he would be draft eligible, Torra was projected as a possible fifth-round pick. He quickly laid waste to those predictions. UMass opened its season on February 25 at the University of New Orleans. Torra pitched seven innings of shutout ball, striking out ten. Back north, he dominated. He struck out sixteen batters in one game, fourteen in another. He pitched a complete game shutout over Temple, facing just one batter over the minimum. Scouts began showing up en masse. In unison they cocked their radar guns as Torra released the ball. They liked his focus on the mound, a body language that never betrayed concern. He had shaved seventeen pounds off his now 221-pound frame, and his endurance was startling. Scouts were wowed by his ability to maintain velocity deep into games—ten innings against Duquesne, eleven against Saint Joseph's. Torra was gaining a reputation as, in baseball parlance, a horse.

The scouts were not the only new spectators. While Torra warmed up before a start against Saint Bonaventure, a couple of teammates raced out to the bullpen and breathlessly exclaimed, "Theo's here!" Sure enough, Boston's Boy Wonder general manager, just months removed from the World Series deliverance, had made the trek across the state to see the top prospect in New England in person. Torra, a lifelong Yankees fan, responded with a two-hit shutout.

On May 20, 2005, with the wind blowing out, carrying the smell of sewage from the adjacent wastewater treatment facility, representatives from fifteen major league teams sat down to watch a terrible UMass team begin play on the final weekend of a 14–32 season. The scouts were all old guys—even the young ones. One cracked open peanut shells on the aluminum stands behind home plate, while another sipped a Schweppes, and a third smoked a cigar.

Jim Masteralexis had a special fondness for these grizzled baseball lifers. They were skilled readers of the game's innumerable nuances: how well the catcher blocked balls in the dirt, how short a batter kept his swing, what kind of late break a pitcher had on his slider. These were the things Jim loved to kick around with scouts, many of whom came to regard him more warmly than they did the typical slick agent. That connection proved advantageous on this Friday afternoon when one of the scouts called Jim on his cell phone. Snapping it open in Boston, where he was checking out another prospect, he heard the familiar voice of a National League scout,[2] saying, "Jim, you better get over here fast. There is a Scott Boras representative who is all over Mr. and Mrs. Torra."

Jack Toffey, an elegantly dressed man in a yellow sweater, perfectly pressed slacks, and penny loafers, actually no longer worked for Boras. But capitalizing on his recent experience with the über-agent, and also a stint working for the large Woolf and Associates agency, he had struck out on his own. Now he was trying to swoop in before the draft to snatch Torra out of the nest. In the agent world, as apparently in love and war, it's hard to hit a ball foul.

Two hours away, Jim felt a sense of panic. He speed-dialed Lisa and pleaded with her to intervene. Lisa raced over to UMass and found Torra's mother, Pat, utterly flustered. She mouthed the word "Help" to Lisa, who charged right into the conversation. Upon hearing the story, Jim Masteralexis described it as "a battle between a female Jedi Knight and Darth Vader."

Matt Torra struck out fourteen batters that day as UMass defeated La-Salle. He finished the season with a 6–3 record and a 1.14 ERA, best in the nation among Division I schools.

At dinner at Bertucci's in Amherst a couple of days later, the Torras described the encounter with Toffey to Steve McKelvey and the Masteralexises. "I felt that he was just there all of a sudden because of the money, because Matt was doing good," said Pat, a teaching assistant at Conte Elementary School in Pittsfield. "It totally turned me off." Pat said that Toffey had been very damning of DiaMMond Management, claiming they had no experience with athletes who were expected to be drafted as high as Matt, that they were unprepared to handle the negotiation or deal with his high-profile career as it went forward, with marketing opportunities, arbitration hearings, and so on.

Jim bristled. The big agents "won't spend the time with you when you're nobody. But when you become a prospect, they decide to get off their ass and pretend they care about you."

Matt laughed and assured Jim he wasn't going to ditch DiaMMond Management for one of the big boys.

Jim Torra, a slim man with a gray mustache and a slight limp from recent knee replacement surgery, went a step further: "We're just regular people. You guys are regular people, too. Believe me, we're not going anyplace. It could be the Angel of God coming down and saying he wants to represent Matt—he's not going."

The Torras had followed Matt's career very closely. They had never missed one of his starts in high school or college, whether that meant driving to Ohio or flying to New Orleans. Since Matt's young days in Pittsfield, Pat had been a fixture in her lawn chair, scorebook in her lap, dutifully recording every K.

For the Torras, the run-up to the draft was an absolute whirlwind. Even Mary Torra, Matt's eighty-two-year-old grandmother, was swept up in it. In the mornings she'd leave her home on the banks of the Housatonic—while her backyard was being dredged on a daily basis to scoop up more PCBs—and head to Saint Theresa's for daily services. There some of the gray-haired regulars would greet her with folded clippings from that morning's *Berkshire Eagle* update on Matt.

Jim Torra was constantly being asked by subcontracting plumbers and his buddies at Dettinger Lumber about his son. Where was he going to be picked? How large a bonus might he get? One morning Jim awakened at four, plucked the Sunday paper from an orange plastic bag in the driveway, and saw Matt smiling at him from page one. He immediately read the large feature story. "The tears were streaming down," he said. "I read it a second time, and then again." At five he went upstairs and found Pat still asleep. He left the paper on the foot of the bed.

Jim's and Pat's families had come over from Italy. They were, he said, "all workers"—shoemakers, custodians, carpenters. Prosperity had been a long climb in the manner of Horatio Alger: lots of long hours, daily discipline, and sacrifice. Jim said he would wait until the draft on June 7 before he really allowed himself to get excited about Matt's future: "That will be the day where I kind of let loose, [when I say] it really has happened. It's not a dream anymore. How many kids dream about it? Every kid that plays sports."

On May 22 Peter Gammons wrote on espn.com that Torra was one of the two players moving up most rapidly on the draft charts: "Teams want arm strength in college pitchers, and Torra throws 91–93 MPH, and has a good slider, changeup, and body to run up innings. Torra, who was considered a fifth-rounder in March, now may go as early as midway in the first round."

For Jim Masteralexis, this was a giddy time. He had never had a pick that high. (Brad Baker's selection as the fortieth pick in the 1999 draft was his best.) Even the twentieth pick in 2004—two-thirds of the way through the first round and selected by the small-market Minnesota Twins—had scored a bonus of $1.5 million. To land someone in the middle of the first round meant not only a fat commission but also greatly elevated status in his beloved testosterone soap opera.

Masteralexis called Matt several times a day. He set up a meeting for the family with a financial planner, vetted the million-dollar insurance policy they had taken out against injury from American Specialty Underwriters, and counseled Matt about what to say—and what not to say—to the media. While Matt had absolutely no intention of returning to UMass for his senior year, Masteralexis told him to keep that option open publicly as a bargaining chip.

Most of all, Masteralexis fielded a barrage of phone calls from scouts, scouting directors, and assistant general managers. He talked about his client's work ethic, family values, and sharp-breaking curve: "It's a fucking hammer." Both sides were feeling each other out for information. Masteralexis wanted a fix on where teams might draft Torra and what they might offer; they wanted to gauge Torra's "signability."

"He really likes UMass, and he'd like to finish his degree," Jim would say, "but the kid wants to play. We're just looking for a fair offer—slot value[3] and a little bit more."

Jim set up pre-draft tryouts for teams that wanted a second look. One day Torra drove down to Augusta, New Jersey, with his parents to throw for the St. Louis Cardinals' top brass at their easternmost minor league facility. Another night Matt flew to Pittsburgh with his father, getting box seats to watch a game against the Marlins and then throwing off the mound the next morning.

There was also a battery of what Matt called "psychologic exams." The Red Sox kept him on the phone for an hour and a half. "They wanted to know do I get angry? Am I sad? What type of emotions do I have when somebody close to me dies? What was my first memory with my father?"

By the time the New England College All-Star Game takes place at Fenway Park on June 5, Jim Masteralexis has put together a range of draft options. At best, he thinks, Matt will be picked eighth in the country, by the Tampa Bay Devil Rays. At worst, the Cardinals will grab him at number twenty-eight. In between there are several teams that have expressed interest: the Pirates with the eleventh pick, the Indians at fourteen, the Marlins at sixteen, the Yankees at seventeen, and the Red Sox, who have picks at both twenty-three and twenty-six. While it is a business, of course, Jim can't help but regard those last two picks with special interest. The Red Sox. His Red Sox.

Three decades ago, when he had exulted in Carlton Fisk's home run to end Game 6, Jim had yearned to make it to the big time at Fenway. And now, in a sense, he had. Striding purposefully into the old ballpark as Matt Torra's agent is not unlike being a trainer leading a prize thoroughbred into Churchill Downs. By association, he commanded respect.

Wearing a red Washington Nationals polo shirt (a badge of belonging in that his lone major league client, Tomo Ohka, toils for the Nats), Jim revels in the scene. He trades good-natured barbs with Buddy Paine, the long-time scout for the Pirates. He gives a warm embrace to Jim and Pat Torra and tells them to get ready for what "might be a multimillion-dollar negotiation." Excusing himself to take a cell phone call from a *Washington Post* reporter, he soon saunters over to Gordon Edes, the Sox beat writer for the *Boston Globe*, to gush about Torra, and to remind him that he also represents Sox minor league prospects Manny Delcarmen and Charlie Zink. Then Masteralexis spots a handsome young man in an untucked olive green shirt and dark slacks walking out to the bullpen to watch Torra warm up.

The stands are closed off beyond the dugouts for a game not expected to draw more than a few thousand fans, but Jim charges through the tiny right field seats, explaining to a gesturing usher that he is Matt Torra's agent. Winded and with sweat beading up on his forehead, he arrives at the visitors' bullpen in time to watch Torra throw his last pitch. Walking right up to the man in the olive shirt, he sticks out his hand and says, "Theo, I'm Jim Masteralexis."

From behind the plate twenty minutes later, Jim hears Torra's deliveries cracking into the catcher's glove, as his prize horse gallops through two shutout innings. He watches as a few rows ahead of him a parade of young women ("babe college women with half-shirts on") approach Epstein for an autograph. He looks out over the big ball field and sees acres of beautiful green.

● There is more beautiful green on Tuesday, but, driving into the verdant Berkshires, Jim Masteralexis is oblivious to it. He grips the wheel of his blue Lexus wagon—yes, Masteralexis in a Lexus—heading west on the Mass Pike, thundering along at eighty-three. He is on his way to Lanesborough, to the Torras' small cottage on the shores of Pontoosuc Lake, just across the way from their home in Pittsfield. It is a trip of about an hour and a half, and en route he stares at the road from behind Rudy Project sunglasses and takes a series of calls from scouts and scouting directors. They proffer illegal, but common, pre-draft deals. If Torra is selected with pick number x, would he sign for a bonus of y? Talent alone will not dictate the day.

"I think we can do business. The kid wants to play."

"Theo told me there are scenarios where the Sox would pop him at twenty-three, and scenarios where they would pop him at twenty-six."

"I'd be surprised if he gets past the Cardinals, but you never know. If he does, we'd love to talk to you."

At one point Jim talks with animation to one of his favorite scouts, John Koziak, who works the Northeast for the Los Angeles Dodgers. The Dodgers are not expected to be a player for Torra—they don't have a pick until number forty—so Jim speaks freely. He tells Koziak about an earlier conversation with Cardinals scout Tommy Shields, a former student of Lisa's at UMass, who had called that morning to say that he had been authorized by his bosses to offer bonuses of $1 million for the twenty-eighth pick and $850,000 for the thirtieth pick. Jim was outraged. Given that Torra "schlepped down to New Jersey," the Cardinals in his view were singularly ungrateful. Their front office, he says, consists of "people in power trying to take advantage of a working-class family. . . . They gave us $200,000 below the fucking slot last year. . . . The kid wants to play. . . . Those people who haven't seen him pitch don't know the fucking monster that he is. He's a fucking monster—don't you think?"

Lisa Masteralexis sits in the passenger seat, occasionally smiling at the Type A tension to her left. She knows what she's got. She drapes her long, slender fingers with their trademark blood-red nail polish over the back of the seat. One of her key roles in the agency is to bond with a player's parents, telling them that as a mother she totally understands their concern for their child's well-being. It's not all nurturing nice-nice, though. As the daughter of a union carpenter, she has been a tough fighter in negotiations, sometimes surprising even Jim with her even-tempered fierceness. "I get a kick out of the reaction on the other side of the table," she says. "They don't know quite what to do with me. They try to clean up their language. It kind of throws them off."

The agency had been her idea. She had come to UMass as a dance major in the early 1980s, then found her way into sport management. She became enamored with the idea of representing professional athletes, even though her well-regarded professor Bernie Mullin scoffed at the ambition, telling her male jocks would never stand for it. When she and Jim fell in love in law school, she tried to persuade him to take courses in sports and entertainment law. He responded over and over, "I have no interest in this." Deep down, she knew that wasn't true.

"His not making it in baseball was still raw, and he couldn't deal with that," Lisa came to realize. "In the same way that I had started as a dance major and I dropped it, I still couldn't go see a ballet performance . . . because you have these hopes and dreams, and then they don't work out."

By the end of 1992, Lisa's powers of persuasion had won out, and the fledgling agency was launched. Their first client was a young man named Billy Hartnett, a pitcher who had been offered a signing bonus of $5,000 as a twelfth-round pick in the 1993 draft. The family didn't know what to do. Billy's dad was terminally ill with cancer. Money was tight. Jim and Lisa met with the family at Bickford's in Braintree and told them they would do everything they could. They wound up convincing the Astros to increase their offer to $15,000, and the Hartnetts were thrilled. Jim and Lisa spent much of their summer driving up to Auburn, New York, to watch Billy's starts in the New York Penn League. Though Billy never got anywhere close to the majors, Jim and Lisa were hooked.

● In a real sense, their relationship, their marriage, their whole family story has revolved around the game from their first date at Fenway forward. This morning had seen the usual craziness. The twins had been up several times during the night. Justin had been screaming with an ear infection, then Taylor started yelling when she saw her brother getting the attention. Jim and Lisa tag-teamed a few hours of sleep apiece. She awakened at seven, panicked that she had overslept, then took Justin to the 8:30 walk-in appointment at the pediatrician's up in Amherst, a half-hour from their home in West Brookfield. The nanny arrived. Jim got Nathan a bowl of Cap'n Crunch, walked him out to the bus stop for kindergarten, checked out Matt Torra's current draft projections on the Internet. One site had him going twenty-third, the first pick by the Red Sox. *Baseball America*, which had pegged him twenty-first just the day before, now had Torra slotted at number thirty-two with the Colorado Rockies. Printing out that list, Jim gulped, knowing it meant a difference of hundreds of thousands of dollars in signing bonus money—4 percent of which would have been a commission for DiaMMond Management. His cell phone was buzzing like a beehive all morning. Was Torra hurt? Was he going to be a "hard sign?" Did he really want to play?

Lisa returned, sensing Jim's blood pressure beginning to soar. They showered, dressed, gulped some coffee while reviewing strategy. They then sped over to UMass to meet up with McKelvey, who was preparing a fact sheet on Torra for the press conference they planned to hold later in the afternoon at Pittsfield High School. McKelvey would spend the draft day down in Chicopee with Scott Barnes, the top high school prospect in the area.[4] They were running late, but right outside the Isenberg School of Management, McKelvey gave both Jim and Lisa a hug. It was a big day.

● Truth is, the odds are stacked against DiaMMond Management. The business of baseball, like most American businesses, gives huge advantages to the big boys—in this case agencies like the one run by Scott Boras. A former minor leaguer in the St. Louis Cardinals organization (where he was a teammate of UMass baseball coach Mike Stone), Boras has transformed the economic landscape of the game over the past few decades. Deified by some, vilified by others, he has leveraged some astonishing contracts, most notably the ten-year, $252 million deal for Alex Rodriguez with the Texas Rangers. Boras and some of the other large agencies could offer services that were just impossible to match: a state-of-the art training facility, a battery of sports psychologists, nutritionists, tickets to elite concerts and sporting events. The big agents have tentacles that reach all throughout the game. If a player's stock is rising in the minors, he often will be courted by fat-cat agents. There will be a red light blinking on the hotel phone, an invitation to dinner, and offers that are hard to refuse. The business, predicated on trust, can be an absolute snake pit.

Lisa has a close friend, an accomplished lawyer, who had tried to make it as an agent for a year or two before leaving it all behind, telling her, "There's no way I can handle this. It makes your stomach turn." At a presentation on being an agent at Western New England College the following November, Lisa will tell the eager crowd of students, "It is not a nice business to be in. People are not fair."

Still, she loves it. So do Jim and Steve. There is something audacious about the challenge of trying to make a go of it around their full-time jobs and busy family life. They have a model that they think can work. They strive for a modest-sized agency with lots of personal attention, getting to know a small group of players and their families much better, they believe, than the big agencies ever will. They will focus on the New England area, concentrating especially on western Massachusetts. Granted, this is not exactly baseball's Fertile Crescent, but it has landed them clients like Peter Bergeron, who played for the Expos for a couple of years; and Doug Clark and Brad Baker, both prospects now at Triple-A. Through word of mouth, they figure they can pick up some other quality players. To a degree it is working. Through Manny Delcarmen of Boston they had picked up knuckleballer Charlie Zink. Through Ryan Cameron of Williamstown, they had connected with Randy Ruiz, who is having a monster season in Double-A.

Their skill sets are complementary. Jim is the front person, the charmer, with the pedigree of being both a former college catcher and a lawyer specializing in labor and employment. As head of the sport management program at UMass, Lisa connects with lots of on-the-rise baseball executives. Steve McKelvey adds a creative spark and a bevy of marketing ideas. It is an uphill battle, of course, but they think it can work. Baseball, after all, has become a multibillion dollar industry.

Getting those billions to trickle down, though, is an ongoing struggle. Even when a player breaks through to the big leagues, it doesn't necessarily mean money for the agents. Bergeron was a classic example.

He had been drafted in 1996, got called up to the Expos in September 1999, and served as the team's starting center fielder for most of the 2000 and 2001 seasons. That had meant a significant infusion of money for a working-class kid from Greenfield, Massachusetts: a salary of $201,500 in 2000 and $242,500 in 2001. Of course this was great news for the agents, giving them recruiting clout with other clients, legitimacy at baseball's winter meetings, a certain swagger—but not much in the way of cash. The Collective Bargaining Agreement of Major League Baseball stipulates that an agent cannot claim a commission until the player has cleared the big league minimum, and almost no player makes much more than that until he has three years of service. That's when the life-changing money really kicks in, when players become "salary arbitration eligible" and begin to see contracts in the millions. Bergeron never got there. He didn't hit enough, even by the lowly standards of the Expos: .245 with five home runs in 2000, .211 with three in 2001. Thereafter he struggled in baseball quicksand: thirty-one games in the bigs in 2002, none in 2003, eleven in 2004, then back again to the minors, struggling to find his way.

Jim had been with him since the beginning. Bergeron's surprise call in 1996 ("Mr. Masteralexis, my name is Peter Bergeron, and I was just picked in the fourth round of the draft by the Dodgers. I was wondering if you might be able to help me with the negotiations") had been the first real foothold for DiaMMond Management. Jim had agreed to hop on board and take nothing out of the $240,000 bonus, seeing this as a golden opportunity to build the business. He logged on each morning to monitor Bergeron's progress in Yakima, Washington, and Savannah, Georgia. He traveled to see him play in Harrisburg, Pennsylvania, and in the Arizona Fall League, and to his big league debut at Montreal's Olympic Stadium. McKelvey dutifully ran Bergeron's off-season clinic each winter in Greenfield, arranging for the equipment, the staff, the advertising, the door prizes. All three principals of DiaMMond Management made the trek to Bergeron's wedding in Indiana, Pennsylvania, in November 2003.

But by the end of the 2004 season, with Bergeron's baseball stock tumbling, Jim found it increasingly difficult to find his client a job. That December, Jim was standing amid the teeming masses at Penn Station when he heard the call for the 6:40 p.m. Amtrak to Springfield, Massachusetts, where his car was waiting—just as Theo Epstein's number came up on his cell phone. Jim had been trying to reach Epstein for weeks, hoping to convince him that Bergeron would be a good replacement for soon-to-depart reserve center fielder Dave Roberts: good speed and defense, a spray hitter, a solid team guy. So Jim took the call and missed the train. It was the last one of the day to Springfield, and Lisa, back home with the three young kids, could only shake her head.

The Sox were not sufficiently interested in Bergeron, and Jim ultimately negotiated a minor league deal with the Cubs. Bergeron headed out to Scottsdale, Arizona, in February 2005 with his wife, Jen, pregnant with their first child. On the last day of spring training, he was released. He slung a duffel bag over his shoulder, went out to the parking lot, and called Jim, while Jen sat crying in the passenger seat.[5]

● The real jackpot for agents, representing a decent arbitration-eligible player, had been hit exactly once in the thirteen years of DiaMMond Management. That was Tomo Okha, a mustachioed control pitcher from Kyoto with an array of sinking and cutting pitches, none of them thrown exceptionally hard. Jim referred to him as "the Japanese Greg Maddux."

The connection with Ohka came through a sports law student of Lisa's who also hailed from Japan. The timing was great. In November 1998 the Red Sox purchased Okha's contract from the Yokohama Bay Stars of the Japanese Central League. The next year he cut an astonishing swath through the Sox' minor league circuit, going 8–0 at Double-A Portland, and 7–0 at Triple-A Pawtucket. On July 19 he got the call from the Red Sox, making the often torturous climb through the minors look like a walk in the park. He became DiaMMond Management's first major leaguer (beating Bergeron by seven weeks).

But getting big league hitters out proved to be another story. Back and forth between the big leagues and the minors during the next two and a half seasons, Ohka posted an unimpressive 6–13 record with an ERA of 4.61. In the summer of 2001 he was living alone in a small apartment in

Braintree, Massachusetts, essentially equidistant from Boston and Paw-tucket. He was playing with the Triple-A PawSox in late July when the team traveled to Kentucky to take on the Louisville Bats. There, on Mon-day, July 30, one day before the trading deadline, he learned he was being dealt to the Expos, who wanted to promote him to the big leagues. That deal ushered in the kind of logistical chaos that fans never get to witness.

The Expos had played at home on Sunday, and were off on Monday, fly-ing west to Arizona to begin a series with the Diamondbacks on Tuesday night. Given the off day, Ohka flew back to Boston, where he was met at the airport by Masteralexis. Since Ohka spoke only a tiny bit of English, the two men drove mostly in silence to Braintree to pack up some things from Ohka's apartment. Jim made the calls to shut off the utilities. Ohka then flew west to join the team.

He was scheduled to make his first National League start on Saturday night at Houston. Early on Saturday, Jim and Lisa made a two-hour drive from their home in the sleepy central Massachusetts town of West Brook-field, first dropping off two-year-old Nathan with Jim's parents, then driv-ing down to Braintree to spend hours packing up the rest of Ohka's apart-ment. They then drove Ohka's car five hours north to Canada, explaining at the border that they were relocating a Japanese-speaking pitcher—now in Houston, Texas—to French-speaking Montreal. They dropped off his stuff at Olympic Stadium and finally found a hotel room, a struggle be-cause of a huge French rock and roll festival taking place in the city. That night they watched Ohka pitch against Roy Oswalt of the Astros on tele-vision. He matched the young ace pitch for pitch through six scoreless in-nings before surrendering three runs in the seventh and taking the hard-luck loss. At the end of a long day, Jim and Lisa sank into bed, but the rock festival blared outside their window deep into the night, and Lisa wound up grabbing about an hour of sleep on the bathroom floor, pillows pressed against her ears.

Such was the life.

But in 2002 Ohka broke through with a 13–8 record and a 3.18 ERA. In the winter he was asked to play on a major league tour of Japan, and was allowed to bring one guest. Jim was wide-eyed the entire trip, asking Jason Giambi to sign a ball for Nathan, riding a tour bus with Bernie Williams to a Japanese castle, gawking at two sumo wrestlers who went into the locker room at the Tokyo Dome to meet the comparatively svelte Barry Bonds.

In 2003 Ohka's numbers fell to a mediocre 10–12, 4.16 ERA, but he now had the requisite three full years (516 days) of big league service, arriving at the golden gate of salary arbitration eligibility. One season after making

$340,000, Tomo Ohka signed a 2004 contract for the magical total of $2,337,500.

But in the testosterone soap opera, you never know what drama is lurking around the corner. In June 2004, Ohka was hit just above the right wrist by a screaming line drive off the bat of Carlos Beltran, then of the Kansas City Royals. He reached down to pick up the ball, and couldn't throw it to first. The "Major League Baseball" imprint was branded on his arm, right next to the radius bone, which was shattered. He was flown to Melbourne, Florida, for surgery. Jim met him there, and the two of them spent four days together.

Ohka worked hard on his rehab and surprised many by returning to pitch, albeit ineffectively, in September. Now in 2005, the team having fled Montreal to become the Washington Nationals, he was trying to fight his way back to form. Masteralexis felt that some of his client's problems stemmed from the language barrier, and he tried unsuccessfully to convince general manager Jim Bowden that the team should hire a full-time translator, just as the Yankees had for Hideki Matsui and the Mariners had for Ichiro Suzuki. Hit hard early in the year, Ohka was banished to the bullpen by old-guard manager Frank Robinson. In May, though, Ohka seemed to right the ship.

He took the mound against the Braves on Memorial Day. The game was nationally televised on Fox, which turned it into a grand patriotic occasion. There were numerous homages to soldiers fighting the brutal war in Iraq. There were many allusions to the last Memorial Day game played in Washington in 1971, in the midst of the Vietnam War. And there was abundant reference to World War II, even a look back at FDR's "Green Light Letter" to baseball commissioner Kenesaw Mountain Landis, expressing his view that the national pastime should continue its games throughout the fighting. The sixtieth anniversary of the end of the war was just a few months away: the horrific detonations in Hiroshima and Nagasaki; a sailor and a nurse kissing for eternity in Times Square.

And here on the mound for the Washington Nationals was Tomo Ohka, a soft-spoken young man from Kyoto. He was absolutely brilliant. After the seventh inning he walked off the mound, his work complete, and yielded to a rousing rendition of "God Bless America" from Master Sergeant Regina Coonrod of the U.S. Air Force Band. Ohka's line: 7 innings, 1 unearned run, 2 hits.

Back in Massachusetts, Jim Masteralexis was soaking it up in front of a wide-screen TV. Washington, D.C., was a big market, a new market, an international market. If Tomo could thrive there, the agency could flourish. At last, perhaps, Jim could leave the soulless world of labor and employment law behind him forever and turn to baseball full-time. He could almost taste it.

In his next start, on Saturday, June 4 (just one day before Matt Torra's appearance at Fenway), Ohka struggled to find his rhythm at home against the Marlins. He was nibbling, missing his spots, pitching slowly and poorly as the Marlins scored single runs in each of the first three innings. Robinson was stewing on the bench. In the fourth with one out, Ohka surrendered a single to Luis Castillo, then walked Carlos Delgado, and Robinson had seen enough. Just three months shy of his seventieth birthday, Robinson still walked purposefully, storming out to the mound, where Ohka was speaking haltingly with journeyman catcher Gary Bennett, his back to the home dugout. Robinson, taking it as a sign of disrespect, thundered, "Give me the fucking ball!"

Before his next start, Ohka was traded to the Milwaukee Brewers.

● It is exactly 12:59 when Jim and Lisa pull up at the Torras' cottage in Lanesborough. They are greeted by a smiling young man who is wearing his UMass baseball jersey with the number 31 on the back, shorts, and untied Nike sneakers. The draft is set to begin in one minute.

Held the first Tuesday in June, the first-year player draft is a day dripping with promise. Thousands of young men, many of whom have known the glory of being the best player in their town, or high school, or college, wait to hear from major league teams. Through fifty rounds, over two days, some 1,500 players get the treasured call, while many more face the stinging rejection of being told, essentially, that they are not good enough at the thing they most love. Those players who do sign all receive the standard first-year player contract of $850 a month, housing not included. But at the top of the draft there are some sizable signing bonuses; at the very top, it's life-changing money.[6]

In 2005, unlike the drafts for the NFL and the NBA, the first-year player draft for Major League Baseball is not yet a major media event.[7] In part this is true because amateur baseball, even at the college level, lacks the impassioned national following enjoyed by NCAA football and basketball, which are essentially the minor league systems for those sports. Drafted players often go right onto NFL and NBA rosters, sometimes right into a starting lineup. In baseball that almost never happens. Even top picks typically toil in the minors for a year or two or three. In truth, there is no guarantee that even the elite picks will eventually make it. *Baseball America's* 2001 study of the draft from its inception in 1965 through 1995 showed not only that more than 35 percent of first-round picks failed to make it to the big leagues, but also that by the fifth round some 88 percent would never get to The Show.

Since that first draft in 1965 (instituted to prevent bidding wars and distribute amateur talent more equitably), the event had been held by conference call. For years, teams would not even announce their picks beyond the first round for a couple of weeks. But since 1998, when selections were first posted in real time on mlb.com, the draft had gained traction with fans. Throughout the country lots of people are logged on to computers as of one o'clock.

At Pittsfield High School, vice principal JoAnn Soules and her secretary both follow the action on screens in the main office. Next door to the Torra cottage, Gabe Levy, a thirteen-year-old Floridian with braces who is visiting his grandparents, follows the draft on a desktop computer using a broadband connection. And on the Torras' dining room table, the modem connected by dial-up, sits a small Compaq laptop, the focus of all attention.

Matt Torra sits on one side of the table, his arms folded behind the short-cropped black hair on the back of his head. On the opposite side, Jim Masteralexis digs in, uncapping a blue Sharpie and placing the morning's *Baseball America* projections on the table. He neatly checks off the opening selections, announced in staccato fashion from the computer: Justin Upton by the Diamondbacks; Alex Gordon by the Royals. In Chesapeake, Virginia, and Lincoln, Nebraska, a couple of families go wild.

Elsewhere in the tiny cottage that Jim Torra built, a couple of articles about Matt's baseball prowess are displayed beneath a magnet on the refrigerator. Matt's two betta fish, Tito and Willie, swirl over colorful pebbles in separate tanks (so they don't kill each other), while his beloved golden retriever, Hoops, sits outside on the grass, watching the scalloped waves on Pontoosuc Lake with Matt's older brother, JT, who flew in from Kentucky the night before to surprise him. On the couch, Pat Torra and Lisa Masteralexis are thumbing through Matt's baseball scrapbook. Nearby a television set pumps in ESPN's Tuesday afternoon fare, a film of the 1999 Home Run Derby, flashbulbs igniting Fenway Park as Mark McGwire takes his hacks. (Afterward, a TV voice says, "Superman's with Stuart Scott.")

At number eight, Jim Masteralexis's best-case pick, Tampa Bay opts for the first right-handed pitcher in the draft, Wade Townsend from Dripping Springs, Texas. With the next pick the Mets take another right-handed hurler, Mike Pelfrey, someone they will ultimately reward with a bonus of $3.55 million. Jim dutifully checks off both players on the list. Jim Torra sits down in the chair next to Matt, and over the next several minutes runs his finger through his gray mustache over and over again.

At number eleven the Pirates go for Andrew McCutchen, an outfielder from Fort Meade, Florida. Loudly, almost violently, Jim Masteralexis puts a check on the page that *Baseball America* had projected with the words, "This time, Pirates scouts want the athletic McCutchen and apparently will be allowed to take him, though upper management would prefer a college player such as Texas A&M shortstop Cliff Pennington or Massachusetts righthander Matt Torra."

Matt remains silent as the picks unfold, though his cheeks slowly begin to redden when the Yankees bypass him at number seventeen in favor of a shortstop from Putnam City High School in Oklahoma.

The first-round selections are spaced about two minutes apart, the bonus money silently dropping by $50,000 here, $100,000 there. Through the halting reception of the computer's audio, phrases break through: "solid pitching class . . . Second Baptist School . . . from Springville, Utah . . . such a great package."

By the time the Red Sox take Jacoby Ellsbury with their first pick at twenty-three, little beads of sweat have bubbled up beneath Matt Torra's brown eyes. His mother sits on the couch, tugging on her necklace. Jim Torra twirls a coaster with a picture of a rooster and the words "This is the day the Lord has made." Older brother JT stands outside with Hoops, looking at a small boat bobbing on the lake on a sun-splashed day with temperatures in the low nineties.

Just before the Sox announce their next first-round pick at twenty-six, Jim Masteralexis proclaims, "Here we go."

Indeed, the Sox grab a right-handed college pitcher, but it is Craig Hansen from St. John's. Projected by many as a top ten pick, Hansen has dipped because he is represented by Scott Boras, and teams fear a hard negotiation. From the couch, Lisa Masteralexis says simply, "They'll go to war."

The Cardinals pick Colby Rasmus at number twenty-eight, then close out the first round with Tyler Greene at thirty. Lisa mutters, "Oh, Jesus."

Matt stares down at the table and says, "It's okay."

During the fifteen-minute break before the start of the supplementary round picks,[8] Jim Masteralexis swings into action. He confers briefly with Matt, checks a file of last year's bonuses for supplementary picks, and heads out to the deck, snapping open his cell phone. He first speaks to Tommy Shields, the Cardinals scout and former student of Lisa's. The Cards will pick again at forty-three.

"How confidential is this? . . . Would your scouting director accept, or be willing to negotiate between those two parameters, 725 and 800,000? . . . I know you work for the guy, and I know this isn't coming from you, but Matt Torra has been straight up with everybody. If he wants Matt Torra, he's got to show me some good faith and come up."

Moments later Jim persuades Shields to turn over the phone to the Cardinals scouting director, Jeff Luhnow, and turns on him with the full force of his fury: "I want you to justify why you're paying seventy-five less than last year after my client schlepped down to New Jersey! You tell me why right now! We want $800,000, which is what last year's slot was. You were in the World Series. Deep in the playoffs, and you need pitching. Is this the way you do business? . . . Do you want the kid to come in with a good attitude, feeling good about the organization? . . . Eight hundred–plus!"

Jim cracks the cell phone closed. The ensuing calls begin to take on a tone of desperation. "What would you guys give us at fifty?" Click. "He's not hurt! He pitched in the All-Star Game and did fine. He hit ninety-four four times!" Click. "For $600,000 at the sixty-third slot? I'd say very likely. . . . Thank you." Click. "Fuck them."

Pat Torra comes out on the deck and announces that the draft is about to resume. Jim begins to trudge back in. He knows that a huge amount of money has fallen off the table. And while Matt Torra might well have a fortune in his future, Jim knows that it is also possible that his signing bonus will be the only big payday of his baseball career. For evidence Jim doesn't need to look any further than his highest-ever pick, Brad Baker, who scored $832,500 as the fortieth pick in 1999, but now, six years later, is still making under $3,000 a month at Triple-A.

He is absolutely mystified about Torra's fall. What had happened to all of that goddamn helium?

But before Jim even sits down, before there is any news from the Compaq computer, he hears cars honking from next door and wild shouts of "They got him!"

The Levy family is the first on the lake to learn that Matt Torra has been selected with the thirty-first pick by the Arizona Diamondbacks. There could be no more effective advertisement for high-speed Internet.

When Jim Masteralexis realizes what has happened, the stress vanishes from his face. He grabs Matt Torra in a tight embrace—catcher greeting pitcher on the mound after a no-hitter—and shouts, "That's a million-dollar pick!"

Pat Torra rubs her hands together, saying over and over again, "Unbelievable. Oh my God. Unbelievable." Tears well up in Jim Torra's eyes. JT comes to give his brother a concussive high five.

An hour later Matt is sitting in the front of the Lexus with Jim driving and Lisa sitting in the backseat. The agents, who had first persuaded Matt to change into tan slacks and a white shirt with a collar, are now prepping him for the press conference scheduled to begin in twenty minutes at Pittsfield High School.

No, Matt is told, he shouldn't express any disappointment about being bypassed by the Yankees and the Red Sox. This is a great opportunity. Still, he shouldn't publicly rule out returning to UMass for his senior year, either. Any questions about money should be referred to Jim.

Lisa thumbs through a *Baseball America* directory and tells Matt that in all likelihood his professional career will begin with the Diamondbacks' short-season Single-A team in Yakima, Washington.

"Shall we say," Jim asks with a mischievous smile, "that you're single, without a girlfriend?"

"Yes," Torra answers. "Blond hair. Blue eyes."

"Once they see your signing bonus," Lisa pipes in, "they'll be coming out of the woodwork."

Driving into downtown Pittsfield, Jim asks Matt about a sign advertising the "Sheeptacular Celebration." Informed that it is a tourist attraction featuring lots of "sheep art," Jim replies, "A lot of people, mostly Greek people, are touring the country looking for sheep."

"James," Lisa scolds, "watch yourself." She then adds with a laugh, "That's what I live with, day in and day out."

Pittsfield High School is a brick building with a gray façade. In the front hallway a plaque from 1930–31 proclaims, "Erected by the City of Pittsfield that her youth may here acquire the knowledge which makes for a larger life."

Vice principal JoAnn Soules, whose mother, fresh off the boat from Italy, had once lived in downtown Pittsfield with Matt's grandmother, Mary Torra, reaches up to give Matt a hug. In brushing ever so briefly against his right shoulder, the same shoulder that had been firing ninety-three-mile-per-hour fastballs all spring, she leaves a little smudge of lipstick.

On the exact day of the death of Anne Bancroft, the famed Mrs. Robinson from *The Graduate*, Matt Torra spends the next few minutes trying to wipe an older woman's lipstick off his shirt.

After a while the Torras walk out to the front steps of the school. It is late in the afternoon on a beautiful June day. The old beech trees in front of the building are in full leaf, casting shade on the TV trucks with their satellite dishes. The crowd of almost one hundred people includes high school friends and former coaches, Matt's grandmother Mary, and his first babysitter, Mickie Turner. There are Little Leaguers and old-timers here to bask in the day as Jim Masteralexis walks up to the microphone:

> Welcome, everybody. Hello. My name is James Masteralexis. I'm an attorney, but please don't hold that against me. I'm Matthew's family adviser for this journey into professional baseball. We're just very proud to be associated with the Torra family—a "*hahd*-working" family from Pittsfield . . . Today in baseball was the first day of the amateur draft. There are two days to the draft, and there are fifty rounds in the draft. There are thirty teams, and each team has selections up to the fiftieth round. That's 1,500 players, and today Matthew was the thirty-first player drafted in the entire nation, . . . In the next two or three weeks, it's going to be my responsibility, along with Matthew and his family, to negotiate in good faith with the Arizona Diamondbacks. Matt's a junior, so he always has the option of going back to school, but playing professional baseball is one of the great honors here in our society. And I know that Matthew values it, as do we.

Afterward, to thunderous applause, Matt steps to the microphone. He is three weeks shy of his twenty-first birthday, the wide world already spreading out before him. He thanks his parents, who have never missed a game, his brother, and the city of Pittsfield: "You guys have been great for me."

Soaking it up, he takes questions from the local media, then mingles with the crowd. A pretty blond woman tells a friend, "I have the funniest picture of me and him from preschool."

Jim and Lisa stand off to the side, letting it all sink in. Lisa looks at her watch. It is time to get back to the kids. As they walk toward the Lexus, Matt comes up to them one more time and says triumphantly, "We did it!"

Jim claps him on the shoulder. "You did it, man. We were just along for the ride."

During his junior year at the University of Massachusetts, Matt Torra records the lowest
ERA of any Division I pitcher in the country, 1.14. *Courtesy of UMass Media Relations*

The stress of draft day is etched on the faces of Matt and his father, Jim Torra, as agent Jim Masteralexis goes over his notes. Berkshire Eagle, *courtesy of Jim Torra*

With Masteralexis looking on, Matt celebrates with his family immediately after getting selected with the thirty-first pick of the 2005 draft by the Arizona Diamondbacks. Berkshire Eagle, *courtesy of Jim Torra*

It's a deal: Matt signs with Arizona Diamondbacks' scout Matt Merullo. His signing bonus is $1,025,000. *Courtesy of Steve McKelvey*

In 2008, Matt reaches the top of the minor league ladder with the Triple-A Tucson Sidewinders. *Courtesy of the Tucson Sidewinders*

The DiaMMond Management team: Steve McKelvey, Lisa Masteralexis, and Jim Masteralexis. *Shaowei Wang*

10 Waiting (on Deck) for Godot

Portland, Oregon; Selah, Washington

On the first full day of summer, Wednesday, June 22, 2005, there is still a cascade of sparkling sunlight as the 7:05 game time approaches at PGE Park in Portland, Oregon. The Beavers, the Triple-A affiliate of the San Diego Padres, are hosting the Fresno Grizzlies, top farm team of the San Francisco Giants. While the Grizzlies stretch in right field, taking sidestep leads on the foul line, crossing over, then running three-quarter sprints into the emerald outfield, the PA system pumps in an anthem from the Summer of Love: "If You're Going to San Francisco (Be Sure to Wear Some Flowers in Your Hair)."

Lineup cards are exchanged. The Beavers run out to their positions to the words of John Fogerty: "Put Me in, Coach." Hats cover hearts. *The perilous fight . . . gallantly streaming . . . the home of the brave.* "And now from PGE Park," says PA announcer Mike Stone, "let's play ball! Leading off for the Fresno Grizzlies, the left fielder, Doug Clark."

Toting a walnut-colored Louisville Slugger, Clark steps in from the left side, assuming his closed stance, digging his back foot into the chalk line at the rear of the batter's box. He wears his age on his back—29—and his left pant leg is frayed to threadbare above the hamstring.

Across the country in a 1958 ranch house on Piedmont Street in Springfield, Massachusetts, night has fallen. Bill Clark has set up the computer for the webcast, and he listens to the now familiar voice of Doug Greenwald describing the leadoff hitter working a walk on a 3–2 fastball. On the next pitch, Doug steals second. With two outs, he steals third. There he is stranded.

It is another night of baseball in yet another year filled with nights of baseball. Doug is still grinding away at the goal. These are team games composed of individual moments. Every pitch offers the possibility of something new. Tonight is no exception. In the home sixth inning, with two outs and the bases loaded, Pat Misch uncorks a wild pitch, and the runners, led by Adam Hyzdu on third, dig hard for the next base. Catcher Justin Knoedler retreats toward the backstop. But the ball shoots past him yet again, having hit a tiny square of brick on the fly, and rebounds back toward the third base side of the plate. Misch scoops it up on the dead run and slaps the tag on Hyzdu. His erstwhile wild pitch has turned into a putout to end the inning. Jogging in toward the dugout from left field, Doug Clark can only smile. Funny game.

Doug goes 1-for-2 on the night with a booming triple, walks twice, and scores the Grizzlies' lone run in a 3–1 loss. He ends the game in the on-deck circle, waiting.

● Sitting on a grassy bank above the Willamette River the next morning, Doug lifts his Arnette sunglasses to his freckled brow and considers his prospects of getting to the big leagues. For the first time in his eight-year minor league career, he is playing every day at Triple-A. The team's starting left fielder, he is batting .321. Up in the big leagues, the Giants are searching for outfield solutions. Just ten days earlier, on June 13, they had called up two outfielders from Fresno, Todd Linden and Adam Shabala. Doug says he is happy for his teammates. They have worked hard. They have earned the promotion. "I wasn't going to dwell on the fact that 'That could have been me,' or 'Why wasn't that me?' I'm not that person. I'm not the person that's going to look at other people and compare them to myself and be jealous, or do anything that's going to cause my mind to be polluted."

His time, perhaps, will come. After all, San Francisco is struggling mightily at the plate. The starting left fielder has been out all season with no return in sight. His name is Bonds. Barry Bonds.

● On years of Tuesday nights from May through August, Bill and Peggy Clark headed over to the entrance of nearby Van Horn Park on Carew Street, right on the edge of an Irish Catholic neighborhood in Springfield known as Hungry Hill. All seven Clark kids, Doug third in the order, were there in shorts and sneakers, bustling with energy, fired up about the weekly Richard W. Childs trail race. Often the Clarks were met by all eight Joyal cousins, the children of Peggy's sister Kathy, who lived nearby, and once in a while by all nine Howard cousins, the children of her other sister, Maureen, who lived outside Boston. By the time he was in kindergarten, Doug was used to jostling for position at the starting line, waiting anxiously for the gun.

When it went off, so did he, thundering through the trails, 2.4 miles up and down. Deep in the woods, sucking in air, striding as hard as he could, Doug would listen at all the checkpoints to hear his time, to see if he was moving faster than last week's pace. He feasted on that challenge, and was determined to be the hungriest kid on Hungry Hill.

To a point, of course. "There's this one corner where nobody is there to check your time," Doug recalls from that grassy bank in Portland all those years later. "You can go down this path, which would cut a corner and cut a pretty good chunk off your time. Some kids would take it, and some wouldn't. I remember always telling myself: 'I don't care. I'm not going to walk it. I'm not going to take that shortcut. If I come in whatever place, that's fine.'"

It is that same discipline, he says, that keeps him away from the dangling apple of performance-enhancing drugs. "I think that something has to be said for the people that just go at it the right way. That's something I try to strive for on an everyday basis. No matter what I do, I just try to do it the right way. If you come out on the short end of the stick, at least you have that to fall back on. These kids who have done [steroids], who have gone to the major leagues and had great seasons, it's something they still have to fall asleep to at night."

● As a kid, he went to sleep in a makeshift bedroom in the basement on Piedmont Street in the lower berth of a bunkbed his dad made, older brother Andrew up on top. Eldest brother Will got the single bed on the other side of the room. The walls were lined with sports posters. (Ultimately Doug would put up the one with the thirty-three baseball cards from the 1998 Salem-Keizer Volcanoes, his first professional team.) Out in the hallway, near the washer and dryer, was a small stall with a shower. Upstairs in the main part of the house were three bedrooms and one bathroom to accommodate his four younger siblings and two parents.

Growing up in a city made famous by Dr. Seuss, the seven Clark kids came of age in a family whose beloved relatives included Grandma Honey and Aunt Bunny. Their red-haired, freckle-faced mother, Peggy, was referred to all the time in public by their father, Bill, as "Mother Goose." A former fourth grade teacher who went back to work years later as the alumni director at her alma mater, the College of Our Lady of the Elms in nearby Chicopee, Peggy liked to sneak in a few pages of a mystery novel in the living room, propped up on a couch with pillows proclaiming "Moms Make Memories" and "A Man's Home Is His Castle—Until the Queen Arrives."

The Clarks' values were simple. Family came first, always. If there was a family event, which there often was with seven kids and seventeen first cousins, you went to it. School mattered. There was no question that all the Clark kids would be going to college. Religion was a big part of the equation, though not one without complications. Every Saturday meant going with their mom to Our Lady of Hope. On Sundays they were off with their dad to Trinity United Methodist. (Doug says they coexisted peacefully across the Catholic-Protestant divide, even after his decision at age thirteen to cast his lot with the Catholics.)

Finally, there was sports. Competition was the great leveler, the separator, the way to stand out. There were fierce battles in the basement: wrestling matches and floor hockey, Doug trying to hold his own against his two older brothers. At Central High School he was a standout three-sport athlete. In the fall he was the quarterback of the football team, leading the Golden Eagles in his senior year to an undefeated season. In the winter he was the lone white player on the school's varsity basketball team, a tenacious rebounder. And in the spring, of course, Doug played that great American game.

Tennis.

● The conventional wisdom is that if you don't start baseball early, you'll never be any good. The game's subtle and specialized skills, such as fielding a grounder and hitting the curve, do not have universal athletic translations. Witness the minor league career of Michael Jordan, named by ESPN in 1999 as the greatest American athlete of the twentieth century. In 1994 he stepped away from his mastery of the NBA to play a year of minor league baseball for the Double-A Birmingham Barons. He poured himself into the challenge with all of his legendary competitive zeal. He batted just .202 and struck out 114 times in 436 at bats.

Doug Clark never played an inning of Little League. As a kid he played casually on church teams for a couple of summers, but he never went to baseball camp. In high school, during baseball season he donned his tennis whites. He was good enough to become the team's top singles player, but in the state tournament he would always fall in one of the middle rounds to some suburban kid who grew up taking lessons at the country club.

Of course he followed the Red Sox with avid interest, and loved to take his brothers deep in Wiffle Ball, but playing baseball just didn't seem to provide the intensity he was craving.

The summer after his junior year of high school, at age seventeen in 1993, he decided to try out for the American Legion team, just for something to do with his friends. The other players all were coming off of high school seasons. At the tryouts Doug was coordinated and competitive, but completely out of his league. Coach Tom Nicholson thanked him for coming by but said he just didn't see where Doug would fit in. A few days later Nicholson had a change of heart. He called the house on Piedmont Street and said, "Doug, you know what? I've got a uniform for you. Let's give this a try."

Doug was surprised by how much he enjoyed playing baseball. It offered the team camaraderie of football and basketball, but also the *mano a mano* of tennis, an inner contest of pitcher and hitter on which the whole drama was poised. The game forced Doug deep into himself, a challenge he loved.

Still, his primary focus was elsewhere. His size and speed and power were paying dividends most of all on the football field. He loved those Fridays in the fall: wearing his jersey into school, leading his team's crash through the banner held up in the end zone by cheerleaders. By the end of his senior year he had been offered a scholarship to the University of Massachusetts. Granted, the Division I-AA level was a notch below the elite, but within the small speck of the planet that he occupied in western Massachusetts, this was still a considerable achievement. He figured he would go to UMass, play as hard as he could, and see what happened. Sure, the NFL was the longest of long shots, but he would back up that distant dream by majoring in biology. If he couldn't play for his beloved Steelers, he figured he could pursue a more reasonable route and become a dentist.

The college science classes were a massive step up from what he had known at Central High, and the demands of college football were imposing. His days often ran from seven in the morning until ten at night: an early morning lift, then classes and labs, practice, meetings, film, a team dinner, and study time. Even in a raucous dorm, he slept like a baby.

Like almost all freshmen, he was redshirted. That meant dealing with the bruising and boring repetition of football practice but with none of the rewards of actually getting into a game. Then, before his second year, he was converted to wide receiver. On a team that almost never threw the ball, this was the athletic equivalent of being the Maytag repairman in the old TV commercials.

After the season Doug awkwardly approached his coach, Mike Hodges, with a question. He had been playing summer baseball now for three years, and some of his teammates thought he should consider trying out for the team at UMass as a walk-on. He knew that would mean missing spring football, but he promised he would study the playbook hard, keep himself in great shape, and be raring to go when practice began in August. Might it be possible?

Hodges had watched Doug focus hard for two years with few opportunities and zero complaints. He told him that if he wanted to talk to baseball coach Mike Stone,[1] that was okay with him.

So on a blustery December day in 1995, as students were getting ready for finals and winter break, Doug rapped on Stone's door. He shook the coach's hand firmly and spelled out his story.

Stone knew that two-sport college athletes in the modern era were exceedingly rare, particularly when they had ambitions to be serious students as well. Still, the football-baseball combination was familiar to him. His top UMass alum, Ron Villone, had played football for the Minutemen, and had already broken through to the big leagues as a hard-throwing left-hander. Stone himself had played both sports. A former minor leaguer in the St. Louis Cardinals' organization—where he roomed for a time with a hypercompetitive infielder named Scott Boras—Stone had come to UMass as an older student who played football. So he wasn't going to dismiss earnest young Doug Clark right away. "Where did you play in high school?" Stone asked.

"Actually, sir, I didn't play in high school. I played tennis."

Say what?

Doug spent winter break at home in Springfield, going to indoor batting cages and working out for hours at the YMCA. When he returned to campus in January, he beat almost everyone on the baseball team in the mile run. He then plunged into indoor practices, drawing startled looks from guys who had been playing organized ball almost since they could walk. "When he swung the bat, it looked stiff," recalled Ryan Cameron, a pitcher from Pittsfield who would become a close friend and a minor leaguer himself. "When he threw the baseball, it looked painful. When he ran the bases, he looked like he should have a helmet and shoulder pads on. You sat there and scratched your head, and said, 'How does he do it?'"

Remarkably, Doug earned a starting outfield berth, and batted .313. "I enjoyed the whole challenge of taking it on," he said. "It was exciting for me, and I was good at it. I was hungry for it. Every day it was something new."

The next year he was a third-team All-American, and the scouts were coming out in force. A year later he was picked in the seventh round of the draft by the Giants. All the Clark siblings and lots of the cousins crammed into the house on Piedmont Street, toasting Doug on that June night in 1998. Doug's brother Andrew strummed his guitar, and Jim Masteralexis—recently enlisted as Doug's agent—invented lyrics about Doug playing in the outfield alongside Barry Bonds. The beer was flowing, and the horizon had no limits.

A few days later Aunt Bunny—actually his mother's widowed cousin Barbara Hood—came over to help pack Doug's bags, beginning a tradition that would always mark the beginning of his professional seasons. She stuffed in the clothes, the baseball equipment, the white blanket from childhood, and Doug's Bible. The next morning he was winging west.

He began his professional career going 0-for-17. He called home virtually every day, running through phone cards like candy, chewing up big chunks of his $850 a month salary. He lived with a host family, sharing a basement room with teammate Ryan Vogelsong, the tight quarters nothing new to Doug. Although he found host father Ray Johnson to be a little uptight with curfews, it was still all a big adventure: the bus trips under a huge western sky, the Little Leaguers pleading for autographs, the pretty girls in tank tops hovering over the railing. By year's end Doug had hit .335, second best in the Northwest League. He felt like he was on the right path.

And in a way he was. In the coming years he would move up to Double-A, touch the highest rung of the minor league ladder at Triple-A, even get invited to big league spring training. It was heady stuff, getting dressed just a couple of lockers down from Barry Bonds, the game's greatest hitter.

While his six siblings stayed close to the nest, Doug lived out of suitcases. "Home" for the summer meant Salem, Oregon, or Shreveport, Louisiana, or Fresno, California, with a bevy of bus trips and Quality Inns on the road. Truth is, Doug liked the travel. He felt enlivened by the novelty in whatever form new cities could provide it: a zoo, a Civil War battlefield, a Hooters restaurant. The nightly minor league game, with all its attendant rituals and schlock and yearning, was the centerpiece of his life. He poured himself into it. Still, at season's end it was always a deep comfort to head home, back to Springfield. He would immediately take his parents out to their favorite restaurant, Lido's, where Doug always ordered the chicken parmesan and asked for extra green peppers on his salad. He stayed in the basement in the house on Piedmont Street, finished up his biology degree at UMass, and began substitute teaching at Central High School for $55 a day. In February, Aunt Bunny would come over and pack the suitcases—blanket, bats, and Bible—and Doug would stay up late, leaving notes for all his siblings. Then he was off for another year of the quest.

One year he surprised his family by returning in mid-March, taking the red-eye from Arizona on the sixteenth. He was met at the airport by Aunt Bunny, who handed him his tuxedo. He then showed up at the church in time for his brother William's Saint Patrick's Day wedding. The pews were packed with Clarks and Joyals and Howards, as Doug walked his grandmother, Mildred Dwyer, down the aisle. "It was one of those days," Doug would later reflect, "when how things are and how they should be come together."

By a certain point, though, it was hard to say that about his baseball career. Competing in the high minors, he found that the learning curve was beginning to flatten. He hit a point of diminishing returns on effort. This was a ferocious competition, with young men not just from the United States but from baseball-mad countries in Latin America and Asia vying for one of the 750 golden tickets given out to major league baseball players. Every year the talent pool was replenished in the draft by the next group of hometown stars. Big league rosters generally carried four or five outfielders, and on some teams guys were not budging. Barry Bonds, for instance, had been with the Giants since 1993, the year he won his third Most Valuable Player award.

Doug hit .272 in his first full year at Double-A in 2000, then .275 the next year in the same place. He began 2002 at Triple-A for the first time, hitting .269 in sporadic duty for half a season before dropping back to Double-A, where he hit .261. He had become a good outfielder and a base-stealing threat, but he didn't have the power the Giants wanted at the position, never hitting more than eleven home runs.

Doug had always felt that he had an unusual capacity for work. Once he really put his mind to things, he was generally able to accomplish them, even when the goals were extraordinarily hard. He had completed a demanding biology degree alongside two intensive Division I sports commitments. He had made it to the high minors—much further than most kids with a baseball dream—despite having given an immense head start to his competitors. But to get the treasured call, to make it up to the big leagues, he realized he had to do more. Somewhere, somehow, he had to find an edge.

• In December 2002, back from his fifth season of minor league ball, he settled into the usual rhythm in Springfield. There were long days of substitute teaching, followed by hours in the gym to keep his body taut. Often there were family dinners, usually cooked by Mother Goose. Weekends might mean a trip to UMass with his brothers to take in a basketball game.

One afternoon he got a call from Jim Masteralexis, who told him there was a new baseball opportunity if he was willing to act right away. Reed Johnson, one of the American "imports" for a top winter league team in the Dominican Republic, had been injured. They needed a replacement immediately. The pay was $5,000 a month—more than twice what he had ever made in the minors. It might last for only a few weeks, and it would mean missing the Clark family Christmas for the first time in his life. Was he interested?

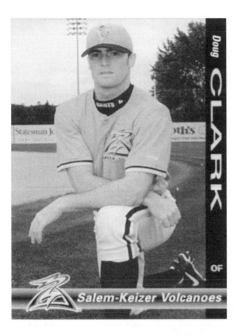

Doug Clark begins his professional career with the Salem-Keizer Volcanoes in 1998. *Courtesy of the Clark family*

In spring training 2005, Barry Bonds is very much the center of attention with the Giants. Doug is on the right, looking straight at Bonds. *AP Images/Eric Risberg*

In 2005, his eighth pro season, Doug is playing for the Fresno Grizzlies when his cousins Carlin, Conrad, and Cooper Joyal come down from Massachusetts to see him play against the Memphis Redbirds. *Courtesy of Kris Joyal*

In September 2005, the call finally comes. Doug's parents, Peggy and Bill Clark, fly down to Washington, D.C., to see the Giants play the Nationals. *Courtesy of R. J. Joyal*

In 2006 Doug leaves the Giants organization, after eight years. When his new team, the Oakland A's, visits San Francisco, Doug finally gets the chance to play left field—in front of a rather imposing background. *Courtesy of Doug Clark*

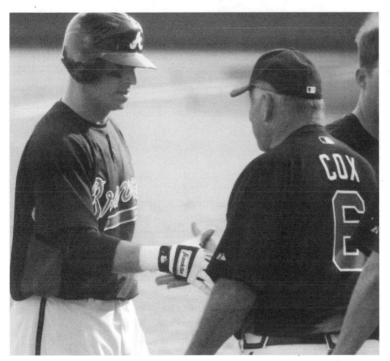

In 2007 Doug signs with the Braves and hits over .400 in spring training, impressing longtime manager Bobby Cox. He spends the entire season, however, in Triple-A with Richmond. *Courtesy of R. J. Joyal*

In 2008 Clark's baseball odyssey continues when he joins the Hanwha Eagles in South Korea. *Courtesy of Doug Clark*

Though he stands out as one of two imports allowed on his Korean team, Doug works hard to blend into the culture. *Courtesy of Doug Clark*

Arriving at the airport in Santo Domingo, Doug thought he had landed in a flea market. People swarmed everywhere, hawking little trinkets, jabbering to him in Spanish far faster than he remembered from his classes at Central with Mena DeCarvalho. The scene at the ballpark was intense: the beating of drums, the waving of flags, the people with painted faces hanging onto the light poles in the outfield for a better view. Los Leones del Escogido were a famous Dominican team, and Doug had joined a roster that was laced with major league talent. There was the sleek shortstop Rafael Furcal, the burly outfielder Jose Guillen, and a larger-than-life first baseman whose deep laughter seemed to make the clubhouse vibrate: David Ortiz. (Not known yet as Big Papi, Ortiz still was wearing his Minnesota Twins gear in practice, but just a few weeks later he would sign a free agent contract with the Boston Red Sox.) All had come from a place of poverty to unimaginable wealth, and all were deified by the fans.

It was a mesmerizing experience for Doug. The game was still the game, the sixty feet, six inches to the plate, the ninety feet between bases, the four hundred or so to dead center still the same, but the atmosphere was supercharged. "That's what they love," he says of the Dominican fans' passion for baseball. "That is their major leagues down there. That's all they have. They're going to root for it until the death."

A couple of months of winter ball became part of his routine. As of 2003 he began playing for a team in Navojoa, Mexico. There was just one paved road leading into town before dirt roads fanned out to the barrios. The rickety buses meandered through the desert, mountains rising in the distance, stars all around. The driver would tell ghost stories about things he had seen falling from the sky. Doug wore uniforms covered with advertising for oil companies and convenience stores, making him feel like a race-car driver. At home in Navojoa he stayed in El Rancho Motel, each morning practicing the rolling of his "r's" on "huevos rrrrevueltos" with a waitress he referred to simply as "Bonita."

At times his life felt as arid as the landscape. He read for long hours: *The DaVinci Code, The Moral Animal: Why We Are the Way We Are*, sports biographies. Sometimes he found a major league classic on television, noting guys he had played with in the minors. He used phone cards sparingly because they were expensive. He looked forward to the road games against Aguilas de Mexicali, where he would see a mile-long line of people massing at the border. As a U.S. citizen, he went right through. He reveled in the Wal-Mart on the other side of what was now called Calexico, finding treats like Snapple iced tea and Pop-Tarts, calling home from his cell phone which magically worked. He brought back a Nintendo Game Boy for the son of the clubhouse attendant, Dante Lugo, and was greeted with one of the biggest smiles he had ever encountered.

Doug considered the whole thing to be a grind, an inner challenge. "It's a test," he explained. 'Are you going to be able to handle this? Are you going to be able to do what you need to do to get through it?'" Doug was searching for that edge, imagining what it would be like to go into a big league clubhouse for the first time, to see that ball rolled back into the dugout after his first major league hit.

He spent the entire 2004 season at Double-A in Norwich, Connecticut, leaving tickets almost every day for family. He hit .292 with ten home runs, a league-leading thirteen triples, and thirty-three stolen bases. At season's end, though, there was no call-up by the Giants yet again. This was seven years now of minor league ball.

He flew out to California to spend a few days with a young woman from Monterrey he had met during one of his stints at Triple-A. They walked the streets of San Francisco, taking cable cars, going out for a walk along the Golden Gate Bridge as fog rolled in over Alcatraz. One evening they went out to SBC Park and picked up a couple of scalped tickets. They settled into their seats in the left field bleachers. Doug stared down at the precious real estate. Right there before him was the immovable object. Barry Bonds had turned forty that year, and he was completing a remarkable fourth consecutive MVP season, the record seventh time he had won the award. He hit forty-five home runs in just 373 at bats, walking 232 times—by far the most in major league history. Every time he came to the plate, the stadium shook with excitement.

The leaking of Bonds's BALCO testimony would come a few months later. Then the 2005 season would launch with the congressional hearings— and Bonds on the sidelines for months.

Doug settled in for 2005 with the Fresno Grizzlies. He shared a two-bedroom condo just off the highway with pitcher Pat Misch, first baseman Mike Cervenak, and shortstop Jamie Athas (knowing that living with fellow outfielders was an invitation for poison—at least figuratively). They labeled their food in the refrigerator, pitched in for gas for rides in Athas's Mitsubishi Montero, and tried their damndest to make it up just one more level.

● On this morning of June 23, Doug watches a host of healthy Portlanders glide by on inline skates on a narrow path that hugs the Willamette River. All he can do, he says, is keep plugging away, control what he can control. "Every day I try to visualize myself as a big leaguer, going into the locker room, getting that call, and just being there," he says. "It's something I can't really worry too much about. It's out of my control. I just try to keep running after it."

Later that very same day the Giants will make a roster move to add another outfielder. It will not be Doug, though. Instead they claim Alex Sanchez off the waiver wire from the Tampa Bay Devil Rays.

Sanchez had been in the news once before this season, earning the dubious distinction of being the first major leaguer ever to be suspended for a positive steroid test. On the eve of the 2005 season—not even three weeks after Mark McGwire told Congress he wasn't there to talk about the past—MLB had announced its first suspension. The player was a skinny twenty-eight-year-old outfielder with four career home runs, someone who, just one month before, had been reunited with his mother and brother for the first time since he left Cuba on a raft eleven years earlier. Sanchez proclaimed his innocence, saying that he had never taken steroids, only "stuff I buy over the counter. Multivitamins, protein shakes, muscle relaxants. That kind of stuff."

Now, a couple of months after his ten-day suspension, Sanchez has been picked up by the Giants. "[The suspension] doesn't concern me," Giants manager Felipe Alou tells C. J. Bowles of MLB.com. "He has plenty of company. The fact that he's clean now puts him in big company, too. . . . It's not like he murdered somebody or stole Mona Lisa."

● A few hours later that same evening of June 23, the sweet smell of apple fries permeates the Central Washington State Fairgrounds. The fairgrounds, situated near a trailer park, a pawnshop, and the Thunderbird Casino, host both monster truck shows and baseball games in the low minors. This is the home of the Yakima Bears, a short-season Single-A affiliate of the Arizona Diamondbacks.

The Bears are managed by thirty-eight-year-old Jay Gainer. Back in 1993 Gainer made it up to the Colorado Rockies, earning fleeting fame as the fifteenth player ever to hit a home run on the first pitch he saw in the major leagues. He wound up batting .171 that year in forty-one at bats and never got back to the bigs again.

The general manager is twenty-six-year-old Ken Wombacher, who started with the Bears as an intern. He says that he truly likes Yakima, but like everyone else—the players, the umpires, even the broadcasters—he hopes to move up: "I definitely have bigger dreams." During the game he roams the stadium, overseeing between-innings promotions such as the "Waffle in Your Face" contest and the catapulting of rubber chickens into the stands, the latter of which he terms "very popular."

The team is owned in the mom-and-pop fashion of pre-Wal-Mart America. Co-owner Mike McMurray sits up in the press box, serving as the game's official scorer. His wife, fellow co-owner Laura McMurray, runs a concession stand on the first base concourse. On this night the stand features discounted items that had been stored in the McMurrays' garage after not selling in years past. Fans can get bargains on a Damian Rolls bobblehead doll, and a T-shirt that says "Major League Dreams . . . do come true." It lists the fifteen players from the Bears' inception in 1990 who have played for Yakima and ultimately made it to The Show. (One of the guys on the shirt is DiaMMond Management client Peter Bergeron, who during this summer of 2005 is now toiling for the Double-A Bowie Baysox, trying to get back to the bigs.)

A sizzling day begins to cool as the sun drifts toward the Pacific. The fans take their seats, many of them on this night wearing green "Four Square Baseball Camp" shirts. The camp is part of the mission of the Yakima Foursquare Church, whose motto is "making it hard to go to hell in Yakima." Thus supported, the starters for the Bears run out to their positions to the piped-in theme music from *Field of Dreams*.

Matt Torra sits in a folding chair in the bullpen down the third base line, spitting sunflower seeds. He is now a pro.

Arizona's regional scout, Matt Merullo, had arrived at the Torras' house in Pittsfield on Sunday, June 19, toting the standard minor league uniform player's contract, six foldout pages on blue paper. It called for the universal first-year salary of $850 a month,[2] but added a one-time signing bonus of $1.025 million. "It was phenomenal to see the money thing in writing," Pat Torra said later that day. "To look at it was something else."

After surveying the contract, Jim Masteralexis told Matt Merullo that long ago he had been scouted by his grandfather, Lennie Merullo. One day when Jim was catching for the University of New Hampshire, Lennie gave him a business card from the Major League Scouting Bureau and told him that he had soft hands and that he received the ball well. They were words Masteralexis had shared with many people long after his playing days were over.

Packing up, Matt Merullo shared a favorite family story about his grandfather. Back in the mid-thirties, he said, Lennie had gone to college, an American Dream come true for his immigrant family, which had—like Jim Torra's parents—arrived the previous generation from Italy. Still, the pride wasn't without some complications. It was in the midst of the Great Depression, and all of the family were working, except for Lennie, who was off studying and playing baseball at Villanova University. One day in 1935

Lennie came home and banged on the door. He walked in, sat down, and put his feet on the table, to the consternation of his mother. Then he smiled at her and slapped a check down on the table. It was a $1,500 signing bonus from the Chicago Cubs (who also threw in a new suit and a pair of shoes). Lennie's mom took one look at the check, then started yelling in Italian, "Everybody—go play baseball!"

Later that day, Jim Torra teared up while reading the Father's Day card from his youngest son. Matt also handed a thank you card to Jim Masteralexis (the cover depicting a guy with a hairy butt and the words "Muchas grassy-ass") and another one to Lisa ("I just hope you didn't get the same card for her," said Jim).

Matt left the next morning. Jim Torra slung his son's belongings into the back of his truck, picked up thirteen-year-old Gabe Levy (the neighbor on Pontoosuc Lake whose high-speed Internet had first informed the Torras of Matt's fate on draft day), and drove over to the small airport in Albany. Jim hadn't missed one of Matt's games in years, but that was about to end. They hugged farewell. Matt high-fived Gabe and then began the journey, crossing the Mississippi River for the first time in his life. He flew to Chicago, then took an Alaska Airlines flight to Seattle, followed by a prop jet inland to Yakima. The scenery was startling: the snow-covered spike of Mount Hood to the south, the hollowed-out peak of Saint Helens, the verdant Columbia River gorge, the majesty of Rainier.

After dropping his bags at the no-frills Oxford Inn for a day and a half, he moved in with his host family and was introduced to the world of Cynthia Keur.

A forty-four-year-old single mother with frizzy red hair and light blue-green eyes, Keur plays the role of Susan Sarandon's famous *Bull Durham* character Annie Savoy—minus the sex. She lives in nearby Selah in a yellow ranch house high up a rocky driveway, just a couple of houses down from a Baptist church. On her front door is a wooden plaque that reads, "We interrupt this family for baseball season."

The interrupted family consists of her fourteen-year-old son, Chandler, a dog named Shadow, and various salvaged beings—a smattering of cats (eight, she believes), and one of her teaching colleagues in the Yakima Public Schools who was fleeing from an abusive spouse. Then there are the ballplayers. In addition to Torra, there is Garrett Bauer, a redheaded pitcher selected out of Missouri Baptist in the twenty-seventh round a year ago; Derek Bruce, a nineteenth-round infielder from Clarkston, Washington; and Adam Howard, a forty-fourth-round pick from Ooltewah, Tennessee. The players live two to a small room in the basement, but Cynthia expects more as the summer progresses. "We get mattresses for whoever wants to stay," she says.

The house is a shrine to the Yakima Bears. The walls are covered with framed baseball cards featuring Bears of the past. Atop the large-screen TV are two relics: a bat emblazoned with the name of Chris Carter, a Northwest League All-Star a year ago, and a ball signed by Boomer, the team mascot. The microwave supports rows of baseballs signed by former Bears who have slept here. The shelves are jammed with scrapbooks. Cynthia almost never misses a game, the nine innings usually providing occasion for some five hundred digital photographs, all of which she dutifully downloads in the wee hours—after making an eleven o'clock home-cooked meal for hungry Bears. No Bear leaves the season without a personal CD from Cynthia. Some get what she calls "dream books," collections of articles and photos and fan letters: "I'm very big into affirmations."

There are few limits to her devotion. When the team hits the road, she and Chandler attach a trailer to the ball hitch on the back of her Ford Expedition, and off they go to see the Bears in action against teams such as the Tri-City Dust Devils and the Salem-Keizer Volcanoes. They take in the game, cheering their hearts out for the Bears, snapping photos galore, then taking a rotating crew of players out to dinner. At night she parks the trailer in a Wal-Mart lot and sleeps under a riot of stars.

She knows most of the players for only a few weeks of their lives, but she takes her role quite seriously. In part, that's to play mother hen. Once a catcher named Bryan Loeb, already finished with pro ball now at age twenty-seven, had taken a vicious backswing to the mask. Cynthia woke him up every two hours to check on his eye, dabbing it with a compress. "There is a connection," she says. "When they have a bad game, or life just ends because their ERA went through the roof, you are the one they come home to. You're mom, you're grandma, you're the nurse."

And not just that. Cynthia also serves as unofficial matchmaker and screener for the Bears. The halter-top hopefuls from Yakima Community College often approach her at games, and she dispenses—or doesn't dispense—"her" players' cell phone numbers. Many of the young women appear at the frequent pool parties on her deck, and more than a few have stayed for breakfast.

Nearing midnight, Matt Torra munches on one of Cynthia's homemade tacos and pages through a scrapbook. He sees photos from a year ago, strapping young men in their first or second year of pro ball, holding bottles of beer, surrounded by bikini-clad talent. Matt inquires about a pair of blond twins in one picture who he thinks look like Anna Kournikova. He is cautioned away from another young lady Cynthia refers to as "too germy."

While Jim and Pat Torra are back in Pittsfield, tuning in to the 10:05 EST starts on the webcast, Cynthia Keur is right up close, rooting for her surrogate sons. And she is there, worried, when Matt comes home one night in July, shaking his head. His just-turned-twenty-one swagger is gone. There is, he says, "a giant knot in my shoulder."

He is diagnosed at first with "dead arm" and told not to throw for a few weeks. A subsequent MRI, though, reveals a tear in the labrum, a ring of cartilage in the back of his shoulder. He will need surgery.

His first pro season, just ten innings old, is now over.

The Second Half

11

Suspended Disbelief

Reading, Pennsylvania

The full-page ad on the back of the sports section of *USA Today* on Monday, July 18, 2005, looks slick. The ad consists of three images. On top is a picture of a handsome man with a dark mustache, designer sunglasses atop the brim of his Baltimore Orioles cap, his expression calm and focused. On the bottom, the same man is captured completing his graceful swing, the top hand coming off the bat, the ball heading deep in a hurry. The photographs are separated by the middle image, two seams of a baseball. On the pristine white surface are printed these words: "Only 4 men in the history of Major League Baseball have recorded 3,000 hits and 500 home runs. Congratulations, Raffy, you never cease to amaze us." The note is signed by Allan H. "Bud" Selig.

Indeed, Rafael Palmeiro joined some elite company when he recorded his three thousandth hit the previous Friday night, a double down the left field line in Seattle. Only Hank Aaron, Willie Mays, and Eddie Murray had managed the dual 3,000–500 milestone. Palmeiro had fashioned a great success story. He had fled Cuba with his parents at age six, leaving behind an older brother, someone he would not see again for twenty-one years. Learning the game from his father, a construction worker, Palmeiro went on to become a three-time All-American at Mississippi State, where the baseball training complex now bears his name. Over a twenty-year career in the big leagues, he had been one of the game's purest hitters. His late-career success was particularly impressive. No player in baseball history could match his string of nine straight seasons of thirty-eight or more home runs, which he accomplished from 1995 to 2003, seasons in which he turned thirty-one to thirty-nine years old.

Other than his surprising stint as a pitchman for Viagra in 2002–3 (becoming the first prominent athlete to tout a treatment for erectile dysfunction), Palmeiro mostly eluded the glare of the bright lights throughout his first nineteen seasons. He played almost all his career with low-profile teams in Texas and Baltimore. He never won a home run title, never finished in the top four in the MVP voting, and never set foot on the grand stage of the World Series. Though his hard work was unquestioned and his numbers had carved a near-certain path to Cooperstown, he remained the game's most quiet superstar.

All of that changed in 2005 when Rafael Palmeiro became a shining knight–like symbol for baseball's integrity. He railed about the accusations of steroid use leveled against him in Jose Canseco's book *Juiced*, which had been released on Valentine's Day. In the congressional hearings the next month, Palmeiro's defiant statement of innocence stood in sharp contrast to the tortured "I'm not here to talk about the past" testimony of Mark Mc-Gwire.[1] Resplendent in a blue pinstriped suit, his dark hair flecked with just a hint of gray, Palmeiro said: "Good morning, Mr. Chairman and members of the committee. My name is Rafael Palmeiro and I am a professional baseball player. I'll be brief in my remarks today. Let me start by telling you this: I have never used steroids. Period. I don't know how to say it any more clearly than that. Never." His words were delivered with a stony glare and a memorable wagging of his index finger at the camera.

For Major League Baseball, Palmeiro's three thousandth hit on July 15 seemed like healing waters. One could well understand Commissioner Selig's desire to bask in the moment. He had felt ambushed by the congressional hearings and the raft of negative publicity that followed. Within his office, many felt that baseball was being unduly targeted in an American society that had become enraptured with pharmaceutical enhancement, from Rogaine to Ritalin, from Botox to Viagra. Other sports seemed to be getting close to a free pass. How was it that football, for instance, was suddenly producing all of these three hundred–plus-pound linemen who could run the forty-yard dash in 4.7? But baseball, still identified by many with that charmingly archaic phrase—the national pastime—had become the focal point, perhaps the whipping boy, of the American discussion on performance-enhancing drugs.

In a year in which the game's reputation had taken a body blow, Rafael Palmeiro stood tall. Well respected both on and off the field (his abundant charitable works had earned him awards named for two of the game's social pioneers, Branch Rickey and Roberto Clemente), Palmeiro was now going to bat for the sport itself. In the spring he had agreed to join the Zero Tolerance Committee set up in the aftermath of the congressional hearings. He seemed to be a crusader for baseball at its pastoral best.

● Late on that same Monday morning, Randy Ruiz awakens groggily in his room at the Doubletree Inn. He is back in Portland, Maine, site of the Eastern League All-Star Game five days earlier, this time with his teammates on the Reading Phillies, who had arrived late the previous evening after a seven-hour bus ride from Binghamton, New York. Over breakfast in the lobby, Randy thumbs through the sports pages of the complimentary *USA Today*, paying no particular attention to the MLB ad congratulating Rafael Palmeiro, if he even sees it at all. A few hours later at Hadlock Field, Randy sparks a 7–1 victory, going 2-for-3 with his third home run in as many days. Remarkably, he has now leapfrogged the entire Eastern League in both home runs (twenty-five) and RBI (eighty-three)—despite serving that fifteen-game suspension to start the season. With those stats plus his league-leading .359 average, Randy is, in his first year at Double-A, on pace to win the Triple Crown. No one has accomplished that feat in the Eastern League in twenty-nine years.

The whole time, of course, there is a hammer hanging over his head.

● There is an undeniable toughness about Lisa Pike Masteralexis. Forget for a moment the blond hair and the deep red nail polish. She has more than proved her mettle in a man's world. She is a tenacious lawyer with an expertise in labor relations. In the academic old boys' network of sport management, she became the head of the well-regarded program at the University of Massachusetts before she turned thirty. And she is among the 1 percent of agents without a Y chromosome who have been certified by the Major League Baseball Players Association.

With her toughness, though, comes a constitutional warmth. She is a naturally affectionate mother with her three young children, a hugger and a soother. In the classroom she manages to be warm and approachable without lowering the bar; twice she has won the university's Outstanding Teacher of the Year award. In her varied professional pursuits, she has a rare ability to connect with people on a personal level, a willingness to look you in the eye, to laugh, to feel your pain. She has always had a soft spot for hard luck cases, for people she perceives to be victims. Yes, her ambition runs deep, and her competitive zeal is apparent, but she is also drawn, in an almost tidal way, to fairness.

From her dad, Butch Pike, a union carpenter, she has inherited not only her love of baseball (and of the Yankees, to her husband's chagrin) but also an abiding belief that workers need to fight the injustices of management. Her mother's experience of being harassed on the job fired Lisa's indignation; several of her published articles take aim at sexual harassment in the sports world. Her highest-profile moment as a lawyer was an amicus curiae brief she helped to file in the U.S. Supreme Court in 2000 on behalf of the golfer Casey Martin. The PGA Tour had fought for years to require Martin to walk the course rather than use a cart, despite a degenerative circulatory condition in his legs that made such walking an excruciating experience. When Martin won his case, Lisa felt a delicious sense of triumph.

To Lisa's mind, baseball's policy around steroids and performance-enhancing drugs was filled with unfairness—particularly in regard to minor leaguers. She felt that many were placed in an extremely difficult spot: either cheat or let go of the dream. Making the big leagues was unbelievably hard, and there was no way to get there without the ability and desire and some good fortune, but it was also clear that a pharmaceutical shortcut had helped a great many players. It was a huge part of the culture of the game. By no means was she condoning the use of steroids. Without question, she felt that players were responsible for their own decisions. But she also believed that in an ultracompetitive world where minor leaguers made so little money and major leaguers made so much, it wasn't easy to just say no.

What's more, Lisa believed, management had been complicit in the proliferation of performance-enhancing drugs. Despite all the finger pointing, there had been essentially no admission on the part of the baseball establishment that steroids had been, in a real sense, good for business. Hadn't that been established during the great home run derby between Mark McGwire and Sammy Sosa in 1998? It wasn't just chicks who dug the long ball (a phrase made famous by a Nike commercial in the late nineties). At a minimum, Lisa felt that baseball executives had "waited far too long to address the problem, in other cases turned a blind eye to performance enhancing drug use, and in the most extreme cases may have sent messages that encouraged athletes to use steroid precursors in supplements or steroids themselves."[2]

Several weeks before she had even heard of Randy Ruiz, Lisa had been captivated by the congressional hearings in March. She was particularly moved by the testimony of Denise Garibaldi, the clinical psychologist whose son Rob had grown up idolizing McGwire, often videotaping his at bats. Told by a series of scouts and coaches that he would need to get bigger in order to have a chance in baseball, Rob began an aggressive course of steroid use. He became addicted. His behavior became erratic, and he was often full of rage, which he ultimately turned on himself. Now here was Denise Garibaldi in Washington testifying, "There is no doubt in our minds that steroids killed our son," then listening from a few rows back to McGwire's sputtering claims about not being here to talk about the past.[3]

Riveting theater as this was, Lisa felt that the hearings had an element of McCarthyism. "What I see happening in Congress," she would later write, "is a witch hunt to make players out to be bad human beings for using steroids."[4]

In the aftermath of those hearings, it seemed to both Lisa and Jim Masteralexis that the commissioner's office needed to take some immediate action to address the public relations crisis. The easy targets were minor leaguers, who, unlike their major league counterparts, were not protected by collective bargaining. Jim described the environment as "a climate where the commissioner is looking to save face on the steroid issue and bag some minor leaguers who don't have the wherewithal to oppose him." When the first round of suspensions was announced in early April—one major leaguer (Alex Sanchez) and thirty-eight minor leaguers—the imbalance seemed to the husband-and-wife agent team patently unfair.

Two and a half months later that feeling of inequity hit them in a much more personal way. After Randy's anguished call from the bus, Lisa had called the commissioner's office in New York to announce her intention to appeal his suspension. She reached a lawyer from the Minor League Health Policy Advisory Committee, whose response had astonished Lisa: *Don't bother—he's guilty.*

Whatever happened to innocent until proven guilty? Where was due process? How come Randy didn't get to present his case in person? And why was it that the three members of the Health Policy Advisory Committee all had ties to Major League Baseball, which, she felt, had a vested interest in assigning blame and thereby conveying the notion that the testing policy was beyond reproach? As she would later write, the HPAC could be seen "as both prosecutor and judge."

However hastily, the appeal had been filed. But before there was even time for a hearty exhalation of relief, here was Randy on the phone on Saturday morning, broiling with anger. His name was in the paper for failing the drug test. Lisa couldn't believe it. How had that happened? Wasn't this supposed to stay under wraps until the appeal played out? Randy's reputation was getting ravaged. He would be abused by fans on the road. More important, his chances of ever getting called up to the big leagues—a subjective judgment always—were vanishing before his eyes.

Randy's story struck a raw nerve with Jim and Lisa. He had grown up with so little: no money, a mother who had abandoned ship, a dad who—however loving—was not living at home. He had clung tight to a difficult quest, bouncing around the country for community college baseball teams, getting signed for $1,000 at a tryout camp, enduring years of the grind in the low minors. Now he was clinging tight to his story, insisting over and over again that he hadn't gone back to the steroids.

Of course, adamant does not equal innocent. They knew that Randy's credibility was not unimpeachable. When the original suspension in April was revealed to be for a failed steroid test in 2004, he had told Mike Drago of the *Reading Eagle* that it must have stemmed from some over-the-counter drug: *I've never taken steroids. . . . I know everybody says that, but I've never taken that. I'm not into that stuff.* He had admitted otherwise to Jim and Lisa.

But, they figured, no one was publicly admitting steroid use at that point. Hadn't the Phillies—who had full access to the drug test results—explained Randy's absence in April by concocting a story about a groin injury? Hadn't their veteran assistant general manager, Mike Arbuckle, someone well regarded throughout the game, told Drago that the unidentified drug in question (which Jim and Lisa knew to be a heavy-duty steroid) was "not something that was particularly concerning to me individually, or to us as an organization"?

Jim and Lisa did have some good reports on Randy's character from sources they trusted. Jim had known John Brickley, the scout who had signed Randy, for almost thirty years. Brickley, a former high school math teacher, told Jim that he believed in Randy, and had maintained a relationship with him for years. Randy had always seemed so grateful for the opportunity. Sometimes, Brickley said, Randy called him out of the blue on holidays, sending regards to Brickley's wife and son.

They also had a window into Randy on the Reading Phillies. Teammate Ryan Cameron, a self-proclaimed "mama's boy" from Williamstown, Massachusetts, had been an excellent student of Lisa's at UMass and a client of theirs since he began his minor league career in 1998. They considered him a shrewd judge of character. He told them that Randy was a good guy, someone well regarded in the locker room.

From the Reading trainer and team doctor, people who observed Randy up close, Lisa says they got more support: "Keep going, keep going. Do this. Push this." At the team level, she insists, there was "a sense of injustice."

Certainly that's what she was hearing from Randy night after night. "He was so hurt through this. He kept calling and talking to me." It felt to Lisa not unlike the "emotion of somebody who was [being] harassed: that raw, up-at-night, no-sleep 'What did I do wrong? How come these people are just out to get me?' There's something that's just so inherently wrong in how he was treated."

Was he innocent? Deep down, Lisa had no idea. But Randy's obvious anguish "made me feel like either he's an unbelievable actor, or this guy honestly didn't do it."

● As Randy continued to play on appeal, the clock ticked louder and louder. Lisa and Jim worked hard to find possible explanations and loopholes. Perhaps the test results that Randy had heard about on June 23 could have represented a false positive. After all, the test they had him take with Quest Diagnostics just two days later on June 25 came back negative for performance-enhancing drugs. Of course, that was going to be a tough argument, given that the steroid in question was exactly the one for which he had tested positive the year before.

Another possibility was that traces of the drug from his 2004 use had lingered in his system. "There is controversy, even among the experts, of even this water-based steroid, getting it out of your system," Lisa says. "Apparently [steroids] connect to your fat cells in your body, and everybody's body composition is different. So it's very difficult to know when these things flush out of your system. . . . Randy swore up and down to me that he had not used, that this [test result] went back to that initial use."[5]

That argument, too, was tricky. Randy had been tested in spring training and had passed. Thus he had gone in less than a year from positive to negative to positive to negative. To suggest that the second positive stemmed from lingering residue from the initial use would cast some doubt on the accuracy of the testing in spring training. Was it possible that the tests themselves were not fully reliable?

In truth, Jim and Lisa did not know what to believe. They felt certain that minor leaguers were being scapegoated, and they believed that Randy was being bullied by Major League Baseball. The prejudgment and press leak struck them as particularly callous.

The practical question, of course, was whether or not they were willing to go to bat for Randy. If the appeal were denied, would they consider going toe-to-toe with the commissioner's office? Would they consider suing Major League Baseball when Randy's goal, when the goal of all of their clients—when their goal for that matter—was nothing less than a golden spot in the rarefied world of Major League Baseball?

● On Friday night, July 22, the Reading Phillies open a homestand against the Erie Seawolves. Fans pour into FirstEnergy Stadium on that hot summer night, sprung from a week at the factory or the mall or McDonald's. Some of the early arrivals splash in the pool behind the right field wall, next to the big sign for the Powerball lottery. Some trade their hard-earned dollars for hot dogs, peanuts, plastic cups filled with Budweiser. Little children sidle up to Screwball the Seamhead for photos. While the PA system blares out timeless minor league classics like "Y-M-C-A" and "My Angel Is a Centerfold," the Phillies take batting practice. Many watch as No. 54, the story of the summer, smashes balls into the alleys and the grassy berm beyond the left center field wall.

Then Randy Ruiz wipes the sweat off his forehead and walks quietly through the gate on the first base side. He signs an autograph or two in the concourse, then slips into the clubhouse. Changing back into street clothes, he disappears into the parking lot, staring at the ground, and then drives away before the national anthem and the timelessly hopeful cry of "Play ball!"

● One week into Randy's unpaid thirty-game suspension, more news comes out. On July 29 the *Eagle* has a four-story package by Mike Drago about Randy and steroids. Drago has spoken to Jim Masteralexis. Clearly frustrated, Jim lets down his guard. He tells Drago that the drug Randy tested positive for this season was the same one for which he had tested positive the previous year, stanozolol, known on the streets as Winstrol, or "Winny."

Drago's articles put forth an array of possible explanations for the positive test. He mentions the "lingering in the system" argument, quoting an article from Bodybuilding.com that says Winny "can be detected for quite some time after last use, so it's not advisable for drug-tested athletes. Many have assumed otherwise . . . but [traces] can be found up to five months after the last injection." Drago quotes Jim as wondering if Major League Baseball had mixed up the tests (citing the "seven other Ruizes" in pro ball), and Lisa as speculating that the positive result might have been triggered by a prescribed corticosteroid, dexamethasone, which Randy had used for his wrist—an argument disputed by the MLB appeal board. Drago even mentions Randy's recent claim that perhaps the positive was produced by his use of Viagra.

The articles are informative and well sourced, and hold to a mostly objective edge. Randy comes across as defiant and somewhat evasive, while Jim is depicted as frustrated and ultimately resigned. "Basically," he says, "the athletes [at the minor league level] have no rights here." He had considered a court challenge over the test results, but has come to realize that such a case would be difficult and expensive, and possibly counterproductive. "There's an element here of baseball blackballing Randy Ruiz," Jim says. "Major League Baseball doesn't appreciate people who fight them in court."

Three days later, on August 1, MLB comes out with a startling announcement: Rafael Palmeiro will begin serving a ten-day suspension after testing positive for steroids. As it turns out, Palmeiro was informed of the positive test weeks before and had filed an appeal. In the shadows, outside of the public eye, an anguished drama had played out. During this time he achieved his milestone three thousandth hit, and MLB ran the "Congratulations, Raffy, you never cease to amaze us" ad in *USA Today*. But now he has become the seventh big leaguer—and by many miles the biggest name—to be suspended for testing positive for performance-enhancing drugs.

A few days later the *New York Times*, citing unnamed sources, says that the drug in question was stanozolol.

● For Randy Ruiz, the dog days of August are freighted with the weight of what might have been. He is allowed to practice with his teammates, but then he has to leave the ballpark before the game begins, a journey that seems to sting more every single night. After so many years of frustration, this had been the breakthrough season. Everyone knew it. He had loved hearing the sense of anticipation and excitement when he talked on the phone with his father in Ohio and his grandmother, Luz, back in the little apartment in the Bronx. He was feeling great at the plate, brimming with confidence. The doubts and disappointments had given way to a reemergence of his boyhood dream, so close he could taste it. Now that taste could not be more bitter.

For his part, Rafael Palmeiro returns to the Orioles later in 2005 and plays just seven more games. One day in Toronto he wears earplugs to block out the booing. He vehemently denies ever knowingly taking steroids. Palmeiro never officially retires but exits the game quietly with 3,020 hits and 569 home runs. He goes into an all but complete exile from the game, making very few public comments. One of those few comes in June 2006, when he tells the *Baltimore Sun*, "The tragedy of all of this is that it happened to me, and it shouldn't have happened. It ruined my life and my career. That's the tragedy of this. Three thousand, it's just a number. It's just a game. The other deals with my life and my livelihood and my family and all that I stand for. All of that is gone."

The similarities between first basemen Raffy and Randy are striking. Still, there is at least one dramatic difference. Over the course of his baseball career, Rafael Palmeiro made over $89 million.

The Three Hardest Outs in the Game

Portland, Oregon; Leyden, Massachusetts

Broadcasting on the evening of July 13, Dave Barnett tells his audience: "Tonight, fans will be treated to the best in minor league baseball. It's the 2005 Triple-A All-Star Game presented in stunning high definition on ESPN2. . . . It is one level below, one phone call away from The Show. There are prospects and journeymen, phenoms and veterans, all with one goal in mind. Most future stars make their last minor league stop in Triple-A, one final plateau before they can call themselves major leaguers. The Triple-A All-Star Game has played host to many of baseball's brightest stars before they shined on the national stage."

● For Brad Baker, it was an honor to be named to the Pacific Coast League All-Star team. It would be cool to play in a game on ESPN2 with some of the league's rising stars, guys like B. J. Upton and Ian Kinsler. But just one day after receiving the invitation on June 22, Brad began to have second thoughts. He wanted to get home to see his grandfather one final time.

Although Donald had been symptom-free when Brad departed for spring training in February, the cancer had coursed through his body with savage speed. Whenever Brad spoke to his parents, or his uncle Jeff, or his grandmother Irene, the picture they painted was bleak. There was no more walking down the hill to sweep the floors at the Pearl Rhodes Elementary School, no more heading out to the pasture to feed Purdy, his favorite cow. And there was no way Donald was going to hang on for bear hunting season in the fall. It was at best a matter of a few weeks.

So Brad said a polite thanks but no thanks, and the league gave his All-Star spot to teammate J. J. Furmaniak.

That best-laid plan, though, didn't work out. Donald took his last breath in the wee hours of Saturday, July 2. For his eldest grandson, there was no making it back.

Brad proceeded to have his best week of the season, with five scoreless outings and four saves. He capped the first half with his twenty-fifth save on Gilligan's Island Night, July 7, and then his twenty-sixth to close out the first half on "Proud to Be a Padre Day" on Sunday the tenth. He came to the All-Star break with twice as many saves as any other pitcher in the Pacific Coast League, and just six away from the league record for an entire season.

● The next day Brad flies home, fraught as home now is with family loss and the quiet fraying of his marriage with Ashley. It is a world he is still drawn to; the closeness of family, the serenity and wildness of the landscape are imprinted on his soul.

His mom, Vicki, and sister, Jill, pick him up at the airport in Windsor Locks, Connecticut, and they drive up to Massachusetts. The beckoning green of Franklin County is all so familiar. The stone walls. The hardwood forests. Cortlands and McIntoshes ripening on gnarled branches. Wheels of hay specking the pastures. Crickets whirring. Red-tailed hawks riding the thermals. The *Greenfield Recorder* curled in a roadside chute beside daylilies, brown-eyed Susans, and the first bittersweet sprays of goldenrod.

They drive past the covered bridge where Jeff made his fateful dive, past the elementary school with its wild raspberries growing by the basketball court, and up Baker Hill. They slow as they pass his grandmother Irene's house with its neatly stacked cordwood, and Jeff's with its swing set out front for Brad's cousins Kyle and Brooke, and then turn into the gravel driveway that has always been home. There are the fishing poles on the porch, the deer racks and bear pelt on the living room wall, the loft up above he had shared with brother Colby still lined with game balls in cases.

He spends two days up on Baker Hill, the nights down with Ashley and her parents in neighboring Bernardston. On Tuesday morning the family descends on Irene's house, as Brad peers around the corner and announces, "Colby wants pancakes." It is an old joke, the same thing Brad has said for years, but Irene laughs heartily and hugs her grandson. He has always been Irene's golden boy. To Irene, who had been so devastated by Jeff's injury, watching Bradley grow up before her eyes had been a thing of wonder. She often says, "It's like the Lord put him in our family."

That evening Brad and Ashley sit at Uncle Jeff's watching the Major League All-Star Game from Detroit. It has been a rough year for the sport, sullied by the steroids hearings in March, but the midsummer classic still casts its spell up on Baker Hill, with the game's brightest stars on the screen: A-Rod and Big Papi, Manny and Roger the Rocket.

On Wednesday morning, after a family breakfast at Denny's, Brad drives up past the volunteer fire department, Leyden Town Hall, and the Methodist church, down Zimmerman Hill past a dairy farm, and then north on a winding road, crossing into Vermont just a couple of miles from his home. After signs for the Guilford Fair—the Labor Day ritual of rides and sheep shearing and Bingo—Brad makes a left on unpaved Sweet Pond Road. He climbs up a steep hill and pulls his truck into a little clearing by a fence atop some clover and Queen Anne's lace. The rectangular plot in front of him is known locally as Baker Cemetery. Although other families are represented, the Bakers are right there in front: Clyde Baker and Elwin R. Baker, Clayton H. Baker, a lichen-covered stone for B. Baker. The new black granite stone for Donald Clayton Baker, like many of the stones in the cemetery, is accompanied by a metal stand with an American flag, commemorating his grandfather's service in the Navy during the Korean War. The design on the stone is a pastoral scene his grandfather would have enjoyed, a U-shaped grassy field in the foreground and some trees, leading out to a dappled lake into which the sun is setting. Brad stands for a while, breathing in the clean air, hearing the gurgling music of running water from the other side of the dirt road.

He cannot stay long. There is a plane to catch.

● Jeff Baker is sad, as always, to see his nephew go. They are far closer than most uncles and nephews; having lived next door to each other, Jeff had seen Brad grow up. Brad's baseball career had become one of the guiding forces of his life. He had loved parking his wheelchair behind the backstop at Brad's high school games and watching as all the scouts pointed their radar guns at the mound. After Brad's first professional game in 1999 in Fort Myers, his first phone call had been to Jeff. It has been a long haul since, but Jeff remains optimistic that 2005 will be the year. On the night of Brad's return to the Northwest, Jeff expresses confidence that a call-up will come, at least in September, when major league rosters can expand from twenty-five to forty. "It seems like a very reasonable possibility. I'm wondering if he'll get called up sooner. I really am." Brad didn't talk about it much, Jeff says. "But I think he knows, deep down, that a September call-up is pretty likely. There's a possibility that he has just a month and a half left in the minor leagues."

Jeff's most fervent hope all year has been that Brad will be up with the Padres when they made their one swing to the Northeast. He has envisioned wheeling up the ramp into his silver van, fitting in the pins on his right wrist to work the levers for gas and brakes, and driving down to Shea Stadium.

The day before the Padres arrive in New York, they have an open date on July 18. It is no off day in the front office, though, as general manager Kevin Towers makes a flurry of moves. Two players are recalled from minor league rehab assignments. Two pitchers are released. Another is placed on the fifteen-day disabled list. An outfielder is optioned to Triple-A Portland.

And there is a right-handed pitcher called up from Portland who has never before spent a day in the big leagues. He had been named to the 2005 Pacific Coast League All-Star team.

Two days later, on July 20, that pitcher makes his major league debut. Clay Hensley, the guy who spent the first fifteen days of the year suspended for failing a steroids test, pitches two scoreless innings against the Mets.

That same day Brad Baker gives up a ninth inning run to the Sacramento River Cats, blowing his eighth save of the year.

● Ted Williams, who may or may not have lived up to his stated goal of becoming the greatest hitter who ever lived, was an indisputably devout student of the game. In his book *The Science of Hitting*, he expressed his first commandment as simply "Get a good pitch to hit."

Brad Baker has always studied pitching closely. He has come to believe that the biggest key to success is simply not giving the batter that good pitch to hit. Velocity is important. Movement is important. But nothing is more important than location. He has seen Trevor Hoffman become a dominant closer with an average fastball, a great changeup, and absolutely pinpoint control. That is his model.

It worked out exquisitely a year ago, but Brad has struggled throughout 2005 to find the same precision. It isn't as if he is walking a lot of hitters, but his control within the strike zone is slightly off. Instead of being right on the corner of the seventeen-inch-wide plate, his fastball might be two inches in. Instead of being at the knees, the pitch might be thigh-high. If he were throwing harder, these subtle misses might not cause much damage. With a ninety-mile-per-hour fastball, hitters have about 0.4 seconds to react, to send the impulse from eye to brain to hands. But with Brad throwing in the mid-high eighties, there is an extra smidge of time, meaning that fastballs that aren't located perfectly are, too often, flying fast in the other direction. He still has the nasty changeup he developed in the backyard with Colby all those years ago, a delivery his current pitching coach, Gary Lance, refers to as mystical. But without the blazing heat and with no consistent third pitch, his margin for error has become too narrow.

● In times of poor performance, minor league life can stretch out interminably, like hospital time. Over the next week, Brad logs just one inning of mop-up duty. July 28 is Mullet Night at PGE Stadium, featuring a hubcap-tossing competition, toilet seat horseshoes, and a redneck dress-up contest. Brad sits and stews in the bullpen, an eighth straight game without a save opportunity.

The next night, finally, he gets his chance as the Beavers host the Omaha Royals. The Blues Brothers, the cult band formed by Dan Aykroyd and John Belushi, are scheduled to give a postgame concert, and Brad, in a certain sense, becomes the opening act, trotting in from the bullpen to start the ninth inning with the Beavers in front, 6–4. With the webcast playing on Baker Hill, Brad melts down: a walk, a couple of singles, a wild pitch, and then a two-run home run. He is booed off the mound.

The next morning's *Oregonian* is not gentle. The headline reads, "Baker Breaks Down in Ninth as Royals Rally." Portland manager Craig Colbert is quoted as saying, "We're up 6–4 going into the ninth and expecting to close the game out, but obviously Brad has blown nine saves this year, and that's quite a few. But he's our closer, and he's got to be able to go out and get the job done."

It is an extraordinary level of public criticism from a minor league manager.

That night things go from worse to disastrous, as Brad comes on in the ninth with a 5–3 lead against the Iowa Cubs. The inning begins with a strikeout. There is a force play wedged in there. But also four singles and two walks, the last of which forces in what proves to be the winning run. Colbert stomps out to the mound and grabs the ball. Brad walks into the dugout, head down, fans raining abuse on him. His days as the team's closer are over.

● By the middle of August, the strain of a minor league season is usually apparent. Players have been living out of suitcases for months, and most stops on the road hold little appeal. The Portland Beavers had played in temperatures over a hundred degrees in Tucson. They had slept at the La Quinta Inn in Tacoma, the Sleep Inn in Memphis, the Valley West Inn in West Des Moines. They had been to Nebraska and New Orleans. They had taken on teams called the Salt Lake Stingers and the Fresno Grizzlies and the Albuquerque Isotopes. But on Saturday, August 20, they arrive at a spot on the road that lots of the players are finally looking forward to: Las Vegas.

It has been exactly one hundred years since the city was established as a railroad town in the rocky, dusty Mojave Desert. A century later, Sin City is flourishing with its resorts and live entertainment, its showgirls and glitter, the smoky vastness of the gaming rooms with slots and roulette and craps all holding out their tantalizing promise of something for nothing.

The Beavers are not staying on the famed strip, but the Golden Nugget Hotel & Casino on Fremont Street offers no shortage of over-the-top. It has almost two thousand rooms. There are slots clanging round the clock, blackjack cards slapping down, wads of cash being laid down in the faith that some baseball player a couple of thousand miles away might bloop a late inning single to help his team beat the spread. The Golden Nugget is the hotel that provided the backdrop to the chase scene in the James Bond film *Diamonds Are Forever*. In the lobby, one of the largest gold nuggets in the world is on display, the "Hand of Faith."

Ashley flies out to meet Brad on Saturday night, the moon one day past full. She watches him throw the last two innings against the Las Vegas 51s at Cashman Field, allowing one run in a 15–3 victory. Manager Craig Colbert is no longer using Brad in situations when the game is on the line.

They stay in Vegas for four sluggish August days, the end of a year that started with such promise. Brad knows that the Beavers are not headed to the playoffs, and that when the season ends on Labor Day, there is not going to be any September call-up.

As seen from outer space, Las Vegas is said to be the brightest place on earth. It doesn't feel that way to Leyden's favorite son, however. The glittery promise, the vast possibility, the shining sense of what might have been have all started to fade.

13

Goose Bumps
Pawtucket, Rhode Island

The MBTA's number 23 bus is Javy Colon's usual route. Back and forth he goes, driving between Ashmont Station in Dorchester and Ruggles Station on the site of the old South End Grounds, home a century ago of the Boston Braves. This is one of the three busiest routes in Boston, carrying over twelve thousand passengers a day. It is also one of the most dangerous, passing through areas of Dorchester and Roxbury with boarded-up buildings and plenty of drug dealing. Once in awhile, that spills onto the bus, but Javy rarely has problems. He has been at this job for more than five years now, and he knows the ropes. Passengers like Javy. He has a natural effervescence, a slightly gap-toothed smile, and an easy rapport with people from the inner city. This is his world. Plus, he is—like so many of his passengers—a Red Sox diehard.

On this Tuesday night, July 26, he has to roll the dice with MBTA policy and smuggle a radio on board. The Sox are down in Tampa Bay, taking on the Devil Rays, their one hundredth game of the 2005 season. It is a wild one. Javy is somewhere on Washington Street in the first inning when Manny Ramirez crushes his twenty-eighth home run of the year, a two-run blast. In the second he is heading west on Malcolm X Boulevard when the Sox extend the lead to 5–0. But in the home third, as the bus approaches Ruggles Station on Tremont Street, starting pitcher Matt Clement, just two weeks removed from his first All-Star appearance, is struck in the head by a vicious line drive off the bat of Carl Crawford. He is down for eleven minutes in a near-fetal position, both hands over the sides of his head. He is conscious and alert, but he has to be strapped to a stretcher and carried off the field.[1]

Tampa Bay surges in front, 6–5. The Sox tie it. Javy Colon picks up people from Boston, young and old, and moves them from point A to point B. The doors swing open. Cars honk. A siren or two wails. Back Javy goes to Ashmont Station, then to Ruggles, and back again. The Yankees, just one game behind Boston coming into the night, have already shut out Minnesota. After "God Bless America," Jeremi Gonzalez takes the mound for the Sox in a 6–6 game and gives up a pair of runs as Javy pulls back into Ashmont for a twenty-minute break.[2]

He pops out of the bus briefly to get a snack, then returns to hear from announcer Joe Castiglione words the bus driver can hardly believe: "And Manny Delcarmen is set to make his major league debut."

Oh my God!

Javy has known Manny all his life. His dad, Mingo, had played softball with Manny's father, Kuki. The two boys were constantly around the diamond, throwing a ball back and forth. Javy, almost five years older than Manny, became, in effect, his big brother. They bowled on the same candlepin teams at Ron's 20th Century in Hyde Park, enjoying a frappe on their way out. Sometimes they took the "T" to Kenmore Square, and finagled their way into bleacher seats at Fenway Park, hovering over the Sox bullpen in right center. Fenway felt like the place where the game they loved mattered most. Playing for the Red Sox had been Javy's dream, too; that was a standard issue dream for baseball-addled kids growing up in the city. And just as standard issue was the end of that dream. Despite distinguishing himself as a strong-armed shortstop at West Roxbury High School, Javy soon realized that his future was not on the diamond.

Watching Manny come along behind him, drawing all those scouts and their radar guns to West Roxbury High, had been a once-in-a-lifetime spectacle. Javy was over at the Delcarmen family home on Sunnyside Street the day Manny was drafted by the Sox in 2000. "It was," he would say years later, drawing out the word to savor it, "un-be-lic-va-ble."

They stayed in frequent contact during Manny's five years in the minors. Manny often called him from hotels in Florida and Georgia, yearning for details about who was seeing whom, who was driving what. Their families were tight, often getting together for Dominican dinners of yams and plantains, *chicharrón*, and red beans and rice. So close were they that the guy taking the mound right now for the Boston Red Sox is the godfather of Javy's two-year-old son, J.J.

Jonny Gomes is at the plate. Twenty-three-year-old Manny Delcarmen, chewing gum furiously, jiggles the baseball behind his back as he gets the sign from Jason Varitek. Then he fires a fastball for strike one.

Javy knows he has to start up the bus in a moment, but he can't turn the key quite yet. He paces anxiously up and down the aisle. On a 3–2 pitch, he listens as Manny blows a fastball by Gomes.

Unbelievable.

● Down at Tropicana Field, the Delcarmen contingent is going crazy. Manny's fiancée, Ana Silva, is screaming so hard it hurts her throat. Manny's mom, Belen, is crying; his spirited sister, Sabrina, pumping her fists;

a few other friends are whooping it up. And of course, beaming with ridiculous pride, unable to sit down for a moment, is the former minor leaguer, Manuel "Kuki" Delcarmen.

Just shy of his fiftieth birthday, his thick hair tinged with gray, Kuki still believes he didn't get a fair shake in baseball. As a seventeen-year-old shortstop, he had signed with the Phillies out of the tiny Dominican town of San José de Los Llanos back in 1973. He played through 1977. Scrappy and stylish in the field, he hit for neither average nor power, and never advanced beyond Class A. He loved the game but struggled with the life. He decided to pack his bags for good after batting .254 with the Peninsula Pilots, the 1977 Carolina League champions.

"The decision to leave baseball was devastating," he said in an April 2001 TV mini-documentary on WGBH that focused on Manny Jr.'s post-draft negotiations with the Red Sox. "I cried like a child, because baseball was the only thing that I knew how to do. I loved playing the game. I got bored playing in the minor leagues. I knew that I could play at a higher level, but I never got the chance. So I got tired of trying, and decided to quit."

Kuki was sometimes haunted by having let the baseball quest fall short. "I often dream that I am packing my suitcase, that I am leaving for spring training," he said. "I have to battle these dreams. Sometimes I wake up and I have to tell myself that I'm not going anywhere, that I'm here right now."[3]

Without the game, he was lost. He moved to Boston at the recommendation of a minor league teammate who told him that some neighborhoods in the city had become havens of Dominican culture. But arriving just in time for the Blizzard of '78, he felt far from anything resembling home. He worked for a while at an auto parts store near Kenmore Square, not half a mile from Fenway Park. He felt an ache in the pit of his stomach watching the throngs pour into Fenway to root on a colorful Sox team: Yaz, Eck, Dewey, El Tiante, and Bill "The Spaceman" Lee, not to mention Pudge Fisk, Jerry Remy, Freddie Lynn, and Jim Rice. They led the Yankees by fourteen and a half games in mid-July, then coughed it up, ultimately losing the one-game playoff on the home run by Bucky Dent. Kuki was caught up completely in the drama, in all of the immense caring and heartache around baseball. He couldn't help feeling the pangs.

Ultimately Kuki scraped together enough money to open a small shop in Hyde Park at the southern end of the city. "WE FIX FLATS" proclaimed a big sign near the hydraulic lift at Kuki's Auto Repair. He worked six long days a week, walking to the shop, often coming home in greasy coveralls.

It wasn't a bad life. He had always liked cars, but not in the passionate way he cared for baseball.

He poured his love for the game into his first son, his namesake, the one he liked to call "Manelito." Seemingly out of the crib, Manny had a competitive and stubborn streak. He thrived on the challenge of the game. Even in the earliest days of Little League, there was a fluidity to Manny's motion, a whiplike arm action which produced fastballs that had hitters bailing out in fear. Kuki would tell anyone who would listen, "That boy is going to be special."

Their bond was of the iconic father-son baseball variety. The game was the subject of virtually every conversation. Trips to Fenway were largely study sessions: Look at the bite on that curveball. Look at his body language when they make an error behind him. Look at the way he doesn't give in on 3-and-1. When Manny was in high school, his dad sometimes scored tickets for starts by Pedro Martinez. The atmosphere was intoxicating: the Dominican flags waving, the "K" cards accumulating in the stands, the pulsing *bachata* from the bleachers, the matador's flourish on the mound.

The day that Manny got drafted by the Sox was as happy a day as Kuki could ever remember. There had been great days and terrible ones since. Manny's first start as a minor leaguer. The call in the middle of the night from the South Bronx, his boy stranded with two flat tires and a heart filled with shame. The tears streaming down Manny's cheeks when he was told he needed reconstructive elbow surgery. The deliciousness of his first game back. All the while, making it up to the Red Sox was the shared obsession of father and son.

And now, here in Tampa on a late July night in 2005, there he is, No. 57 in the Red Sox' classic gray road uniform, "BOSTON" right across his chest. And there is Travis Lee bouncing out to second base. Two up, two down. Kuki always believed that this day would come, yet he can hardly believe it is here.

● For Manny, the 2005 season was a whirlwind. It had started with so much excitement, the invitation to his first-ever big league spring training, basking in the glow of David Ortiz and company. The newly minted world champs were gods to the fans in Fort Myers. Manny soaked it up. But he also knew there were goods to be delivered, and that first exhibition game had proved an unmitigated disaster. Five runs in just one-third of an inning—against Boston College.

And just like that, spring training began to spiral out of control. His return not just to minor league camp but to Field 3. Girding himself every day for that gauntlet down Edison Avenue. Shagging fly balls with anonymous prospects slated for Single-A. Chafing at the team's claim that he was overweight. Raging at the words of assistant director of player development, Peter Woodfork, to his agent: *Jim, have you seen his butt?*

He had been tempted, sorely tempted, to bolt, to tell the Red Sox where they could stick it. It felt to Manny like he had been at this a long time, entering his fifth year of the grind of pro ball. But he was still a kid, only twenty-three, and deep down he knew that he held no cards. He ran extra sprints on the outfield warning track, kept quiet, and threw hard.

Just before camp broke, Manny was transferred up to Double-A with the Portland Sea Dogs, and his world began to turn. Double-A, he figured, was good progress. This was the high minors now, higher than his father had ever gone. He knew that the Sox didn't rush prospects to the big leagues, but he figured if he performed well, before the season was over he might get a little taste of Triple-A ball in Pawtucket, a mere phone call away from the dream come true.

Portland turned out to be pure fun. It was great to be back up in New England for the first baseball season since his days as a star at West Roxbury High. His people regularly made the two-and-a-half-hour trip to Hadlock Field: Kuki and Belen, his buddy Javy Colon. And Ana, beautiful Ana.

He was on a team loaded with prospects. There was his quiet housemate, Jon Lester; the feisty midget at second base, Dustin Pedroia; and the glittering shortstop prospect, Hanley Ramirez, whose locker looked like a sporting goods store from all the freebies sent by his agent. There was also the intensely wound right-handed pitcher with the gravity-defying hair, still a starter then, Jon Papelbon.

Best of all was the fact that he got to reconnect with his baseball buddy, Charlie Zink. They hadn't been able to spend any significant time together since Zink's first year in the minors in 2002 in Augusta: that bizarre year of a knuckleball breaking glasses and a bat bashing tire rims in the South Bronx. Now they were back together again, sharing a condo loft up in Yarmouth, Maine. They were in different places in their baseball trajectories—Charlie awash in doubt, Manny's stock surging—but after the games, they soaked in the life as equals. They enjoyed the salty camaraderie at Gritty McDuff's and Fore Play Sports Pub, talking trash while shooting pool, their status as quasi–Red Sox affording them as many possibilities as late nights in Portland could hold.

Manny had taken a little while to adjust to his new role, working exclusively out of the bullpen for the first time in his life, every pitch from the stretch. It was a different mindset, less of an all-day buildup, more of an adrenaline rush. He liked the confrontation with game-deciding pressure. His arm felt fresh. He was able to let it fly, holding nothing back. It forced his focus. And while the results were up and down early on, his stuff was impressive. The organizational reports were glowing, and in 2005 that meant the chance of some doors getting kicked open a crack.

A year removed from glory, the '05 Red Sox were bumping into adversity. The pitching staff had been hammered by injuries all year, forcing all kinds of adjustments within the organization, including Charlie's brief and disastrous call-up to Pawtucket in May. On July 6 those shifting tides rippled back to Manny. Keith Foulke, the bullpen savior of the '04 postseason, was shelved for arthroscopic knee surgery, and the Sox reached down to Triple-A to activate a skinny right-hander, Scott Cassidy. That opened a spot at Pawtucket. The next thing Manny knew, he was cleaning out his half of the loft in Yarmouth and bidding farewell to Charlie. He arrived at McCoy Stadium to a pumping handshake from Pawtucket's jovial manager, forty-nine-year-old Ron Johnson. RJ was a classic minor league lifer, now in his fourteenth year as a manager. Back in the early 1980s he had made it to The Show as a player for all of twenty-two games.

That night, with squadrons of friends and family sitting behind the plate, Manny was thrown right into the mix against the Ottawa Lynx, Triple-A affiliate of the Baltimore Orioles. He channeled the adrenaline, his fastball exploding into the glove of Kelly Shoppach. Pitching two innings of scoreless and hitless relief, he struck out five batters in helping the PawSox snap a seven-game losing streak. His next appearance on the Sunday before the All-Star break was almost as dominant: two scoreless innings, one hit, and four strikeouts.

While teammates scattered to the winds for the only vacation a baseball season affords, Manny was home already. He and Ana basked in the free time, spending it with friends in Hyde Park and Brockton and Jamaica Plain. They enjoyed a little taste of domestic life in the apartment in Randolph they had rented back in November, hoping for just this day when Manny might make it up to Pawtucket. The place was not much to speak of—a brick complex whose parking lot was filled with older cars and shopping carts from a nearby Shaw's. They ate their meals sitting on rickety chairs at a tiny square table just inside the front door. They drank from plastic Dunkin' Donuts cups commemorating the Red Sox 2004 World Series title. The cats, Precious and Little One, sometimes sipped out of the cup honoring the World Series clincher, showing a picture of Keith Foulke. Manny and Ana, like so many in Boston, had heard the radio replay of the final pitch dozens of times: "Swing and a ground ball, stabbed by Foulke.

He has it. He underhands to first. And the Boston Red Sox are the World Champions. For the first time in eighty-six years, the Red Sox have won baseball's World Championship. Can you believe it?"

And now Keith Foulke was on the disabled list, and as a result, Manny was up at Triple-A. He had made only two appearances, but in four innings he had allowed no runs on one hit with an eye-popping nine strikeouts. Watching the All-Star Game on television—lots of guys in Red Sox uniforms—it was hard not to get excited

Almost two weeks later, on Monday, July 25, Manny took the mound at McCoy to start the seventh inning, against Ottawa once again. The game was a 12:05 start because it was getaway day. After the game, the PawSox would shower, grab a bite, and gird themselves for the 448-mile trip to Buffalo, where a doubleheader awaited them the next day. Maybe that was why the usually upbeat RJ seemed so steamed when he came out to the mound. Manny had struck out the first two batters, then surrendered a double to Bernie Castro, when he saw his manager storm out of the dugout and reach for the ball. "That's what you get for giving up a base hit!" he snapped, yet Manny detected just a curl of a smile beneath the words.

In the clubhouse after the game, RJ clapped his hand over Manny's shoulder and handed him the phone. It was Red Sox director of player development Ben Cherington, the guy Manny had once hung up on while storming away from his team in Augusta.

"Manny, it's Ben. Don't get on that bus. We're going to be making a move after the game in Tampa Bay, and as it stands now, we're going to call you up. That could change if a position player gets hurt or something; then we'll fly you to Buffalo. So watch the game tonight, and be ready to fly to Florida in the morning. Okay?"

"Sure."

"Keep your cell phone on, and don't say anything to the media today, since we haven't made a move. And one other thing."

"What's that?"

"Get a haircut."

RJ congratulated Manny, then walked with him to the parking lot, where the bus sat, its engine idling. Family members and autograph seekers hovered around the door while duffel bags were tossed into the undercarriage. When Manny's bag was removed by a clubhouse attendant, his parents looked over at him. "Aren't you going to Buffalo?" Kuki asked.

"Let's take a walk," Manny said.

One step away: Manny Delcarmen pitching for the Pawtucket Red Sox in 2005.
Courtesy of Bill Wanless, Pawtucket Red Sox

Manny gets set to throw his first pitch off the mound at Fenway Park as a rookie in July 2005. *Kelly O' Connor/sittingstill.net*

A couple of Hyde Park guys: Boston mayor Thomas Menino and Manny at Manny's candlepin bowling fundraiser for Boston Public Schools in January 2006. *Courtesy of Steve McKelvey*

After a game in September 2005, Delcarmen and the other Red Sox rookies submit to the team's annual hazing ritual. *Courtesy of Angela Gagne*

Manny's baseball dreams were always about Boston.
Courtesy of the Boston Red Sox

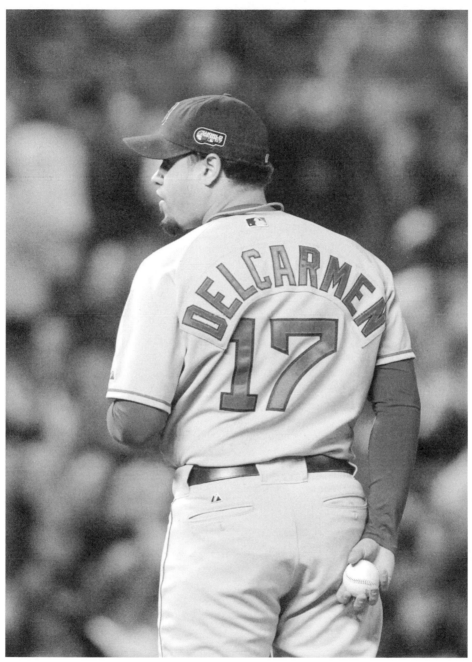

In 2007 Manny gets to pitch for the hometown team in the World Series as the Red Sox sweep the St. Louis Cardinals. *Courtesy of the Boston Red Sox*

The Delcarmens in 2009: Manny I (Kuki), Belen, Ana (pregnant with Miley), Manny III, Manny II. *Courtesy of Steve McKelvey*

They strode through the parking lot and slid into Kuki's car. Manny explained the situation and looked at his father. "Papi, don't get all teary-eyed!" Manny pleaded. "There's cameras everywhere."

That night the Delcarmens gathered for a cookout in Brockton at the house of Manny's older sister, Sabrina. They scrambled for plane tickets, rooted mightily against any slight hamstring pull to a position player, and watched the Sox fall in ten innings, 4–3. Afterward the phone call came. The Sox were releasing thirty-three-year-old John Halama and calling up Manny. His flight would leave from Logan on US Airways at ten o'clock the next morning, and he'd get to Tampa by one.

Except that didn't quite happen. When Manny arrived at the airport, checked his bags, went through security, and got to the gate, he found that his flight had been canceled because of mechanical problems. The next flight out wasn't for a couple of hours, a Delta route that went through Atlanta, meaning he wouldn't arrive in Tampa until almost five for a 7:05 game. Manny called Cherington, who was none too pleased.

He slept for most of the flight, his nerves on hold. Arriving at the carousel for his luggage, he got more bad news: the luggage hadn't been transferred onto his flight. Here he was, off to make his big league debut, a twenty-three-year-old baseball emperor without his spikes or glove.

Waiting for a cab, Manny signed autographs from Red Sox fans who had flown down for the game. In the taxi he checked his cell phone and found it jammed with messages. One came from Charlie in Portland: "Dude, we were supposed to do this together. Don't forget about the little people."

Heart pounding, Manny stepped into his first big league clubhouse and found his uniform hanging in a locker between those of Mike Timlin and Tim Wakefield, both of whom had made their major league debuts when Manny was in Little League. Timlin lent him a glove. Manny scrounged some Nike spikes from a coach. In the manager's office Terry Francona shook his hand, told him to be ready.

Chewing gum ferociously, he sat in the bullpen down the left field line and watched the game's drama unfold: the monster home run by Manny Ramirez in the first inning, the frightening line drive off Matt Clement's temple in the third. Midway through the game, the call came that his bag had made it from the airport, and Manny ducked back into the clubhouse to lace up his familiar Adidas spikes and pound his fist into the pocket of his Rawlings glove, as comfortable as a childhood blanket. Back in the bullpen, he sat down. Curt Schilling told him to breathe. In the top of the eighth, with Boston trailing, 8–6, the phone rang. If the Sox didn't rally, the plan was for Delcarmen to pitch the bottom of the eighth. If they did, Schilling was in. Boston went down 1-2-3, David Ortiz ending the inning by popping to third as a pinch hitter.

Manny jogged in, repeating over and over to himself, "I've got to throw strike one, I've got to throw strike one." With Javy Colon pacing back and forth on the bus at Ashmont Station, Hyde Park homies glued to the screen, and Manny's family on their feet at the Tropicana Dome, he blistered in strike one to Jonny Gomes. The strikeout followed, then the grounder to second.

Now here he is with a 2–2 count on shortstop Alex Gonzalez. The next pitch is ripped on the ground right back through the box, looking like a sure single. The bounce off the mound, though, deflects off Manny's backside to Julio Lugo at shortstop, who throws on to first for the out. It has been a 1-2-3 inning. Manny walks off the mound trying to suppress a smile. That big butt had come in handy.

After the Sox claim a dramatic 10–9 victory in ten innings, Manny's family flocks to the team bus along with a pack of autograph seekers and short-skirted groupies. His mom and dad see Ortiz and Ramirez walking out of the stadium and call out jubilantly in Spanish, but amid the clamor the Sox stars don't seem to hear them and just climb aboard. Manny the younger follows and gets a big embrace from his parents.

On the way back to the hotel, Ortiz says, "Hey man, was that your family?"

Manny nods.

"I'll have to have them over sometime."

● For the next week, Manny is the biggest story in Boston—Manny Ramirez, that is. In his four and a half years with the Red Sox, Manny had become a Fenway favorite. He had come to Boston as a twenty-eight-year-old a couple of weeks before Christmas in 2000, agreeing to an eight-year, $160 million contract with the Red Sox, by far the biggest in club history, as well as the second largest in the sport (behind only Alex Rodriguez's $252 million deal over ten years). On the very first pitch he saw at Fenway in a Red Sox uniform, Manny began etching his legacy, rocketing it over the Green Monster for a home run.

Sure, he could be exasperating. The Sox had seen him stay in the batter's box after hitting a ground ball, and then jog to first with all the urgency of a kid going to the dentist's office. They had seen him opt out of a key game against the Yankees with a sore throat, yet appear the same day in a hotel bar with New York infielder Enrique Wilson. Once he had stead-fastly refused to pinch-hit, a level of insubordination that would not be tolerated by many junior high school coaches. It was in Boston, however, for the simple reason that Manny had become one of the greatest right-handed hitters in the history of the game. In each of his four seasons with the Sox he had batted over .300, blasting over thirty home runs and knock-ing in more than 100. In the magical season of 2004 he had smashed forty-three homers and driven in 130 while batting .308. Then he topped that off by becoming the MVP of the first World Series the Red Sox had won in eighty-six years. So by the summer of 2005, fans were well accus-tomed to looking the other way. Conventional wisdom held, at least back then, that Manny was slightly more charming than he was infuriating, and that in the end, he was worth it.

Back on July 18 Manny had disappeared inside a door in the famed scoreboard below the Green Monster when pitching coach Dave Wallace visited Wade Miller on the mound. The bathroom break ended in the nick of time as Manny jogged back into position while Miller was delivering the next pitch. This was considered just another example, as people in Boston were fond of saying, of "Manny being Manny."

But as young Manny Delcarmen is making his debut in Tampa on the night of the twenty-sixth, things are beginning to turn for Manny the el-der. Word is circulating that night that the forthcoming issue of *Sports Il-lustrated* contains an article in which Ramirez states his desire to leave the Red Sox. Sure, he has made such trade requests before, but this one feels different. Now he is part of the World Champion Red Sox. He is part of a sacred trust. He had damn well better appreciate it.

The next day, the twenty-seventh, Ramirez insists on taking a day off, even though the Sox are shorthanded in the outfield after an injury to Trot Nixon.

With Boston at home for an off day on Thursday the twenty-eighth, the rumors begin to fly that a deal is imminent before the trade deadline on Sunday the thirty-first. Ramirez isn't talking to the media, but the media are certainly talking about him. Talk radio and newspaper columns tear into his perceived ingratitude. At $20 million a year to play a game, he is quitting on the team. He is a cancer in the clubhouse. He needs to go. And yet . . .

Terry Francona benches Ramirez on Friday night the twenty-ninth, and then again on Saturday night the thirtieth, taking him out of the lineup just five minutes before the game is set to begin.

The drama surrounding Manny R. preoccupies almost all ardent fans of the Red Sox during that week, save for one: Manny D. This is his first week in the big leagues, and he is breathing the most rarefied air he has ever known. Ted Williams could be reincarnated in the Red Sox clubhouse and Manny might not notice.

He loves driving in to "work" in the early afternoon, getting waved into the players' parking lot down the right field line next to the finest cars he has ever seen in his life. He revels in the time-honored pregame routines: jogging with clattering spikes down the concrete tunnel from the clubhouse to the dugout and seeing that first shaft of light reaching out to the Green Monster; stretching with pitchers down the right field line; shagging flies in the outfield while sluggers drop down a few bunts, then smack the first round of batting practice to the opposite field; watching four members of the grounds crew hook up a huge hose to a spigot beneath a square of sod behind the mound and spray the infield dirt. The stadium fills as daylight fades. Manny doesn't mind the pregame rookie routine of having to carry the flowery pink backpack out to the bullpen, filled with gum and sunflower seeds. He sits there on the bullpen bench while fans hover over the back fence and tap beach balls through the bleachers.

Sunday the thirty-first is a 2:05 start against the Twins. The trading deadline is set for four o'clock. Once again Manny Ramirez is not in the lineup. The ballpark, sold out as always, is pulsing with even more energy than usual. Making his major league debut on the mound is young Jon Papelbon, who starts the day by striking out the first two batters he faces. In the fourth inning David Ortiz ignites the place with a majestic home run soaring over the Sox bullpen.

In the top of the sixth inning, the clock approaching four, Papelbon surrenders a home run to Jacque Jones that ties the game at two. After a strikeout, a single, and a walk, Papelbon leaves to a standing ovation.

Manny Delcarmen jogs in across the expanse of outfield grass for his second big league appearance. He arrives on top of the mound he has stared at for so many years, and manager Terry Francona hands him the ball.

In the box seats behind the plate, Kuki Delcarmen can't help getting teary-eyed as Manny strikes out the first batter he faces, Nick Punto. An error by third baseman Bill Mueller and a walk follow, and then Manny is done for the day.

A couple of innings later he is sitting next to Papelbon on the bench in the home eighth inning with the score tied at three. With two outs and a runner on second, Ortiz comes to the plate. The Twins elect to walk him intentionally, with Adam Stern due up next. As Juan Rincon delivers ball two, Manny Ramirez walks up the dugout steps. Fenway starts to pulse with chants of "Man-ny, Man-ny!"

On a 1–2 pitch, Ramirez sends a topspin ground ball back through the middle for an RBI single. He stands on first, saluting the crowd.

Terry Francona describes the atmosphere afterward as having been "as electric as you'll see it."

"Just the reaction from the fans, it was like a movie," Manny Delcarmen marvels. "I look over and Papelbon has goose bumps on his neck. Then he looked at [me] and said, 'Dude, look at your arms,' and I'm like, 'Dude, look at your neck."

After Curt Schilling takes care of the Twins in the ninth for the save, Ramirez agrees to an on-field interview with NESN's Eric Frede. The opening exchange goes like this:

Frede: "Where we can hear the chant of 'Man-ny, Man-ny,' the smile is wide here. What about this moment here for you at Fenway, delivering a win for the Red Sox?"

Ramirez: "Man, forget about the trade, man. This is the place I want to be, man. And, um, it's great, man, you know, they love me here, man. And I don't know, man. This is the place to be. Manny being Manny. It's great, man."

● After the game, the Delcarmen family and several friends, including Javy Colon, wait with wives and family members in Fenway's VIP room. When Manny walks in, David Ortiz claps him on the shoulder and says, "I want you guys to come over for dinner tonight."

Manny conveys the invitation to his family and says good-bye to his buddies, who head back to Jamaica Plain in two fully packed cars. When Manny arrives at Ortiz's sprawling Colonial-style house in the leafy suburb of Newton, Ortiz looks at him and says, "Where are your friends?"

"I thought it was just for family," Manny stammers.

"No, no, no," says Ortiz. "Get them on the phone."

Manny calls up Javy and tells him he is invited to dinner at David Ortiz's house.

"You can't be serious."

Ortiz grabs the phone and says, "Do you know how to get to Newton?"

"Yeah," Javy Colon squeezes out of his windpipe. "I drive a bus."

The night is lush with midsummer, sizzling steaks and chicken on the grill, bowls of *sancocho* (Dominican soup), the beer flowing. Javy Colon can't believe the place. When he sees the pictures of Big Papi on the soap in the bathroom, he laughs out loud.

Kuki Delcarmen accepts the gift of a hat from Ortiz and poses with his monstrous World Series ring, his smile so broad his cheekbones hurt. He looks across the living room and sees a strapping young man wearing a T-shirt that reads, "How does never sound?"

His boy, Manelito.

14

"If You Make It, We Will Come"

Portland, Maine

On a sparkling Saturday, July 16, 2005, Charlie Zink stands in the home dugout at Hadlock Field, "Sea Dogs" across the front of his jersey, a familiar logo and the words "Boston Red Sox" on his left sleeve. He stares long and hard at the pitching mound. It is a place where he has known some dazzling success. The mound can be, he knows, the most treasured terrain in sports, literally elevated over the playing surface. When things are going well as a pitcher, you are the king of the mountain.

He also knows that the mound can be a terribly lonely place, a hill from hell. Just the night before had featured the latest dispiriting performance in a season and a half of descent: four and one-third innings, five runs, two home runs, another loss, his ERA bloating to 5.56. Those Double-A numbers didn't even count his meltdown during his brief call-up to Triple-A— the 0–1 record, the 32.40 ERA, culminating in that awful moment in the bowels of McCoy Stadium when he had to fight back the tears in front of Jim Masteralexis and his five-year-old son.

But looking out at the mound now prior to an afternoon game, he can't help breaking into a smile. There stands a paunchy, balding middle-aged man in a brown suit. His salt-and-pepper Fu Manchu is all salt at the tips. The crowd springs to life as he goes into his familiar motion, toeing the rubber, rocking back with his left foot, pivoting with his right, then swiveling around to look at center field, before rotating to deliver the ball to the plate. The fans chant, "Loo-ee, Loo-ee!"

This, too, is part of Red Sox Nation up in Portland, Maine. The emotion in the crowd stems not from the zeal of the fresh convert (though the 2004 championship had sprinkled magic dust on the whole region). This is a more ancestral bond. Some of these fans remember Luis Tiant's greatness in the 1970s. They recall his two wins in the '75 World Series, the shutout over the mighty Big Red Machine in Game 1, and the remarkable 163-pitch complete game in Game 4. They easily summon the flair of the guy Reggie Jackson once called "the Fred Astaire of baseball." Along with that panache had come a rich personality and a childlike love of the game. Tiant was the guy who would roller-skate around the ballpark, or emerge from the shower wearing only a lit cigar. He had an almost tangible sense of soul, a sadness in his eyes born of separation from his family in Cuba, and a barrel-chested laugh when his teammates would strike back at his frequent practical jokes. There were colorful tales of Carl Yastrzemski crawling across the locker room floor to light Tiant's Sunday paper on fire, or teammates hovering in wait to see his reaction to the small alligator they had placed in his locker. More than twenty years after his career had ended, he remained a beloved figure in New England, the one and only El Tiante.

Charlie remembers him in a different way. Twice before, Luis had given him a glorious gift: he had made the game fun again.

● Charlie's first taste of college baseball was an oddly bitter one. Odd because he played on an absolute powerhouse at Sacramento City College, just a half-hour from his childhood home in El Dorado Hills. Sac City had already produced more than two dozen big league ballplayers. Of all their great junior college teams, none was greater than the 1998 squad that went 44–2 and won the national junior college championship. Ten players that year were drafted from Sac City, and that total didn't even include future big leaguers Matt Riley (drafted in the third round in 1997 but not signed until after the 1998 season) and Joe Thurston (drafted in 1999). But even with all that talent and success, there was nothing fun about the experience for Charlie. He found the coaching staff to be dictatorial, running the team through endless bunt defenses, first-and-third drills, pick-offs and cutoffs. It went on for hours and hours every day. "It was like boot camp," he said. "It made you question if you ever wanted to play baseball again."

Living at home was also wearing on him. Lots of his friends had gone away to college and were reveling in newfound freedom. Though he loved Big Ted and Joyce, Charlie wanted to taste a new life.

Luis Tiant had just taken the coaching job at Savannah that same year. To many it seemed a bizarre choice: a former big league star, who had spent almost four decades in professional baseball, leaving a minor league coaching job with the Chicago White Sox to coach Division III ball at an art school. But if ever there had been a pitcher with an artistic sensibility, someone for whom the act of delivering pitches was creative and unique, Tiant was the man. At fifty-seven he felt ready for a quieter pace, one that would allow him to spend more time with his family after so many years on the road. So he moved to Georgia with his wife of thirty-six years, Maria. Their son Luis IV (known as "Junior"), came along to help run the team, relocating from Florida with his wife and little Luis V. The serenity of Savannah and its low-key baseball team would provide an oasis for Tiant for four years.

After his first season in 1998, Tiant traveled out to California to recruit some junior college talent. That's where he found Charlie, coming off his spring of discontent at Sacramento City. If not fate, exactly, it was glorious coincidence. Charlie was all arms and legs then, a rock-back-and-fire pitcher, and he put forth his best stuff from the JV mound at the high school in Rancho Cordova, the tryout pitches smacking hard into the catcher's glove. Tiant looked on, nodding his head.

Ted Zink, the former associate warden at Folsom, had never imagined his only son going to art school, but the full scholarship (dressed up as a "presidential grant") and Tiant's baseball résumé presented an irresistible package.

Charlie was excited, but also hesitant, as the family began the long drive down I-80, through desert and heartland, then dipping into the South. It didn't take more than a few weeks, though, for him to realize he had made the right decision. Tiant "made me feel real comfortable out there," Charlie recalled. "I mean, I was lost. I'd never left California, and all of a sudden I was in Georgia on the other side of the country. I was over there by myself. I didn't know anybody. Louie took care of me."

Charlie loved Tiant's irreverence but also sensed a deceptively calm fire that felt familiar. Tiant was mellow but also quirky and outspoken. And there was within him a yearning that had known its greatest expression on the mound.

● Charlie's experience at Savannah College of Art and Design went deeper than Tiant, though. He liked the spirit of the school. It was populated by original thinkers, iconoclasts, people who hadn't always fit into the social world back home. In elementary school some had found the playground a crucible, a jock proving ground. In middle school they had endured chambers of conformity worthy of a Stanley Milgram experiment. By high school, lots of artistically minded kids, if they were lucky, had found a little enclave of likeminded souls.

From the time it opened its doors in 1979, one week after Charlie was born, the college had been a bastion of the unconventional, a safe haven for free spirits, a point of convergence from so many roads less traveled. Charlie, of course, came with the athletic badge of cool, but his background had given him a deep appreciation for originality, and SCAD for him was a festival of newness.

He made friends easily. Many were baseball players, the guys who traveled around with him on Tiant's magical mystery tour, but Charlie's connections transcended the team. One of his close friends was Marya Milton, an effervescent photography major whose background was almost as unusual as his.

Marya spent the first six years of her life in Yuma, Arizona, near the Mexican border, a place the *Guinness Book of World Records* would dub "the sunniest place on Earth." One day her parents, both of them teachers, told Marya and her older brother that they were considering a major move. One scenario had them hitting another spot with a blazing climate. Phil Milton had been offered a lucrative teaching job in Riyadh, Saudi Arabia.

They decided, instead, to go with Plan B: heading north. After what seemed to the kids like an interminable drive, the Miltons crossed the Canadian border and reached the beginning of the famed Alaska Highway in Dawson Creek, British Columbia. They climbed switchbacks, crossed raging rivers, and saw the heave of the permafrost as they drove up past Whitehorse in the Yukon and continued on. Seemingly on another planet to little Marya, they passed back into the United States in Delta Junction, Alaska, then kept going. Ultimately they wound up in a little city named after a local Dena'ina chief. The five thousand residents at the time made Wasilla the fifth-largest city in the state.

Lots of neighbors worked as fishermen or toiled in the North Slope oil fields. Marya's dad ultimately became the assistant principal of a nearby high school, her mom a school nurse. The Miltons became friends with Sally and Charles Heath, both of whom worked in local schools. Their daughter Sarah was something of a celebrity, known as "Sarah Barracuda" when she led Wasilla High to the state girls basketball championship in 1982, known as "Miss Wasilla" after winning the beauty pageant in 1984, and known, after eloping with her high school sweetheart in 1988, as Sarah Palin.

After graduating from Colony High School in nearby Palmer, Marya returned to the lower forty-eight, enrolling at Memphis Christian Brothers University. A year later she transferred to the Savannah College of Art and Design. At SCAD she became a photography major—spending a semester studying in France and Italy—as well as a college volleyball player, while setting her sights on law school.

Marya became friendly with a number of the baseball players. She would tease them about the preferential treatment they got under Luis Tiant, who seemed to have an unlimited budget from SCAD president Richard Rowan. Once the whole team came back from a lengthy trip with beautiful new watches because Tiant felt that the players weren't getting out of bed early enough. "We have to sleep with five in a room on road trips and stay at the Comfort Inn, and they're sleeping at the Hilton and getting free watches," Marya scoffed.

She was drawn to Charlie Zink's sense of humor, his unpretentious intelligence, and his laid-back nature. She spoke easily about her plans to become a lawyer one day, and sensed Charlie's genuine interest. Marya was good friends with Charlie's girlfriend at the time, Naomi, and they hung out a lot with the guys on the baseball team, a quirky bunch of misfits who always seemed to have fun when they were wearing the yellow and black pinstripes of the SCAD Bees. Charlie was the biggest talent on the team, but truly that didn't say much; they lost most of their games against little-known Division III opponents.

After the 2000–2001 school year, Charlie's final year of eligibility, the pack dispersed. Tiant left the school and ultimately accepted a position as a minor league instructor with the Red Sox, where he remained an icon. Marya, a year away from graduating, began to study for the LSATs and headed west to spend the summer with her family. Charlie was mildly disappointed, but not surprised, when he wasn't selected in the 2001 draft. He had set strikeout records at SCAD, but he knew that a career record of 9–17 with a 3.76 ERA in Division III was not exactly the stuff that made scouts salivate. Still, through Leon Lee,[1] a connection in California, Charlie did get an offer to play for an independent minor league team in the Western League, the Yuma Bullfrogs. It was the lowest rung of pro baseball, unaffiliated with any major league team. Still, he figured it would be an adventure. He would make $600 a month for playing ball. It could be a fun summer job before he returned to Savannah to complete his degree. What's more, he could always tell people that once he had made it as a professional baseball player.

He knew right away it was going to be a disaster. Yuma was ungodly hot, with average July high temperatures of 107 degrees. It was always high on the lists of American cities with the worst unemployment rate. Despite some tourist traffic from the nearby Colorado River, the Mexican border, and (of special significance to Charlie, given his background) Yuma Territorial Prison,[2] the atmosphere of the city was beleaguered. His house father worked as a "repo man" and took Charlie out on some runs, going through parts of the city once inhabited by brothels and saloons. Charlie found his host family's house peculiar, crawling with ferrets and cats. He had to step over litter boxes in the bathroom. He slept on a little kid's single bed, his feet hanging over the edge.

The baseball scene was also discouraging. Charlie was the youngest player on the Bullfrogs' roster. There were plenty of guys in their late twenties and thirties, even forty-one-year-old former big league pitcher Dave Johnson. The team was a renegade crew of hangers-on. Charlie sensed that they were not pulling for one another; the success of a teammate made it that much less likely that you might be the lucky guy signed to a minor league contract with an affiliated team. There was absolutely nothing of the camaraderie and free-spirited fun he had cherished about playing for Tiant at SCAD.

Just a few days into the experience, already lonely and filled with regret, Charlie began to reach out to his friends from Savannah. Most of them weren't even aware of his summer plans, since they had come together so suddenly. When he found Marya, she told him she was visiting her grandmother in Arizona.

"You're kidding," Charlie said. "Where exactly?"

"A city called Yuma."

"No way!"

They got together and spent a few hours shooting pool and drinking beer. She wound up seeing his professional debut, which was pretty amazing timing, given that his manager, former big league catcher Bill Plummer, pitched Charlie only five innings all summer. He wanted out in the worst way, even though he suspected that this was the last time he would ever don a baseball uniform. So be it. He was just miserable.

When he got back to Savannah to start the school year, he felt an immense sense of relief. He spent tons of time with Naomi, and hung out quite a bit with Marya and his former teammates. Classes were enjoyable enough. He studied some architecture, some historic preservation, analyzing the paint he had scraped from old buildings, and re-chiseling worn-down headstones in an old cemetery. He purchased a thick LSAT study guide and figured that he, like Marya, would head for law school in a year or so. He didn't pick up a baseball for months. There was no point. Tiant was gone. He was out of college eligibility. Instead he tossed footballs and Frisbees, and played golf pretty much every day. In a few months he would graduate; Big Ted and Joyce would come and beam, and then it would be time to move on.

Those plans were derailed by the ring of a cell phone. The familiar Cuban accent. Louie.

At first, Charlie thought the idea was preposterous: Come try out with the Red Sox. The Boston Red Sox? He had won one-third of his decisions at the Savannah College of Art and Design. He wasn't drafted. He had pitched all of five innings of independent baseball.

But why not? He flew down to Florida and threw for a couple of days, wearing a spare Red Sox uniform with no number. Then he returned to school. The Sox would get back to him, director of player development Ben

Cherington said. Yeah, right. But then, sure enough, the second phone call came. The second trip to Florida. And on April 1, 2002, a one-year contract for $850 a month. Amazing. All of his friends at SCAD told him he had to go for it. Sure, it was the low minors, and many of them knew it was a huge long shot to advance, but this was the Red Sox. This was Louie's team. This was the lore of Fenway Park. They told him that he could always come back and finish his degree, that he didn't want to face the regret of knowing he hadn't tried.

On Thursday, May 23, 2002, ten days before the SCAD graduation, the Red Sox' Single-A team in the South Atlantic League, the Augusta Green-Jackets, played at Lake Olmstead Stadium against the Savannah Sand Gnats. It was a "Thirsty Thursday" promotion, common in the minors, and Charlie's friends, including Naomi and Marya and lots of teammates, descended en masse, thirst intact. Two of them were chosen for a "rat race" before one inning, placed inside two gigantic plastic balls in center field and told to race to third base. Instead they made a beeline for the mound and almost knocked over the pitcher taking his warm-ups. Charlie Zink laughed out loud and delivered two and two-thirds innings of scoreless relief.

Afterward, his friends gathered round and told him that they would miss him at graduation, but if he ever made it up to the Sox, they would be cheering from up close. "If you make it," they said, "we will come."

● Maybe it's not like working in a lighthouse or living in a monastery, but there is plenty of time to think in the minor leagues. Even arriving three hours before game time, figuring three for the game and another hour at the ballpark afterwards, you find there is a lot of day left. Eastern League cities like New Britain, Connecticut, Akron, Ohio, and Altoona, Pennsylvania, are, for all their civic virtues, hardly places where talented, ambitious men in their twenties would choose to hang out. Unless the players want to fork over cab fare, they are mostly confined to the hotels anyway, the antiseptic lobbies of Holiday Inn Expresses and Days Inns. For some non-ballplayers who travel rarely, a few nights in such a place can be a refreshing break from routine; for those who live the minor league grind, they become a blur of blandness, separated one from the other by hours and hours on a bus.

The games, often contemplative and slow-moving affairs themselves (this being baseball), are nevertheless the sport's sharpening stone. These are the grounds where young men put on display what for a great many of them is their most recognized ability, the thing that has, historically, fueled their self-esteem like nothing else: playing baseball. There is a whole scene around the game—the kids seeking autographs, the old folks basking in stories of a bygone day, the groupies looking for love and a ticket, perhaps, to a more promising future. But it is the nine innings of the game's subtly unfolding challenges that provide the heart of the life.

All the more reason why the three weeks that Charlie Zink sat stewing on the phantom disabled list earlier in the year had been an internal hell. He was with the team—the Portland Sea Dogs—but he was not. He was at the ballpark, going through the motions, but then he had to change out of his uniform come game time and sit in the stands, holding a radar gun or charting pitches. At Hadlock Field he sat listlessly among the faithful. He watched Slugger the Sea Dog stand atop the third base dugout and lead the fans in the somehow still popular "Y-M-C-A." He heard the PA announcer press the button for shattered windshield noise on a foul ball over the grandstand and say, "Uh-oh. Better call Portland Glass." He looked out at the "Maine Monster" replica of the famed green wall in left, topped by its own Citgo sign. He saw outfield fences prominently displaying the jackpots for Powerball and Megabucks. He heard fired-up fans clapping to the piped-in "If You're Happy and You Know It," and he heard them belting out "Sweet Caroline" before the bottom of the eighth. Somewhere along the way he saw the sun set over the third base grandstand.

Charlie couldn't believe how slowly the days were passing. He became, he admitted, a little too fond of online poker games. He drank more than he should. Every day there was the gnawing sense of being alone, of the dream dying on the vine.

If you make it, we will come. During Charlie's four years in the minors, from 2002 to 2005, that thought had gone from being absolutely absurd, to bizarrely likely, to now once again the longest of long shots. Certainly by the summer of 2005, the long-ago mastery of the knuckleball that had elevated him to "Top 50 Prospects" status seemed like another lifetime. He had struggled through a season and a half of woeful performance. Half-expecting to get released by the Red Sox, Charlie called Marya Milton one day. "So," he said, "what's law school like?"

After three weeks of solitary confinement, the Sox put Charlie back on the active roster, the mythical groin injury now healed, and gave him what he regarded as one more chance. There was, he figured, nothing to lose.

There were some good moments. One day in mid-June he pitched five innings of shutout ball as a starter. On June 30 he logged five and one-third innings of one-run ball in a 7–0 loss, for which he was named the Allied Mortgage "Big Dog of the Day." That should count for something.

Charlie Zink at his first
home on the grounds of
Folsom State Prison.
Courtesy of Joyce Zink

Charlie's first sporting
love, tae kwon do.
Courtesy of Joyce Zink

Then a so-called conventional pitcher, Charlie rears back and fires for the Bees of the Savannah College of Art and Design. *Courtesy of Joyce Zink*

Charlie's former college coach, the legendary Luis Tiant, comes to throw out the first ball when Charlie plays for the Double-A Portland Sea Dogs in 2005. *Courtesy of Joyce Zink*

Sometimes minor league life is almost too much for
Charlie to bear. *Kelly O' Connor/sittingstill.net*

Other times, it's a blast. *Kelly O' Connor/sittingstill.net*

But in July 2005 he tumbled back over the precipice. He made three straight starts in which he didn't get through five innings, picking up the loss in each one. The last of these was Friday night, July 15. The next day was the sparkling Saturday when the fans at Hadlock Field chanted "Loooo—eeeee!"

There is one story about Tiant that Charlie could not know. In 1975, Senator George McGovern of South Dakota, two and a half years removed from his landslide loss to Richard Nixon, paid a visit to Cuban leader Fidel Castro. McGovern carried with him a letter from Senator Edward Brooke of Massachusetts, requesting permission for Tiant's parents, Luis and Isabel, to visit their son, who was pitching for the Red Sox. Tiant, an only child (like Charlie), had not seen his dad in fourteen years or his mother in seven.[3] For some reason, Castro agreed. On August 21, in a scene captured by reporters and cameramen, the two Tiant men embraced and wept openly at Logan Airport. Five nights later at Fenway Park, the elder Tiant, wearing a brown suit, removed his coat and handed it to his son. From the mound he delivered the ceremonial first pitch, a fastball low and outside to starting catcher Tim Blackwell. Once a great pitcher himself, starring in the Negro League for teams such as the New York Cubans and the Cuban House of David, the elder Tiant, then sixty-nine, was visibly frustrated. Calling for the ball back, he decided to take a second pitch as the fans roared. That one floated in for a strike   a knuckleball.[4]

Almost exactly three decades later, here is Tiant in a brown suit of his own, throwing out the first ball at Hadlock Field. The pitch has decent velocity and lots of spin.

● In the closing weeks of the 2005 season, Charlie Zink somehow puts it back together. It's hard to say what the turning point is. The reunion with Tiant doesn't pay immediate dividends. His next start, a few days later, is hardly a gem: three innings, four earned runs, seven hits. Perhaps you can point to July 25, the day his buddy Manny Delcarmen gets pulled off the bus in Pawtucket. (*Dude, we were supposed to do this together. Don't forget about the little people.*) That night Charlie works five innings of scoreless relief for the Portland Sea Dogs in New Britain. Or perhaps the turning point comes a week or two later when Charlie is thumbing through a copy of *ESPN The Magazine* in a hotel lobby and sees a picture of the Hall of Fame knuckleballer Phil Niekro. The angle of Niekro's grip on the ball is ever so slightly different from Charlie's. Although Charlie still clings to his unique hybrid grip with one nail and one knuckle, he decides to experiment with positioning his fingers just a tad differently, moving his middle nail past the seam. It seems to Charlie to give him just a bit more command, perhaps a bit more bite.

One of the things the Red Sox establishment has always touted about Tim Wakefield is the knuckleballer's versatility, the way he adds value to a staff that almost no other pitcher can match. In the dog days of August, when many minor leaguers are running on fumes, aching for the finish line, Charlie puts the same sort of versatility on display. On a humid Sunday, August 21, the Sea Dogs are extended deep into extra innings in Manchester, New Hampshire, against the Fisher Cats. Charlie comes on in the bottom of the thirteenth inning in a 3–3 game and pitches two innings of hitless relief, getting the win when Portland scores in the fifteenth. The next night, an off day for the Red Sox, their cable channel, NESN, televises the Sea Dogs' home game against the Yankees' Double-A affiliate, the Trenton Thunder, throughout Red Sox Nation. Charlie's housemate, Jon Lester, has a rough night, getting chased after three innings, and manager Todd Claus has to go to his bullpen much earlier than expected. Charlie comes on and pitches brilliantly, throwing six innings and allowing just one unearned run and one hit while striking out eight.

Six days later, with just one week of the minor league season left, Charlie gets the news that the Sox are going to give him one more shot at Triple-A. Boston has promoted Abe Alvarez from Pawtucket, so the PawSox need a starter on Monday night, August 29, at Ottawa against the Lynx. Charlie is the guy. He can't help but be excited. What's more, he will be reconnecting with Manny, who was sent back to Triple-A two weeks earlier. This will be fun.

Of course, there is the little matter of getting from point A to point B. Charlie arrives at the Portland International Jetport ("One Stop to the World") at five in the morning and waits for his flight to New York, which is running late. The jeans and Tevas crowd from Portland flows into the suits and briefcases of LaGuardia, and Charlie gets lost in the scene. There are businessmen striding belligerently on the moving sidewalks, barking into cell phones; officers in uniform sifting by suavely; some beautiful blondes going somewhere, the hint of possibility. Charlie finds the whole thing amusing, a little bizarre, and then, suddenly, overwhelming. He gets turned around, finds himself in the wrong terminal staring helplessly at banks of monitors, unable to find Air Canada. He retraces his steps, gets some wrong directions, then finally arrives at the gate just in time to watch his flight lift off into the smog.

He calls Jim Masteralexis and explains his predicament.

"You are fucking kidding me," says Jim.

It has been a year filled with poignant phone calls. There was the call from longtime client Peter Bergeron from a parking lot in Arizona, released by the Cubs on the last day of spring training, his pregnant wife crying in the car. There was Brad Baker, his voice hesitant and halting in Oregon, blown saves chipping away at his confidence. There was Randy Ruiz's call from the back of a bus heading from Akron to Trenton, a dream season suddenly imploding.

Jim hears Charlie out, then braces for the call to Ben Cherington. He has known Cherington and his wife, Boston area sportscaster Wendi Nix, since they had been graduate students of Lisa's at UMass in the mid-nineties. They had weathered some awkward phone calls in the years since. Three years before, almost to the day, Cherington had called Jim when Manny Delcarmen kept hanging up on him after going AWOL from his team in Augusta—the call he took when Lisa was having contractions with the twins. In spring training this year Jim had tried to humor Cherington and Peter Woodfork with the "Jenny Craig updates" when a brooding Manny was sent down to Field 3. They had spoken about Charlie in the past, Cherington expressing concern that the knuckleballer was too mellow, that he didn't want it enough; Jim insisting that his California calm merely masked an intense competitive drive. And now it is time to call up Cherington and explain that Charlie is running just a tad late.

Charlie dozes on the terminal floor, picks his way through some overpriced airport food, finally takes off around five o'clock. He lands, goes through customs, and takes a cab to the ballpark. The game is already under way, manager Ron Johnson having gone to emergency starter Juan Perez for the first few innings. When Charlie gets to the bullpen, he sees Manny tapping a mythical watch on his left wrist and smiling. He gives Charlie a quick hug, then lets him warm up. Several minutes later, Charlie is jogging onto a Triple-A mound.

The last time had been a disaster ("I just remember going out there and feeling like I was overmatched, like I didn't belong there"). This time, at the end of a marathon day, he feels an odd sense of calm. He works four innings, the fifth through the eighth, allowing no runs on four hits, striking out four. When his catcher, Kelly Shoppach, blasts a two-run homer in the ninth, Charlie becomes the winning pitcher. He spends the night at the hotel with Manny and several other teammates, drinking Canadian beer and playing poker. Manny scores most of the chips, and the next morning he heads back to the big leagues.

• A week later, Monday, September 5, is a picture-perfect New England day, seventy-four degrees, sparkling and dry. It is Labor Day, the traditional season-ender in the minors. Devotees of the PawSox park their cars by gray cinderblock warehouses, parallel to train tracks alongside hip-high weeds, and walk past the windowless Tommie's Club Vision Lounge, with its advertisements for a pig roast, karaoke, and Keno. At McCoy Stadium they have their tickets torn at the turnstiles and march up the concrete ramp past the line score of the famed thirty-three-inning game. Many come down to the box seats, elevated above the sunken dugouts. Observing a long-standing McCoy tradition, fans place a ball and a pen inside cut-out detergent jugs, which they lower by pulley down to the field for autographs.

Charlie Zink stands for most of the game in the bullpen on the left field side. He had pitched the day before, three innings of scoreless and hitless ball, posting another win when the PawSox scored five runs in the home eighth. Now he hangs out with his buddy, Manny Delcarmen, back again in Triple-A. They take turns tapping a baseball with a bat-turned-putter, the barrel filed down to a flat end.

In the stands, Jim Masteralexis sits with five-year-old Nathan, watching the PawSox lose, 6–0. He talks a bit with Kuki Delcarmen. Kuki tells Jim that a local radio station called him the other day, and that he was tempted to lash out at the Red Sox for twice calling Manny up and sending him back down. Jim swallows hard, says he understands, but assures Kuki that this is standard procedure for the Red Sox, the so-called "Pawtucket shuttle." It doesn't mean that they view Manny as a minor leaguer.

Manny pitches the ninth inning, allowing no runs and no hits. His fiancée, Ana Silva, cheers boisterously, though less so outside the stadium a half hour later when a long-legged college student holding a homemade sign, "Marry me, Manny," asks to pose for a photo with the pitcher.

Pawtucket is done for the year, and the players, toting duffel bags, head out to the parking lot. Jim says good-bye to his two clients. Manny is being called back up to the Red Sox for the big league season's final weeks.

Charlie is told to rejoin the Portland Sea Dogs for the playoffs. He is heading back to Double-A, but deep down he is fine with that. He is, after all, back in the game.

15

At Heaven's Door

Springfield, Massachusetts

Doug Clark steps out of a gray Ford Escort in the familiar parking lot at Springfield Central High School. It is Monday morning, September 12, and it is already steamy at 6:50 as he enters the building, his brain fuzzed with jet lag. He didn't get home until Saturday night, and after seven months out west, his body is protesting: *C'mon, man, it's not even four o'clock.* Still, he knows it's time to go to work.

The days when major leaguers had to work an off-season job—Pirates' third baseman Richie Hebner used to dig graves back in the 1970s—are long gone. In 2005 the average big league salary climbed to $2.63 million, and even the minimum of $316,000 afforded an extremely comfortable lifestyle.

But for minor leaguers like Doug, off-season jobs remain a fact of life. For years he has been coming back to serve as a substitute teacher at his alma mater, and by now he is up to eighty bucks a day, pretty decent money by his standards. That is the equivalent of four full days of minor league meal money. True, he is no longer playing for proverbial peanuts, finally making something of a living wage from baseball at the age of twenty-nine. Qualifying for minor league free agency for the first time after the 2004 season, he re-signed with the Giants for $6,500 a month, from Opening Day until the final game. That meant he made $32,500 playing for the Fresno Grizzlies in 2005—more than twice what he had made in any of his seven previous minor league seasons. Still, the day after he got home he was on the phone with Dolores Crinella, the peppy seventy-two-year-old head secretary at Central High School, letting her know he was ready to go to work.

Granted, substitute teaching is not the top choice of off-season employment for most minor leaguers, particularly at an inner-city high school like Central. It is not an easy place. Regrettably situated less than a quarter-mile from the Smith and Wesson firearms plant, an ominous set of gray buildings ringed in razor wire, Central is Springfield's largest high school. The two thousand students bustle through gray halls lined with narrow maroon and orange lockers under jarring fluorescent light. In a city with the highest violent crime rate in the state, one deemed the nineteenth most dangerous in America in a recent survey,[1] the high school maintains a constant police presence: "Two when things are going well," says assistant principal Tad Tokarz. "Five when things are rocking."

There is not a feeling of menace in the school, but there is a premium placed on order. Teachers are asked to sign passes for students both before they go to the bathroom and once they return—the extra disruption deemed worthwhile by the school administration. And if students are seen without a pass, they are approached by Tokarz or by teachers who have drawn the short straw of hall duty. Always the question is the same, always asked without irony: Where do you belong?

Doug is happy to be back. Central is connected with lots of good memories for him. In truth, it has been a formative place for all seven Clark kids. They were sharpened in the classroom, toughened on the athletic fields. Back in 1993, Doug had been the quarterback for the Golden Eagles when they went undefeated and won a Super Bowl, western Massachusetts style, an achievement that still mattered. The appeal of returning, though, has little to do with basking in past glory.

Teaching is in his blood. His mother, Peggy, taught third and fourth grade for years. Three of his six siblings teach in local schools. Eldest brother Will, his hair already flecked with gray at thirty-three, teaches science at the Van Sickle Middle School, a block and a half from the family homestead on Piedmont Street. Connell teaches math to middle schoolers just over the Connecticut border in Enfield. And here at Central, younger sister Molly has just started the week before as a special education teacher.

Students accustomed to viewing substitutes as fair game quickly learn not to give Doug any guff. He knows what it's like to navigate the adolescent maelstrom at Central High. At six foot two and a rock-hard 207 pounds, he is also a commanding physical presence. His curly black hair, freckles, chiseled grin, and lively laughter make many a teenage girl's heart race. There is no denying Doug's twinkle, his easy confidence. The guys are impressed when they hear the news: their teacher is a professional athlete.

Doug enjoys the kids. He likes their vitality, their energy. He respects their fight. And in ways that transcend the cliché, he believes in what he is doing.

"I don't forget about the type of things you have to deal with at that age," he says. "It's not easy. You're still trying to figure out what you want and who you are."

Part of what he likes about the teaching, he admits, is the immersion in another world. Baseball can be so intense, so consuming. Yes, he loves the life, more so than most minor leaguers. He thrives on the challenge of the game, the daily competitiveness of it. Moreover, he truly enjoys taking in the new cities, the new adventures, the new women. Still, at season's end, he finds something refreshing about stepping into another realm. That has always been the case, but never more so than this year.

This year he needs the distraction, the buffer from a disappointment that borders on heartbreak. *Where do you belong?* Yeah, this was home—this would always be home—but this year, surely, he belonged somewhere else. How could the Giants not see that? All year at Triple-A. A .316 average. Thirteen home runs. Thirty doubles. Twenty-nine stolen bases. What else, exactly, did he have to do?

● All season he had heeded the advice of his manager, Shane Turner: Be ready. Put yourself in position. You're one phone call away. You never know what's going to happen with the big club.

The Giants' outfield had been a revolving door. Barry Bonds, within reach of the most hallowed record in sports, had spent the entire year tucked away on the disabled list, dealing with three knee operations and a swirling cloud of suspicion. In his absence the team had floundered. General manager Brian Sabean had tried to plug the gap with an array of moves: call-ups and trades and waiver acquisitions. Prior to September 1, ten people had played outfield for the 2005 Giants, four of them rookies.

Doug had reacted without bitterness, the minor league equivalent of Boxer, the horse in Orwell's *Animal Farm*, who says over and over again, "Just keep working." Of course, Boxer works himself to death.

Through seven and a half years in the minors, Doug had seen that professional baseball was not a pure meritocracy where people always got what they deserved. Some guys (the high draft picks, the ones anointed "prospects") *did* get more chances than others. Some guys seemed slotted merely to fill out minor league rosters, the so-called organizational players. Some got labels that were hard to remove.

Was *he* in that category? He knew that Turner, who had been dealing with him for a year and a half now, admired Doug's professionalism, his preparation, the way he comported himself off the field. The Giants' major league manager, Felipe Alou, had asked Doug in spring training about his experiences playing winter ball in Mexico and the Dominican Republic; he seemed impressed with Doug's willingness to work.

But in the Giants' front office, where the decisions were really made, who knew? Despite having been invited to major league spring training four times, he had never spoken more than a couple of words with Brian Sabean.

He had never gotten a particularly warm vibe from the general manager's old-guard assistants Jack Hiatt and Dick Tidrow. Just this past March during a chance meeting with Doug's agent, Jim Masteralexis, at Sky Harbor Airport, the sixty-two-year-old Hiatt (a former catcher who played with Willie Mays on Giants teams in the late sixties) had broached the subject of Doug's decision to leave spring training for two days to attend his brother's wedding back in 2001. Wasn't that story old news? Didn't Hiatt realize that Doug hadn't even asked to go? Didn't he know that Doug was merely making a video as a present for his brother, asking veteran players to comment about marriage, and that some of those veterans, without even telling Doug, had gone to manager Dusty Baker? Wasn't he aware that Baker (knowing Doug was about to be sent to minor league camp anyway) was the one who suggested making the trip? Didn't he know that Baker had directed the team's traveling secretary to make the arrangements, and then paid for Doug's ticket? Was Hiatt serious when he told Masteralexis that the Giants weren't sold on Doug's commitment because of that incident?

This was not a line of thinking Doug liked to explore. If Orwell's statement "All animals are equal, but some animals are more equal than others" fit minor league baseball to a T, one thing was clear: it made no sense to dwell on it. Over and over again, baseball had taught Doug to focus only on what he could control. Sometimes you hit four line drives right at people and go hitless. Sometimes you get three hits on bloopers. At their core, Doug believed, major league teams wanted to win. There was money in winning. If he could just prove to them that he could help them win, his time would come. That was the only healthy way to think about it.

Even when the Giants had signed the controversial free agent outfielder Alex Sanchez,[2] the first major leaguer ever to be suspended for failing a steroids test, Doug bit his tongue. His agent, though, almost popped a gasket. Jim Masteralexis fired off an e-mail to Giants minor league director Bobby Evans: "Do you guys think you are going to win that many more games with Sanchez as a backup outfielder rather than Clark? Clark would be a minimum salary guy and give you more pop and the same speed as Sanchez. And all he has ever done is work hard and eat his Wheaties if you know what I mean."

Evans's reply was curt. What Doug Clark should be playing for, he said, was a September call-up.

● Ah, September. Teachers and students at Central High School might greet the word with misgivings, but for minor leaguers on the rise, "September" is sweet music. Major League Baseball rules allow all teams to expand their rosters on September 1 from twenty-five players to as many as forty. Many teams will wait until the minor league season ends on Labor Day (September 5 in 2005), and most squads don't wind up adding a full fifteen players, but the transaction wire is always active. Almost every team will call up a half-dozen or more guys, many of whom will make their big league debuts.

The Fresno Grizzlies' season was set to end in Colorado Springs with a four-game series on Labor Day weekend. By that last weekend, lots of players are tired of the grind. The brutal travel of the Triple-A season—with the road trips that begin on game day with airport shuttle pickups at 3:30 in the morning (so the teams can avoid having to pay for an extra night in hotels)—has taken its toll. The dinners at Subway and Pizza Hut have grown old. The lure of home is profound.

But for those who have had big seasons, there is still hope.

Doug figured the Giants were apt to call up a couple of outfielders, and deep down, he felt he was positioned to be one of them. None of the remaining outfielders in the Giants minor league organization had put up numbers that were as impressive. He just wanted to finish strong, to run through the tape.

On Sunday, September 4, the Giants made their first move, and to many it came as a surprise. They elevated Dan Ortmeier from Double-A in Norwich, a twenty-four-year-old former third-round pick who had hit .274 with twenty home runs. He had never played even a single day at Triple-A. Ortmeier was the fifteenth rookie the Giants had activated, the largest total since the 1996 season.

The next day, in western Massachusetts, the Clark family waited for Doug's call. Labor Day for the Clarks represents the end of summer more than for most families with grown kids. It's still back to school the next day. It's a day of barbecues and Wiffle Ball, yellow jackets buzzing around cans of Coke, the first maple leaves beginning to fire. This time, though, dangerous as hope always is, it was hard to tamp down the anticipation. Eight years into this baseball journey, the grand day—maybe, just maybe— had arrived.

Outside the Le Baron Hotel in Colorado Springs, players gathered in the parking lot, slinging duffel bags over their shoulders. They all seemed to be on their cell phones, making plans. As they tossed their bags on the bus, though, word began to spread: "They called up Julio."

This was astonishing news. Julio Ramirez had had, by any definition, a mediocre season at Triple-A. He had batted just .241. He did hit twenty-three home runs, but he also struck out 113 times, by far the most on the team. At twenty-seven, Ramirez was getting called up for the fifth season by his fourth organization. His play at the major league level had been anything but impressive. In ninety-two at bats, he had managed just fifteen hits (a .163 average), while striking out thirty-five times. But he was the choice, and he was off without farewells to join the Giants in Los Angeles, where they were set to open a series against the arch-rival Dodgers.

Doug swallowed hard and snapped open his cell phone. He spoke to his dad and to his cousin R.J. "You could sense the disappointment in their voices," he said. "It didn't help."

● The last game of a minor league season—or a major league one for that matter—is usually a simplified version of baseball. It's not that players aren't trying; it's just that pitchers don't tend to nibble as much, and hitters often become first-pitch swingers. Two-hour games are common. Guys just want to leave. But if this was to be the end of his eight-year journey with the Giants, Doug was determined to go out in style. "I just knew that there was nothing I could do about it," he later said. "It was out of my control. I wasn't going to let this moment define my season as a failure. I knew what I had done that year was a success, something great for me. . . . I wasn't going to take away from that. I wasn't going to let myself do it."

He led off the game against Wilton Chavez, a sinker-slider pitcher from the Dominican Republic. He went up looking for a sinker out over the plate, found one, and drilled it over the left fielder's head for a double. By game's end he was 3-for-4, putting the wraps on a season in which he led the team in games played (127), runs scored (81), doubles (30), and stolen bases (29), while finishing second in batting (.316), hits (149), and triples (5), and hitting a career-high 13 home runs. If that wasn't good enough for the Giants, so be it. He knew in his heart he was ready.

Doug flew back to Fresno and packed up his things from the two-bedroom apartment that he had been crammed into all summer with three teammates. While stuffing his clothes into a bag, he got a panicked phone call from Matt Kinney, a pitcher who was the team's other New Englander (born in Maine).

"Yo, Doug, are you flying back from Phoenix?" (the Giants' spring training site).

"Yeah, man, what's up?"

"Can you drive my car?"

The Giants had decided that they needed one more pitching arm for the stretch run, probably someone to burn some innings if they were getting pounded.

"Sure. No problem."

Doug wasn't quite ready to head home. He had to close down the apartment in Fresno, ship his clothes and his baseball gear back to Springfield. He also needed some time to decompress, to get the long season out of his system. A first cousin, Tab Howard, who lived in Los Angeles, had invited Doug down for a couple of days. It was kind of on the way to Phoenix anyway. Late on Tuesday he packed up Kinney's green Jeep Cherokee and headed south.

Tab had been out in L.A. for four years now. Like Doug, he had grown up in a large Irish family in Massachusetts, one of nine children. The two cousins were just a year apart, and they shared a bond at the big family gatherings. Both had played college football; both had an itch for a bigger life. For Tab that had meant moving to L.A., working as a bartender and a personal trainer. He would go into the *Architectural Digest* homes of the super-rich, flashing chiseled arms and a winning smile. Sometimes he met bikini-clad clients at the beach.

Tab had followed Doug's career closely and had made it out to Fresno for a few games. He knew that not getting the call this time was a bitter pill, and he was determined to show Doug a good time to help him wash the whole thing away. Doug called Tab from the road and agreed to meet him at Nacional, a bar on the corner of Wilcox Avenue and Hollywood Boulevard. Normally Doug didn't need a lot of arm-twisting to go out, but he felt a little resistant after the flight from Colorado, the time suck of packing, five hours on the freeway, and the cumulative toll of a long season. And while he had grown comfortable presenting himself in the hot spots of Pacific Coast League cities like Fresno, Colorado Springs, and Portland, this was a whole new world. Nacional was right in the heart of Hollywood, pulsing with slick, self-important types. There was a long line outside the door, and lots of attractive, well-dressed, self-assured young people were being turned away.

Tab was there with some friends, and he was confident he could get a few people in. He suggested to Doug, though, that he should use his "player's card" for entry.

Feeling a bit embarrassed, Doug said, "It doesn't work, guys. There's a big league card and a minor league card." This was definitely not a minor league establishment. Pressed by Tab and his friends, though, Doug reached into his wallet and took out the blue card that he had covered in plastic, the one that read "Association of Professional Ballplayers of America" and "This is to certify that Doug Clark, 7-year-member, has paid dues."

Doug knew that if he had the other card—the laminated one with the picture ID in the Giants uniform, reading "Major League Uniform Personnel" and "Doug Clark, San Francisco Giants," and "Please extend courtesies and conveniences usually granted Major League players"—there would be no problem. But what the heck? When he got to the front of the line, he flashed the minor league card and, to his surprise, found himself ushered in.

Nacional is a Cuban-themed bar with marble and stone floors and a sensual Spanish flavor. Tuesdays are "Owner's Nights" with "list only" parties. Doug watched the easy mixing of beautiful women with celebrities like Eddie Murphy and former NFL Pro Bowler Keith Byars. The place was electric. After a drink or two, Doug began to feel at home, catching up with Tab, starting to let loose. But in the next moment the warm glow gave way to a startling sight.

In walked some of Doug's former minor league teammates: Noah Lowry, Jason Ellison, and Kevin Correia. They were all up with the Giants now. Doug had forgotten that the big league club was in Los Angeles playing the Dodgers. They had just suffered a galling loss, a 4–2 ten-inning decision on a walk-off home run by former Giant Jeff Kent, snapping the team's longest winning streak of the year at six. The loss, which thinned the Giants' slim hopes of catching the first-place Padres (they were just five games out, despite a 63–74 record), did not stop the players from heading out to Nacional. Of all the gin joints in all the towns in all the world . . .

But if Doug was stung by the reminder, he didn't show it. According to Tab Howard, Doug reveled in the company of other baseball players that night. "Hey Doug," they said, "you got screwed. You should be up here with us."

He stayed in L.A. through Thursday night, watching the NFL opener at a bar with Tab as the Super Bowl champion Patriots defeated the Raiders. It was time now to go home.

The next day he drove a major leaguer's car out of L.A. on Route 10, through the desert, past Blythe, California, and Hope, Arizona, and then on into Phoenix, the Valley of the Sun. This was where his season had begun seven months ago. Next year when he returned to spring training, here or in Florida, he would be turning thirty years old.

On Saturday he boarded a Southwest Airlines jet and flew into Hartford. His brother Will met him at the airport with an Italian grinder and a six-pack of Bud Light. They hung out for a while, then Will drove Doug back to Springfield, to the homestead on Piedmont Street. There, still stuck to the refrigerator by a magnet was a photo from a distant Halloween with the three elder boys in costume: Andrew as Batman, Will as Robin, and Doug, a pudgy kid in a baseball uniform, his left hand on a red bat.

He insisted on taking his parents out to Lido's. The conversation flowed freely. Doug asked about Grandma Honey and Aunt Bunny and all of his siblings. He talked a little bit about baseball. It had been the season of his life, and despite the disappointment at the finish line, he said he was optimistic. He would be a minor league free agent again in October, and after a full season of shining at Triple-A, there was sure to be some interest. In six weeks or so he would return to Mexico for a fourth season of winter ball, but for now it was time to forget about the game. On Sunday, he said, he would call Dolores Crinella and sign up for subbing. It was good to be home.

He slept in the basement that night, in the room he had shared for so many years with Will and Andrew, now both married, fathers of young kids. On one wall still hung the poster made of baseball cards from the 1998 Salem-Keizer Volcanoes, thirty-three fresh-faced kids starting out their pro careers, all determined to make it to the top. Almost all had fallen by the wayside. Arturo McDowell, one of the Giants' first-round picks, never made it past Double-A. Sammy Serrano, the national batting champ in college baseball at Stetson, was the sixty-eighth player picked in the country but never got out of A-ball. Jeff Urban, a left-handed pitcher from Ball State, had topped out at Triple-A before developing arm trouble. On and on it went. As a rule, Doug said, he liked to look at the poster when he got home, comparing it to the reality show *Survivor*: "You're X-ing guys off. You just try to be that last man standing."

● On Monday morning he drives over to Central with his sister Molly. Doug is in this day for math teacher Elmore John. It will be a day of algebra and geometry, of immersion in the teenage world, of conversation with his buddy Tad Tokarz, the assistant principal.

The scene as always is bustling. The kids are packed into tight jeans, packed into classrooms, packed into the cafeteria at little round tables with orange plastic chairs. Cops patrol the building. (Last week they had spoken to the school administration about the dangers of one student returning; his jaw was wired shut from a summer drive-by shooting that had killed a Central High graduate in what was thought to be a gang-related incident.) The ROTC office is busy. A teen mother or two shows up with a pacifier-sucking baby on her hip. It is hot in the school building, the air almost too heavy to breathe. By afternoon, Doug is beat.

Sluggish that night, he talks to friends and channel surfs. Late at night, watching SportsCenter, he shakes his head in amazement at the top story. Barry Bonds's shadowy season of exile has finally come to an end. Without a second of minor league rehab, Bonds has rejoined the Giants after almost a full year between games. In his first at bat, leading off the second inning, he got a standing ovation that lasted fifty-two seconds, then lasered a double off the top of the left center field wall. The guy is amazing.

Doug sleeps fitfully but gets up early on Tuesday, September 13, ready to go. Today he will be subbing for social studies teacher Matt Dowd, one of his former instructors. He drives in with Molly, turns off his cell phone, and heads to Room 218. There is a cluttered feel to the room: desks filling the floor space, maps (Britannia 55 BC–AD 409) covering the walls, texts with names like *American Journey: The Quest for Liberty since 1865* haphazardly strewn on a shelf. In the front of the room, an American flag hangs limply on a wooden pole. As the day goes on, Doug feels the jet lag burning away, his energy coming back. He is finding his rhythm with the kids. He begins each class by telling the students that Dowd is out because he is accepting a National Teacher of the Year Award (he is actually out because one of his children is sick).

Between classes he spends time with Tad Tokarz. They hatch plans for Saturday: make a few bucks by helping Doug's brother Andrew with a landscaping job at seven in the morning, grab a bite, shower, then head up to UMass to tailgate before the home-opening football game, a night contest against Albany.

After lunch, during sixth period, the second floor of Central is sweltering. Doug rolls up his sleeves and carries out Matt Dowd's lesson plan for U.S. History II. The class is discussing a Declaration of Human Rights. If the students were in charge of a brand-new colony, what rights would they guarantee? How could they set up a society where things were truly fair, where virtue was rewarded, where cheating was punished, where people got what they deserved? Just then, Doug hears a rapping on the door, and through the thin sliver of glass he sees the familiar bald and freckled head of his father.

Bill Clark is out of breath. Ten minutes earlier he had gotten a call at home on Piedmont Street, and had driven right over to Central. He checked in at the office, found out where Doug was teaching, and raced upstairs. As it turned out, Molly Clark was on hall duty, talking to another staff member at the time. "Dad!" she said. "Is everything all right?"

"I've got to talk to Douglas," he said, charging past.

The unexpected arrival of a family member can portend bad things, and Doug fears the worst. It wasn't all that many years ago, really, that he had been living it up at a high school graduation party—singing in a makeshift band—when his brother Andrew called and told him he needed to come right home: their cousin Maura Howard (Tab's older sister) had been killed by a drunk driver. What now?

"This is my dad, Bill Clark," Doug says, nervously introducing him to puzzled students. "He's a retired civil engineer. He put the lights on the Central High football field."

"I need to talk to you," Bill says, staring right at his son.

Doug nods, then hears his father quietly add, "You have to call the Giants!"

Bill explains that minor league manager Shane Turner had been trying to reach Doug on his cell phone, and that he then tried the house on Piedmont Street. The call is urgent.

Moments later Doug is out in the hallway he has been walking for half his life. He dials up Turner and gets some news he can hardly believe. On Sunday, Moises Alou strained his groin while scoring on a wild pitch. Then last night, first baseman J. T. Snow, one of the team's better left-handed hitters, strained his hamstring while approaching first base on a seventh-inning single. Both players are going to miss some time, and the Giants might need another outfielder and a left-handed bat off the bench. Nothing is guaranteed, Turner warns. The team front office is going to meet in a little while. "But if that is the decision, can you be ready?"

"Absolutely."

Moments later Doug strides down to Tad Tokarz's office, tells him the news, and watches his friend's face light up. Tad pulls a calculator out of his desk, and they start figuring out the difference between Doug's substitute teaching salary of $80 a day and his prorated major league minimum of $316,000, just under $2,000 a game.

Time slows down. Doug stares at the phone like a nervous high school freshman with his first crush. The final bell sounds—still no call. He drives home in the gray Escort—nothing. The house on Piedmont Street is alive with anticipation. The bags that have just arrived are picked over like road kill by a crow, some socks here, some pants there. Doug's mother, Peggy, raids her younger son Connell's dresser for more undershirts. Doug places his phone on the kitchen windowsill, where he knows he will get reception. Everyone waits for the call.

When it comes, Doug sees the caller ID from San Francisco, takes a deep breath, and answers. It is Bobby Evans, the Giants' minor league director. He starts out the conversation casually.

"Doug, what have you been doing with yourself?"

"I've just been home here substitute teaching."

"Well, I've got another job for you."

The Giants have made arrangements for him to fly from Hartford on a Delta flight through Cincinnati, leaving at 5:36, just two hours away. Can he make it?

It is fantastic and frantic all at once, the moment the family has been dreaming about for years, and not a second to savor it. After some rib-crushing hugs, Doug is off with his dad in the truck. On the way down to Bradley International Airport, Doug calls Tokarz and tells him that indeed he will have to find a different substitute teacher tomorrow. Can't do the landscaping job on Saturday morning. Will have to miss the UMass game. Sorry, dude.

At Bradley, his father pulls up in front of the Delta terminal, and Doug takes his two suitcases and bat bag out of the back. He goes to check the bags at the curb, accustomed to paying eighty bucks for the third bag, the overweight one filled with bats. When the skycap punches his information into the computer, though, he says, "You're all set, sir."

For the first time in his life, Doug Clark is flying first class.

He shakes his dad's hand, nods at his "Go get 'em," and heads into the airport.

The whole trip is out of some other world. At the gate he goes to buy a magazine for the flight and sees former UConn and NBA player Donyell Marshall, who had once thrown out the first ball at one of Doug's minor league games in Norwich, Connecticut. Doug introduces himself and says, "Listen, man, I just got called up. I'm going to the big leagues." Marshall speaks to him about his own excitement when he first played in the NBA. Moments later Doug is sitting down in seat 3A and watches Marshall walk back into coach.

On the tarmac he calls up people who have been part of the journey. He leaves a message with Jim and Lisa Masteralexis and one for Steve McKelvey, thanking them for years of support. He reaches his former UMass coach Mike Stone and reminisces about the fateful day when the bemused coach agreed to let a young man who hadn't even played baseball in high school try out for a Division I team.

During the layover in Cincinnati he fields a phone call from Garry Brown, the veteran sports columnist for the *Springfield Republican*, who has been writing about Doug for years. "The year I had, I admit I felt a little dejected when I didn't get promoted right after the season ended, but now here I am, on the way to San Francisco," he tells Brown.

When he arrives, there are instructions from the Giants' traveling secretary on his cell phone. He claims his bags and takes a forty-two-dollar cab ride to the Omni Hotel. He stands for a moment on the marble floor of the lobby beneath chandeliers of the finest Austrian crystal. The Days Inn this isn't. Upstairs, his bed is amazingly comfortable. He can hardly sleep.

The Giants have an afternoon game on Wednesday against the first-place Padres. Doug is out on the sidewalk shortly after dawn, getting his hair cut as soon as a barber shop opens. He grabs a cab to SBC Park,[3] fog shrouding the harbor. The locker room door is open, and he steps inside to find a dimly lit place, no creature stirring. He walks around the room and sees the home shirts hanging: Snow, Vizquel, Benitez, Bonds. He can't resist—looking left, looking right, then plopping down ever so briefly in the legendary leather recliner in "Bonds's Corner." Then he bolts up, looks around some more, and finds pure gold: a major league jersey, No. 40. CLARK.

He snaps open his cell phone and makes a quick call to his cousin R.J., telling him where he is.

Finally, equipment manager Mike Murphy comes in. At sixty-three, Murph is a Giants legend. When the team moved west from New York in 1958, he began working as a sixteen-year-old bat boy. In 1960, when the team moved to Candlestick Park, he became the visiting clubhouse attendant. For the last twenty-five years he has been the equipment manager. He's been with the team through Mays and McCovey, through Bobby Bonds and Barry, making all the road trips for a generation and never missing a single home game in forty-eight years. The place where rookies in their first game and would-be home run kings hang their hat is known simply as the Mike Murphy Clubhouse.

Murphy, a tall, bespectacled, slightly stooped man, knows Doug from spring training. He congratulates him, then fits him for some pants and gives him a helmet with his name on the back.

Veteran catcher Mike Matheny, who had once taken Doug out to dinner in Arizona, comes up and shakes his hand. Moises Alou, with whom Doug had talked a lot about winter ball, gives him a hearty welcome. And hitting coach Joe Lefebvre, always a supportive presence at spring training, approaches with his hand extended, saying, "It's about time."

● At Central High School that morning, Dolores Crinella begins the announcements over the PA system in this fashion: "First of all, we'd like to congratulate Central High graduate Doug Clark, who was in here yesterday substituting. He got called up to the major leagues by the San Francisco Giants. Congratulations." She then pauses for a second, before continuing, "Detention has started. It will be held on Mondays, Wednesdays, Thursdays, and Fridays from 1:52 to 2:28 in Room 128."

Over at the house on Piedmont Street late that afternoon, the Clark clan gathers in the wood-paneled living room, photos of all seven kids prominently hung on the walls. Bill had just ordered the prorated MLB package through Comcast, the most gleeful he has ever been at spending $49.95. He sits on one couch wearing Giants shorts and a white T-shirt. His eldest son, Will, comes over after teaching science at Van Sickle Middle School, clutching a roster sheet off the Internet that lists the team's outfielders alphabetically: "18—Moises Alou; 25—Barry Bonds; 40—Doug Clark . . ."

When the camera pans to the Giants dugout, the room comes to full alert. From three thousand miles away, cousin Colleen Joyal exhorts Doug to stand next to Barry Bonds, who has not started this one, a day game after a night game, just back after all those months away.

Since Bonds has returned, the Giants have won the first two games of the series over the Padres, pulling within five games of first place. A win today would cut that gap to four, the footsteps getting louder and louder. Things are not going well for the Giants, though, who trail 2–1 going into the seventh inning stretch. With one out, they send up a pinch hitter, and there is tense silence from the Clarks until they hear "Dan Ortmeier."

"Who's he?" says Colleen.

"Double-A, Norwich," says Will matter-of-factly, crossing him off the roster list.

Ortmeier flies out to left, and the Giants go down in order.

In the bottom of the eighth, against new pitcher Akinori Otsuka, Lance Niekro walks with one out and gives way to pinch runner Julio Ramirez; Will crisply sends another line through another name. Ray Durham walks, and then the crowd buzzes to life as Barry Bonds emerges on the top step of the dugout, bat in hand. Out in McCovey Cove, the kayakers paddle around excitedly. In the dugout, Doug Clark has chills. But on this occasion Bonds does not deliver, hitting a couple of weak fouls and then getting called out on a borderline pitch, leading to shrieks of injustice from the home crowd.

But just as the air seems to have come out of the balloon, Pedro Feliz slams a two-run double to give the Giants the lead, and Mike Matheny follows with a bloop single to make it 4–2.

The stadium is dizzy with joy. The living room is muted with ambivalence. A Giants lead means no bottom of the ninth—no chance for Doug to get into a big league game.

Bill Clark looks at his watch and sees that his seven o'clock tennis match is fast approaching. He disappears to take a shower to get himself loose. Will puts his roster sheet on the arm of a chair. Cousin R.J. shares some pictures from Doug's frenzied packing of the day before.

Largely escaping notice at first is the meltdown of Giants closer Armando Benitez, who surrenders a double and a couple of walks to load the bases with two outs. Then Sean Burroughs drives a 1–2 pitch to the left center field gap for a two-run double. The Giants fans are silent as the game spills into the bottom of the ninth, tied at four.

After two minutes of commercials, the big screen shows this: Rudy Seanez on the mound, pitching to a smooth-swinging No. 40. "Oh my God!" calls out Colleen. Will and R.J. look at each other with wonder and send an explosive high five echoing off the walls. Doug takes the first pitch for ball one.

Then Will looks around and sees an empty spot on the couch. "Dad!" he thunders. "Where the hell is he? Dad!!!"

Moments after Doug walks on four pitches, Bill arrives, clad only in shorts, his torso still taut at sixty-eight, his gray chest hair moist from the shower. "Nice job, Billy Boy," Will says. "You just missed his debut."

While R.J. croons, "On base percentage—one thousand" and exhorts, "Send him!" his uncle Bill watches intently as Randy Winn strikes out, and Omar Vizquel grounds into a double play, Doug sliding hard into second to try to break it up.

The Padres wind up winning in ten innings, 5–4.

● The stadium empties. Doug takes off his uniform, looks at his name on the shirt and the dirt on the back side of his pants. He showers, gets dressed. Then he calls a cab and reluctantly steps out into the parking lot. The day of baseball is over.

For so long there had been this unquenchable thirst, and now finally, deliciously, here it is, the sweetest nectar. His cell phone is full of messages, but he isn't ready to call anyone quite yet. The sun is dropping into the Pacific as Doug gets out of the cab near Nob Hill and walks deliberately past the cable cars, taking in the scene, breathing slowly, savoring every step.

Interlude
The Off-Season

16 | There's Always Next Year, Sometimes

The 2005 minor league baseball season was a mixture of the puerile, the peculiar, the pure, and the poignant.

In New Britain, Connecticut, a between-innings promotion featured a competition of "Musical Toilets," involving four kids and three plumbing fixtures as the PA system blared out "Go Johnny Go." The Bowie (Maryland) Baysox went one better—or worse—with their third annual attempt at an alleged record for whoopee cushion use on the Fourth of July. ("Thousands of baseball fans will create simulated flatulence as they attempt to enter the *Guinness Book of World Records* by simultaneously sitting on whoopee cushions during a Bowie Baysox–Harrisburg Senators game at Prince George's Stadium on Monday, July 4, beginning at 6:05 p.m.," the team's website proclaimed. "The current record of 3,790 participants was set on October 17, 2004, in Kusatju, Japan. . . . 'With one of our largest crowds this season anticipated, we hope to flatten the record by allowing our fans to have a little fun making whoopee,' said Baysox General Manager Brian Shallcross.")

The mosaic of the baseball season included other stories, of course. In 2005 Adam Greenberg was called up to the big leagues for the first time, joining the Chicago Cubs from their Double-A affiliate in West Tennessee. A scrappy undersized outfielder with dark curly hair and an All-American smile, Greenberg had been good enough to become the Connecticut Player of the Year in high school, the ACC Rookie of the Year in 2000 at the University of North Carolina, and a ninth-round pick by the Cubs two years later. Now, fulfilling his most fervent childhood fantasy, he was digging into a big league batter's box for the first time on a warm and windy night in Florida on July 9. His mother, Wendy, sat in the stands, snapping picture after picture to preserve the moment for posterity. There was one out in the top of the ninth, the Cubs leading, 4–2, when the pinch-hitting Greenberg dug his spikes into the dirt and stared out at journeyman lefty Valerio de los Santos. The first pitch was a ninety-two-mile-per-hour fastball that exploded into the back of Greenberg's helmet, the loud crack resonating all over Dolphin Stadium. He writhed around on the ground, hands over his helmet, "trying to hold my head together," as he would explain two years later to ESPN's *Outside the Lines*. Greenberg suffered a concussion, debilitating headaches, and what was ultimately diagnosed as positional vertigo.

(Playing minor league ball in the Kansas City organization in 2007, Greenberg told ESPN that he was fully confident he would one day return to the big leagues. "I'm going to get back," he said. "I've worked too hard in my life and my career for that to be it for me." But as of 2009, which found him playing outfield for the independent Bridgeport Bluefish, that goal seemed far away.)

Another player who got a one-game call-up in 2005 was a pitcher from western Massachusetts named Matt White, then a client of DiaMMond Management. White, twenty-eight, had previously pitched a total of five and two-thirds innings over five games in two big league cameos in 2003 while trolling around various minor league stops over nine years. On Saturday afternoon, August 27, he joined the Washington Nationals to make his first major league start. He lasted four innings and got the loss, surrendering four runs in a 6–0 shutout by the Cardinals in front of 44,254 fans at RFK Stadium. Immediately after the game White was sent back to the Nationals' Triple-A team in New Orleans, whose doubleheader that day against Iowa was listed in the line score on minorleaguebaseball.com as "Cancelled: Tragedy." White joined his teammates in Oklahoma City, his belongings stranded in an apartment as Hurricane Katrina blasted ashore.

(As of 2009 White had not made it back to the bigs, but he had become famous around the game for another reason. A surveyor had determined that there might be millions of tons of mica schist rock on fifty acres of property White had purchased for $50,000 in the small town of Cummington, Massachusetts. The rock, valued at $100 a ton, led some minor league teammates to refer to White as "The Billionaire.")

Most minor leaguers, of course, were not so fortunate. The vast majority didn't get the call at all in 2005. Some would never be back, having played a season or two, or ten. They had come a long way. They were still young men. They had reached the end of the road.

For others, though, the hard hopes still sprang eternal. Pitchers and catchers were due to report to spring training in just a few months.

● Randy Ruiz's bid to become the Eastern League's first winner of the Triple Crown in twenty-nine years fell just short in 2005. Despite playing in only 89 of the Reading Phillies' 142 games—mainly because of the two suspensions—Randy finished tied for second in the league in home runs with twenty-seven, seven behind the leader, Shelly Duncan (who played

142 games). He was fourth in RBI with eighty-nine, just four behind the top spot.

Randy did, however, win the batting title with a .349 average. Along with it came his second "powerized" Louisville Slugger bat mounted on a plaque, joining the one he had earned in rookie league (Class A) with the Billings Mustangs in 2000. Back in the South Bronx, his grandmother, Luz, was hoping to put the plaque up on the wall of Randy's childhood room on 136th Street.

Randy's overall numbers were by far the best of any minor leaguer in the Phillies organization that year. Still, the Phils wanted no part of him. They did not tender him a new contract for 2006. On October 15, four days shy of his twenty-eighth birthday, he became a minor league free agent.

For over three months he twists in uncertainty. At times he wonders if his baseball career is over. At one point he drives up to Amherst, Massachusetts, to stay with Jim and Lisa Masteralexis. The agents have moved to a new house on a cul-de-sac in the woods, leaving behind their home on the common in West Brookfield.

Randy's visit is a good one, an opportunity to decompress and to try to map out the future. Lisa is struck by how playful Randy is with the three children: six-year-old Nathan and the three-year-old twins, Taylor and Justin. At six foot three and 240 pounds, Randy bounds around the house "like he [is] one of them." She sees him throwing a football in the backyard for hours with the kids, then sitting on the couch watching television while Nathan cuddles up close to him.

When Randy leaves, he hugs everyone and heads home. That doesn't mean a trip to the Bronx to be with his grandmother, or a trek to Ohio to be with his dad, or even a jaunt to Belleview, Nebraska, where he has spent recent winters working at the No Frills Supermarket. Instead he returns to West Reading, Pennsylvania, to a small row house on a crowded block that has become the center of his life. During the abyss of his second suspension in August, Randy started pouring his heart out to Lena Covel, a local woman who had graduated from nearby Alvernia College with a degree in criminal justice and a minor in forensics. ("I've got to keep my nose clean," he says laughing.) Lena has straight red hair and lots of freckles around the tattoo of interlocking sunflowers on her right bicep. She grew up in Muhlenberg Township, participating in the Miss Berks County pageant, and crying as a child because her grandfather ("my father figure growing up"—her dad left when she was five) always had the Phillies games on television throughout the summer. Lena listens to Randy in a way he has never been listened to before. She refuses to let him dissolve into self-pity.

"You need to stay positive," she says. "Prove to them that you're not going to let this beat you."

On New Year's Day they pick up the *Reading Eagle* and see the sports department's ranking of the top ten local stories of 2005. The wild ride of Randy Ruiz checks in at number one.

The story brings back lots of memories for Randy. Some of them are great. Some are terrible. He thinks about tearing up the article but decides in the end to keep it. Why?

"To say I was the number one story somewhere."

● By the last week in January 2006 the rumors are flying. The Red Sox are in desperate need of a center fielder for the upcoming season. Johnny Damon, the heart and soul of the "Idiots" who had won the 2004 championship, has just signed with the Yankees, of all teams, a business transaction that feels in Boston like the height of betrayal. The Sox hope to fill the void eventually with their top draft pick from the previous June, an extraordinary athlete of Navajo descent named Jacoby Ellsbury, but he is almost certainly a few years away from the big leagues. In the meantime, the Sox have a gaping hole in the middle of the outfield, and the player whom general manager Theo Epstein has set his sights on is Covelli Loyce "Coco" Crisp of the Cleveland Indians. For days the prospective deal percolates, debated fiercely on WEEI radio. What combination of players and prospects will the Sox have to part with to land Crisp, a stylish outfielder who is coming off a .300 season with sixteen home runs?

For lifelong Red Sox fan Manny Delcarmen, these kinds of prospective trades had often been the heart of wintertime discussions. The so-called "Hot Stove" truly blazed in Boston. As a kid, Manny liked to kick around possible trades with his friends. It was boyish barter, as if the players were baseball cards. Things are different now. The Indians want a right-handed reliever as part of the package, and as talk of the trade heats up, the name that keeps emerging is none other than Manny Delcarmen.

At one point Jim Masteralexis fields a phone call from Cleveland's assistant general manager, Neal Huntington, who asks straight up, "Would Manny be brokenhearted if he were traded out of Boston?"

Even at the tender age of twenty-three, Manny has seen proof many times over of the reality that baseball is a business. But it is a business predicated on passion, and nowhere is this more true than in the heart of Red Sox Nation. Manny Delcarmen is a special case. That house on Sunnyside Street in Hyde Park is just nine miles from Fenway. Players have always spewed clichés about living their dreams, but this really is the only life that Manny has ever wanted. Against ridiculous odds, it has come to pass.

He has pitched only nine innings in the big leagues, but the memories are etched indelibly. Hyperventilating in the bullpen down in Tampa Bay. That first game at Fenway: running in across that familiar expanse of green, the goose bumps at Manny Ramirez's pinch hit, the dinner with his family and friends at David Ortiz's house in Newton. It was mesmerizing stuff. He couldn't believe how loud the booing was at Yankee Stadium. When they were in Toronto, he was dumbstruck when Big Papi told him and Venezuelan rookie infielder Alejandro Machado[1] that he wanted to help them look like big leaguers. They went out to a Lacoste shop and Ortiz bought them $5,000 worth of clothes. What do you say? Thanks?

Even the rookie hazing was, in its own bizarre way, a thing of wonder. After one September getaway game, he and other rookies came back to their locker and found their clothes missing. In their place was a bag containing a costume. Manny had to roll on the oversized pantyhose, don a frilly blue skirt, stuff socks into his off-the-shoulder black and blue blouse, and top off the ensemble with a pointy black hat. From the parking lot at Fenway, Tiffany Ortiz texted Ana Silva, "You just missed your man in the best witch's outfit ever." And, according to Manny, that wasn't all. "We had to serve on the plane. The flight attendants didn't do anything. Johnny Damon wanted a drink. . . . That wasn't even the end of it. We got to Tampa. A limo picked us up and they took us to a strip club. They made us get up on the table. I was hoping that no guy was going to grab my legs."

He has, in a sense, arrived.

Even after just those nine innings, the off-season opens up with unprecedented possibilities. He buys a silver BMW. He and Ana, now engaged, purchase a house that is being built in the quiet South Shore town of East Bridgewater. It sits just down the street from the Our Lady of Sorrows convent, amid stone walls and a gurgling stream, a place visited by wild turkeys and what Manny calls "deers." At restaurants in Hyde Park and Jamaica Plain he hears again and again, "Your money's no good here." Just in case, however, there are plenty of opportunities to earn extra cash. One day in November he shows up at a warehouse called the Connecticut Expo, site of upcoming bridal fairs and antique arms shows. This day it hosts memorabilia dealers who hawk photos of people like Ted Williams, John Havlicek, and, inexplicably, Jamie Lee Curtis. Red Sox fans young and old shake Manny's big right hand, pose for photos, tell him how proud they are. Afterward Jim Masteralexis whisks his client behind a blue and white curtain and starts counting out from a huge wad of bills. Manny is now commanding $3,000 for a two-hour signing.

● About 7:00 on Thursday morning, November 24, Manny is awakened from a deep sleep by the cell phone he had forgotten to turn off.

"What?" he mumbles.

"I just wanted to be the first to say 'Happy Thanksgiving!'" It is Charlie Zink's drunken voice greeting him from California.

"Dude, do you know what time it is?" Manny shouts. "Get some sleep!"

Charlie comes east for a few days in early January, just before the trade rumors begin to fly. Manny meets him at Logan, showing off the new BMW, and puts Charlie to work right away, hoisting boxes onto a U-Haul truck and helping Manny move from the apartment in Randolph to the new house. He doesn't have a ton of stuff. There is the remote-control car that Manny races at seventy miles an hour, the remote-control helicopter he is looking forward to flying out in the open fields, piles of video games, mounds of sports equipment. One of the first pieces of furniture set up in the new house is the Ping-Pong table upstairs in what Ana calls the "man room." It sits next to a mural of Manny on the mound for the Sox, ticket stubs from his first big league game and first game at Fenway tucked into the frame.

The next morning, Saturday, January 6, they meet Jonathan Papelbon, Bronson Arroyo, and a few others outside Fenway Park at the popular entertainment complex known as Jillian's. As part of the "New Stars for Young Stars" Jimmy Fund event, they play pool in the morning with a number of kids with cancer. Then comes the fundraiser autograph session, the platinum tier tickets (including lunch and a game jersey) going for $149. Charlie sits at a table with Manny and Jim Masteralexis as the line snakes out the door. Charlie marvels at the reaction Manny is getting. In the afternoon he walks with Jim through the Back Bay on swanky Newbury Street, breathing in the sense of possibility should he ever master the knuckleball.

The next day is more of the same. They go to the World of Wheels, and Charlie pockets $1,000 for signing with his friend. (Unbeknownst to Charlie, the money came from Manny.) They are busy for two hours, then pose for photos with the other featured guests, long-legged women in high heels who lie languorously across the hoods of hot rods, their two-piece tops featuring a lone white star atop each ample right breast. Charlie Zink, the flutterballing former art school student, is hanging out with members of the "Texas Bikini Team." He could get used to this.

• He left in a gorilla suit. Back on Halloween, Red Sox Boy Wonder general manager Theo Epstein escaped Fenway Park in costume. Just thirty-one, the Boston native and lifelong Sox fan had already delivered a World Series championship after that little eighty-six-year hiatus. But after a grinding 2005 season that saw Boston fall just short of the playoffs, amid unrelenting scrutiny of his private life and some backstage bickering in the front office, Theo stepped away, saying that he couldn't be "all in."

He couldn't be all out, either. Just two and a half months later, toward the end of January, he returned, reclaiming the post from co–general managers Ben Cherington and Jed Hoyer. His first order of business, his first transaction, would be to acquire a center fielder to replace Johnny Damon. The Coco Crisp rumors filled the airwaves.

Jim Masteralexis had introduced himself to Epstein back at the New England College All-Star Game at Fenway just before the draft in June. Still, Jim recognizes his place, and knows he has to be careful about not calling Theo's cell phone with casual business. This time feels different.

"Theo," Jim says, "first of all, welcome back."

"Thank you."

Jim then explains that he is helping to organize a bowling event with Manny Delcarmen that is a fundraiser for the Boston Public Schools in a few days. "So I was just wondering if I should be contacting some bowling alleys in Cleveland, Ohio."

There is a pause.

"Jim, tell Manny that he's not going anywhere. We really like him. Tell him to have a good bowling event, and we'll see him in spring training."

It is hard to believe that it's almost that time. For Manny, 2005 spring training feels like a lifetime ago: the five runs against Boston College, stewing at Field 3 with the Wilmington work group, the "Jenny Craig updates." Before flying down to Florida for the beginning of the 2006 season, though, Manny heads over to the candlepin bowling lanes on Hyde Park Avenue where he used to bowl in leagues with his father, the former minor leaguer. Ron Covitz's ice cream–bowling establishment is less than a mile from both Kuki's Auto Repair and the old family home on Sunnyside Avenue. The familiar ten lanes are there, same as ever. The famous frappes. The Keno tickets for sale, just as always. The handwritten posters saluting the people who had whipped the three-pound balls down the lanes effectively enough to make the "Women's 150 Club" or the "Men's 165 Club."

Ron Covitz, a plump gray-haired man whose father opened this business back in 1962, practically gushes with pride. He talks about the way

Manny "led our junior boys team to two state championships." According to Covitz, Manny's ascent to the Red Sox is a seismic event in the neighborhood: "More than anything else, it's a local kid. A local kid going to a Boston public school made it big. That's really, really exciting for everybody here."

Another local Hyde Park resident pops in for a while. Recently elected to his fourth term as Boston's mayor, Tom Menino is happy to deflect attention from the recent spate of gun violence in the city and heap some praise on Manny: "We need more athletes to be role models."

Dental technician Sabrina Delcarmen talks about her brother's volatility as a kid and the uncanny bond he had with their father: "My brother does not work without my father. He knows what it's like to go through the minor leagues. He knows the heart and soul."

Fiancée Ana Silva watches Manny flit around from lane to lane, laughing with people he has known since he was a child. He sends balls blazing down the lane with explosive speed, his follow-through bringing his pitching arm way up over his head as the pins clatter. His brown curls are pearled with sweat, his smile constant.

"It could be ten years from now," Ana says. "He could be making millions of dollars. He'll still be in here with his friends."

After a while Manny comes over to chat with his agents Steve McKelvey and Jim Masteralexis. (Lisa is back in Amherst with the kids.) He looks over the raffle prizes: the signed David Ortiz bat in the yellow triangular DHL box; the signed baseball from Manny Ramirez; the certificate offering the opportunity to be a Red Sox bat boy for a day—something he would have loved to do as a kid.

Jim hands Manny a blue Sharpie, and he begins to sign glossy photos of a certain rookie right-hander pitching from the mound at Fenway.

MBTA bus driver Javy Colon, wearing a gray Sox World Series sweatshirt beneath his beige Red Sox cargo hat with both flaps up, smiles broadly to reveal a big gap in his front teeth. Long ago he, too, played baseball at West Roxbury High School, and like Manny he entertained ideas of one day playing for the Sox. "I like my job," he says, "but baseball: I would love to do that. For him to be able to do that is unbelievable."

● This is not the way Matt Torra expected his 2005 season to end. The year had started off as a magical ride. He had emerged as one of the best college pitchers in America. The scouts had flocked to the University of Massachusetts to see his ninety-three-mile-per-hour heat, his hammer curve, his pinpoint control. Preseason projections of being drafted in the fifth or sixth round had been blown away as he showed a capacity to keep his velocity late in games, well past a hundred pitches.

And if he hadn't quite been selected in the middle of the first round as Peter Gammons had forecast, he still had been the thirty-first pick in the whole country, good enough for a bonus of a million dollars. He had signed quickly and flown out to the Northwest to begin his new life, living in Cynthia Keur's basement and launching a pro career that, he felt confident, was destined for the big leagues.

But three months to the day from that flight, he sits on a hospital bed in Tucson, preparing for surgery on his precious right shoulder. Matt knows enough about pitching to realize that there are some types of surgery to pitchers' arms that have a very high success rate. For instance, the reconstruction of the ulnar collateral ligament in the elbow—Tommy John surgery—leads to full recovery in 85 percent of cases. In quite a few of these cases, including Manny Delcarmen's, the pitcher winds up throwing harder than he did before the surgery. Shoulder surgery is trickier terrain. This is especially true when it involves the labrum, the critical shock absorber and connective structure in the back of the shoulder. Just the year before, baseball injury guru Will Carroll had written an article for *Slate* magazine in which he described the torn labrum as a "fearsome modern baseball injury" that "almost without fail . . . will destroy a pitcher's career." Carroll said that "if pitchers with torn labrums were horses, they'd be destroyed."

Facing the surgery, Matt clings to a hope that because his injury is a "tiny, tiny tear," he might have a chance to get back on track. Still, he admits to some fear. He has just turned twenty-two, and he wonders, "Am I going to come back to what I used to be?"

● On one level, it is awkward for Brad Baker to come home to Leyden after the 2005 season. Partly that is because his year with the Portland Beavers felt like a failure to him. Sure, he led the Pacific Coast League in saves with twenty-seven. Yes, he was named to the league's All-Star team. Still, he knows in his heart that he didn't pitch well. His velocity was down. His mechanics were messed up. His confidence was teetering. He lost his role as the team's closer in such humiliating fashion, called out by his manager in the next day's newspaper: *Obviously Brad has blown nine saves this year, and that's quite a few. But he's our closer, and he's got to be able to go out and get the job done.* Down the stretch, he got relegated to mop-up duty. Only a couple of decent outings at the finish line brought his ERA down to a still bloated 4.75.

Back in Leyden, he remains the great hope. In a rural town of under a thousand people, everybody knows his name. He is the guy who was going to put the place on the national map, the former first-round draft pick of the Red Sox. He is that "fabulous Baker boy" who got the signing bonus of over $800,000. Sure, it had taken him a while to navigate his way through the minors, but 2005 was going to be the year when he finally broke through. Hadn't *Baseball Prospectus* said at the beginning of the season that he had "a devastating change-up that baffles opposing hitters" and that he had "gone from serviceable to nearly unhittable"? Hadn't Padres general manager Kevin Towers said that "he realizes that it's now not that far away," that "it's not just a dream"?

Well, then, what was it, exactly? At season's end he was dropped from the Padres' forty-man roster.

Coming home is hard in other ways, too. Baker Hill just isn't the same without his grandfather. Donald Baker had been a drinker and a two-to-three-pack-a-day smoker, but he and his eldest grandchild always had a special bond. This time of year used to mean bear hunting and scouting for deer, just the two of them. They could stand together on the side of a mountain for hours without speaking a word and consider it time well spent. Brad had always seen Donald's softer side, the way he kept cows as pets, the way he spoke about the cycles of nature with such reverence. In the snow pack of February, Donald had seemed healthy when Brad left for spring training. By the time he returned to swollen milkweed at the All-Star break, Donald was gone. Now, with the maple trees starting to turn, his absence feels jarring.

Brad also has to face a major scare in November when the phone rings from the trauma center at Baystate Medical Center in Springfield. His kid sister, Jill, has been in a car accident and has been airlifted to Baystate with fractures in her neck and spine and ribcage. It is a harrowing re-creation of Uncle Jeff's injury. Remarkably, she manages to escape any lasting damage.

And of course there is the music that Brad has to face with Ashley—the lack of music, actually. They haven't even been married a year, and already it is clear that this has been a big mistake. Their relationship doesn't have a solid foundation. It has the storybook veneer—small-town high school sweethearts, the Hallmark trimmings of the wedding in the old stone church—but no real connection at the core. Always in minor league limbo, they have never set up home, never merged worlds that in any case contain an inherent clash. Ashley is a vivacious person, eager to embark on a bigger life. Brad is trying to make a go of it in an enormously public profession, but at heart he is a solitary soul who craves his time in the woods. When they talk, they don't meet. That was obscured through years of dating, most of which took place long distance, but it has been laid bare by marriage.

Coming home means dealing with small-town gossip in a place where everybody knows your business, or thinks they do. Coming home means admitting to his family struggles that he has suppressed all season. "He had nobody to talk about [his marriage] to, because he never said a word to us," his mother, Vicki, later recalls. "He really desperately wanted it to work out." That burden, she suspects, carried onto the field. "You really have to focus on [the game]. Mentally, you've got to be there."

Still, being back in Leyden is, for Brad, the truest meaning of home. Part of that has to do with family, the unique three-house horseshoe on Baker Hill with his mom and dad at the top, his grandmother Irene and her legendary pancakes down below, and his inspirational uncle Jeff and his family in the middle house, set back a bit in the woods. Whenever Jeff, the former star athlete, comes wheeling up to see Brad, he is always smiling, filled with the faith that things will work out soon.

Beyond family, what calls to Brad most deeply is the land: the mountains, the river, the autumn leaves pirouetting into the woods. He loves to get in his black pickup and drive past the weathered barns with the white silos, seeing the plumes of wood smoke curling into the crisp air, the dry cornstalks sticking out of the snow, and head deep into a hardwood forest with his bow and arrow. Sometimes he will spend the whole day in the woods without taking a shot; these days themselves are more than enough. And when the ice freezes just enough to be safe, maybe five inches, when the metabolism of the trout and perch beneath is still active, he loves to go up to the Harriman Reservoir, auger open a hole, and sink a line. This is peace for him. In truth, he loves it more than baseball.

But baseball is still the fuel of his self-esteem. It is the reason why people in Leyden have always regarded him as special, the polite young man with the golden right arm. After signing a minor league contract with the Atlanta Braves for 2006, he gets ready to start again.

First, though, he has to endure one of those public-speaking events that, frustratingly enough, come with the territory. He has agreed to speak at the Amherst Youth Baseball banquet in late January. He knows there will be some other local players there, as well as his agents, Jim Masteralexis and Steve McKelvey. This isn't quite the same as the indignity of having to buy the cowboy hat and plastic pistols at Wal-Mart and sing "Save a Horse, Ride a Cowboy" at Padre Idol, but it comes close.

So on a starlit Saturday night he dons a pair of khaki pants, a blue blazer, and a baseball tie, and heads over to the student union ballroom at the University of Massachusetts. There are more than a hundred T-ballers and Little Leaguers, coaches, and dads sitting at banquet tables behind buffet troughs of chicken and pasta. Brad shakes hands with Jim Masteralexis, on whose placecard someone has scrawled "S. Boras." Politely, he poses for grip-and-grin photos with starstruck youngsters, some of their fathers telling Brad they remember having watched him pitch in high school. Then Brad sits down unassumingly at the far right end of the head table in front of a red curtain. He is a young man still, just twenty-five years old. He eats his dinner quietly, then listens to the first few speakers, including fellow minor league pitcher Ryan Cameron. Brad steels himself for the introduction from eighty-one-year-old Stan Ziomek, who founded Little League Baseball in Amherst in 1952. Ziomek tells the crowd how Brad's charity golf tournament had raised over $12,000 for Big Brothers/Big Sisters of Franklin County. He says that Brad ranked in the top ten of all minor leaguers this past year with twenty-seven saves. He asks for a big hand for the local kid who "will be going to spring training trying to earn a spot in the bullpen with the Atlanta Braves."

Stepping slowly to the dais, Brad thanks Ziomek, then speaks, somewhat haltingly, about the past season. He says that he lost too much focus and didn't put himself in the right position to get called up when the Padres had a need. When others got the call, Brad says, he was happy for them. "But deep down I was hurt. That should have been me." In a flat, tentative tone, he claims that he is still optimistic: "I still have an opportunity. I'm young. I've got plenty of years ahead of me. . . . It's up to me. No one else is going to make it happen."

A roomful of kids look up at the dais as Brad stumbles a bit through his speech. Some of them have tasted the nectar of youthful glory. The prospect of someday being a first-round draft pick of the Red Sox like Brad Baker is tantalizing. "Go in with that mindset that you're going to make that team," Brad urges them softly. "Not only just be there, but be the best. You want to be the best at whatever you do. In the end, if you aren't, as long as you try your hardest, you'll be happy with yourself. . . . You should always be happy. . . . Enjoy what you're doing. Once again, thank you for having me. It's a pleasure being here. I hope to be back next year. Thank you."

Amid polite applause, Brad walks back to his seat and waits for the evening's final speaker.

● Doug Clark has been coming to these Amherst Youth Baseball banquets for years. He had gotten onto Stan Ziomek's radar when he was drafted by the Giants out of UMass in 1998. In the early years, Doug's speeches were a bit on the hokey side, even by his own admission. His brothers razzed him unmercifully for the B-A-S-E-B-A-L-L acronym he spouted one year: "*B* is for believe in yourself. *A* is for have a good attitude . . ."

In time, Doug hit his stride. His regular stints as a substitute teacher at an inner-city high school have forced him to develop an easy authority in front of a group. As an eight-year professional ballplayer, he has grown comfortable with the public part of the role, turning in an engaging interview. His years of playing winter ball in Mexico have required him to think on his feet so often that talking to a big room full of fawning Little Leaguers seems like hitting a hanging curve right over the heart of the plate. Though he just returned late the previous night after an all-day trip from Navojoa, Mexico, Doug looks rested and energetic. Beneath his black curls, his tanned and chiseled face almost glows with anticipation. Wearing a blue suit and a vibrant yellow tie, he sits at a table with his father and listens to Stan Ziomek provide the introduction: "Last September, he was at Central High School in Springfield doing some substitute teaching when he got a phone call that everyone dreams about."

Doug practically charges up to the podium. "Thank you very much, Stan. As always, I'm very excited to come here and speak to you guys. . . . For the past five, six, seven years, I was talking about my minor league experience. Well, tonight I get a chance to tell you a little bit about my major league experience."

He had been in the big leagues for all of nineteen days. He hadn't started a single game, hadn't played at all in the field, and had gone 0-for-5 at the plate in pinch-hitting appearances. That treasured first big league hit, that iconic moment when the umpires call time and roll the ball into the dugout, remained beyond his grasp.

But there had been some unforgettable memories, and tonight they pour out of him like sweat in a sauna. He likens getting the phone call from the Giants to having the prettiest girl in school agree to go to the dance with him: "an unbelievable feeling." He speaks with wonder about boarding the flight to San Francisco: "I was sitting in row 3, not row 26 or 24. It was row 3. The seat was two times bigger than it usually was." He recounts his debut the next day, the four-pitch walk to lead off the bottom of the ninth, which ultimately led to his being erased on the front end of a double play. "But I ran hard to second, slid in hard to second, and tried to run off that field like a major league baseball player. And that's what it's like. It was a dream come true."

● A few days after that slide, Doug had watched from the Giants' dugout as Barry Bonds, barely removed from more than five months on the disabled list, smashed his first home run of the year against the arch-rival Dodgers. Later that night Doug came in as a pinch-runner in the tenth inning and wound up scoring the winning run. Friends who saw the highlight on *SportsCenter* filled his cell phone with texts and voicemails.

Doug's first road trip as a big leaguer was to Washington, D.C., when the Giants played the Nationals. A *USA Today* story the next day began, "Once Barry Bonds got past the discomfort of that first cross-country plane ride, he simply wanted to make the nation's capital just like any other road trip." For Doug, that trip was a thing of wonder. The food never stopped coming. Steak. Lobster. Ice cream. Doug kept looking across the aisle at Scott Munter, a pitcher with whom he had played at Double-A, "making sure that everything I was doing was kosher." When they touched down, he was amazed to watch team personnel pick up his bags. He floated through the lobby to the team bus, then arrived twenty minutes later at the team hotel, the Ritz Carlton.

The visiting clubhouse at RFK Stadium was a parlor for millionaire ballplayers. Above the big-screen TV sat an odd assortment of videotapes: *There's Something About Mary, Sea Biscuit, The Manchurian Candidate, A Few Good Men, Forrest Gump.* By the food spread in front there were major leaguers playing cribbage and chess and backgammon. Four or five Panasonic laptops drew only idle interest, showing the release times of Washington's catchers. A young clubhouse assistant unscrewed bottles of Aquafina and microwaved plates of chicken. In one corner, relatively untouched, sat a child's Halloween fantasy come to life: Dots, Atomic Fireballs, Reese's Pieces, Skittles, Rice Krispie Treats, Butterfingers, Kit Kats, Twizzlers, Rolos, Tootsie Pops, Starbursts. Barry Bonds shuffled to the back right corner of the locker room, sitting in slowly, dressed all in black, to get his right knee massaged by a trainer. Mike Murphy, the team's equipment manager, a tall man wearing bifocals, black polyester pants, and a white Giants shirt with a big food smear, took a moment to stir some iced coffee. Doug's locker was at the end of the middle row. A single jersey hung on a plastic hanger: the MLB symbol over the "A" in "CLARK," the black number "40" trimmed in orange. On the top shelf lay a couple of folded newspapers and a Wilson glove beneath a neatly brimmed black hat with "SF" in orange. There were two bats, Rawlings Big Sticks emblazoned with his name, "Doug Clark."

In the dugout there were blue bins full of David Sunflower Seeds and Bazooka gum. Helmets were stacked in preschool-like cubbies: "Clark" between (Pedro) "Feliz" and (Edgardo) "Alfonzo."

Doug spent much of the pregame time schmoozing with his family down the right field line. His parents, along with some of his siblings and cousins, had descended, as well as his best friend from high school, Mark Gaffney. Doug signed baseballs for them, posed for photos over the railing, and laughed out loud at their signs: "Clark is in the Park" and "D.C. in D.C."

That same day, September 20, 2005, Joe Bauman died in Roswell, New Mexico, at the age of eighty-three. Roswell was on the American pop culture map for two things. One was the alleged recovery of a UFO in July 1947. The other was the seventy-two home runs that Bauman hit for the Class-C Roswell Rockets, a record in professional baseball, major or minor leagues, for almost half a century—until Barry Bonds smashed seventy-three in 2001. Bauman never made it to the big leagues, but his long balls launched into the desert air one summer lived on as a slice of Americana, every bit as present as the gas station he owned for many years on the legendary Route 66.

Fittingly, Bauman bade farewell on a day when the long ball was flying. In New York, Alex Rodriguez hit number forty-five for the Yankees, making his then-richest-in-sports $25.2 million a year seem like a bargain to some.[2] Manny Ramirez, making $20 million a year, smashed home runs thirty-seven and thirty-eight, helping the Red Sox pound Tampa Bay, 15–2.[3] Not to be outdone, his popular teammate David Ortiz (then making a mere $5.25 million) cracked his forty-fifth and forty-sixth home runs of the season.[4]

Shortly before the game in the nation's capital, a PA announcement from drugfree.org was projected onto the scoreboard at RFK Stadium: "Steroids don't make great athletes; they destroy them."

In the fourth inning, Barry Bonds ($22 million) rocketed his 706th career home run deep into section 468 in the upper deck.

● It had all gone so quickly for Doug, but the preciousness of those nineteen days remains fresh with him months later as he speaks to the crowd in Amherst. The entire room is transfixed by his words. Strong-armed nine-year-olds and their balding, well-educated dads lean forward on the edge of their seats. Jim Masteralexis stares intently at Doug, resting his chin in his hand. Bill Clark, who had charged into Central High School that memorable day to find his son after years of listening to the webcasts from Keizer, Oregon, and Shreveport, Louisiana, and Fresno, California, sits in the back, his right index finger poised between his lips. Silver-haired Stan Ziomek smiles broadly with each anecdote. Everyone wants a taste of this.

"It takes time," Doug says. "It takes dedication, and ultimately a word that I want you to really, really listen to is 'perseverance.' That word means the most to me. One of the words I've had to stand by the whole time I've been playing baseball. Baseball taught me to persevere. Now 'persevere' means when things aren't going your way, when you aren't getting what you want, you stay on course. You stay true to what you believe in, and you keep pushing forward. That's what it takes to get to places where you really, really want to be—and places where not a lot of people get to go."

When the crowd of kids asking for Doug's autograph finally disperses, he puts on his coat and walks out into the January night to go out for drinks with his dad, Ryan Cameron, and Jim Masteralexis. Brad Baker politely declines, saying he has to head home to Leyden.

But on his way back to his truck, Brad admits that when he listened to Doug's speech, there were tears in his eyes. "I want to make it so I can tell a story like Doug," he says. "I'm like every kid out there."

Opening Day 2006 to August 12, 2008

17 Going Home Again

Boston

Big beams of sunlight shine through the ominous purple clouds that roll into Boston in the middle of the afternoon on Tuesday, August 12, 2008. The natural spotlights touch down everywhere: on the sailboats bobbing along the Charles River, on the brownstones of Beacon Street, on the scalpers hustling tickets on Yawkey Way.

Manny Delcarmen parks his Hummer in the players' parking lot down the right field line. The kid who grew up leaning worshipfully over the bullpen in right center is now, if not a bona fide star, an established member of the Boston Red Sox. At the age of twenty-five, he shares a locker room every night with the likes of David Ortiz and Jonathan Papelbon. Shopping for shoes on swanky Newbury Street or ordering takeout amid the pulsing *bachata* on the street corners of Jamaica Plain, he is often asked to sign an autograph or to pose for a picture.

Manny's wild days are apparently behind him. He is married now to Ana, his former classmate at West Roxbury High School. There is no more storming off, leaving the team, blasting his tire rims with a baseball bat in the South Bronx. There is no more brooding at Field 3 in spring training, bristling at the team's insistence that he lose weight. He is a big leaguer now, channeling all of his competitive drive into his pitching.

After his ten-game, nine-inning cup of coffee in 2005, Manny spent most of the 2006 season in the big leagues, pitching in fifty games for the Red Sox. He was by no means a dominant force (2–0 with a hefty 5.06 ERA), but he demonstrated an upside that was appealing: a fastball that touched ninety-seven, a sharp-dropping curveball, an occasionally reliable changeup with deceptive arm action. On June 11 of that year he blanked the Texas Rangers in the eighth and ninth innings, then watched from the dugout as the Red Sox came to bat, trailing, 4–2. With two outs and two strikes, David Ortiz launched a three-run walk-off home run. As teammates raced to greet Big Papi in a mosh pit at the plate, Manny Delcarmen, author of his first major league victory, tripped over the railing in front of the dugout, falling flat on his face.

If anything, 2007 began even less gracefully. Manny started the year in Pawtucket, in part because of a spotty spring training performance and in part because of general manager Theo Epstein's numerous off-season acquisitions in the bullpen (Joel Piñeiro, Brendan Donnelly, J. C. Romero). With Ana pregnant at home with their first child and Manny yearning to join her, things went miserably. He struggled with his command, constantly facing 2–0 and 3–1 counts. On Cinco de Mayo, a festive day back in his childhood haunts, Manny hit rock bottom against the Buffalo Bisons. In the stadium where *The Natural* had been filmed, Manny and equally touted Craig Hansen collaborated on one of the worst bullpen collapses in professional baseball history. Hansen took the mound in the bottom of the ninth, Pawtucket cruising with a 14–6 lead. He faced seven batters. All reached base. Then Manny was summoned with the score 14–11 and two runners on. He got the first batter to pop out. The next five reached, and the winning run scored on a walk with the bases loaded.

But from those ashes, Manny Delcarmen (1–2 with a 7.24 ERA) rose with a vengeance. Suddenly he was delivering one lights-out performance after another, dominating hitters for weeks, not coming close to allowing another run. On Father's Day, June 17, he was called back to the big leagues for good. That day the Sox played an interleague game against the Giants in a jam-packed Fenway Park, before a crowd that included his dad and his pregnant wife. In the sixth inning of that game, Barry Bonds moved closer to becoming the game's all-time home run king, smashing a blast off Tim Wakefield. Manny came on in relief later in the sixth and pitched two-thirds of an inning of scoreless ball as Boston went on to win, 9–5.

Before long, Manny became established as a key cog in the Red Sox bullpen machine. Increasingly he gained the trust of manager Terry Francona. There he was, blowing away Sammy Sosa on a 3–2 fastball with the bases loaded and two outs in the seventh in a 2–1 game. There he was, fanning Alex Rodriguez in a tight spot against the Yankees. Sometimes Francona would have him pitch the eighth inning as the set-up guy for Jonathan Papelbon; when he retired the side and walked into the home dugout, he would hear the entire stadium burst into Fenway's unofficial anthem, "Sweet Caroline." It was an amazing thing to be a part of, what his hometown team had become. They were by now a Nation, followed with the zeal of a religion. There was sellout after sellout at home, an entourage of thousands on the road, Sox fans often outnumbering the local patrons in Baltimore and Tampa Bay. A front-page *USA Today* story that summer referred to the Red Sox as "America's New Home Team."

If he was not quite a Red Sox A-lister, Manny was certainly gaining attention. Sox backup catcher Doug Mirabelli told the *Boston Globe* that Manny had the second-best stuff on the pitching staff—behind Josh Beckett and ahead of Papelbon. While Manny sat at home with Ana and watched the All-Star Game in July, he heard Joe Buck tell America at the start of the eighth inning: "It's a three-run American League lead. And it's Jonathan Papelbon, the closer for the first-place Red Sox in the game. Third season, second All-Star Game, with an ERA of under one closing for the Red Sox last year. And after an attempt to go back to the rotation early in spring training, they put Papelbon back where he belongs. And with Delcarmen now and Hideki Okajima setting up Jonathan Papelbon, that's about as good as any bullpen gets."

Manny finished up the regular season with a sparkling 2.05 ERA in forty-four appearances. In Game 2 of the Division Series sweep of the Angels, he pitched scoreless ball for an inning and a third of a contest then tied 3–3. When he came in against Cleveland for the first time in the American League Championship Series, commentator Tim McCarver relayed a conversation he had recently had with Theo Epstein, who'd told him, "Every trade the Red Sox are contemplating, Manny Delcarmen is the number one guy other teams want—and with good reason."

By then Manny had another job. Early on the morning of September 9, he had been awakened in a Baltimore hotel room when his cell phone rang. "Manny," Ana said from the bathroom of their house in East Bridgewater, "my water just broke." After a quick call to traveling secretary Jack McCormick, Manny was heading home. He made it to South Shore Hospital in time to hold Ana's hand as she got the epidural injection, which she responded to by biting him in the ribs. That afternoon Manuel Delcarmen III arrived fifteen days ahead of time by cesarean section.

Little Manny paid his first visit to Fenway Park in October, hanging out in the family room with Ana while some tense postseason baseball games played out on the field. Juliana Ramirez, like Ana a native of Brazil, was particularly warm and welcoming.

The baby did not make the trip out to Denver in mid-October. He was sitting in Ana's lap back in East Bridgewater when his dad came on in relief in Game 4 against the Rockies. On some level, perhaps, he was taking it all in when Ana began screaming in delight a little while later, as she watched Manny pour champagne over his teammates' heads, the Boston Red Sox having won their second world championship in four years.

A few days later the little guy was riding in one of the duck boats at the tickertape parade. And a couple of weeks after that, he was sitting in Ana's lap at King's Lanes, Manny's "Bowlin' Strikes for Schools" having added a second fundraiser to the neighborhood event at the ten-lane candlepin alley in Hyde Park. This time it was upscale bowling at a glittering place in the Back Bay, where Harpoon I.P.A. and Stella Artois were available on tap. Sure, friends like Javy Colon, the MBTA bus driver, were still showing up, but so were some of Manny's new buddies. Kevin Youkilis was there to help out. Curt Schilling, wearing a Junction City, Iraq, cap, bowled some frames with wife Shonda and their towheaded children. Even Terry Francona was in the house, saying, "Manny is a special story, being a local kid. We're kind of watching him grow up and mature into a pretty good young man right in front of our eyes."

Manny soaked it all in, looking poised and confident as he spoke to the TV cameras from New England Cable News and Fox 25 and NESN. At the silent auction nearby, dinner with Manny was claimed for $600. "Thank you, guys," Manny said, taking the microphone. "We've got the World Series trophy out front if you want to come up and take some pictures." Sure enough, out in the lobby fans posed with the trophy, supervised by a guard who repeatedly asked people not to touch or kiss the polished metal.

From a slight distance, the original Manny Delcarmen, known to all as Kuki, took in the scene. It was almost incomprehensible to the former minor leaguer how his son's life had taken off. The World Series share alone would be worth more than $300,000. In a few weeks Manelito would be joining his teammates for a trip to the White House to meet the president of the United States! Kuki could only shake his head. He talked about his own playing days in A-ball for the Phillies at places like Pulaski in the Appalachian League. He said he was still proud of the ring he'd earned as part of the Spartanburg team that won the Western Carolina League championship in 1976. "It's a one-in-a-million chance to become a professional baseball player," he said. "And making it to the major leagues is an even greater challenge." Beaming at his son across the room, he added, "It gives me a great honor just to say that I'm his father."

In 2008 Kuki's pride and joy would be with the Red Sox from start to finish, his minor league days apparently in the rearview mirror. Ana and the baby even made the season-opening trip to Tokyo. Months later they were long since asleep when Manny climbed into bed in the wee hours of August 12, having flown in after a night game in Chicago. He awakened at noon, a bit groggy from the grind but excited nevertheless. This night, at Fenway, was apt to be something special.

18

A Giant among Legends
Somewhere over the Pacific Ocean

While the Red Sox get ready to take on the Texas Rangers on the night of August 12, 2008, Doug Clark heads back to join his team, far, far away. Over eleven seasons as a professional baseball player he had known hundreds of thousands of miles of travel, much of it bad. There had been the numbing bus rides in the low minors, some of them ten hours or more. In Triple-A he had endured some galling early morning flights, shoving shirts in a duffel bag after a night game at home, getting picked up in a van a few hours later, and wedging his six-foot-two frame into a coach seat for the first leg of a trip from Fresno to Oklahoma City. Down in Navojoa, Mexico, where he played winter league ball for years, the travel could be even worse. Some buses had shock absorbers that were ground to nubs. Cigarette smoke would waft to the back of the bus; beer was tossed everywhere. Drivers seemed to accelerate down the windy roads, always a good time in the back for a gringo with a little bout of Montezuma's revenge. Once, well after midnight, the bus broke down so far from anywhere that Doug felt he was on another planet; beneath a canopy of a million stars, he watched the driver remove his belt and tie it to an axle on a wheel that was billowing smoke.

But of all those trips through all those years, this one on August 12—well August 11 *and* August 12—has proved the longest. It started with a farewell back in Springfield, Massachusetts, after an exceedingly rare summer visit with his family. Bill Clark had given Doug a ride down to Bradley International Airport late on Monday afternoon, the eleventh. He flew first to Cincinnati, before boarding Delta Flight 1789 for Los Angeles. On board, high above the heartland, headphones over his ears, Doug drifted into a deep sleep. Awakening to the captain's voice and the increased air pressure from descent, he figured he was arriving in L.A., only to learn that the plane had been diverted to Albuquerque. A woman up front had been having trouble breathing. According to Delta spokesman Anthony Black, "no medical emergency was declared," but a doctor onboard felt that the passenger should receive attention quickly. When the plane finally arrived in Los Angeles just after midnight, most of the groggy passengers picked up their bags to head home, while Doug raced across the airport to another terminal. His connecting flight, though, was already gone.

Back he traipsed to the Delta counter, only to find that it didn't reopen for business until four in the morning. He hauled himself over to McDonald's, grabbed a couple of burgers, a chicken wrap, and a Sprite, and crashed at the food court amid other frustrated travelers and airport itinerants. It was not until 12:30 the next afternoon that his thirteen-hour flight to Seoul began to climb over the Pacific.

When Doug finally broke through to the big leagues with the San Francisco Giants in September 2005, he never imagined that a few years later he would be playing ball in South Korea. Sure, there was a little bit of family history there (stationed just south of the Thirty-eighth Parallel with the Army Corps of Engineers, Bill Clark had helped to build a wood and wire bridge to an orphanage more than forty years before); but Doug was not looking to follow in his father's footsteps.

Doug began the 2006 season with more than one thousand minor league hits, but he was 0–5 as a big leaguer. He signed that year with the Oakland A's, finally cutting the cord from across the Bay after having spent his first eight seasons in the Giants' organization. He started the year with the Sacramento River Cats, Oakland's Triple-A affiliate in the Pacific Coast League. They were managed by Tony DeFrancesco, a ninth-round pick by the Red Sox back in 1984 who had spent eight years in the minor leagues, never making it to the bigs. Doug connected well with his new manager, who told him not to define the success of his baseball career on the basis of his big league experience. "I won't, Tony," Doug told him, "but I still want that one line drive up the middle."

He was blazing hot out of the gate, playing in six of the seven road games to begin the year, hitting in all of them. Then came the home opener at Raley Field, which had led all minor league ballparks in attendance the last few years. An overflow crowd of 13,932 jammed into the park that night. Players on both teams stood on the baselines with their caps over their hearts as Sacramento's own Stevie Scott, a nineteen-year-old brunette who had recently competed on *American Idol*, sang the national anthem. In his first two trips to the plate Doug blasted home runs, the only two hits allowed over five innings by William Juarez, starting pitcher for the Las Vegas 51s. Two nights later, during the first Sacramento rainout in three years, Doug called his parents from Denny's, where he was having his Easter dinner. He was the leading hitter in the Pacific Coast League at .457.

His bat cooled off, but he kept grinding away, hoping for an opportunity, aware that the A's outfielders were struggling at the plate. After a loss on the night of June 19, Doug was toweling off from the shower when De-Francesco came into the locker room and announced, "Clarkie's going to the big leagues." His teammates broke into spirited applause. Frank Thomas had just been placed on the fifteen-day disabled list retroactive to June 15, and it looked as if Doug would have at least a brief stint with the A's, still seeking his first major league hit.

He went 0-for-2 in two games as a pinch hitter in Colorado. The A's then flew home for three games at San Francisco against his former team. With two outs in the bottom of the eighth inning on Saturday afternoon, June 24, 2006, Doug was sent out to left field in a double switch, running out for the first time to a treasured piece of real estate he had long imagined inhabiting. Back in September 2004, after his seventh professional season, he and a girlfriend, Mindy, had purchased tickets from a scalper and sat in the bleachers one day, looking down on Barry Bonds, who walked all five times he came to the plate—the ultimate show of respect for a batter. In September 2005 he had memorably gotten the call directly from the high school classroom, and arrived in the Giants' locker room before anyone else, plopping down briefly in Bonds's Barcalounger, just to be able to say he did it. He never got to play in the field during his brief stint with the Giants. But now, there he was, standing on hallowed ground before a sellout crowd of 42,866 fans, including his brother Connell and sister Nora, who had flown across the country to stay with him at the hotel in Oakland. After Omar Vizquel struck out to end the inning, Doug trotted in as Bonds reclaimed his spot.

With two outs in the top of the ninth, Doug came to the plate against Tim Worrell. It would be, he knew, a grand moment for that treasured hit, but he grounded to second base to end the inning. Returning to left field for the bottom of the ninth, he heard a voice screaming: "Hey Doug! Doug! Doug Clark!" He looked up to see Ray Johnson, the man who had been his house father back in Keizer, Oregon, during his first summer of pro ball in 1998. It was, indeed, a small world.

The A's led the game, 7–5, as the Giants came up for the final time. Mark Sweeney dumped a single to left center. Up came Bonds as the potential tying run. He was already 2-for-2 with home run number 719, a double, and two walks. Doug had never in his life heard a crowd so loud. While the kayakers swirled around in anticipation in McCovey Cove behind the right field wall, Doug moved back in left, playing just a few feet in front of the warning track. Behind him on the fence was a huge mural depicting Bonds facing Aaron, Ruth, and Mays next to the words "A Giant among Legends." Doug leaned forward, staring in at the plate at the guy who had kept him out of the big leagues for so long. Bonds walked again on a 3–1 pitch. Moments later Ray Durham crushed a walk-off three-run home run. Amid the mayhem in the stands and the celebratory mosh pit at the plate, Doug Clark quietly jogged into the visiting dugout and disappeared into the clubhouse.

He realized that he was running out of time when the A's traveled to San Diego for a three-game set against the Padres beginning on June 27. He was getting only sporadic pinch-hitting duty, still never having started a big league game, and Frank Thomas was due to come off the disabled list in a few days. Teammate Bobby Kielty, who had befriended Doug in spring training, assured him that first major league hit was coming, likening it to the Holy Grail from *The Da Vinci Code* (both had seen the movie, released just weeks before).

On the night of June 28 the A's fell behind the Padres, 5–1, in the bottom of the fourth inning, and bench coach Bob Geren told Doug that he would pinch-hit the next inning for starting pitcher Joe Blanton. Doug quickly disappeared into the tunnel, where he found Kielty waiting for him in the cage. "All right, here it is," said Kielty, setting up baseball after baseball on a tee. "This is it." Ten swings later, Doug was out in the on-deck circle.

After leadoff hitter Marco Scutaro grounded to short, Doug was announced as the pinch hitter and hurried into the box, concerned that home plate umpire Derryl Cousins would otherwise have time to look up at the scoreboard, see all the zeroes (0–4 on the season, 0–9 in his career), and "broaden the zone." He dug his spikes into the batter's box and looked down to see future Hall of Famer Mike Piazza "glaring through his mask. I kind of gave him a head nod, and said, 'What's up, Mike?' But he didn't respond."

Doug looked out to the mound at San Diego pitcher Clay Hensley. The year before, Hensley had been one of the largely anonymous group of minor leaguers suspended for violation of the performance-enhancing drug rules. On this night, though, Hensley was a dominating major league pitcher, hurling seven innings of five-hit ball in an 8–1 rout of the A's.

Doug swung over the top of the first pitch, then managed a feeble tip on the next one for an 0-and-2 count. The third pitch was a fastball away that stayed up. Doug stepped in and swung, and felt the clean break of the ball off the bat. Running toward first, he saw center fielder Mike Cameron racing in, but then, at the last instant, pulling back, as the ball plunked cleanly onto the grass.

For just a few seconds Doug stood on first, savoring the moment. "This was something I had lusted over for a while," he later said, "not knowing if it was ever going to come true."

Across the country on Piedmont Street in Springfield, just before midnight, Doug's brother Connell started screaming in the kitchen. Bill and Peggy Clark awakened, startled. Well into the night they watched the game's statistics flash periodically across the *SportsCenter* crawl: "Clark 1–1." The baseball from that "1" would soon reside in a case in their dining room.

Sent back to Sacramento two days after the hit, Doug reentered the familiar grind of minor league life and never got called up again by the A's. He finished the Triple-A season batting .283 with a career-high fifteen home runs and twenty-five stolen bases.

Page 376 of the 602-page *Baseball Prospectus* for 2007 included this two-sentence account of a certain minor leaguer: "Doug Clark, all 30 years of him, picked up his first major league hit (a single up the middle off Clay Hensley) and his first major league stolen base on June 28. Both were also his last of the season, and quite likely of his major league career."

He signed with the Braves for 2007, and stayed at major league spring training right to the final cut, batting a team-high .441 in fifteen games. Manager Bobby Cox told Doug that the Braves were trying to work out a trade to send Ryan Langerhans to another team, in which case Doug would begin the year in the big leagues. The trade did not materialize at that point, though, and he began the season as the third-oldest player on the roster of the Triple-A Richmond Braves. From Florida they flew to Buffalo to start the season, arriving in a blizzard, and wound up mostly sitting in their hotel rooms as all four games to start the year were postponed.

Doug struggled in the early going but rallied late for another solid season, earning the team's MVP award with a .275 average, fifteen homers, and twenty steals. He never got called up by Atlanta, however, not even when the rosters expanded in September. It was his third straight season spent productively at Triple-A, but the big league life remained tantalizingly out of his reach.

After a summit with his agent, Jim Masteralexis, Doug decided to take the plunge and accept an offer to play in 2008 as one of two imports for the Hanwha Eagles in Daejeon City, South Korea.

"It just got to the point where I had to be honest with myself," he said over a Reuben sandwich at a diner in Chicopee, Massachusetts, the day before he left. "I know this is a game. I know this is a dream. But I really had to think along the lines that these organizations are thinking. They have the leverage to offer to kids: 'This is your dream. You want to play ball? Here is your opportunity.'" Doug had heard that before. "I understand the dream. I understand the opportunity—or lack thereof sometimes. But I had to be real with myself. I didn't want to keep making a parallel move to keep putting myself in that same situation of maybe being held down. There is that slim hope of what happens if somebody gets hurt, . . . [but] those are things that are out of my control. I think right now I wanted to put a couple of hands on the steering wheel."

He knew, of course, that many other talented players on the cusp of a major league career had steered their lives in other directions. For every Mark McGwire and Rafael Palmeiro and Roger Clemens, there were tons of lesser-known players who had also taken pharmaceutical shortcuts. Some had tested positive and received "education and counseling." Some had been suspended. A great many had simply gotten away with it. In one sense, Doug knew, he had paid the price of his convictions, but in another he felt proud: "It's just something that's not worth it for me. . . . [Playing professional baseball is] something I'm going to do until I can do it no more, but I'm not going to push the envelope."

He would make slightly over $300,000 playing in Korea, not quite the 2008 major league minimum of $390,000, and vastly below the 2008 major league average of $3.15 million, but more than five times as much as he had ever made before. In stepping away from baseball in the States, he knew that he ran the risk of closing even further the door that was barely ajar on a big league career (out of sight, one year older), but he came to the conclusion that it was a move he had to make. "It seems like I've been holding my breath for ten years when I go out to eat, or try to decide to buy a computer or get a car," he said. "Right now, life is starting to make a little more sense. Before, my teachers said, 'You work hard: things will pay off.' My coaches said, 'You work hard, things will pay off.' Where's the second half?"

He arrived in Korea on the night of March 5, his thirty-second birthday. After long hours over the ocean, a three-hour bus trip from Seoul to Daejeon City, and a confounding cab ride, he arrived, stiff and achy, at a high-rise apartment building on a busy street. He hauled his stuff up to a second-floor hallway cluttered with kids' toys. It was dark outside when he turned the key and stepped into a small apartment, heavy with stale air. He was all alone.

Even after five straight seasons of winter ball in Mexico, his new life seemed incalculably hard. The most basic decisions—how to order food, catch a bus, find a bathroom—required an exhausting level of alertness.

Even the baseball field, his oasis, was filled with adjustments. He had to stay loose during the fifteen-minute break after the fifth inning. He had to learn to bow to his manager. When players made mistakes—swinging at a breaking ball in the dirt—they had to submit to a public tirade in the dugout. "When you screw up," he said, "it's like, 'Go to your room.'"

But the game is the game, and Doug Clark, who never even played baseball for the Central High School Golden Eagles, quickly became the starting center fielder and number three hitter for the Hanwha Eagles. Back home, his six siblings all lived within a short drive of their parents' house on Piedmont Street, but Doug had come to be a baseball ambassador, mindful of his place: "Respect their culture. Respect the people. Try to fit in. Don't be a person who is going to be walking into their clubhouse as a pompous American who just wants to play baseball his way, and that's it."

In short order Doug became a big deal in Daejeon City. Fans, lots of them young and female, would wait for him as he left the clubhouse, chanting "Clock-Clock-Clock" (their pronunciation of his name, since there is no "r" sound in Korean). They offered him gifts and asked for his autograph.

Over the short course of his baseball career, the technology of communication had changed drastically. He had gone from using phone cards in Oregon, to waiting for weeks for his Navojoa team to play Mexicali so he could cross the border and use his cell phone to call home, to lots of late-night chats with family and friends on the computer via Skype. Streaming technology also allowed him to take in some American TV shows on his computer. Through the MLB package he often watched the Red Sox game from the night before, falling asleep to the sound of the Fenway crowd, like New England kids hovering over their transistor radios generations before.

Doug played in the All-Star Game in Seoul in early August, then gladly flew all the way home, taking advantage of the fact that the Korean League suspended play for three weeks during the Olympics (where South Korea ultimately claimed the gold medal). It was an unusual feeling for Doug to be home at this time of year, but he soaked it up. He went with a couple of his brothers to see an Irish band, the Saw Doctors, in an outdoor concert in Northampton, and rode on the toy train with his godchild. He yukked it up on the bumper boats and competed fiercely with his brothers at mini golf. He ate big portions of his mom's roast beef. He saw Aunt Bunny—who always packed his suitcase so well—and Grandma Honey. He heard his dad refer to his mom over and over again as "Mother Goose." He went out drinking beers with friends he had not seen in too long. Then he'd fall asleep late at night down in the basement in the room he had shared with his two older brothers, one wall still decorated with a poster of the 1998 Salem-Keizer Volcanoes.

That all makes it hard to get back on the plane once again. When it finally lifts off, the one from L.A. to Seoul, he can't sleep. He wishes he could listen to the Sox game on August 12 as his plane soars toward the international date line. Instead, he pulls out a book and reads. It is a thin volume by Phillies catcher Chris Coste recounting his long years in the minors: *The 33-Year-Old Rookie.*

19 Knockin' after Midnight

Minneapolis, Minnesota

The post on waswatching.com, a blog billed as a "laconic commentary from a Yankeeland zealot," came from "hopbitters" on April 25, 2006. It read: "I never heard of Randy Ruiz before, but, my God, is the guy the ultimate loser."

Hopbitters was responding to the signing of Ruiz that week by the Trenton Thunder, the Yankees Double-A affiliate in the Eastern League. The post referred to a claim attributed to Ruiz that his positive drug test in 2005 might have stemmed from his use of Viagra. "Viagra has nothing to do with steroids," hopbitters wrote. "Though the young man no doubt used Viagra because Stanozolo [*sic*] makes you go limp. Just ask Raffy 'Former "And I Use Viagra" Spokesman' Palmeiro, who used the same drug."

The criticism didn't come just from the cruel anonymity of the Internet. Mike Drago of the *Reading Eagle* wrote on his blog, "Like a bad dream, Randy Ruiz just won't go away. Now comes word out of Trenton that the New York Yankees have signed the former Reading slugger and are ready to put him in a Thunder uniform. Provided they've got one big enough."

A week later, with Ruiz struggling at the plate, Drago wrote:

Even after he had been suspended for a second time, and even after his agent admitted that Randy Ruiz had tested positive for taking steroids, the big first baseman said last summer that the only substance he had knowingly taken was Viagra.

Apparently Ruiz is off the little blue pill, because his bat has been rather impotent this season compared to last year, when he tore up the Eastern League, winning a batting title while playing for the Reading Phillies.[1]

● The cover of *Sports Illustrated*'s 2006 "Baseball Preview" edition claimed, "The Game Is Good, Clean Fun Again." After the various assaults on the integrity of the national pastime in 2005, Major League Baseball had taken some strong measures, *SI* clearly felt, to address the culture of performance-enhancing drug use that had been quietly thriving for years. Twice in 2005 the players and owners had amended their Collective Bargaining

Agreement to toughen the drug policy. The first time a player tested positive would now cost him fifty games, the second time one hundred; the third time he would be banned for life. What's more, former Senate Majority Leader and federal prosecutor George Mitchell had been appointed by Commissioner Bud Selig to do a thorough investigation of the use of performance-enhancing drugs in baseball.

Had baseball truly cleaned its house? Between innings of an Opening Day game in San Diego, a fan tossed a syringe at a certain Giants left fielder. Barry Lamar Bonds—author of 708 home runs, a man who had never been identified as testing positive for steroid use, and the subject of the just released *Game of Shadows* (which compellingly chronicled his alleged use of a huge array of performance enhancers dating back to at least 2001)—simply picked up the syringe and tossed it off the field "so no one would get hurt."

In June federal investigators seized shipments of human growth hormone that had been sent to the Scottsdale home of Arizona Diamondbacks reliever Jason Grimsley. Jason Grimsley? For many fans, this was a puzzling development. Grimsley was no larger-than-life slugger. He was a pitcher, and not a very good one by major league standards, a defining example of that marvelous baseball term, "journeyman." A onetime Reading Phillie, Grimsley had broken into the big leagues in 1989. He had played in parts of fifteen seasons with seven different teams, assembling a record of 42–58 with a 4.77 ERA.[2] How much help could performance-enhancing drugs provide? Perhaps enough to have kept him in the big leagues all that time, allowing him to claim a precious roster spot while talented minor leaguers—who may or may not have chosen to juice—were kept down in the agonizing world of "almost." Over the years, Grimsley made more than $10 million in major league salary.

Cooperating with the feds in the early stages of the investigation, Grimsley admitted that he had switched from steroids to an exclusive regimen of HGH because there was no test for the latter. He asserted that personal trainers were supplying players with enhancers by the "boatful." He also identified other users; ten names were redacted in the affidavit, unleashing an avalanche of speculation.

In January 2007 the Hall of Fame vote was announced. Mark McGwire, eligible for the first time, did not receive even 25 percent of the vote, despite his 583 home runs, seventh then on the all-time list.

On August 4 of that year, Bonds tied Hank Aaron for the all-time lead, blasting number 755 against San Diego pitcher Clay Hensley (the same guy who had served a fifteen-game suspension in the minors in 2005, when he had been Brad Baker's teammate; the same guy who surrendered Doug Clark's only major league hit in '06). Three days later, against Mike Bascik of Washington, Bonds hit number 756. In December the new all-time home run leader, with 762, was arraigned on charges of perjury and obstruction of justice.

The Mitchell Report, twenty months in the making, was released the following week. Senator Mitchell cited a "collective failure" on the part of owners, players, and the commissioner to address the pervasive culture of performance-enhancing drug use. In one section of the four hundred-plus-page report, Mitchell wrote: "The minority of players who used such substances were wrong. They violated federal law and baseball policy, and they distorted the fairness of competition by trying to gain an unfair advantage over the majority of players who followed the law and the rules. They—the players who follow the law and the rules—are faced with the painful choice of either being placed at a competitive disadvantage or becoming illegal users themselves."

Mitchell expressed a hope that people in the game, the media, and fans would focus most of their attention on the report's recommendations[3] rather than on the section that identified users of performance-enhancing drugs. "Knowledge and understanding of the past are essential if the problem is to be dealt with effectively in the future," Mitchell admitted, before emphasizing that "being chained to the past is not helpful" and stating, "Baseball does not need and cannot afford to engage in a never-ending search for the name of every player who ever used performance-enhancing substances." In subsequent interviews he acknowledged that the eighty-nine players mentioned in the report represented just a small percentage of overall users, and that there was a danger in singling any one person out.

That said, the public's attention inevitably turned to the evidence against the biggest name in the Mitchell Report: Roger Clemens. One of thirty-one pitchers named in the report, the Rocket had likely concluded his remarkable twenty-four-year career a few months earlier, his $1 million per start rental by the Yankees having fallen flat (he was 6–6 in seventeen starts with a 4.18 ERA) in their quest to overtake the Red Sox. Clemens had won 354 games in his career and struck out 4,672 batters, second on the all-time list. He was renowned for his ferocious work ethic and incredible competitive drive.

But now, thanks to Mitchell's interviews with Clemens's former personal trainer Brian McNamee, the Rocket would gain another reputation altogether. In the compelling, if unseemly, congressional hearings that followed, Clemens and McNamee both testified live on national television.

Those hearings memorably involved Clemens's assertion that his close friend and former teammate Andy Pettitte must have "mis-remembered" a conversation about Clemens's interest in performance-enhancing drugs; the reference to a "palpable mass" on Clemens's buttocks; McNamee's claim that he had injected Clemens's wife, Debbie, with HGH in the couple's bedroom prior to the 2003 *Sports Illustrated* swimsuit edition photo shoot that featured a particularly buff Mr. and Mrs. C.; and Congressman Elijah Cummings's admonition to the Rocket: "It's hard to believe you, sir. You're one of my heroes, but it's hard to believe you."

No one doubted the ability or the commitment of Barry Bonds and Roger Clemens. They were clearly two of the game's all-time greats. But now the enormity of the Steroid Era was symbolically captured at full force: the game's only seven-time Most Valuable Player and the game's only seven-time Cy Young Award winner—the best player and best pitcher of their generation—were, at least in the court of public opinion, guys who had cheated to get an edge.

Did people care? Which of the dual American yearnings—for justice and for victory—would prevail? Certainly some fans turned away from the game, but during the 2006 and 2007 seasons, both major league and minor league baseball again set new attendance records. MLB was now a $6.2 billion industry.

The landscape of performance enhancement was growing more complicated by the day. While Mitchell implored everyone involved in the game to "join in a well-planned, well-executed, and sustained effort to bring the era of steroids and human growth hormone to an end and to prevent its recurrence in some other form in the future," it was clear that those other forms were already massing on the horizon. There was talk about new generations of performance enhancers, including gene therapy. Some young pitchers were opting for elective Tommy John surgery to tighten ligaments, enabling them to throw faster fastballs. *ESPN The Magazine* opined that there might come a day when athletes seeking a competitive edge would opt for elective prosthetics, as we approached an era when manmade limbs might be capable of outperforming natural ones.

● Amid that landscape, Randy Radames Ruiz tried to put the pieces of his life back together after the tumultuous season of 2005. The Phillies had no interest in re-signing him for 2006, a startling rejection given the fact that he had won the Eastern League batting title with a .349 average, the highest in club history, while blasting twenty-seven home runs and knocking in eighty-nine runs in just eighty-nine games. They had apparently seen enough.

His 2006 season began, instead, in the very center of the country with the Wichita Wranglers, Double-A affiliate of the Kansas City Royals. Randy's agent, Jim Masteralexis, thought this was a promising fit. The Royals had been a struggling organization for years, having posted the game's worst record in 2005, 56–106. They clearly needed help.

Things did not go well. After playing just six games, Randy was released. He had become involved in a dispute with the team's trainer, Charles Leddon, who told manager Frank White that Randy was in the clubhouse on the exercise bicycle rather than out stretching with his teammates—something Randy claims was an innocent mistake. White, a well-respected second baseman for the Royals for many years, was a no-nonsense manager, and he quickly fined Randy $200. When Randy muttered to Leddon that he would go to the bank and get twenty thousand pennies, Leddon reported that to White too. Summoned into the manager's office, Randy started yelling at the trainer. Just like that, he was out of a job, deemed a "bad influence" on young players by Frank White.

Certainly there were questions about Randy's character. He had now been given the pink slip by three teams. He had twice tested positive for steroids. Some saw in him a selfishness, a laziness, a capacity for brooding.

Others saw his frequent effervescence, his playfulness with young children, his luminous smile, and his abiding love of the game—and couldn't help rooting for him. Hawk Harrelson, the White Sox broadcaster and former major league outfielder (and father of Randy's former college teammate Casey Harrelson), refers to Randy as being "like a second son." John Brickley, the Reds scout who signed Randy out of a tryout camp in 1999, had maintained close contact ever since. Brickley and his wife, Julia, had frequently had Randy out to their Melrose, Massachusetts, home and watched him treat John Jr. like a kid brother. They had come to expect his cheerful phone calls from winter ball on Thanksgiving and Christmas mornings. And even after the Phillies had washed their hands of Randy, his Reading manager, Steve Swisher (also not brought back for the '06 season), invited Randy to spend time with him and his sons (including big leaguer Nick) in West Virginia in the off-season.

Jim Masteralexis was puzzled by the divergent reactions Randy sparked, and yet he felt both extremes himself. Here was a young man who had overcome so much, someone who was in some ways so delightful, who could also be, at times, a colossal pain in the butt. Jim regarded Randy's flameout with the Royals as a huge missed opportunity and warned him that he might be running out of time. "You do the hitting," Jim told Randy as he arranged a deal with the Trenton Thunder for the rest of 2006. "I'll do the talking."

So Randy returned to the Eastern League, scene of the previous year's drama. After a slow start, he began to hit the ball with authority.

Playing in Trenton allowed him on several occasions to return to the Bronx. His former high school coach, Mike Turo, had invited him back to talk to the baseball team at James Monroe High School, and Randy volunteered his time at Little League clinics that Turo ran. Randy frequently visited his seventy-one-year-old grandmother, Luz, a.k.a. "Mamá," at the old two-bedroom apartment on 136th Street, the walls still adorned with his trophies and plaques. During one off day he even went to Yankee Stadium, having got complimentary tickets from Ruddy Lugo, a kid he had grown up with, who had just been called up by the Tampa Bay Devil Rays. Sitting behind home plate in the section reserved for friends and family, looking out over the most famous stadium in sports, jammed with more than fifty thousand fans, Randy couldn't help wondering what it would be like to get the call: "It would be a sweet moment. It would be a book-writing story, coming from nowhere, working, going through ups and downs—and making it. And getting my first hit, or my first home run, or going into a big league locker room with your name up there and looking at it. That would be amazing."

He feared, though, that, already behind on the count, he now had another big strike against him because of his drug-related suspensions. Sure, the Yankees' first baseman, the guy whose position he was vying for, was Jason Giambi, someone who was widely suspected of steroid use[4] (and someone making over $20 million that year—and more than $100 million in his career), but Randy knew his situation was different. "I could have had everything last year," he said over dinner one night in May. "I could have been called up. . . . If it wasn't for that suspension, I probably would have had a lot of opportunities. That's tainted my name, and I think it's going to be with me for a long time." He knew that success in baseball was about going straight ahead—the next game, the next at bat, the next pitch—but he couldn't quite take his eyes off the rearview mirror. "I was so up," he said again later in the season. "I was just right there. . . . You never know what would have happened to me, where I would have been at."

The Eastern League schedule eventually took him out to Akron, site of the painful memory from the year before of being notified by Steve Swisher about the second positive test, a result he still bitterly disputed. The Aeros played just forty minutes from his dad's house in Middleburg Heights. Lifelong Yankees fan Randy Ruiz Sr. was on hand for all three games to cheer on his Mets-rooting son, who went 6-for-13 with six RBI.

And of course Trenton also played some games in Reading. On August 1, at FirstEnergy Stadium, Randy rocked Baseballtown with two doubles and two home runs. Taking in the scene with the Crazy Hot Dog Vendor, the five mascots, and 5,060 other fans was Randy's girlfriend, Lena Covel. The former Miss Berks County pageant contestant was almost eight months pregnant.

Despite his hitting a very respectable .286 with twenty-six home runs (one behind the league leader) and a league-best eighty-seven RBI, there was, yet again, no September call-up for Randy, no chance to suit up at Yankee Stadium. That, however, allowed him to be on hand at Reading Hospital, bringing donuts and cider to the nurses during breaks in Lena's three days of labor. Finally, by cesarean section, Randy Joseph Ruiz III came sliding into home.

● Randy's 2007 season began with yet another organization, the Pittsburgh Pirates. He was assigned to the Pirates' Double-A squad in Altoona, Pennsylvania: the Curve (so named because of the famed Horseshoe Curve of the railroad, a 220-degree hairpin turn in the Allegheny Mountains). The Pirates were another team in need of help. They had endured fourteen straight losing seasons, and they were coming off a 67–95 year in which they'd finished twenty-ninth of thirty teams in runs scored. Randy was back for another go-round in the Eastern League, a circuit he had led in slugging percentage for two straight years. He still hadn't spent a day at Triple-A, let alone the big leagues, and he feared his time was drawing short. At twenty-nine, he was the second-oldest player on Altoona's roster, and he had been around the minors enough to see the strong preference for young prospects on the way up.

Randy homered on Opening Day at Akron in front of his dad, and settled in as Altoona's cleanup hitter. After he got two hits on May 1 in Norwich, Connecticut, his average was up to .342. The next day Altoona promoted from Single-A one of the organization's top prospects, first baseman Steven Pearce, who had been a high draft pick in 2005. For the first time all season, Randy sat on the bench the following day. Through May his playing time became sporadic as Pearce was showcased. Randy was stewing. He remembered Jim's directive about letting his agent do the talking, but he thought he had to advocate for himself. The clock was ticking.

The Pirates did not choose to release Randy, but they made a curious transaction to accommodate him on May 31. He was traded for what was termed "no compensation." To the Pittsburgh organization he was, evidently, worthless.

More curious still was the recipient of the trade, the very team that was playing against the Curve in Altoona that night: the Reading Phillies. Switching locker rooms and donning a familiar uniform with a train above the logo, Randy Ruiz went 4-for-6, with a home run and a double.

"Randy Ruiz, easily one of the most productive and controversial players in Reading Phillies history, is back with the club," wrote Mike Drago in the next day's *Reading Eagle*. Drago recounted Ruiz's history, culminating with the organization's decision not to bring him back after the 2005 season. "Less than two years later they have accepted him back, ready to let bygones be bygones, according to farm director Steve Noworyta. "Basically, we feel that's in the past," Noworyta told Drago about Ruiz's "checkered" involvement with steroids. "We just move forward from there."

Randy's return to Baseballtown was brief and memorable. He immersed himself in the old scene: walking through a gauntlet of fans from the clubhouse to the field; the Crazy Hot Dog Vendor winging wieners before the home half of the second; the train lighting up in right center field after every Reading run. And as usual, there were fans galore on summer nights, including Lena Covel and little RJ, not even a year old, dressed in a Phillies jersey with "Ruiz" on the back. Randy proceeded to hit .378 in twenty-two games. Coming home to Lena and RJ was one of the sweetest feelings he had ever known.

Less sweet was the feeling he got upon opening the *Reading Eagle* on June 10 to see Mike Drago's column headlined "Ruiz's Return, Its Message Hard to Forgive, Forget."

The column reviewed a litany of what Drago considered to be terrible decisions by the team over the years, one of which had been bringing in Steve Swisher as manager back in 2005. ("He was psychologically unstable, a danger to himself and anyone who he came in contact with.")

The brunt of Drago's judgment, though, focused on the decision to bring Randy back to Reading:

Are the Phillies so desperate down on the farm that they actively pursue known baseball cheats and readily stick them in the middle of their Double-A lineup?

Apparently so.

The transaction was a jaw-dropper, for sure.

The last thing this Reading club needed was another big slugger to clog up the first base/DH slot, a guy who's a defensive liability and a non-prospect. Ruiz is twenty-nine and has crushed the ball everywhere he's been, yet no organization ever has moved him to Triple-A. Why?

Forget about homers and slugging percentages for a moment. Why would the Phillies want to reach back into their dark past and regurgitate this episode with Ruiz? When he was here the last time and tested positive some people in the Phillies organization were furious over it. They hated being associated with the dirty side of the game.

No doubt, baseball is full of cheaters—always has been. Pitchers have illegally loaded up the ball for a century. Hitters have countered by doctoring their bats. In some ways, there was a charm to all that.

But the steroid era has been one of the uglier chapters in the game's history. There's nothing romantic about it.

Baseball did its best to turn a blind eye to the subject of performance-enhancing drugs, but now we know better. We know guys did it; we know guys still do.

But going back into the player pool to fish out a two-time loser such as Ruiz indicates to me the Phillies simply don't care. They don't care about their image. They don't care that players cheat. And they don't care about the vast majority of the guys in their own system who have played by the rules, with integrity and with respect for the game.

That's the message they send each time they let Randy Ruiz lumber to the plate in Phillies pinstripes.

It's a message that's hard to forgive, or forget.

An athletic-looking middle-aged man whose brown hair is graying at the temples, Drago comes across as a genial fellow. He grew up outside Baltimore, but by 2007 he had been with the *Reading Eagle* for twenty-four years, covering the Reading Phillies for fourteen of them. He is a hard-nosed and enthusiastic reporter.

Back in 2005 he had never heard of Randy Ruiz, and was startled by his early season power show. "He became an instant story," said Drago. He was proud of his investigative work which uncovered the fact that Randy had missed the first fifteen games of that year because of a steroid suspension rather than the reported groin injury, a deception he laid squarely at the feet of the team: "They tried to sneak it through—no doubt about it." As Drago explained it, the story kept growing because of the concealment on all sides, coupled with Ruiz's startling performance. "It was a sort of Perfect Storm of a news story," he said, "the way the Phillies reacted, the way he reacted, and the way he produced." The detail about the Viagra, re-ported first in a New Jersey paper, only made the saga more compelling.

Drago insisted that he didn't dislike Randy, but he didn't trust him ei-ther. When the Phillies failed to invite him back for the 2006 season, Drago was confident that the parting was forever. When the team reacquired him in June, Drago was "totally astonished." He wrote the column in which he called Ruiz a "two-time loser" ten days later. Before the next game, Drago remembered, he was out in the Reading bullpen doing an interview when Randy approached him and said, "Hey, man, when are you going to stop dogging me? Why don't you give me some good pub?"

Drago's response: "As soon as you are ready to admit what you did was wrong and confess your crimes, etc., I'll be glad to write about it. Until then, forget it."

Bracing for rage, Drago was shocked to see Randy smile broadly and of-fer his hand. "Randy is an unusual guy," remarked Drago. "He said, 'Okay, that's fine,' and went about his business."

● That business hadn't included Drago for very long. After a 4–3 victory over Altoona on Monday afternoon, June 25, Randy emerged from the locker room still in uniform to greet Lena and RJ, who were standing by the cinderblock wall with all the pictures of Reading Phillies teams of the past. "I have some bad news and some good news," he announced. Sling-ing his arm around Lena, he told her that he had to move out for a while. The good news? He had been promoted to Triple-A. His manager, P. J. Forbes, had come up to him after the game with a smile on his face. "It's about time, big guy," said Forbes. "Get the hell out of here."

Not quite four months shy of his thirtieth birthday, Randy was now one step shy of his dream.

But not even one month later, on July 24, the report on minorleague-baseball.com read, "The Philadelphia Phillies have released Lynx IF/OF Randy Ruiz." It was a stunning development. Granted, Randy had not yet hit his stride against Triple-A pitching, batting just .215 with four home runs. But he had played only twenty-two games. It was a paltry sample size for someone who had batted a combined .320 on the season in sixty-nine games at Double-A, someone who was a career .301 hitter in his ninth sea-son of minor league ball, someone who had been the best hitter in the Eastern League now for three years in a row.

More than any of his previous three releases from teams, this one rocked Randy to his foundation. Lena would later say that it "almost de-stroyed him." In reacquiring Randy and then promoting him, the Phillies had dangled both hope and forgiveness before him, then given him essentially no chance to prove himself. Even Mike Drago acknowledged, "The whole thing was curious. I hope that in some way they got him out of here because of things I wrote and said—I hope. I like to take credit for that. But once they did move him up finally—it was his first time ever at Triple-A—they didn't give him a chance. He only had a limited number of at bats. That didn't show me anything. I think they were looking for him to fail so they could finally wash their hands of him."

Phillies minor league director Steve Noworyta told Randy that day that the team was making some changes, that there were some guys coming off the disabled list, that Ottawa wanted to go with more speed, and that Randy looked "a little heavy up top." They didn't want to send him back to Double-A, so they figured they would release him. Randy couldn't believe it. In the locker room, he scattered everything in his possession that had the Phillies' red on it—a duffel bag, spikes, socks, batting gloves, shirts—and stormed out, fighting back tears. Maybe this thing just wasn't meant to be.

Jim Masteralexis talked Randy back from the ledge. He told him that the Phillies were being unfair, that he too was pissed off. He would make some calls on his behalf. And sure enough, in a couple of days Randy was back in the Eastern League with the Connecticut Defenders, the Double-A affiliate of the Giants, his fourth team and third organization of the year.

Over lunch on a sparkling day in late August in Norwich, Connecticut, Randy turned philosophical. He still loved the game, he said. It was still fun for him to see how new teammates were always startled by his resemblance to Muhammad Ali. ("Yeah, that's my uncle," he liked to kid.) But the grind was taking its toll. It just wasn't a level playing field, he said. Certain guys—the young ones, the high draft picks, the prospects—got all the breaks. Labels were so hard to shake, and he knew that after a year in which he had been traded for no compensation by one team and released by another, his time might be running out. "I understand it, but I feel like it should be my turn. I should have opportunities. Put me up there, see if I can do it. If I can't, then I had my chance."

● Jim Masteralexis again worked the phones in the off-season while Randy played winter ball in Venezuela. Lots of teams didn't even return his call. But one day Jim had a promising talk with Rob Antony, the assistant general manager of the Twins, someone he and Lisa had connected with nicely at baseball's winter meetings a year ago. The Twins were a small-market team that had won ninety or more games in four of the past six years, in part by finding diamonds in the minor league rough. They were in need of right-handed power. Jim urged Antony to look outside the box at someone who had over a thousand minor league hits, 150 home runs, three straight years of excellent production in the Eastern League. The steroids issue, Jim insisted, was in the past. Antony checked with people in the Twins' organization and got good reports, including one from longtime minor league skipper Stan Cliburn, Randy's manager in Venezuela. Cliburn would be the manager of the Twins' Triple-A team in Rochester for 2008.

The next day Jim called Randy down in Maracaibo with great news: he had gotten him a deal with Minnesota, including a first-ever invitation to big league spring training. "But," Jim cautioned, "you have to be ready from day one. This is probably your last chance."

On March 21, 2008, the first day of spring, Randy cleaned out his locker at Hammond Stadium in Fort Meyers, Florida. Despite the fact that he had just learned he'd been sent down to minor league camp, he was in high spirits. He looked good, a healthy glow on his face between pencil-thin sideburns, an undeniable power in his barrel chest beneath a tight blue Mizuno shirt. "It's been an awesome spring [training]," he said. "Can't ask for more."

Randy had reveled in getting a few weeks of major league meal money. He enjoyed the one-on-one instruction from former Twins greats like Harmon Killebrew and Tony Oliva. He was surprised by how welcoming people were in the clubhouse, even the stars like Joe Mauer and Justin Morneau. And on the field, Randy had delivered. In fourteen spring training games he had gone 11-for-28 with two home runs. No one in camp with more than five at bats could top his .393 average. Manager Ron Gardenhire and general manager Bill Smith had just spoken to him in the office, saying that he had opened some eyes. "As you know, Randy, there are no promises in this game," Smith said, "but if you go down to Triple-A and produce, you could be in the mix."

By the time he arrived at the Triple-A field a half-hour later, the nameplate above his locker in the big league clubhouse had already been stripped off.

In starting the year with the Rochester Red Wings, Randy was beginning his tenth season of professional baseball for his eighth different organization (ninth if you count the Cardinals, who released him in spring training in 2004 before he ever played a game in their minor league system). It was, however, his first real shot at Triple-A. Rochester had a family-oriented feeling to it, with Stan Cliburn as manager and his twin brother, Stu, serving as pitching coach. They had grown up in Jackson, Mississippi.

With Stan as the star catcher and Stu as the top pitcher, they had led Forest Hill High School to the 1974 state championship; since then they had spent most of their lives in the minor leagues.[5] Randy had a long history of turning his baseball mentors into father figures—high school coach Mike Turo, Hawk Harrelson, John Brickley, Steve Swisher—and Stan Cliburn joined the club. Randy liked Cliburn's folksy but authoritative approach. Cliburn said that it was, of course, important to produce, to put up the proverbial numbers, but that equally important to him was Randy's conducting himself in what he called "the Twins way." He challenged Randy to show professionalism on and off the field, to arrive early, work hard, and be a good teammate. This was all part of the package that could give him the opportunity he yearned for. Later in the year, Cliburn would say that no one on the team improved more in these areas than Randy Ruiz.

But in the ruthless world of the minors, being a good Boy Scout is not nearly enough, and Randy was struggling. Triple-A pitching was better than what he was used to. The pitchers attacked weaknesses and showed a willingness to throw changeups on 2-and-0. Randy found himself locked up at the plate, taking tentative swings at borderline strikes while sometimes leaving his bat on his shoulder as fastballs cut through the middle of the zone. At the beginning of May, Rochester traveled out to Ohio to play at Toledo and Columbus. Playing in front of his dad almost always seemed to ignite Randy's bat, but in a six-game stretch to start the month he went 0-for-17, striking out nine times. His average was down to .234. He had hit exactly one home run. Doubts were beginning to overtake him. Maybe he had found his level.

Stan Cliburn pulled Randy aside and told him to relax, to stop grinding the bat to sawdust. The organization liked him, Cliburn said. He had shown them something in spring training. He shouldn't feel like there was some sort of decision hanging over every at bat. Randy summoned a smile and said, "Stan, I'm holding you personally responsible for getting me to the big leagues."

"Now, Randy," Cliburn said, laughing heartily, "I'll do what I can to get you there. But you're the guy who has to go out there and do all the things we've talked about."

Just like that, the hits began to rain down, first in little trickles, and then in torrents. In a nine-game stretch in the beginning of June, he blasted six home runs. His average climbed into the .290s. Though he was held hitless on June 15, the Father's Day game against the Louisville Bats was, Randy said, one of the greatest memories he had ever had in baseball. His father came to Rochester from Cleveland; Lena and RJ came in from

Reading. The oldest and youngest Randy Ruizes then threw out first balls to Randy, absolutely beaming at the plate. To play just one major league game in front of them, he thought, would be the ultimate thrill.

One week later he went on an absolute tear, tying a team record with a twenty-four-game hitting streak. He was now the league's second-leading hitter.

In the fifth inning of a rainy Monday night game on July 28 in Rochester, Randy got set to lead off against Brian Bruney, who had just come into the game for the Scranton/Wilkes-Barre Yankees. Randy was 1-for-2 on the night, raising his average to a season-high .313. Bruney, a burly right-hander who had been back and forth between the majors and Triple-A over the last three seasons, let loose his first pitch, a ninety-seven-mile-an-hour fastball that went crashing right into the back of Randy's helmet. Randy dropped the bat, raised his arms, and called out, "What the fuck?" whereupon he and Bruney were immediately ejected by first base umpire Mike Estabrook.

After the game, Randy lumbered onto the team bus, called Lena, and settled in for the 385-mile trip through the night to Pawtucket, Rhode Island. The beanball incident kept eating at him even as he put on his headset and tried to drift off to sleep. He hadn't charged the mound or thrown a punch. What he had done was to react. The whole thing, he knew, could be taken away from him in an instant.

● On Tuesday night at McCoy Stadium in Pawtucket, Randy had plenty of company. Jim Masteralexis and Steve McKelvey drove down for the game and saw him smack a pair of doubles. They then took him and Pawtucket knuckleballer Charlie Zink out to eat at the Ground Round restaurant adjacent to his hotel, the Comfort Inn. Also there was one of his most loyal mentors, John Brickley, the former Cincinnati scout who had signed him out of the tryout camp at Holy Cross back in 1999. The two men had maintained lots of contact over the years, so much so that Randy invited Brickley to spend the night in the hotel so he could also take in the afternoon game the next day, Wednesday, July 30. They talked well into the night about each other's families, about baseball, about Randy's prospects of finally breaking through. The next afternoon, after Randy slammed his sixteenth homer and another double, Brickley drove him and teammate Francisco Liriano to a rental car agency, said good-bye, and headed home to his wife and son in Melrose.

Randy was feeling good about his own family. He called Lena and RJ a few times every day. His grandmother in New York and his father in Ohio were filled with pride. Randy was even slated to see his mother in a couple of days. After years and years of cutoff, they had reconnected, mostly through Randy's growing closeness with his half brother, Jonathan Morales. Jonathan was getting married in North Bergen, New Jersey, on Saturday, August 2, and Randy had told him he would be there. Rochester was playing just an hour and a half away against the Lehigh Valley IronPigs.

Two days before the wedding, at four o'clock on Thursday, July 31, the Major League Baseball trading deadline passed. There were a couple of blockbuster deals; the White Sox acquired Ken Griffey Jr. from the Reds, and the Red Sox finally parted company with Manny Ramirez. In Minnesota, the Twins sat tight, not making any moves.

Randy continued his tear that night, going 3-for-4 with another home run, and pulling into a tie for the league batting title at .320. After the game, a little past eleven o'clock, he and Liriano sat at the Ground Round eating chicken quesadillas. Unbeknownst to them, a big baseball drama was playing out. Stan Cliburn had been instructed by the Twins minor league director, Jim Rantz, to call Minnesota after the Triple-A game because the team might be making a move. It took him quite awhile to get through, though, because Minnesota, just a game and a half out of first place, was having a wild game with the division-leading White Sox. Down 4–3 in the home seventh of a hotly contested game, the Twins howled in protest about a called strike against Denard Span. Fiery manager Ron Gardenhire stormed onto the field and promptly got tossed by home plate umpire Marty Foster. Gardenhire responded by yanking off his cap and punting it into the air. This unleashed a riotous response from the home crowd of over thirty thousand, many of whom started flipping hats and other projectiles onto the field. The White Sox players raced for the dugout, and the PA announcer warned of a possible forfeit. When the dust finally settled, the Twins rallied with four runs in the inning and wound up posting a 10–6 victory.

In an emotional clubhouse afterward, general manager Bill Smith elected to wait a day before telling two veteran players, pitcher Livan Hernandez and outfielder Craig Monroe, that they were being released. But the rest of the transaction had to be put into motion, and at around midnight eastern time, Smith finally got on the conference call with Jim Rantz and Rochester manager Stan Cliburn. He told Cliburn that the team was promoting Liriano, a left-handed pitcher who had gone 13–2 with the big league club two years ago before Tommy John surgery, and one other player: Randy Ruiz.

Randy was surprised to see Cliburn's number come up on his caller ID at that hour. "What's up, Skip?" he said.

"Congratulations, young man," Cliburn said. "You're going to the big leagues."

The cell phone reception in the Ground Round was sketchy, and Randy shot out of his seat and ran right out to the parking lot. The windy evening carried a faint scent of the ocean. Adjacent to the parking lot, an occasional truck roared along Route 95. Between clouds, some starlight glittered up above. "Are you serious?" Randy asked. According to Cliburn, Randy kept thanking him over and over again.

It was a wild scramble to get ready. Randy's baseball gear was over at Mc-Coy Stadium. He had to pack up his personals. The wakeup call for the morning flight was going to be at 5:30. And there were phone calls to make. He immediately dialed his dad, waking him in Middleburg Heights, Ohio.

"What's up?" Randy Sr. said groggily.

"Hey, man, you'll never guess what."

"What happened?"

"I got called to the big leagues."

"Don't say that—you're lying to me!"

"I'm serious."

"Stop playing with me!"

Over the next couple of hours, Randy Sr. kept calling back and asking Randy if he was serious.

In Jersey City, New Jersey, Jonathan Morales was playing poker with some friends when Randy called him and said he couldn't make the wedding after all. "Oh man, you're kidding me," Morales said. "Why not?" When Randy told him, Morales shouted into the phone, "For real?"

In Sinking Spring, Pennsylvania, Lena Covel left her bartending job at the Bar-B-Q Pit in the wee hours and headed home to Reading, where her mom was watching RJ. As she got in the car, she saw that there was a message on her cell phone. As she played it, the tears started welling up.

In Amherst, Massachusetts, Jim Masteralexis was asleep when the phone rang. In the morning, though, he had a huge smile on his face when he approached his eight-year-old son and said, "Hey Nathan—guess what happened last night?"

By that point, Luz Ruiz had finally fallen asleep on 136th Street in the Bronx. After she had gotten the call, she bolted out of her apartment in her nightgown, banging on one door after another. "Randy made it!" she screamed. "Randy made it! Randy made it!"

● The trip to Minnesota was surreal. Randy had never held a first-class ticket in his hands before. He would save it as a souvenir. He sat up front with Liriano, talking about big league life. Arriving in Minneapolis, they took a cab past signs for the Mall of America, the biggest in the world. They passed over the Mississippi River, watching barges full of wood chugging south. They arrived at the Embassy Suites. Randy got up to his room and answered the phone to hear an exuberant John Brickley. He marveled to Brickley about the accommodations, the note of congratulations from the hotel manager, the crackers and cheese that were waiting in his room.

He and Liriano had been instructed not to arrive at the ballpark before four o'clock for the seven o'clock game so that the team could handle the uncomfortable business of releasing Monroe and Hernandez, and informing the other players about the transactions. A little after 3:30 Randy got into Liriano's white Mercedes ("the nicest car I've ever seen in my life") and drove out past Rod Carew Drive and Kirby Puckett Place, lined with game day establishments such as Sportsman's Walleye Shore Lunch and Famous Dave's Barbecue, known for its famous "Wilbur Beans." They came to the players' entrance before the gray concrete Metrodome; the black security gate lifted, and they were in.

In the locker room Randy got a handshake and welcome from Ron Gardenhire and several of the players he had met in spring training. He tried not to stare. There was Justin Morneau. There was Joe Mauer. And there was a locker labeled "Ruiz" with a big uniform hanging, No. 56.

He got dressed and went down through the tunnel, emerging into a still quiet dome with acres of blue seats. The dugout was stocked with packs of sunflower seeds in flavors like "Dill Pickle" and "Dakota Ranch." Randy did his stretching and some running, then grabbed his all-black Old Hickory bat, unwrapped some Dubble Bubble, strapped on his batting gloves, and went to the cage to hit. The sound of the ball off the bat was, as always, sweet music.

Before the game he signed his first big league autographs, fans leaning over the dugout and calling out "Randy!" and "Mr. Ruiz!" He met with a pack of local media who asked him a little bit about the long journey, all those teams, all those years. During any of the hard times had he ever thought about quitting? "Not at all," he said. "This is what I have always wanted to do. This is my dream."

He was batting sixth that night against the Cleveland Indians' left-hander Jeremy Sowers. With two outs in the home second, the Twins radio broadcaster said, "Well, here is the initial at bat in the major leagues for Randy Ruiz, designated hitter for the Twins. He takes the pitch low and away, one ball and no strikes. Ruiz, who was just called up today from

Rochester, was leading the International League in hitting at .320 with seventeen home runs and sixty runs batted in. . . . Ruiz last year alone played for three different organizations."

He grounded out to shortstop, then struck out in the fifth inning.

Before the home seventh, with the score tied at one, Randy stood as the crowd sang "God Bless America," then "Take Me Out to the Ballgame." There were 33,709 fans in the stadium, far more than he had ever played for. Freshly ordered MLB packages were bringing the game live to Luz Ruiz in the Bronx, to Randy Sr. in Ohio, to Lena Covel in Reading. Leading off, second baseman Nick Punto singled, and then fan favorite Joe Mauer launched a laser to left center for a two-run homer. The place went crazy. Two outs later Randy came to the plate, facing Sowers for the third time. He fouled off a fastball, then flicked his bat at an outside changeup and hit it on a soft line to right field.

Standing on first base with the TV cameras focused squarely on him, Randy tried to keep it cool, to be a professional, to act as if he belonged. But the moment was too big for him. Even as home plate umpire Ted Barrett called time-out to signal for the ball and then rolled it into the dugout,[6] Randy could not suppress the smile that kept blooming on his face. In Amherst, Lisa and Jim Masteralexis were dancing around the living room, as their three kids shouted at the TV. The next thing they saw was Brendan Harris smacking a double to left center, and big, barreling Randy, motoring faster than they had ever seen before, sliding safely into the plate.

It had been a simply dizzying day, and Randy floated back to the Embassy Suites in Liriano's Mercedes. After all of that waiting for so long, everything had happened so quickly. There had been no time for his family to be able to make arrangements to get out to the game. That would not come until the next homestand.

● On Tuesday night, August 12, as Jim Masteralexis and Steve McKelvey arrive at Fenway Park for the Red Sox–Rangers game, Randy gets ready to play a major league contest in front of his father and son and Lena Covel for the very first time.

It comes against the Yankees, the team his dad grew up worshipping in Luz's apartment in the South Bronx. Randy Sr. is on his feet, going wild, when Johnny Damon leads off the game with a home run. Then he is cheering like a young kid for his son's team. Seemingly every play of the game he is applauding. "Everybody must have thought I was crazy," he would later say.

In the home eighth, with the Yankees leading 6–3, one out, and a runner on second, he sees Randy going up to the plate as a pinch hitter. The image of his son's face appears on the scoreboard. More than thirty thousand fans urge him on: "Let's go, Randy! Let's go, Randy!" On a 2–2 pitch, he rips a single to right field. The fans roar their approval: "Way to go, Randy! Attaboy, Randy!"

There is more baseball drama that night. Mariano Rivera comes in at that point and surrenders a game-tying three-run home run to Delmon Young that makes the Metrodome shake with noise. In the twelfth inning Alex Rodriguez hits the go-ahead home run, and Xavier Nady adds a two-run shot for a 9–6 Yankees victory. Randy Ruiz Sr., the former stickball legend in the South Bronx, loves all of it.

The enduring memory, though, comes from seeing his son at the plate, the image of his face on the scoreboard, the sound of his name chanted by fans in a major league ballpark.

"It's strange," Randy Sr. later reflects. "That's my name. It's like the dream I wanted when I was younger."

20

"Just Hoping to Have It Be Over"

Colorado Springs, Colorado

Matt Torra warms up in the bullpen on August 12, 2008, trying to feel strong. He is pitching for the Tucson Sidewinders on a warm and windy night in Colorado against the Sky Sox.

He is barely twenty-four, but at times he feels much older. The path back from shoulder surgery has been far tougher than he thought.

At first, when that "giant knot" in his shoulder had been diagnosed as a labrum tear just weeks after he turned pro in 2005, he thought he could power through it. Sure, it was shoulder surgery, serious business, but wasn't Matt the "horse" everyone had said he was earlier in the year when all those scouts flocked to UMass games? Didn't they gush (even as some cringed) when he maintained his ninety-three-mile-per-hour fastball deep into games, twice throwing at least ten innings, once reaching a whopping 149 pitches? Wasn't he the guy "with more helium than anyone in the draft"? Wasn't he a first-rounder who got a million-dollar signing bonus? And wasn't it just a "small, small tear," worthy of only a couple of arthroscopic cuts and three dissolving screws? How bad could it be?

Four months after the surgery in January 2006 in Tucson, the Diamondbacks let him pick up a baseball once again. Under the watchful eye of head trainer Greg Latta, Matt was allowed to make a few tosses from thirty feet. He had been throwing a ball all his life; nothing had felt more natural. Now it felt as if his shoulder were locked in vise.

It would be months still before he was game ready. Ultimately he managed to pitch just twenty-five innings, his fastball plodding along in the mid-eighties.

After a vigorous off-season workout regimen, Matt was hoping that 2007 would mark his return to glory. He would be able to pitch a full season with no restrictions. He was assigned to the Diamondbacks' high-A team, the Visalia Oaks.

It proved to be a humbling, dispiriting season. Despite a solid 12–10 record, he posted a 6.01 ERA, third worst in the league. He couldn't blow the ball by hitters anymore, and the "power curve" just wasn't as sharp. Many a night he would call his dad, Jim Torra, back home in Pittsfield, Massachusetts, letting down his guard and admitting his doubt. "I got my butt handed to me," Jim would hear his son say. Or, "I just want to crawl and hide. I don't know if it's the injury, or if the competition is just that much better."

Matt knew the Diamondbacks weren't quite ready to give up on him. They had invested in him, after all. High draft picks have more room to fail; that's just the way the game works. Still, he knew their patience was not infinite. There were new draft picks every year in the States. Then there were hungry players from Japan and Korea, Venezuela and the Dominican Republic, all yearning for a shot. Throw in trade possibilities and free agent signings, and he knew he would have to perform. If not now, then soon. Real soon.

● Going into 2008, Matt came to a hard reckoning. He was never going to be a power pitcher by major league standards. He was going to have to rely on finesse. He had always had great control. The fastball might not blaze the way it once had. The power curve might not have that wicked north-south drop. But he would develop a slider, work on his changeup, learn not just to pitch but to, as the scouts liked to say, "become a pitcher."

Through the first half of the year, the results were encouraging. The Diamondbacks had given him his first promotion to the high minors, at Double-A in Mobile, Alabama, and Matt had gone 5–5 with a nifty 2.85 ERA. On June 15 they promoted him to the Sidewinders.

For Matt, this was thrilling news. For almost two years he had been dating a woman named Jessica Reed, whom he had met during his rehab in Tucson (where she worked in human resources for the Diamondbacks).[1] The Sidewinders had also recently called up Matt's friend Frank Curreri, who used to catch him at UMass. And of course Tucson was Triple-A ball, the highest rung of the minor league ladder. Maybe with a good performance he could earn a call-up to the big leagues when the rosters expanded in September.

It meant another adaptation, of course, pitching against older guys, many of whom had already been to The Show, all of whom were determined to return. He was hit hard. But on August 6 in Oklahoma he tasted the kind of success that fueled his hope. He pitched eight innings of shutout ball and got the win. His Triple-A stats now looked okay: 3–3 with a 4.47 ERA. So when he takes the mound on this Tuesday night in Colorado, he is brimming with optimism.

Things start out terribly when the first batter, Mike McCoy, hits an inside-the-park home run. Then they get worse. Matt lasts just four innings and surrenders nine runs on twelve hits, three of them homers. The game spirals so far out of control that in the home eighth inning, Tucson manager Bill Plummer puts in catcher Frank Curreri to pitch. Tucson loses, 21–5.

Matt is not headed to the big leagues anytime soon, he knows, after a game he will never be able to forget. "You're just hoping to have it be over," he says. "It was awful, one of those days that you just wish you didn't play baseball."

21

On the Big Screen

Greenfield, Massachusetts

The first phone call Vicki Baker received on May 14, 2006, came from her eldest son, Bradley. He was down on the field with his Richmond Braves teammates, getting ready for a game against the Toledo Mud Hens. He just wanted to wish her a happy Mother's Day.

All was well up on Baker Hill. Brad's sister Jill had made a remarkable recovery from the car accident in November that had fractured vertebrae in her neck and between her shoulder blades. Uncle Jeff was doing fine, driving down to his financial planning job in Greenfield every day. Grams was in good spirits; Irene would be out on the riding mower soon now that the grass was greening up. At night she listened to all of Brad's games.

Through the first month of the season those broadcasts had been filled with good news. Brad had started the year at Double-A with the Mississippi Braves in the small city of Pearl. After just two relief outings, both of them scoreless, he was elevated to Triple-A with the Richmond Braves. He wasn't closing games for Richmond, but he was being used in significant innings. In nine appearances he was 1–0 with a 2.40 ERA.

Vicki thought Brad sounded upbeat on the phone. He didn't seem burdened or preoccupied in any way. The divorce paperwork was going through, and he and Ashley were both eager to move on. Brad said he enjoyed being back on the East Coast and had already spent some days fishing and golfing. He liked the coaching staff, and he had some nice teammates. Earlier in the month, when Richmond had hosted Scranton/Wilkes-Barre, he had gone out to dinner with Dan Giese—his old friend whom he had not seen since the wedding. It had been great to catch up with Dan, to compare baseball journeys. Last winter Dan had decided that selling cars was not for him after all. There was nothing like playing baseball for a living.[1]

Brad was also enjoying his situation at home. His younger brother Colby, who had been working for a commercial roofing company in Boston, had been transferred in December to work on some buildings for Phillip Morris in Richmond. Brad moved right into the apartment in April. So the Baker boys were roommates once again, just as in their childhood days in the loft in Leyden with the baseball card sheets and the posters of Lou

Gehrig and Pamela Anderson. Sometimes Colby would sit behind the plate at the stadium known as The Diamond and watch his older brother uncork his signature changeup, the pitch that had first plunged south in a catch with Colby up on Baker Hill years ago.

"Anyway, Mom, I gotta go shag some flies. I just wanted to say happy Mother's Day."

An hour later the phone rang again. "You're not going to believe this, Mom. I was just traded."

Brad had become the "player to be named later" that the Braves were providing after acquiring pitcher Franklin Nuñez on April 5. That baseball I.O.U. was now paid up as Brad cleaned out his locker and got into his truck.

"What are you saying?" Irene Baker yelled at her daughter-in-law a few minutes later. "You've got to be kidding me!"

Jim Baker just sat there shaking his head.

Jeff Baker, who had wheeled up to Jim and Vicki's house with his wife, Cheryl, sat silently for several moments before his face softened into a smile. Then he let out two words: "Oh, wow."

Brad was on his way to Pawtucket. He was back with the Red Sox.

● It seemed like another lifetime to Brad, the day when Sox area scout Ray Fagnant had sat in the Baker living room in the summer of 1999. Brad had just been selected with the fortieth pick in the draft, and Fagnant had driven out to Leyden with a big briefcase. He told the Bakers how impressed he was with the family. He said that the Red Sox had scouted every single pitch that Brad had thrown during his senior year. Before putting the team's initial signing bonus offer on the table, he showed the family a series of photos. First there were pictures of the Sox' spring training complex in Fort Myers, where Brad would start playing that summer in rookie league. Then there were pictures of the team's Single-A facilities in Augusta and Sarasota. Waterfront Park, the Double-A home of the Trenton Thunder, was next.[2] At each rung of the ladder, Fagnant explained, Brad would get closer and closer to Boston. Triple-A was at McCoy Stadium in Pawtucket, just forty miles from Fenway. As Brad had said in that summer of '99, "He sold the dream."

When he had been traded away in 2002, Brad had yet to climb into the Northeast. Now, four years later, he was back at the top of the Sox' minor league system, one step away from where he had always wanted to be.

It had been seven years since Brad had played a baseball game in New England. His family came out in force. The first time Jeff drove his silver van to McCoy Stadium, he got lost on the way home. He and Irene talked baseball for hours, not pulling back onto Baker Hill until 1:30 in the morning. On off days Brad drove back to Leyden. He wanted to get his tree stand set and scout for deer. One day Jeff and Cheryl let their twelve-year-old son, Kyle, skip school to go fishing with Brad on the Green River. Afterward, Brad worked with Kyle on his pitching motion under Jeff's watchful eye, and then went out to his game for the Masonic Lodge in the Greenfield Little League. There the coach and the league president had arranged to have baseballs signed by Brad for all the kids. "It was pretty cool," said Kyle. "He talked about what he did to get to where he is now. After the game, all the kids were chanting, 'Bradley, Bradley.'"

Brad was way past the point of awe himself, but he recognized that his teammates at Triple-A included some guys on the verge of stardom. Wearing the same Pawtucket uniforms with the "33" patch on the left shoulder (commemorating the twenty-fifth anniversary of the longest game ever played) were Dustin Pedroia and Jon Lester. The pitching staff also included fellow DiaMMond Management clients Manny Delcarmen and Charlie Zink. And once in a while on injury rehab, Red Sox players Brad had grown up rooting for on Baker Hill shared the small locker room at McCoy Stadium, guys like Jason Varitek and Trot Nixon. Now it all seemed to be within reach.

Except that in thirty appearances Brad stumbled, with a 2–4 record and a 6.02 ERA. His fastball had never returned. Even with the ever nasty changeup, he was too vulnerable against good Triple-A hitters. He surrendered an average of 11.7 hits per nine innings, the worst ratio of his career. In September there was no hope of a call-up to the Red Sox. At season's end, there was no contract tendered for 2007, either.

● What was there left to do but come home and try again? Jim Masteralexis made lots of calls on Brad's behalf, and got him an offer from the Minnesota Twins. It wasn't a spot on the forty-man roster, and there was no guarantee even of playing Triple-A. Still, the Twins were a well-regarded organization with a good reputation for developing pitchers.

Brad lived with his grandmother in the off-season. He caught up with old high school friends, and noted that Ashley Kachelmeyer had gone back to school, playing varsity basketball at Westfield State College. ("She's doing real well for herself," Brad said. "She's coming around. She's everything I expected her to be.")

Brad got a puppy named Ruby, a Rhodesian Ridgeback he was hoping to train for hunting coyotes. Around the edges of various hunting seasons (bow and arrow, rifle, primitive arms) in various states (Massachusetts, Vermont, New Hampshire, Maine, and Pennsylvania), he worked out and readied himself for another season. He drove down to Amherst College and worked with head coach Bill Thurston, a nationally recognized pitching guru who had once featured Brad in an instructional video because of his perfect mechanics. He listened to Jim Masteralexis's suggestion about talking with a sports psychologist. He spent a lot of time at a small gym in Greenfield. Then in February he flew down to Florida to give it one more shot.

The Twins placed him with the Double-A New Britain Rock Cats. As the season approached, the Twins gave him some surprising news: he would go back to being a starting pitcher. "It's a new day for Brad," declared Masteralexis.

On April 10, in his first start since 2003, Brad pitched shutout ball over five and two-thirds innings against the Portland Sea Dogs, allowing just two hits and striking out five. He got the win.

Brad impressed again in a few more outings, but then the bats started catching up, and the season started getting long.

As he careened from team bus to hotel, another year of the numbing minor league odyssey, Brad began, at times, to think about other ways of living his life. He was determined that he didn't want to do construction like his dad. He had considered studying for his broker's license in real estate during the off-season. He launched a hunting supplies website for a while, and even briefly tried his hand at becoming a distributor for a fruit juice drink called Mona Vie—citing Roger Clemens and Jonathan Papelbon as "current users of this product."

None of it, though, was really from his heart. In his ninth minor league season, he felt adrift.

To his own surprise, he was promoted from Double-A to Triple-A in Rochester on July 6. The press release from the Rock Cats referred to him as "the popular hurler," noting, "The versatile Baker made 17 mound appearances for the 2007 Rock Cats, 13 of which were starts. A reliable workhorse, Baker tossed 77⅔ innings in New Britain, compiling a 2–5 record and 5.33 ERA."

It went well at Triple-A, then not well at all. On August 25 he made his final appearance of the year, pitching in relief against the Pawtucket Red Sox. It was a pretty solid effort: one run on two hits with four strikeouts and no walks in two and two-thirds innings. Nevertheless, his Triple-A numbers stood at 0–2 with a 7.56 ERA.

He rode out the last week of the season, spitting seeds in the bullpen as Rochester ended the year with games against the Ottawa Lynx and the Buffalo Bisons. On September 3 he cleared out his locker and headed home.

● It had been almost a decade since Brad had felt the earth soften in western Massachusetts. In 2008 he soaked it in. He heard the tapping of sap dripping into maple buckets and smelled the sweet smoke curling up from the sugarhouses. He felt his boots getting sucked loudly into the ground during the singular pleasure of what New Englanders call "mud season." He heard the extraterrestrial screams at dusk of mating peeper frogs. With the rivers running wide and fast, he went fishing every single day.

He spent lots of time with his girlfriend, Chelsea, a wholesome young woman from Leyden who lived on a horse farm and worked at a hospital just over the border in Brattleboro, Vermont. Inside the barn in the winter, he gave private pitching lessons to local teenagers.

That was all the baseball he wanted to play, though. He said he had no regrets about not taking the offer that Jim Masteralexis had found for him in the off-season to pitch professionally in Italy. The money would not have been any good, he explained, and he really wanted to be home.

In the late spring a couple of the teams from the Tri-County League came calling. He had played for one of those teams, Manny's Appliances, briefly in the summer of 1999 while his agents had been negotiating his signing bonus with the Red Sox. He liked the spirit of that league, the way the players passed the helmet around during the game to help pay for the umpires and the equipment. But this time around Brad just said a polite "No thank you."

He hadn't made it. Not to the big leagues, anyway, not the way the locals had hoped for back in that golden year of 1999. He didn't know why. He figured there wasn't any one explanation. There were times when he wondered if maybe he hadn't loved it enough, really loved it the way he loved the outdoors. "That's always excited me more," he said. "I liked baseball, but I was never like, 'Oh my God, baseball season is coming up—I can't wait.' That's how hunting and fishing is for me."

Deep down, he knew that he had taken the quest further than the vast majority of kids with baseball dreams. He was a guy from a tiny rural town who had become a pro. He had been a first-round draft pick. He had been a winning pitcher in the minors. Some 90 percent of all minor leaguers never play in the bigs, but Brad Baker had come close. He had gone all the way to Triple-A. He had been named a Triple-A All-Star. There was no shame in that.

What's more, baseball had given him some big rewards. He had traveled around the country. As a high draft pick, he had made money in the game, a signing bonus that had provided the foundation for a comfortable life. Part of that bonus consisted of a $100,000 college fund. It was something big league teams routinely offer to top high school picks, knowing that a very high percentage of them will never wind up using it. But in the summer of 2008, approaching his twenty-eighth birthday, Brad decided that yes, in fact, he would spend the Red Sox' money. He began looking into business courses that were being offered in the fall at Greenfield Community College.

At night Brad worked at the 99 Restaurant in Greenfield. The restaurant was right off Route 2, the so-called Mohawk Trail, with its signs for the Bridge of Flowers. Its walls were decorated with team pictures from Greenfield High School squads, kids who had known a little piece of local glory. The 99 chain was also a big sponsor of one of New England's greatest passions, as indicated by the banner out front declaring, "When Red Sox win, kids eat free."

Most nights the Sox game was on both of the two flat-screens at either end of the big rectangular bar, as well as on the screen perched over the middle of the room. Beneath that screen, the bartender poured Bud Light and Sam Adams lager into frosty glasses. The team that had drafted him, traded him, re-signed him, and let him go was still Brad's team. When talking about the Sox, he used the pronoun "we."

For a Tuesday night, August 12 is unusually busy at the 99. Brad is already working up a sweat a little after seven o'clock as he looks up at the big screen. There stands a former teammate making his major league debut. He is taking his warm-up pitches from the mound at Fenway Park.

22

"The Path of the Knuckleballer Is Rarely Linear"

Boston

"Tickets! Tickets! Who needs tickets?"

It is late on a Tuesday afternoon outside Fenway Park. The Texas Rangers, the top-hitting team in baseball, are in town as the Red Sox, in second place with a 68–51 record, begin a critical home stand. The game is sold out for the 444th time in a row—just eleven shy of the major league record—but there are, of course, tickets available outside the ballpark to fans willing to shell out big bucks.

Three and a half hours before the first pitch, it is already a bustling scene. There are pregame toasts at the Cask'N Flagon. Sox hats and jerseys are flying off the shelves of the Twins Enterprises souvenir shop. A line is already forming at El Tiante on Yawkey Way, where draft beers now go for $7.25. Everywhere there are T-shirts proclaiming messages such as "Ellsbury," "Matsuzaka," and "Love Me, Ortiz Me."

Inside the old brick stadium, the receptionist answers a steady stream of phone calls with "World Champion Boston Red Sox." Grizzled media members take an elevator up to the press box, where a plaque with a quotation from the late baseball commissioner A. Bartlett Giamatti hangs on the wall: "Genteel in its American origin, proletarian in its development, egalitarian in its demands and appeal, effortless in its adaptation to nature, raucous, hard-nosed and glamorous as a profession, expanding with the country like fingers unfolding from a fist, image of a long past, evergreen reminder of America's best promises, baseball fits America."

Down below, the Red Sox locker room is an unpretentious place with old fluorescent bulbs hanging above a stained green carpet. There are black leather couches, a few decks of cards, a cribbage game going on, three television sets blathering ESPN. The cooler is filled with Poland Spring water, Powerade, Coke Zero, and, curiously, little containers of Mott's apple sauce.

There is only sporadic activity here in the hours leading up to the game. Former Red Sox great turned broadcaster Jim Rice reads *USA Today* and sips from a large Dunkin' Donuts coffee. A bare-chested Dustin Pedroia, in the midst of an MVP season, announces to no one in particular, "I'm gonna hit rockets!" Manager Terry Francona, grabbing some Dubble Bubble gum from a white bucket, laughs and says, "Put your shirt on." Holding a Japanese newspaper, Daisuke Matsuzaka ambles over to a pitchers' meeting to review the tendencies of the Rangers' hitters. Occasionally a player peers at the lineup card posted on the front door beneath a photo of Johnny Pesky stepping out of the Red Sox dugout onto the field in 1942. Right beside the card is the man himself: a dapper eighty-eight-year-old with thick white hair and sharply defined features, Pesky still maintains a locker in the room he once shared with Ted Williams.

A gaggle of reporters at one point surrounds Tim Wakefield. The one-time minor league infielder has long since emerged as the most versatile and enduring member of the Sox staff, having helped the team as a starter, in long relief, and as a closer. At forty-two, he is the third-winningest pitcher in Red Sox history, trailing only Cy Young and Roger Clemens. A pitchman for Just For Men (every Sox broadcast includes the spot touting "the hair color Tim Wakefield uses"), Wakefield has indeed seemed ageless. But the reporters are gathered now to hear about the tightness in the back of his pitching shoulder which has sent him to the fifteen-day disabled list, causing him to miss a scheduled start for the first time all year. He seems resigned to his fate: "It is what it is, forty-two years old, and a lot of wear and tear."

Across the way, in the pitchers' wing, between lockers with nameplates for Justin Masterson and Javier Lopez, is a locker whose plate says merely "Boston Red Sox." The locker is spare. Dark jeans with a white belt and a light blue polo shirt hang next to a couple of uniforms with the number 51. On the shelf up above sit a Blackberry and a wallet next to a stack of chewing tobacco tins and two Sox hats. Those are perched above two black TPX baseball gloves. In front, placed atop the Sox logo on the standard-issue blue chair, is an index card with a handwritten message.

Charlie Zink reads the card and smiles. He then heads out the door, spikes clattering down the long, narrow corridor lined with gray plaster. Just ahead of him, he sees the shaft of light reaching out to left field and the Green Monster. He emerges in the Red Sox dugout, where general manager Theo Epstein sits alone, and climbs up the steps onto terra firma at Fenway Park.

● It had been a love-hate relationship. On the one hand, Charlie felt, the Red Sox were probably the best organization for him. They believed in the knuckleball. They had lived with its maddening uncertainty for years. They were aware of the patience it required, and the accommodations: often a roster spot for a light-hitting catcher with soft hands, quick reflexes, and a butterfly net. Many teams steered clear of the knuckleballer, either unintentionally (because the supply was virtually nonexistent) or deliberately, out of a desire to avoid bipolar baseball. But for the Sox, Tim Wakefield had been worth the indulgence many times over. He had given them solid value for fourteen seasons, making him the longest-tenured member of the team. And for Charlie Zink, the very fact of Wakefield's career provided an inspiration, a glittering sense of what could be, maybe, someday.

On the other hand, there was not a tougher organization in which to break through as a pitcher. In recent years the once hitting-happy Sox had become a pitching-first organization. They stockpiled high-priced talent through free agent signings (Curt Schilling), through trades (Josh Beckett), through international auctions (Daisuke Matsuzaka), while also assembling hard-throwing young studs in their minor league system (Jon Lester and Clay Buchholz, among others). Going with the theory that pitching is the most important part of the game and that you can never have enough of it, Theo Epstein put together a mound armada that had helped bring the team two world championships in four years. It was great for the fans at Fenway—the good times never felt so good—but not so great for a longtime minor leaguer trying to break through.

"I get mad that I'm here," Charlie said between sips of a Sierra Nevada Pale Ale one night in 2007. "But there probably isn't another place for me."

For a couple of years now, he had pitched very well in the minors. He closed out the 2005 season strongly (with one stretch in August and September at Double-A and Triple-A of twenty-four and two-thirds straight innings without an earned run). In 2006 he was the top winner at Triple-A Pawtucket, going 9–4 with a respectable 4.03 ERA (plus a 1–0, 1.23 performance in a couple of games with the Double-A Portland Sea Dogs). In 2007, after the Sox had loaded up on pitchers, they sent Charlie not up but down to Portland, where he was an Eastern League All-Star, going 9–3 with a 3.98 ERA.[1] His success wasn't like the wild spree of '03, when he came ever so close to pitching two no-hitters in his first month at Double-A. It was more measured now, but also more sustained. In the high minors he was consistently doing the fundamental pitcher's job of getting outs. With a lot of other organizations, such consistent performance would have resulted in a certain phone call every minor leaguer dreams about. With the Red Sox, it never came.

This was the one life he knew, so Charlie mostly soldiered on. There were times, though, when the grind of minor league life seemed too much, when it was hard to steer away from what psychologists call "learned helplessness," the surrender that comes from believing that one's performance has no impact on the environment. "I would trade everything right now for a marriage and kids, just have a steady job where I was making eighty grand a year doing something," he said one summer night in 2007. "I would trade it for that. I don't have fun living out of a suitcase."

● By spring training 2008, the top fifty prospects listed in the 2004 *Baseball Prospectus* had overwhelmingly borne out the prediction and become the bright young stars of major league baseball. The group included one who had already won a Most Valuable Player award (Justin Morneau), one who had won a batting title (Joe Mauer), and eleven who had already played on at least one big league All-Star team: Morneau, Mauer, David Wright, Prince Fielder, Scott Kazmir, Alex Rios, J. J. Hardy, Cole Hamels, Grady Sizemore, Jason Bay, and Bobby Jenks. Eighteen were under contract to make more than a million bucks for the 2008 season, and a few (Morneau, Wright, Rios) had already signed multiyear deals guaranteeing them more than $50 million.

While only 10 percent of minor leaguers ever make it to the bigs for so much as a day, forty-eight of these fifty had already made it. The thirty-third guy on the list, a former first-round draft pick named Greg Miller, hadn't broken through yet. (He began the 2008 season with the Las Vegas 51s, the Triple-A affiliate of the Los Angeles Dodgers.)

And then there was number fifty, the undrafted guy out of art school who had become a knuckleballer one day, the 166th minor leaguer out of 166 listed alphabetically in the 2008 Red Sox media guide.

Charlie was twenty-eight years old now, about to enter his seventh year with the Red Sox. He was up to $2,700 a month for the five months of the minor league season. If at year's end he wasn't elevated to the team's forty-man roster, he would become a minor league free agent, eligible to sign with anyone.

Driving across the country from California to Fort Myers for spring training, Charlie cracked the precious nail on his middle finger. He arrived in the Sunshine State, though, with a mixture of focus, hunger, and perspective. He had come to believe that his meteoric rise back in 2003 had been a huge obstacle to his advancement.

"It was a really good learning process for me," he said. "The success I was having came so fast and so easy, because I didn't know what I was doing still. I just figured it would always last. When it didn't, I had no idea how to correct it."

The one-fingernail, one-knuckle pitch that was his and his alone— Charlie Zink's spinless original—had been, he concluded back in 2005, nothing but luck. But after changing the angle of his grip on the ball ever so slightly at the end of that year and recommitting to the path, he had slowly, over time, begun to feel differently. The best baseball players at any position talk all the time about "making adjustments" as a key to success, and Charlie had come to realize that he was no different in this respect. If he was falling forward a little too fast, he could slow it down. If the ball was spinning out, he knew how to turn his hand to correct it. If he was too strong going one way and the ball was moving left, he could work it back to the right. "It's just little things like that," he said. "I just feel every pitch."

He was not arrogant enough to believe that he had mastered something as mystical as the knuckleball. If anything, he had developed a healthy respect for the pitch. Every day there were people (fellow pitchers, position players, fans) asking him how he threw his knuckler. He was happy to show them, and he understood their curiosity. It was one pitch, thrown at a velocity a great many people were capable of reaching. It could be worth millions. But almost nobody throughout baseball history had been able to find the way. Charlie, with his second-degree black belt in tae-kwon-do by age twelve and near-scratch golf game, was accustomed to repeating fine motor motions with precision, but even he regarded the knuckleball command as a holy and mysterious art. "These guys who are worth millions of dollars have no idea how to even come close to getting the ball not to spin," he said. "I have no idea. I really don't."

The pitch, whose many nicknames over the years have included "the ghostball," was no longer haunting Charlie Zink. It wasn't an albatross hanging around his neck. He wasn't pleading with the Red Sox anymore to let him go back to the days when he was a conventional pitcher. Whether or not he would ever make it to the big leagues was a question mark, but he had come to a genuine belief that this was his only possible ticket.

"Now I know I have to be what I am," he said. "And I'm comfortable with that."

• Each morning he'd drive down Edison Avenue, past the sparkling City of Palms Park, with its Ted Williams statue and five-dollar bottles of water, past pawnshops and auto graveyards, to the player development complex. Ron Johnson, the jovial RJ, who would be his manager again this year at Pawtucket, thought Charlie's knuckleball looked particularly "dirty" in spring training. (RJ had been managing the Portland Sea Dogs back in 2003 when Charlie had come through for the first time with those two near no-hitters. It was unlike anything he had ever seen in thirty years of professional baseball: "It was unbelievable. Maybe it was too good to be true. . . . It was guys looking stupid for nine innings.")

Goose Gregson, now in his twenty-fourth year as a minor league pitching coach or instructor, looked in on Charlie with curiosity. It was Gregson who had pushed Charlie and the Sox to make the knuckleball conversion after seeing the dramatic evidence of the pitch's movement on a visit to Augusta during Charlie's first year. "He threw one that just splattered this poor kid's face," he remembered about trainer Darren Wheeler, who had been having a catch with Charlie in the outfield. "When he opened this poor kid's face up, I figured we had to at least give this a try." Over the years, Gregson had watched Charlie's sharp rise, precipitous fall, and steady climb back up again with special interest. "I can honestly see Charlie pitching in the big leagues now," Gregson said. "It doesn't necessarily have to be with the Red Sox. We're in the business of developing players and creating value for them. . . . He's right there on the cusp of being able to say that every piece of this hard work and struggle has been worth it."

On a drizzly Saturday morning in late March, two right-handed pitchers with shaved heads beneath their Sox caps were warming up on adjacent mounds in a bullpen that sits between two diamonds at the minor league complex of Boston's spring training neighbors, the Minnesota Twins. Getting ready to pitch a Double-A game was a swirling, sidearming giant named Justin Masterson. At six foot six, he delivered his pitches like a flamboyant matador, snapping his arm across his body, the ball cracking into the catcher's glove. A second-round draft pick out of San Diego State in 2006, the just-turned twenty-three-year-old had pocketed a signing bonus of over $500,000. He was the latest young pitching stud on the rise in the Red Sox organization.

Just a few feet away, Charlie warmed up for the Triple-A game, throwing to George Kottaras. His pitching style suggested playing darts in a smoky bar. His stride was short. His wrist was locked. His signature spinless delivery wafted toward the plate at a speed that wouldn't seem intimidating to the average high school hitter.

Exactly twenty-eight fans watched the action as Charlie took the mound in the bottom of the first. The first batter, Alexi Casilla, was facing a 1–2 count. The pitch came in knee high, then darted down and away at the last second, as if suddenly remembering some very important date. Casilla swung feebly and missed. The ball caromed off the glove of Kottaras, who sprinted after it and flipped to first for the out. Hard to hit, hard to catch, the knuckleball was looking dirty indeed.

Just before the regular season, Ben Cherington, vice president of player personnel, reflected on Charlie's journey. Cherington was the guy who had called Charlie back in 2005 after his flameout in his first start at Triple-A and warned him that he had to find his command in a hurry or else the Sox would have no choice but to release him. Since then, Cherington said, the organization had been pleased with Charlie's commitment, and his results had been steady. Still, there were no guarantees. In 2008, for the first time, Charlie would begin a minor league season in the starting rotation at Triple-A, and that represented an opportunity, but nothing more. "The path of the knuckleballer," said Cherington, "is rarely linear."

In the second inning of Charlie's first start of the 2008 season, at home in Pawtucket against the Indianapolis Indians on April 5, he allowed six runs. After one more inning, he was done.

● Joyce Zink was accustomed to loss. The power of the uncontrollable was wired into her family story. Her Japanese-born parents and two eldest siblings were pulled away from their family farm and herded into an internment camp after the attacks on Pearl Harbor. Joyce lost both of her parents before she turned sixteen. She was used to things being unfair.

She sought a career in corrections. She worked in prisons for thirty years, "around some infamous inmates," as she puts it—Sirhan Sirhan and the "Manson girls." Her husband, Ted Zink, associate warden at Folsom State Prison, was known by the inmates as "Cobra."

Away from the big yard, their world focused deeply on their only child, Charles Tadao Zink.[2] Charlie's youth sports career, in tae-kwon-do, in golf, in football, and ultimately in baseball, became the centerpiece of family life. Ted was the president of the Little League. Joyce, with her "Baseball Mom" business card, worked the snack bar. They never missed a game: in Little League, in high school, during Charlie's first year at Sacramento City College. In 1998, when Charlie was lured away to Savannah by Luis Tiant, the emptying of the nest left an emotional chasm.

Still, Ted and Joyce sensed Charlie thriving at SCAD, and knew that the time away was a necessary part of his growing up. They knew he was having great fun playing baseball with the free-spirited Bees and their ringleader with the Fu Manchu. They visited several times, and on occasion caught up with the Bees during their road trips. In 2002, when Tiant called Charlie and told him there might be a spot in the Red Sox minor league organization, Ted and Joyce were in full support of his going to try out, and ultimately sign, even though it left him a few credits short of his degree.

That 2002 season with Augusta was a piercingly double-edged time for the family. Ted and Joyce followed every game over the Internet, delighting in Charlie's success against professional hitters, even as Ted weakened from the insidious constriction in his lungs. In June there was the hastily arranged flight on Father's Day and the few last hours together at Folsom Mercy Hospital. When Charlie had to fly back to Georgia, Joyce could hardly hold herself together.

Ever since, she had followed the action as a kind of lifeline. That meant listening to the games, pretty much every one, via webcast. The good broadcasters brought the game right into her living room. She built up a big library of microcassettes, dutifully logging Charlie's games with labels. There was a whole inventory of her son's peaks and valleys.

Joyce tried to keep herself busy by puttering in the garden and volunteering at church. She stayed close to Charlie by staying connected with his social world. She often ate lunch with the mother of Charlie's old buddy Dave Russell, who had been killed in a car accident during his senior year of high school. She liked to chat with one of Charlie's teammates from SCAD, Ryan Fickle (who refers to Joyce as "the sweetest, nicest lady I've ever met in my life"). Joyce also became very close with Marya Milton, Charlie's friend from Wasilla, Alaska, whom he had met at SCAD. Marya had gone to law school at the University of the Pacific in Sacramento, not far from Joyce's home in El Dorado Hills. They got together frequently. Joyce often referred to Marya as her daughter, while Marya proudly called Joyce her "surrogate mom."

Mostly, Joyce looked forward to the off-season, Charlie's return from the baseball grind. He always spent it at home with her in El Dorado Hills. Charlie had his own life, his friends, a little fling here and there, lots of hours at the gym. But he and Joyce also spent long hours together, bonding in ways that worked for them. They both liked to watch mixed martial arts competitions, and sometimes they road-tripped together to Reno or Lake Tahoe, Charlie driving fast, Joyce's cares melting away. She had come to dread the farewell in February, the beginning of his long drive to Florida, the migration that took him away for more than half the year.

The 2008 season was the seventh minor league campaign she had followed. All she could do was keep on hoping. On Charlie's first start, on April 5, she listened to the now familiar voices of Steve Hyder and Dan Hoard uttering phrases such as "Charlie Zink getting ready to make his first start of '08," "the very left edge of the rubber," "an All-Star last year at the Double-A level," and "Charlie had a terrific spring." Before the top of the second inning she heard a Blue Cross/Blue Shield commercial that proclaimed, "Life can be unpredictable," then listened as Charlie surrendered six runs, followed by what looked like a home run off the bat of Luis Ordaz, before the ball sailed just foul. "Charlie Zink takes a deep breath, and he'll try again."

After that brutal start, though, Charlie caught fire, and Joyce began hearing one superb outing after another on the webcast. By the end of April he was 3–1 with a 3.76 ERA. When May was done, Charlie was 6–2 with a 2.59. And at the All-Star break in mid-July, he was 11–2 with a 2.22 ERA. He was well on his way to winning the 2008 award as the top pitcher in the International League. He had been featured already in the *Boston Globe* Sunday magazine and the *New York Times*.

He had also fallen in love, for the first time in years, with the vivacious promotions manager of McFadden's Restaurant and Saloon, a beautiful young woman named Madeline Munroe. Upon meeting Charlie, she insisted she would never date a baseball player, but she seemed uniquely suited to date this one. After all, she had grown up in the Rhode Island town of Wakefield. Whenever they went to visit her family there, her two-year-old niece Lilly Manfredi, would always smile, giggle, cover her eyes, and say, "That's Charlie Zink. He throws the knuckleball!"

It was a sweet life in all respects, save one. For some reason, still, the Red Sox had not given him a chance.

His first fire alarm came on the heels of three excellent starts in April. On the twenty-fourth, the Sox suddenly needed an emergency starter when Daisuke Matsuzaka contracted the flu. That happened to coincide with Charlie's turn in the rotation at Pawtucket, but the Red Sox instead turned to Double-A and had Justin Masterson leapfrog his way into the rotation for his first big league start. Masterson validated the decision with a strong outing amid much fanfare at Fenway, while Charlie quietly pitched well at Pawtucket, allowing two runs over six innings in a no-decision.

On May 19 in Scranton, Pennsylvania, Charlie was called into manager Ron Johnson's office. The buzz around the hotel was that the Sox needed spot starters for both the twentieth and the twenty-first, and Charlie was said to be one of those guys. A few friends had picked up the rumor and called Charlie's cell phone, wanting to know if it was true that the big day had finally arrived. Charlie tried to stay calm as he walked into RJ's office. He merely nodded when he heard that the Sox would again use Masterson on the twentieth, then send him to Pawtucket after the game so they could activate Bartolo Colon from the disabled list for the twenty-first. Charlie took his turn in Scranton and pitched one-hit ball over six innings, getting the win against the Yankees' top farm club.

On the night of June 5, the PawSox were down in Charlotte to take on the Knights, Triple-A affiliate of the Chicago White Sox. As usual the night before a start, Charlie was restless. He channel-surfed in search of his favorites: *Seinfeld*, *That '70s Show*, the Kung Fu Channel. He struggled for a long time to find sleep. When he went to the ballpark the next day, RJ called him into the office and said that there was some news that Charlie was not supposed to share with anyone. They were pulling him from his start that night and calling up a pitcher from Double-A. The idea was for Charlie to be on the exact same schedule as Wakefield, who was supposed to pitch at Fenway on June 7 against the Mariners. The plan would be for Charlie to open up the Pawtucket home stand on the seventh, but "something might happen."

And what could that something be? The rumor was that Wakefield's back was stiff, that he might not be able to make his start.

So on a Friday night in North Carolina, Charlie sat in the Pawtucket dugout, watching his teammates post a minor league victory. The next morning was one of those galling adventures in Triple-A travel: up a little after four o'clock for a 5:30 flight. By the time they arrived in Rhode Island, the news was already official: Wakefield would make his start after all.

At McCoy Stadium that night, on an unusually unpleasant evening with temperatures still hovering in the low nineties and high humidity, Charlie took the mound against the Buffalo Bisons. The whole team was exhausted. Charlie had every right to be furious. He went out and pitched eight innings of one-run, four-hit ball as the PawSox cruised to a 9–1 win.

Some 46.71 miles and a world away at Fenway Park, Wakefield pitched seven strong innings as Boston beat Seattle, 11–3.

There was nothing Charlie could do, of course. In a few months he would be a minor league free agent, and it would be time to say good riddance.

He was a no-brainer selection for the International League All-Star Game, and to his surprise, the Red Sox said they would also fly his girlfriend, Maddie, to the game in Louisville. But after Charlie pitched on the Sunday before the All-Star break (one run in seven innings in another win), he got a call from the president of the International League, who said they didn't want him at the All-Star Game since pitchers without rest wouldn't be useful.

So he just stayed back in Rhode Island with Maddie. They watched the game on ESPN2. They spent some time with her family. *That's Charlie Zink! He throws the knuckleball!*

A blister here, a slip in the shower there, a well-timed family crisis—any of these things can open doors. But when word about Tim Wakefield's shoulder problem began to circulate in the Pawtucket clubhouse on August 10, Charlie paid it no mind. Sure, Wakefield was supposed to start the Sox home stand on August 12 against the Rangers, but the fruit had been dangled so many times before. On Monday the eleventh, the PawSox had an afternoon game at McCoy Stadium. Immediately after it was over, Charlie took off, back to his apartment in Providence. He didn't want to face his teammates, the media, the specter of another crushing disappointment. A few minutes from the ballpark, his phone rang. It was one of his agents, Steve McKelvey.

● In many ways, Steve had grown tired of the chase. He was in his late forties now, and though he still looked young, his brown hair had lost some luster and added a little gray, his blue-green eyes were bordered by a faint phone tree of wrinkles. He had a full-time job as a sport management professor at UMass, where he ran the graduate program. He had a wife at home and two girls. The slog of a decade chasing baseball gold had taken its toll.

Over breakfast in January he had seemed disillusioned. The thousands of calls to sponsors, the hustling for deals on Mizuno gloves and Rawlings spikes, the setting up of autograph shows and clinics, the coddling of so many players—it had all seemingly reached a tipping point. He talked that day about "figuring out an exit strategy."

The payoff was so rare. "I'm not recruiting anymore," he said. "I'm not spending another day away from my family chasing another high school kid who has a one-in-a-million shot of making it, and then spending the next three years trying to keep him.[3] It's not worth it."

He sensed the business slipping away. There seemed to be too many obstacles for a small, family-oriented agency to succeed in this savagely competitive world. He had been reminded of that recently through experiences with a couple of younger clients. One was Bubba Bell, an outfield prospect in the Red Sox organization whom the agents had signed through a connection with Charlie. Steve had worked hard to close a couple of card-signing deals for Bell, and equipment contracts with Franklin and Reebok. In January, though, they got a fax of an Agent Designation Form for Bell from Reebok, indicating that he was now being represented by the Beverly Hills Group, one of the biggest names in the industry. Bell hadn't told Steve personally, and Steve gave him a call, blood boiling. He found the young star on the road from his home in Texas, heading to Florida to an elite training center, whose fee was paid by his new agents. It was the kind of thing DiaMMond Management couldn't afford. (That perk had become a standard part of representation now, thanks to Scott Boras, who touted one of his services as "performance maximization.") Steve was appalled, and couldn't help lashing out at Bell. "I want to tell you personally you were a huge disappointment," he said, taking a deep breath. "Thanks for fucking us." Then he hung up, a little satisfied, a little embarrassed.

Then there was Scott Barnes, a local kid from Chicopee, Massachusetts, Steve had been working with for years. When he was just a rail-thin seventeen-year-old, Barnes had been picked in the forty-third round of the 2005 draft by the Washington Nationals. Steve was with the family that night (Jim and Lisa having been with first-round pick Matt Torra). Barnes had taken to referring to Steve as "my older brother." And why not? After all, Steve had gone down to New York at least ten times to see Barnes's starts at St. John's, the school whose full scholarship he had accepted after not signing with the Nationals (as suggested by DiaMMond Management). Steve and his younger daughter had had many a pizza dinner with the Barnes family in Chicopee during the three years when their son was in New York. The agents invited Barnes to golf tournaments and clinics, giving him a taste of the professional life to come. They tried to prepare him for his next foray into the draft in 2008. But shortly before he was selected by the Giants in the twelfth round, Barnes had signed on with Barry Meister, the agent who represented Randy Johnson and Tim Wakefield.

"The term that we use is 'big league,'" Steve said. "When they start to believe it, then everything's out the window, all loyalty." He talked about the way the big agencies would travel to the Arizona Fall League to try to poach clients, and said that DiaMMond Management just couldn't "do it the right way—which is the wrong way."

The struggle, Steve said, was as much as anything generational. It was hard to relate to players who said, "Yo, dude," and tough to "figure out what the friggin' handshake is. . . . This is a fucking twenty-year-old. I'm done fucking around with twenty-year-olds. That's not what I want to do with the rest of my life."

And yet in other ways the quest, no matter how tarnished and impure, continued to cast its spell. Many of the players that Steve and Jim and Lisa represented had become, if not family, alive in their inner sense of what mattered. It was cool for Steve when Doug Clark made it up to the Giants right out of the high school classroom. It was sad to him, really sad, when things didn't work out for Brad Baker. Manny Delcarmen was a bona fide big leaguer, and if he could hang on for another year (and they could keep him away from the sharks), the money would start to flow.

When Randy Ruiz was called up to the Twins on August 1, Steve couldn't help feeling a sense of pride. The guy could be a pain in the butt—whenever he said on the phone, "Steve, question for you," McKelvey knew that some new request for bats or spikes was coming—but he had persevered, and was now, at least for a short while, a major leaguer.

Charlie Zink had become one of Steve's absolute favorites over the years. He was a character. He was a guy with a story. As worn-down and cynical as all three of the agents had become in some ways, there was still something irresistible about Charlie. He took them back to a game they still loved, but more deeply into a realm of yearning they couldn't quite articulate, a childlike kind of hope.

This year had been a vicious tease with Charlie, the dangling of "almost," of "so close." It was not unlike Steve's situation back in October 1986, when he was preparing the Red Sox World Series trophy for presentation, the yearned-for moment finally at hand, and then ripped away.

So Steve was hesitant to call Charlie on August 11, but the rumors about Wakefield were rumbling. Talk radio and the Internet were buzzing with speculation. The Sox would need a starter on the twelfth. It was Charlie's turn. It was all set up. They couldn't deny him again, could they?

No, Charlie told Steve, he had heard nothing, nothing at all. He had left the ballpark right after the game. They knew where to find him. He was just not going to subject himself to this kind of humiliation.

Steve small-talked. He tried to be funny. Maybe Theo Epstein was working some trade for a bunch of starting pitchers. Okay, maybe it wasn't so funny.

Then Charlie's cell phone beeped. The caller I.D. flashed the number of his manager, RJ.

"Steve," Charlie said, his voice strong and determined, "this fucking better be it."

● Fenway Park opens to fans two hours before the first pitch. They hustle past the signs that read "Be Alert: Foul Balls and Bats Hurt" and stream down to the railing with their cameras and Sharpies. They gawk at batting practice and beg for autographs. Tonight they are buzzing about the trade Theo Epstein has just worked to acquire starting pitcher Paul Byrd. They call out to NESN's beautiful reporter Heidi Watney, blond hair billowing over her red sweater atop a lacy shirt and black jeans, who is bustling down the right field line with her microphone.

At 5:15 two smiling friends walk down that same right field line, heading for the dugout and the Boston Red Sox locker room. Manny Delcarmen is wearing his sunglasses. Charlie Zink holds his glove in his left hand. Sunlight splashes all around them.

Not long after, a group of fans gathers in Section 21, Row NN, behind the plate. Steve McKelvey, who had spent the day working on his syllabus for a sponsorship event class, walks in with Jim Masteralexis. Jim tells Steve that he left a message on Charlie's phone about the first inning, when he will be facing three All-Stars right away: Ian Kinsler, Michael Young, and the mighty Josh Hamilton, who put on a legendary display in the home run–hitting contest at Yankee Stadium last month. When Hamilton comes up, Jim advised Charlie, "Look him in the eye and say, 'I'm Charlie Fucking Zink, and here comes my knuckleball!'"

The agents chat with Madeline Munroe and her mom and stepfather, who are both wearing red T-shirts that say "Think Zink." They are introduced to some of Charlie's friends from the Savannah College of Art and Design, who have descended from distant points. Two have arrived from Savannah: Wes Gunn, a construction supervisor with a video and film background, and Randy Rodriguez, the art director of a design press printing department. Then there is Sean from California, and Tony from Connecticut, and the guy they all call Junior, Luis Tiant's son, who had really done most of the coaching back in the day. (El Tiante would not be in the house on this night; it was his thirty-seventh anniversary, and he and his wife, Maria, had plans to celebrate in Connecticut at Foxwoods. The night before, though, when Charlie checked into the hotel in Brookline, he saw Red Sox scout Felix Maldonado in the lobby on the cell phone, which he handed to Charlie. There on the other end was the hearty, soulful laughter of his college coach, and the biggest, warmest congratulations.)

Marya Milton, now a corporate lawyer in Oregon, had gotten the news from Joyce Zink the day before, saying that Charlie might be getting called up. She told Joyce to let her know as soon as she heard. Marya was getting her hair done when the phone rang and Joyce shouted, "He got the call! He's going to pitch tomorrow at Fenway!"

Marya flew in on one red-eye, not sleeping at all, chatting up all the stewardesses about how she was going to see her good friend make his major league debut for the Red Sox. Joyce flew in on another, far too keyed up to sleep. They met at Logan Airport and went to the Marriott in Brookline. There they met Madeline Munroe and, after some hesitation, woke up Charlie, then went out to get some burritos at Baja Fresh. And now here they are, taking their seats as game time approaches.

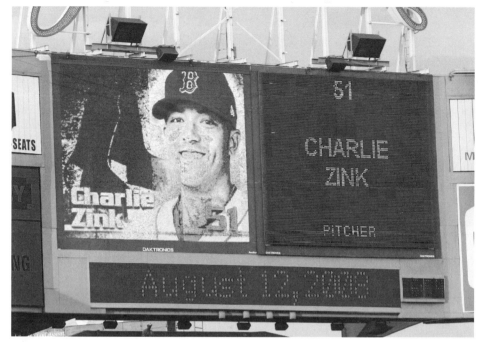

August 12, 2008: the long-awaited day for Charlie Zink at Fenway Park.
Kelly O' Connor/sittingstill.net

Before the game, Charlie reconnects in the outfield with his longtime friend Manny Delcarmen. *Kelly O' Connor/sittingstill.net*

Night falls in Boston as the Nation gathers at Fenway Park.
Jere Smith/a Red Sox fan from Pinstripe Territory

In the bullpen, Charlie gets ready to face a powerful Texas Rangers lineup.
Kelly O' Connor/sittingstill.net

Charles Tadao Zink arrives on the grand stage.
Jere Smith/a Red Sox fan from Pinstripe Territory

Things couldn't have started out much
better for Charlie and the Red Sox . . .

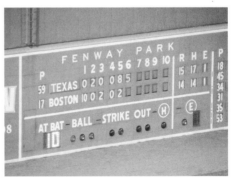

. . . then they take a dramatic turn for the
worse. *Jere Smith/a Red Sox fan from
Pinstripe Territory*

Joyce Zink and Madeline Munroe after Charlie's memorable major league debut. *Photo by author*

Outside the Red Sox locker room, Charlie signs baseballs for friends from the Savannah College of Art and Design who traveled to Boston for the game. *Photo by author*

Joyce looks out over the field, her expression frozen in wonder, disbelief, and fear as the national anthem is played on a saxophone. She says that Charlie's dad is looking down on the game, overcome with pride.

Chris Conti of Barrington, Rhode Island, delivers the ceremonial first pitch as the grand prize winner of the 99 Restaurant Fenway Fantasy Sweepstakes.

At the 99 Restaurant in Greenfield a hundred miles away, Brad Baker pours a beer as the Red Sox game comes up on the flat-screens at either end of the bar. Twenty miles south, Lisa Masteralexis pays the pizza delivery man from Sibies and tells her five-year-old twins they can't watch *Scooby-Doo* right now, tuning in instead to the NESN telecast on their new HD television set. Across the country in California, Charlie's old buddy Ryan Fickle takes in the game on mlb.com, watching with three friends, hanging on every word. The day before he had been making one of his sales stops for Southern Wine and Spirits when his phone rang and he saw Charlie's number. Charlie told him he'd be starting the next night, and when Ryan answered, "Shut up. Get out of here," Charlie responded, "No shit, son," and they both laughed and laughed. ("We giggled like little kids," Fickle later said. "That's the dream right there, that's the call. For one of us clowns to start in Fenway Park—get out of here. Who does that?")

The Boston Red Sox jog out to their positions. Kevin Youkilis rolls a grounder to Dustin Pedroia. The game time temperature is seventy-one degrees.

From behind the pitching rubber, Charlie Zink scratches out the number 16 in tribute to Dave Russell. The Fenway PA system blares the Rolling Stones: "Let's spend the night together, / Now I need you more than ever . . ."

Ian Kinsler steps into the batter's box from the left side. Steve McKelvey mutters, "First pitch strikes," as Maddie Munroe shouts, "Let's go, Tadao!" Joyce Zink stands silently, clutching her camera, trying to hold back the tears.

The first pitch is a knuckleball in the dirt. Three pitches later there is a fly to deep left, but Jason Bay catches it just in front of the Green Monster.

Charlie retires the trio of All-Stars 1–2–3 and walks slowly back to the dugout at Fenway.

The bottom of the first inning proves an absolute bonanza. J. D. Drew walks, and Pedroia singles. David Ortiz then launches the second pitch into the bleachers for a three-run home run.

That is just the beginning. There are hits and more hits, an error, a walk, and then Ortiz is up again, blasting *another* three-run homer. It feels as if Charlie Zink, who has finally gotten to the mound at Fenway Park after so many years of yearning, may never get back there again. When he finally does, the Sox are leading, 10–0.

His whole career, his whole life, really, had been tinged with the bizarre, and his major league debut almost had to follow suit. So maybe it is no surprise that Charlie is gone in the fifth inning, having surrendered eight runs; or that the Red Sox cough up that entire lead and wind up trailing, 16–14 (thanks, in part, to one of the worst relief appearances in Manny Delcarmen's career); or that they come back ultimately to win, 19–17, in a game that ties a fifty-eight-year-old American League record for most runs scored by both teams. With Charlie Zink, that is just how it goes.

It is a long, long night. After the game, Charlie sits by his locker, gladly answering whatever questions come his way. In the first inning, he says, "my heart was pounding out of my shirt." He admits that over the years he has had to ride through a place of deep doubt: "There were definitely times when there wasn't a whole lot of hope." He tells two journalists from Japan that there was a point growing up when he was uncomfortable with his Japanese heritage, when he offered his middle name as "Todd" rather than "Tadao," but that now he considers it to be "one of my proudest parts." The atmosphere at the ballpark was "a new experience for me, something I had never seen. Just amazing, exciting."

Sure, he wishes his pitching line (four and one-third innings, eight runs, all earned, on eleven hits, with one walk and one strikeout) could have been better, but he absolutely treasures the experience. "This will be the best memory of my life, still," he says. "Hopefully, there's more to come, but if there's not, this was still amazing tonight."

He speaks briefly with Terry Francona and Theo Epstein.

Shortly after midnight he emerges from the locker room out into the concourse, where all the concession stands are now closed. There is a crowd waiting for him. Manny Delcarmen claps him on the shoulder, and Charlie hugs Ana and almost-one-year-old Manny III, still awake. Charlie whispers something to his agents Jim and Steve, and they all laugh as he hands them the index card that he found on his chair when he arrived in the afternoon: a note of congratulations from another agent who left his phone number.

There are bear hugs from all the friends from SCAD, including Luis Tiant's grandson, who holds up two tiny Wally the Green Monster dolls. Charlie gives a big kiss to Maddie, and saves a long embrace for Joyce. He poses for picture after picture.

Charlie drops his blue and red duffel bag on the concrete walkway. The bag says "Pawtucket Red Sox" with an address tag reading "McCoy Stadium, Ben Mondor Way." He has already been sent back to Triple-A.

But before saying good night, Charlie agrees to go back into the locker room one more time, pushed by his friends. He emerges with a box and begins signing a souvenir for all of his buddies. They are brand new baseballs. Rawlings.

Major league.

Epilogue

The Strangest Luck

A year later, almost to the day, Charlie Zink is back on the mound at Fenway Park, the words "Red Sox" splashed across his chest. But this afternoon, August 8, 2009, serves merely as a cruel piece of irony. Charlie is starting for the Pawtucket Red Sox in the annual "Futures at Fenway" showcase in the midst of a dreadful 2009 season during which such a future seems impossible. His ghostball has vanished once again.

Today is typical of a lost season: five runs on six hits in five and one-third innings, with three walks, two hit batters, and another galling "L." One year after going 14–6 with a 2.84 ERA, good enough to win the International League's Most Valuable Pitcher award—the Triple-A equivalent of the Cy Young—Charlie walks a whopping ninety-three batters in 135 and one-third innings, while hitting thirty more—twice as many as anyone in the league. He winds up with a 6–15 record and an embarrassing 5.59 ERA.

Those numbers are eerily similar to the ones posted in 1994 by Tim Wakefield in Triple-A with the Buffalo Bisons: 5–15, 5.84. Released by the Pirates' organization, the following April, he signed with Boston, and spent the first month of the season in Pawtucket. Called up in late May, he went 14–1 with a 1.65 ERA in his first seventeen starts, perhaps the most dominant half-season in team history. All these years later, Wakefield is still around, making his first American League All-Star team in 2009 and then signing a two-year extension. So who knows?

Charlie makes $65,000 in 2009, the approximately 400 percent raise coming from spending one day in the big leagues. At year's end, he and Madeline Munroe make the long drive out to California. They live together with Charlie's mom all off-season, shopping for a house and talking about getting married. For almost twenty years, Charlie has kept a ring in a safe. When he was eleven, he had gone shopping with his father at the Sports Authority. In one of the gloves he tried on he felt a hard object. When he shook the glove, out popped a glittering ring. No one at the store knew anything about it. No one responded to an ad in the paper. It was appraised for several thousand dollars. Now Charlie is confident he has found the right woman, but he isn't quite sure if this is the right ring. When Maddie hears the story, she can only shake her head. "He has," she says, "the strangest luck."

Also a tad unusual is the story of the first knuckleballer to sign a pro contract in the off-season, Eri Yoshida, who inks a deal with the Yuma Scorpions in the Arizona Winter League. In the very city where Charlie began his pro career in 2001, Yoshida gets ready for the brief 2010 season, set to begin in late January. Even by knuckleballer standards, the Japanese hurler is a bit unconventional: a sidearmer, just seventeen years old, only five foot one. And female.

After long conversations with Jim Masteralexis, Charlie signs his 2010 contract in January with the St. Louis Cardinals. It's a Triple-A deal, but it includes an invitation to major league spring training, where he will wear uniform No. 99. Charlie is excited to work with renowned manager Tony LaRussa and the Cardinals' highly acclaimed pitching coach, Dave Duncan. Moving over to a National League team, he also spends some winter time in the batting cage after almost a decade without an at bat. He hopes to get a little instruction from the Cardinals' newly appointed hitting coach, a guy whose poster still adorns one wall of Charlie's childhood room: Mark McGwire.

Charlie says he has no remorse about leaving the Red Sox after eight years, and that he didn't hear a single thing from anyone in the organization about the move   other than a congratulatory phone call from Manny Delcarmen. It's time to move on. "I'm just excited," he says, "for what feels like a chance."

● In 2009 Brad Baker also returns to a familiar mound. After sitting out the 2008 season, he couldn't resist the siren call of the game. So early in the evening of July 30, he stands atop the pitching rubber at Frontier Regional High School in South Deerfield, Massachusetts. A decade earlier, Brad had been the star of stars at nearby Pioneer Valley Regional. The scouts had descended en masse to see games that suggested a robust rural optimism of a bygone era: "Pioneer vs. Frontier."

His uniform now reads "Teddy Bear." He is playing for Teddy Bear Pools and Spas against Manny's Appliances in a playoff game of the Tri-County League. Most of his teammates are college players. Brad, at twenty-eight, still cuts an impressive figure. Maybe his mechanics are no longer perfect. Maybe his fastball lacks the heat to get out the best hitters in the world. But on a soft summer evening in western Massachusetts, it still cracks into the catcher's glove with authority.

He had shown up to the team's first practice wearing San Diego Padres gear from a few short years and a lifetime ago. Teammate Mike Cole, a pitcher for Springfield College, said that at first he and his Teddy Bear teammates were intimidated by Brad. As the summer went on, though, Brad invited them out golfing or fishing. He told funny stories about his days in pro ball and spoke occasionally of his classes at Greenfield Community College. Sometimes Teddy Bear players showed up at the 99 Restaurant in Greenfield and watched the Red Sox, with Brad pouring the beers. "We all became pretty close with him," Cole said. "We learned a lot from him, because he has an incredible understanding of baseball. But I think we rubbed off on him, too, in terms of really enjoying the game once again."

This midsummer game is a good one, a tight pitcher's duel between Brad and Jeff Dixon, a six-foot-eight righthander for Manny's who once played pro ball himself, though never above the Class-A level. There are only a few dozen fans in attendance. The crowd includes a high school junior named Matt McKelvey, who raves about the pitching lessons he gets from Brad in the winter in a horse barn in Leyden. Matt's uncle and one of Brad's erstwhile agents, Steve McKelvey, also watches the action. The atmosphere is laid back. Players go into the woods behind the backstop to pee or to fetch foul balls, poison ivy notwithstanding.

Brad surrenders just four hits and a single run in a complete game, but loses, 1–0. The loss eliminates Teddy Bear from the playoffs. Afterward, in the waning light, Brad hangs out for a while in the parking lot with a couple of players, then bids them farewell. Under a waxing quarter moon, he gets into his black truck and drives back up to Leyden.

● It is only one game, Matt Torra knows, this contest in the small town of Sevierville, Tennessee, on the night of August 31, 2009. How much can you really tell from one game? That disaster a year ago, on August 12, 2008— the 21–5 loss in which his starting catcher had finished up on the mound— was only one game, too, and that wasn't the whole story. You make it in baseball, or you don't, based on the long haul. Still, this particular game, more than any he can recall since his labrum surgery four years earlier, gives him a sense of hope, a sense of resolve.

Pitching for the Mobile BayBears, he takes on the Tennessee Smokies, Double-A affiliate of the Chicago Cubs. The Smokies are not terribly well liked in the Mobile clubhouse. They are the first-place team, and they have taken on the fiery personality of their manager, Hall of Famer Ryne Sandberg, who has already been ejected six times this season.

In the top of the fourth inning, Mobile's Bryan Byrne is drilled in the helmet by Tennessee starter Hung-Wen Chen. The ball caroms into the stands over the Mobile dugout as Byrne drops in a heap. He ultimately gets up, dazed, but has to leave the game.

In the home fifth inning, Matt plunks the Smokies' Tony Thomas in the earflap of his helmet, and Sandberg comes tearing out of the dugout. He is screaming at the umpires, screaming at Mobile manager Hector De La Cruz, screaming at Matt Torra. Over three thousand fans in Sevierville seem ready to end at least Matt's baseball career.

Warnings are issued, but Matt stays in the game. He comes to bat in the top of the sixth with two runners on and two outs and Mobile leading, 3–0. Matt hasn't hit very much at all since his days at Pittsfield High School. There was a DH in college, a DH at Single-A, and DHs at the higher levels when the games were played against American League teams. Against National League affiliates this season, he has managed just one hit in thirty-four at bats for an anemic batting average of .029. Hard-throwing reliever David Cales looks in for the sign. Ryne Sandberg glares out at the plate. The crowd smells blood.

Matt Torra blasts the next pitch over the left-field fence and runs around the bases trying to keep the smile off his face. He retires the Smokies in order in the bottom of the sixth, and then Sandberg explodes at the umpires and gets ejected once again.

Matt finishes off a complete-game shutout in the 6–0 win. He allows only four singles, strikes out seven, walks nobody. For the first time since 2005, his fastball tops ninety miles an hour. He is a first-round draft choice who has not made the Show after five years in the minors. But perhaps this horse, and his big league dreams, need not be destroyed after all.

● Doug Clark spends another season in Korea in 2009. Even in his second go-round, it remains a hard and isolated life. Sometimes on the subway he feels all the eyes on him, "like I'm a new species." There are times when the strain feels like too much, particularly when he is not hitting. Of course, that's nothing new for Doug. There have been sleepless nights along the way, not just in a couple of seasons in Korea, but in six years of winter ball in Navojoa, and ten slogging through the minors, when he hasn't been sufficiently comforted by the Bible he brings with him or by the occasional presence of a beautiful woman.

Mostly, though, he is at peace with this life, having "grown comfortable being uncomfortable." Baseball continues to provide irresistible challenge.

"It's brought me to places that I never thought I'd go, in my own head and in the world," he says. "It challenges you in more ways than you ever were challenged in your life. It crushes you. It picks you up. Usually, if you respect the game, the game will somewhat credit you for the work you put in. It tests everything that you stand for in life. It tests your morals. It tests your faith and what you believe in."

Playing this season for the Seoul Heroes, he bows to his manager and joins his teammates after every game in tipping their hats to the crowd. He bats .290, with twenty-four home runs, ninety RBI, and twenty-four stolen bases. When he comes to bat, his fans chant, "Clock-Clock-Clock—What time is it?"

Now thirty-three years old, he returns in the off-season to Springfield and the comforts of home: the room in his parents' basement, the occasional trek into Central High School, UMass basketball games, his baby sister Nora's wedding on New Year's Eve. For the first time in seven years he decides to pass up winter ball in Mexico. He doesn't really need the cash anymore. The Seoul Heroes want him back again in 2010, and he will make almost $400,000.

He admits that he would love another crack at the big leagues. Deep down, though, he knows that's unlikely. His 1–11 big league career and .091 average are likely to remain etched forever as a small part of his baseball legacy. But unlike the vast majority of minor leaguers, Doug knows that, however briefly, he made it to the Promised Land. As his family gathers round and Aunt Bunny comes to pack up his suitcase for the trip to Seoul in late January, there is no denying the reality of a certain major league baseball sitting in a case on the dining room shelf.

● The 2009 season gets off to a spectacular start for Manny Delcarmen. The pride of Hyde Park does not allow a single earned run in his first eleven appearances, stretching over fourteen innings. The streak, dating back to the end of the previous season, is up to twenty-five and one-third innings, almost three complete games. There is lots of talk on Red Sox fan sites about Manny's "closer stuff." With another team, perhaps Manny would be the rock star of the bullpen. Maybe if the hyperkinetic Jonathan Papelbon were to get hurt, or plunge into free agent waters, Manny might become the man at Fenway.

But by the All-Star break, the edge seems to be off, ever so slightly, almost imperceptibly. His fastball is getting a bit too much of the plate, the curve not dropping quite as sharply. As he heads out to an afternoon of golf with Charlie Zink, Luis Tiant, and his agents Jim and Steve, his ERA is still a more than respectable 2.41, but his stock is beginning to sink.

The second half of the year proves to be a disaster. In September, in particular, Manny implodes. Against the Orioles on September 19 he faces four batters, surrendering two home runs and two walks. Two nights later he gives up four runs in just two-thirds of an inning to the Kansas City Royals. Finally, after surrendering two runs in one inning against the Blue Jays on September 30, with his ERA soaring up to 4.53, he admits to manager Terry Francona that he has felt some tightness in his pitching shoulder for several weeks.

With just four days left in the regular season and a first-round playoff series looming with the Angels, the Sox brass is infuriated that Manny has not shared this news earlier. Theo Epstein insists that Manny have a cortisone injection that very night. Francona later says that he spoke to Manny about "his ability to be honest."

Three days later Manny is driving in the left lane of I-93 when a car in the middle lane veers right, causing a driver up ahead in the right lane to lose control and career across the highway. Manny slams on the breaks and turns hard into the left median. The windshield shatters. The left side of the truck caves in. The front left tire bounds away. His beloved Hummer is totaled.

Manny pleads with the paramedics to take him to Fenway Park, but they transport him instead to Massachusetts General Hospital. His back and neck are stiff, but he is fine. The whole thing feels, he says, "like a movie."

Some in Red Sox Nation are none too pleased with the native son. When the story is reported, reader comments are harsh. *His driving is as accurate as his pitching. Why does he have a Hummer? He is a spoiled kid. The Red Sox are better without him.*

Manny is left off the playoff roster and the Red Sox are swept in three games. It is the lowest point of his big league career.

But by the last day of January 2010, the smile is back on his face. He is hanging out at the bowling alley in Hyde Park, Ron Covitz's ice cream parlor and candlepin lanes. He is surrounded by his people. Ana is there, corralling two-year-old Manny III or handing him off to Manny's mom so she can give a bottle to Miley, the couple's two-month-old daughter. Manny jokes around with his older sister and his younger brother, just down the block from the triple-decker on Sunnyside Avenue where they came of age. He bowls on the same team as his old buddy Javy Colon, still an MBTA bus driver. Looking on with pride is the pitcher's dad, the original Manny

Delcarmen. Back when he owned Kuki's Auto Repair, this is where the former minor leaguer used to bring his eldest son in the winter to try throwing strikes. Now in its fifth year, Manny's homespun "Bowlin' Strikes for Schools" has raised well over $50,000 for the Boston Public Schools.

It's a pretty good life, all things considered. Good family. Good friends. Good health—the shoulder is feeling fine. And a job he rather likes. Manny just signed a 2010 contract for $905,000. In a couple of days he'll report for duty. That means a trip to Edison Avenue in Fort Myers, where he gets to be a pitcher for the Boston Red Sox.

● Not that it was ever his (or anyone's) childhood ambition, but after the 2008 baseball season, Randy Ruiz has become one of the most decorated players in the history of the minor leagues. He finishes up with a .320 average for the Rochester Redwings, good enough to lead the International League in hitting. It marks his third Louisville Slugger trophy as a league batting champion, one apiece now at Single-A, Double-A, and Triple-A. He adds the International League Rookie of the Year Award, rather double-edged hardware for a thirty-year-old.

His tenth professional season also marks, at long last, his first taste of the big leagues. In limited duty, he holds his own with the Twins, batting .274 with a home run. That performance, is not good enough for the Twins to keep him, though, and once again Randy finds himself in baseball limbo going into 2009.

Randy wants to accept a Triple-A offer from the Los Angeles Dodgers for $15,500 a month, meaning almost $80,000, the kind of money he can command now that he has some big league time. The Dodgers? This is glitter, if not gold. L.A. Hollywood. Manny Ramirez and Joe Torre.

Jim Masteralexis pushes hard for the Toronto Blue Jays' Triple-A offer of $11,500 a month. Yes, it is less money. Yes, it is Canada—but if Randy wants some glitter, the Blue Jays' Triple-A team is in Las Vegas. More important, Jim says, with the Jays he has a better chance to get back to the big leagues. They need some right-handed power. "Plus," he says, tweaking Randy about his oft-criticized defensive shortcomings, "it's the American League. They have this thing called the fucking designated hitter."

Randy calls up his longtime mentor John Brickley, the scout who had signed him at the tryout camp. Brickley casts his vote for Toronto, and Randy packs his bags. The Blue Jays will be his tenth different big league organization.

All season long he crushes the baseball at Triple-A, ultimately earning the Pacific Coast League's Most Valuable Player award. By mid-season he is at or near the top of all three Triple Crown categories, just as he had been four years before in the Eastern League with the Reading Phillies.

There is hardly any more talk about his suspensions in 2005. Stories of steroid and performance-enhancing drug use continue to plague the sport in 2009—Alex Rodriguez, Manny Ramirez, David Ortiz—but it seems that the public has become more forgiving, or more resigned, to the endless saga. A-Rod is welcomed back to the Yankees with open arms and ultimately leads them to their twenty-seventh World Series title. Manny serves a fifty-game suspension, during which fans come close to voting him a starter at the All-Star Game. And Big Papi dances around a couple of uncomfortable days in the media, before the story seems to vanish.

Randy enjoys his time in Vegas. His girlfriend of four years, Lena Covel, gets the summer off from her bartending job at the Bar-B-Q Pit and comes to live with him in a condo. Their two-and-a-half-year-old son, Randy III, becomes a regular presence in the locker room for the Las Vegas 51s, earning the nickname "The Helmet Bandit." Randy just keeps on hitting. Life is great—except for the fact that the Jays do not seem all that eager to call him up. Randy vents to Jim on the phone, sometimes bringing up the extra money he would be making with the Dodgers. Jim tells Randy that the team is likely to "clean out some contracts" at the trading deadline at the end of July, and that he should be the first right-handed batter they call up.

On the Fourth of July, Randy raises his average to .328 with three hits, including his sixteenth home run, against the Fresno Grizzlies.

The next morning, on the other end of the country, Jim Masteralexis opens up this e-mail:

Dear Mr. Masteralexis,

Thank you for your years of hard work in helping me flourish my career. You have always helped me find a new team when I was released or a minor league free agent. Our pinnacle together was last season when I made the major leagues.

You have been always there for me as a friend not just a representative.

At this time, I have decided to seek player representation elsewhere. Even though this has been an extremely difficult decision for me, I feel that this is best for my career at this time. As such please refrain from advocating on my behalf with any baseball organization.

Very truly yours,
Randy Ruiz

He has signed with Greg Genske, a big player in the agent world. Among others, Genske represents C. C. Sabathia of the Yankees, Vernon Wells of the Blue Jays, and Francisco Liriano of the Twins. A year ago Liriano had taken Randy to his big league debut at the Metrodome in a white Mercedes.

Randy had been torn about the decision. "I told Greg, 'It's tough. I'm with somebody that I don't want to hurt. He's the nicest guy in the world. You don't get nobody better than that.'"

Genske said that he understood, that there was no pressure. He believed that he could offer Randy more than he was getting from his current agents, more experience with big leaguers, more clout, more opportunities, but he wanted Randy to make his own choice. "He said, 'Just make sure you make the right decision.'"

Which way are you going to go, Randy? This way, or that way?

Randy is in Des Moines when he gets the call. His big bat (.320 average, 25 home runs and 106 RBI) will not be needed by Las Vegas against the Iowa Cubs that evening at Principal Park. Instead, early on Tuesday morning, August 11, he boards a plane to join the Toronto Blue Jays, who are playing on the road against a divisional rival. Randy is headed back to the Bronx, to the brand new Yankee Stadium.

He is met at LaGuardia Airport by his old friend and high school teammate Joel Martinez, now a janitor in a New York school. Randy decides against joining the Blue Jays at their plush downtown hotel. He has Martinez drive him past the Willis Avenue Bridge. They go past Restaurante Cuchifritos and La Casa Del Latino Grocer, Puerto Rican flags flapping out front. They drive by buildings with water tanks on roofs, fire escapes angling down, graffiti on the walls. Turning onto 136th Street, they park opposite P.S. 43 and the sweet music of recess, beside a six-story brick building with cigarette butts in the stairwell and jarring fluorescent bulbs in the hallways. Right next to the trash compactor on the second floor, Randy raps on the door. Four locks open, and Luz Ruiz, sparkling at seventy-four, engulfs her grandson in a hug, absolutely refusing to let go.

Luz hates to travel. Other than the occasional bus trip to play bingo at the Mohegan Sun casino, she almost never gets out. She has followed Randy's eleven-year career closely, but only once before (a few years earlier in Trenton) has she seen him play a professional game in person. This, though, is a game she is not about to miss. She joins the throngs at the stadium, and is swept back to those long-ago days of being tugged through the turnstiles by her wide-eyed grandson. In the fourth inning, when Randy slams the ball off the right-field foul pole against Joba

Chamberlain, no one in the crowd of over 46,000 fans is any louder than Luz Ruiz.

The homer is no isolated incident. In 115 at bats, Randy hits ten home runs, while batting a robust .313. Of all major league players with at least one hundred at bats, only one manages a higher slugging percentage than Randy's .635—the guy he helped recruit to Maple Woods Community College, Albert Pujols. The fifty-one games in which he is on the Jays' roster (at the prorated big league minimum of over $2,400 per game) are filled with drama. He becomes a YouTube sensation when he takes a fastball from Josh Towers directly off the cheek ("It's nothing that, growing up in New York City, I haven't experienced"). He hits three of his homers against the Yankees, prompting Derek Jeter to come up to him before one game and say, "Hey, take it easy on us." ("I'm just trying to be like you," Randy replies, before sheepishly asking Jeter for an autograph). The highlight, however, comes on the night of September 30.

● It's late on a Tuesday night, a school night. In a big house on a cul-de-sac in Amherst, Massachusetts, Jim and Lisa Masteralexis are putting their three kids to bed. Both have to get ready to teach in the morning.[1] After saying good night, Jim walks down to the kitchen for a snack and snaps open his iPhone. There he watches the first-ever confrontation between the father of Manny III and the father of Randy III. He sees the high changeup and the mighty swing, and hears the familiar voice of NESN announcer Don Orsillo: "High drive to left, deep, far, and very gone. That clears everything in left field. Randy Ruiz, his second home run of the night, four-for-four. More problems for Manny Delcarmen."

Jim says there is nothing remotely bittersweet about the moment: "It sucked."

The day before, overriding the advice of Lisa and Steve McKelvey, Jim had traveled into Boston to have lunch with Randy at Legal Sea Foods. It couldn't have been much more awkward. Randy thanked Jim for doing a "good job." He told him he respected him as a "family man." It was, he insisted, "nothing personal."

Jim didn't want to remind Randy of all they had been through together. He tried to refrain from telling him what he believed to be true: that Randy would not have made it to the big leagues without DiaMMond Management. He hoped that he could just wish Randy well and cling to the high road.

He couldn't quite do it. "I'm disappointed," he said. "I just don't understand it. The thing that annoys me is I wanted to enjoy this with you."

Randy looked at his feet, stammered some small talk, paid the bill. Then the two men shook hands and went their separate ways. Randy took off for Fenway Park. Jim got in the car and drove home.

He and Lisa have been at this now for seventeen years, eleven of them with Steve McKelvey. Technically it's never been more than a part-time job around the edges of practicing law and teaching. It's been a full-time obsession, though, filling weekends, pushing many a night into the wee hours, shaving precious hours away from family life. The business has become what he calls "marginally profitable," but it is hard to know how to assess the real return on such a colossal investment of his soul. "It's been really interesting," he offers on a Friday afternoon in late October, his voice sounding tired. "It's been a lot of fun. It's not over."

In recent years, he has sensed Lisa recalibrating, investing most of her energy in their kids and in her teaching job, fitting in the baseball when she can. Likewise, he has sensed Steve, the first of the bunch to hit fifty, still pouring in huge hours, but almost viscerally fighting the cynicism, wanting to put up some saner boundaries. And deep down Jim feels the same way. He doesn't get out to nearly as many games now, he admits. He is excited about coaching the Orioles in the 2010 Little League season in Amherst. His ten-year-old son Nathan, he says, can really swing the bat.

He agrees with Steve and Lisa that it's probably time to focus on their veteran clients and leave the chase to others. Maybe Manny will become a closer someday. Perhaps Matt Torra will defy the odds and become a horse once again. And Charlie—who knows? Those knuckleballers can pitch forever.

Of course, once in a while a young player with promise might prove too hard to resist. In 2010, Amherst Regional High School features a senior who is probably the top prospect in New England and likely the best pitcher ever to come out of their hometown. Kevin Ziomek is a tall left-hander who already throws ninety miles an hour and has an arsenal of nasty breaking pitches. He has already been offered a full scholarship to Vanderbilt, and after summer showcases in 2009 he is projected to be a very high draft pick in June. Scott Boras and other big agents are already on his trail.

When they sit down with the family, Lisa tries to bond with Kevin's mother. Steve tells the dad about another client of theirs who grew up in Massachusetts and now pitches for the Red Sox. Jim tells Kevin that it's the beginning of a journey. He says that he and his wife and his good friend will try their level best to make his dreams come true.

Acknowledgments

The baseball metaphor is overplayed. There is no larger meaning, no cosmic significance. It's merely a game: hit the ball with a stick, run counterclockwise.

But then of course, there's all that yearning. All the disappointment. The almost inevitable heartbreak. And once in a great while, that glistening glory of deliverance. It's a game, perhaps more than any other, with a sense of story. I have long believed that the richest baseball stories, the most human ones, can be found in the minor leagues.

Any piece of nonfiction worth its salt requires a tremendous level of co-operation. I have been exceedingly fortunate in that regard. At the center of this drama are nine people (one for each position on the field, one for each inning), all of whom shared their lives quite generously. They knew that I was not there as a public relations agent, that I was going to aim for the real picture, both the wonder and the warts.

I am grateful to the six ballplayers whose stories I have tried to honor. I appreciated Charlie Zink's candor in live interviews in six states over several years; his verbal delivery, like his signature pitch, comes in without spin. Thanks to Doug Clark for his willingness to dig deep and excavate his baseball journey from Springfield to Seoul. I appreciated the kindness and boyish enthusiasm of Randy Ruiz and Manny Delcarmen. Matt Torra and Brad Baker showed me the beginning of the dream.

The three agents who provided the connective tissue for these stories were exceptionally generous with their time and absolutely respectful of my independence. Steve McKelvey kept it real and proved as reliable as Mariano Rivera. Lisa Masteralexis provided great insight and compassion. And Jim Masteralexis made me laugh, made me think, and gave me a front row seat at the testosterone soap opera.

From the very start, I conceived of these as family stories. I wasn't interested so much in what the managers and general managers had to say about these players. I wanted to know what it was like for the wives and girlfriends and family and friends, the village that it takes to raise a ballplayer. Thanks to all of you. In particular, I am indebted to the following individuals: the spirited Joyce Zink and Maddie Munroe; Bill and Peggy Clark; the vibrant Luz Ruiz and Lena Covel; Kuki and Ana Delcarmen; Jim and Pat Torra; and the Baker clan—Jim and Vicki and the inspirational Jeff.

I was very lucky indeed to connect with the talented team at University of Massachusetts Press, who, under the direction of Bruce Wilcox, helped develop this book as if it were a first-round draft choice. Clark Dougan's intelligence, kindness, and tremendous enthusiasm for both books and baseball made him an ideal editor. Carol Betsch worked a skilled pivot on the double play as managing editor. And if Amanda Heller and Mary Bellino have as good a batting eye as they do an editing eye, they should be leadoff hitters in the World Series.

There is no way to even begin to pay the debt owed to my family. Alan Dobrow, my father, taught me that great Roy Campanella lesson that you've got to play it like a man and love it like a boy. Vida Dobrow, my mom, might not be Vida Blue, but the life has always radiated out from her, casting all around her in a better light. My sister Julie and brother Joe continue to be inspirations. Joe's help in particular with this book has been immensely valuable.

On the home front, I have reveled in the father-son baseball saga playing out with ten-year-old Josh, who loves the game—and his Orioles—with his whole heart. Of all the baseball seasons in my life so far, none has been any sweeter than the 2010 Little League campaign for Riverbend Animal Hospital. Sarah, walking around the world with her deep artistic heart, has been a walkoff grand slam since birth. And a Game 7 no-hitter. Jeremiah, likewise ablaze with creative energy, has been the ultimate free-agent signing. Missy-Marie, my muse and my beloved, sometimes turns on the radio late at night to catch the games from the West Coast. Her help with this book has been immense; her help with my life knows no bounds.

I greatly appreciate the kindness of photographers and suppliers of photographs who have made terrific contributions to this book. Kelly O'Connor and Jere Smith were exceedingly generous. Thanks also to Paul Franz, Carol Lollis, and Jerrey Roberts. Also coming through in a big way were Michael Ivins, Marc Kostic, Bob Rosato, Tommy Viola, Shaowei Wang, Bill Wanless, and Jason Yellin.

Parts of this book were adapted from newspaper and magazine stories that I wrote for other publications. I thank the editors at *The Boston Globe*, *The Boston Globe Magazine*, *Sport*, *Hampshire Life*, *Western Mass Sports Journal*, and the *Daily Hampshire Gazette* for their help.

Thanks also to Peter Neumann, for your great friendship and literary guidance for more than three decades. Thanks to Steve Berman, Jerry Mileur, and David Maloof for enormously valuable guidance on the manuscript.

And thanks also to many, many others, including but not limited to: Rob Antony, Andy Ayres, Irene Baker, Mike and Nancy Bean, John Beattie,

Kyle Belanger, Peter and Jen Bergeron, Mark Blegen, Dick Bresciani, John Brickley, Elizabeth Coffin Bynum, Ryan Cameron, Ben Cherington, Will Clark, Stan Cliburn, Mike Cole, the late Milt Cole, Javy Colon, Ron Covitz, Yvonne Crevier, Sabrina Delcarmen, Gabrielle DeMarchi, Mike Drago, Mike Evans, Justin Felisko, Ryan Fickle, Brooke Foster, Jim Foudy, Stephen Gill, Doug Greenwald, Goose Gregson, Hawk Harrelson, Jack Harrison, Rich Hendel, John Hock, Tab Howard, Ron Johnson, R.J. and Kris Joyal, Ashley Kachelmeyer, Cynthia Keur, George Kottaras, Gary Lance, Margaret Lloyd, Rob Manfred, Marya Milton, Jonathan Morales, Doug Most, Mike Murphy, Kelly Polidoro, Carla Potts, Bill Rosario, Debra Scherban, Kristin Schroeder, Dave Scott, George Seaver, Felix and Ginette Serrano, Mike Stone, Joe Sullivan, Neil Swidey, Tad Tokarz, Kevin Towers, Mike Turo, Larry Vale, Dan Wetzel, Darren Wheeler, John White, Ken Wombacher, Julie Zagars, Andrew Zimbalist, and the timeless Stan Ziomek.

Notes

1. Crash Davis Territory

1. Between the beginning of the 2005 season and the end of the 2009 season, five more players joined the five hundred home run club: Frank Thomas, Alex Rodriguez, Jim Thome, Manny Ramirez, and Gary Sheffield.

2. Can't Miss

1. For most of the season major league rosters consist of twenty-five players, but the teams can protect an additional fifteen players in their minor league systems from other teams claiming them in the "Rule 5 draft." These fifteen players are generally considered to be the team's most treasured minor league assets.
2. In recent years, as signing bonuses have soared, teams have selected players not only for their playing ability but also for their affordability. Many teams have bypassed top players because of fears that they would cost too much.
3. This system ended in 2007, when the draft was televised for the first time (on ESPN2).
4. Boston's other first-round pick in the 1999 draft was Rick Asadoorian, an outfielder from Worcester, selected seventeenth. Asadoorian had not signed by this point. He ultimately signed for a bonus of $1.725 million. As of 2009 he had not made it to the major leagues.
5. That total included eighty-four "supplemental" picks. Since 1982, teams that had lost elite free agents had received pre–second round picks as compensation. These supplemental picks were still technically considered first-rounders. At number forty, Brad was a supplemental pick by the Red Sox as payment for the loss of free agent first baseman Mo Vaughn, who had signed a six-year, $80 million contract with the Angels, at the time the richest contract in the game.

3. Fluttering Away

1. In his one season at Sacramento City College, Charlie started just one of the team's forty-seven games. He finished the year with a 6.75 ERA.
2. SCAD left Division III and joined the National Association of Intercollegiate Athletics (NAIA) in 2003, a year after Charlie left.

4. Manny Being Manny

1. At year's end, Woodfork was named assistant general manager of the Arizona Diamondbacks.

5. A Dream Deferred

1. A. J. Sager, who had played in the big leagues from 1994 to 1998, played one game with the Gulf Coast Reds in 1999; he is not included in the five out of fifty-eight statistics, since he had already made it to the big leagues at this point. He would never make it back to the majors.

2. Randy and Jasmine have the same biological parents, Randy Sr. and Julia Franco. Jasmine was raised primarily by Randy Sr. and his wife, Denise, who currently live in a suburb of Cleveland. They have five other children. Julia Franco, who lives in New Jersey, has two other sons.

3. Minor league test results for this and other years come from the December 13, 2007, "Report to the Commissioner of Baseball of an Independent Investigation into the Illegal Use of Steroids and Other Performance Enhancing Substances by Players in Major League Baseball" (the Mitchell Report). The numbers can be found on p. 46.

4. Manfred's testimony took place on July 24, 2003.

5. See the Mitchell Report, p. 46.

6. By season's end, under immense public and legislative pressure, the penalties increased again to fifty games for a first positive test, one hundred for a second, and a lifetime ban for a third.

7. Just two years later Howard would crack fifty-eight home runs and become the National League's Most Valuable Player.

6. "It's the Life—the One Everyone Wants to Live"

1. In September 2008 Hernandez finally got back to the big leagues with the Tampa Bay Rays, a promotion desperately needed to help pay the medical bills for his five-year-old son, Michael, who had been diagnosed with Type I diabetes.

2. Hensley became an intriguing footnote to history two years later, surrendering Barry Bonds's 755th career home run, which tied him with Hank Aaron for the major league record.

3. Bozied played sparingly in 2005, a little Double-A and a little Triple-A. Through the 2009 season he still had not cracked a big league roster.

4. Sparks asked for his release after three starts with the Beavers and then signed on with another Pacific Coast League team, the Sacramento River Cats, believing he had a better chance to get back to the big leagues with its parent team, the Oakland A's. That never happened, and Sparks finished his playing career in the summer of 2005.

5. Bumstead did not go all the way to the big leagues, finishing up his professional career in independent ball in 2008.

6. Over $300,000 went to taxes, and approximately $33,000 went to DiaMMond Management as part of the standard 4 percent cut taken by agents.

7. Despite the geographical anomaly, the New Orleans Zephyrs had been part of the Pacific Coast League since 1998.

7. Opposites Attract

1. Catching knucklers in the big leagues often requires a different level of accommodation. The Red Sox retained light-hitting reserve catcher Doug Mirabelli, his precious roster spot and major league salary secured primarily because of his ability to catch Tim Wakefield's offerings every fifth day. In 2006 the importance of this role was made starkly apparent. After briefly letting Mirabelli go to the Padres after a 2005 season in which he hit just .228, the Red Sox had to bring him back one month into the 2006 season when replacement Josh Bard proved a knuckleball sieve. The Sox overpaid with Bard and Cla Meredith—both of whom would have big years for the Padres—and flew Mirabelli across the country in a private jet. He was met at Logan Airport by a state trooper, who handed Mirabelli his Red Sox uniform and drove him at a startling pace to Fenway Park in time for Wakefield's start against the Yankees. Asked afterward if he had ever been in a police car, Mirabelli memorably answered, "That was the first time naked."

8. Baseballtown

1. The history of Lizzie Arlington, Babe Ruth's visit, and other colorful details have been lovingly researched by Charles J. Adams III, author of *Baseball in Reading* and *Tales from Baseballtown*.

2. The exception here is the fifteen minor leaguers per organization who are on the major league team's forty-man roster.

3. The "steroid hidden in a supplement" argument has been advanced by a number of other athletes who have tested positive, notably J. C. Romero, pitcher for the Philadelphia Phillies, who was suspended for fifty games at the beginning of the 2009 season after testing positive at the end of 2008 (when the Phillies won the World Series). Given the lack of regulation of the supplement industry, such a claim is plausible. Of course, it also can provide a convenient cover.

4. Regarding stanozolol, the drug for which Randy Ruiz (and sprinter Ben Johnson and reportedly Rafael Palmeiro) tested positive, there appears to be some debate. Some suggest that as a water-based steroid with a short half-life, it clears the system quickly. Other sources, however, suggest that in some people it might last quite a bit longer. An extensive article about Winstrol (or "Winny," the street name for stanozolol) put together by Jelsoft Enterprises Ltd. says that it is "not advisable for drug tested athletes" because "apparently some inactive metabolites are easily esterified, so they can be found up to 5 months after the last injection."

5. Wagner was signed by the Red Sox at the city's old Lauer Park. Nicknamed "Broadway" by Ted Williams because of his fancy suits, Wagner pitched exactly one

hundred games for the Red Sox. He later served the team as a scout, minor league pitching instructor, and major league pitching coach. He attended every Red Sox spring training from 1935 until 2006, except for his years in the navy from 1943 to 1945. As the team's oldest living former player, Wagner got to conclude the celebration of the Red Sox' first World Series championship in eighty-six years at the 2005 home opener by calling out, "Let's play ball!" He died of a heart attack in 2006 in the parking lot of FirstEnergy Stadium after attending a Reading Phillies game.

9. "They Got Him!"

1. A couple of generations before, Pittsfield had produced big leaguers Mark Belanger and Tom Grieve.
2. The scout wished to remain anonymous, saying that publicly showing favoritism to agents was bad for business.
3. The "slot value" is the unofficial bonus target recommended by the commissioner's office for each pick. It carries no official weight.
4. Barnes would be picked in the forty-third round by the Washington Nationals. At the advice of DiaMMond Management, he chose not to sign, accepting instead a scholarship from St. John's University. He would work on his craft, pursue a college education, then be eligible to reenter the draft after his junior year in 2008.
5. A few weeks later Jim got Bergeron a job playing for the unaffiliated Nashua Pride, whose preseason extended into April in Homestead, Florida. In one of the sparsely air-conditioned units where his teammates stayed, one player found a snake. Ultimately, Bergeron was signed to a Double-A contract with the Baltimore Orioles. He would never get back to the big leagues, retiring after the 2007 season. Bergeron's case is similar to that of Chad Paronto, a longtime DiaMMond Management client who, despite playing in parts of several big-league seasons, was never eligible for arbitration.
6. The number one pick in 2005, Justin Upton, would set what was then a record with a $6.1 million bonus.
7. As indicated in an earlier note, the draft would eventually be televised. That date came two years later in 2007, when it was carried by ESPN2 from Disney's Wide World of Sports Complex in Orlando.
8. These were the thirty-first through forty-eighth picks in the 2005 draft, awarded to teams as compensation from rivals who had signed away elite free agents. Technically they are still considered first-round draft choices.

10. Waiting (on Deck) for Godot

1. The UMass baseball coach is not related to the Mike Stone mentioned earlier in the chapter (the PA announcer at PGE Park).
2. Salaries for first-year minor leaguers went up to $1,100 a month in 2006.

11. Suspended Disbelief

1. After nearly five years of silence, McGwire finally talked about the past in a series of interviews in January 2010, after he was hired to be the hitting coach of the St. Louis Cardinals. He tearfully apologized for using steroids for many years, including 1998, when he set a then-record seventy home runs. He insisted the drugs were used solely for health purposes, and adamantly claimed that they hadn't enhanced his performance in any way.

2. From Lisa Masteralexis's presentation to the New England Law Review Symposium, November 4, 2005.

3. To his credit, McGwire said in a January 2010 interview with Bob Costas that listening to Garibaldi while remaining silent had been "killing my heart."

4. From Lisa Masteralexis's presentation to the New England Law Review Symposium, November 4, 2005.

5. In September 2005 Seattle Mariners rookie Mike Morse would make the same argument after failing a drug test and getting suspended. He had been suspended in May of the previous year while playing for the Birmingham (Alabama) Barons, in the White Sox organization, a team that evidently tried to dress up the suspension as something else. The *Birmingham News* reported that "a hamstring pull suffered over the weekend has Morse temporarily on the shelf." In late June, he and two other teammates were suspended again for what team officials termed "a violation of team policy." Morse told the *Birmingham News:* "It wasn't anything like drugs or substance abuse or anything like that. I don't want to get into it, but it's a lesson I'll learn from and put behind me." At the time, no minor leaguer had been publicly identified as having been suspended for steroid use. After a trade to the Seattle organization, Morse got called up to the big leagues for the first time in 2005, where he was hitting .287 when he was flagged for failing another test. "Back in November 2003 when I was 21 years old, I made an enormous mistake in my life," Morse said to reporters. "I took steroids while in the minor leagues. My thigh muscle, which I had previously torn, had never healed and I was scared that my career was over. I was desperate and made a terrible mistake which I deeply regret. In May 2004, I was punished and suspended, which I deserved, for my mistake. I embarrassed myself, my family and my team. I am responsible for the mistake of taking steroids and the positive result was not due to some over-the-counter supplement, protein shake or tainted test." Morse went on to insist, though, that both subsequent positive tests resulted from steroid remnants remaining in his system after that initial use. "I am troubled," he said, "that I will be suspended for the third time despite the fact that the scientific evidence supports that I kept my promise that I would never use steroids again. Even the [arbitration] panel states in its written decision that 'the panel recognizes that this result might be viewed as unfair to Michael Morse.'" Still, the suspension was enforced. Morse

made it back to the big leagues for parts of several subsequent seasons, playing sixty-seven games between 2006 and 2009.

13. Goose Bumps

1. Clement returned later in the year, and would make twelve starts for the Sox in 2006, but he never regained his All-Star form, in part because of subsequent arm injuries. He announced his retirement in April 2009.
2. A year later Gonzalez would tell his new team, the Chicago Cubs, that his first name was actually spelled "Geremi." In May 2008 he was killed by a lightning strike on a beach in his native Venezuela.
3. From the WGBH documentary *Going to Fenway*.

14. "If You Make It, We Will Come"

1. Leon Lee, brother of former big leaguer Leron Lee and father of Cubs star Derrek Lee, had a long career in the minors and in Japan. He established a baseball academy in his hometown of Sacramento in 1995. He is a fixture in the baseball community there, and has numerous connections in pro ball.
2. Yuma Territorial Prison was in one sense like Folsom, where his parents had worked: a place with a notorious past. In the late nineteenth century, prisoners were chained to the stone floor of tiny cells in the summer heat, with tuberculosis raging.
3. Isabel had been allowed to visit her son in Mexico City in 1968, while her husband was reportedly detained in Cuba to guarantee her return.
4. Tiant's parents would witness his mastery in the 1975 World Series and stay on in Boston for over a year. That is where the elder Tiant died in December 1976. Just before the memorial service a couple of days later, Isabel also passed away.

15. At Heaven's Door

1. *City Crime Rankings* (12th edition, 2005), published annually by Morgan Quitno Press.
2. Sanchez would last forty-three at bats with the Giants that season. He would never get back to the big leagues.
3. The name was changed to AT&T Park in 2006.

16. There's Always Next Year, Sometimes

1. Machado had ten at bats and one hit for the 2005 Sox. Through 2009 that remained his only big league experience.
2. Rodriguez would opt out of the last three years of his ten-year contract, then sign a new ten-year deal for an average annual salary of of $27.5 million in 2008. Be-

fore the 2009 season he would admit to having taken performance-enhancing drugs earlier in his major league career.

3. When Ramirez was traded to the Los Angeles Dodgers in 2008, he had the misfortune of hitting the free agent market as the United States economy encountered its worst times since the Great Depression. He had to settle for a two-year contract at $22.5 million a season. After leading the Dodgers to a great start in 2009, he was suspended for fifty games for testing positive for a performance-enhancing drug.

4. In April 2006 Ortiz signed a four-year extension with the Red Sox at $12.5 million per year. He went on to hit a career-high fifty-four home runs that season. In July 2009 a *New York Times* report indicated that both Ortiz and Ramirez had been on the supposedly anonymous list of 104 players who had tested positive for performance-enhancing drugs in 2003.

19. Knockin' after Midnight

1. By 2008 Viagra was being seriously studied for its "performance-enhancing" capabilities, not in the bedroom but on the field. A *New York Times* article on November 23, 2008, headlined "New Suspect in Sports Doping Is, No Joke, Viagra" pointed to studies under way to detect possible increased cardiac output stemming from the drug's dilation of blood vessels. It also reported that "some athletes are believed to take Viagra in an attempt to aid the delivery of steroids to the muscles and hasten recovery from workouts. Others take Viagra to counter the effects of impotence brought on by steroid use," according to steroids guru Dr. Gary Wadler.

2. Grimsley was perhaps best known for his involvement in an off-field incident back in 1994 when he was with the Cleveland Indians. Teammate Albert Belle had his bat confiscated by the umpires after complaints from the White Sox. During the game Grimsley, a flashlight in his mouth, crawled through the air conditioning ducts to the umpires' locker room and replaced Belle's corked bat with the uncorked lumber of teammate Paul Sorrento. Five years later he confessed.

3. Bud Selig agreed immediately to follow all of the recommendations. Some involved closing remarkable loopholes, such as the one that gave teams twenty-four hours' notice about forthcoming "random" drug tests.

4. Under pressure from commissioner Bud Selig, Giambi would ultimately become one of the only active players to talk to George Mitchell, speaking about his "personal history regarding steroids." He would be named prominently in the report that was released in 2007. He was never suspended.

5. Both did make it to the big leagues, however briefly. Stan got fifty-six at bats for the Angels in 1980, while Stu pitched for the Angels for parts of three seasons later in the decade.

6. Randy would give the ball that night to teammate Michael Cuddyer for inscription purposes. Cuddyer was known as the player with the best handwriting on the team. He says that he developed his script at Great Bridge Elementary School in Chesapeake, Virginia.

20. "Just Hoping to Have It Be Over"

1. Matt and Jessica were married in November 2009, in Pittsfield, Massachusetts. Jim and Lisa Masteralexis and Steve McKelvey attended the wedding.

21. On the Big Screen

1. In September 2007 Giese would make his major league debut with the San Francisco Giants. In an interview on a Yankees website two years later, he recalled getting the word from his Triple-A manager: "I was in shock. I couldn't believe it. All those years of blood, sweat, and tears had finally paid off. I made it to the major leagues. I immediately called my wife and was weeping like a baby. My entire life I just wanted to get one out in the big leagues and I was able to do just that. Everything now is just a bonus!"
2. The Red Sox moved their Double-A team to Portland, Maine, in 2003.

22. "The Path of the Knuckleballer Is Rarely Linear"

1. Charlie wasn't quite as successful in eight games at Pawtucket, going 2–3 with a 5.89 ERA.
2. In the eighth round of the 2005 draft the Red Sox selected a pitcher out of Everett Community College in Washington known as J. T. Zink. As a joke, Charlie listed him as his brother on a Red Sox information form, and thus in several media guides the two are listed in this fashion. They are not related. J. T. Zink lasted three years in the Sox' minor league system, peaking briefly in high-A ball in 2007. He hasn't played professionally since then.
3. That is, the commission for agents kicks in only above the major league minimum salary, and except in very rare instances, players don't make much more than that until they are eligible for salary arbitration, typically after three years of service.

Epilogue

1   In August 2008, the same month Randy Ruiz and Charlie Zink first got called up to the big leagues, Jim Masteralexis left Brackett and Lucas after almost eight years with the firm. He would have preferred to concentrate on DiaMMond Management full time, but that was too much of a risk. Instead he took a job as an assistant professor at Western New England College, teaching sport management in the School of Business. Far more than practicing law, he figured, the teaching job would allow him time to focus on baseball.

Index

Marty Dobrow writes regularly for the *Boston Globe*. His freelance work has appeared in a wide variety of publications, including espn.com, *Sports Illustrated,* and the *International Herald Tribune*. On five occasions his work has been honored in the annual *Best American Sports Writing* series published by Houghton Mifflin. He has earned national writing awards from organizations such as the Associated Press Sports Editors, the United States Basketball Writers Association, the American Association of Sunday and Feature Editors, and the Sunday Magazine Editors Association. His first book, *Going Bigtime,* was named one of the top ten books on basketball history in Peter Bjarkman's well-regarded *Biographical History of Basketball*.

A graduate of Wesleyan University, Dobrow is an associate professor of communications at Springfield College and a Little League baseball coach. He lives in Springfield, Massachusetts, with his wife, the poet/professor Missy-Marie Montgomery, and their three children, Jeremiah, Sarah, and Josh.